P9-DGJ-350

A HALF-CENTURY OF ELIOT CRITICISM

An Annotated Bibliography
of Books and Articles
in English, 1916-1965

A HALF-CENTURY OF ELIOT CRITICISM

An Annotated Bibliography
of Books and Articles
in English, 1916-1965

Mildred Martin

Lewisburg
Bucknell University Press

Associated University Presses, Inc.
Cranbury, New Jersey 08512

ISBN: 0-8387-7808-9
Printed in the United States of America

CONTENTS

Introductory Note   7
List of Publications   9

Bibliography   19

Appendix   263
Author Index   304
Index to Periodicals   324
Subject Index   333

INTRODUCTORY NOTE

The original intention of this bibliography was to include all books and articles, in both magazines and newspapers, published in English between 1916, the year of the first published notice of T. S. Eliot's work, through 1965, the year of his death. Ephemeral articles were included in the plan as well as substantial material because they give insight into the intellectual history of those fifty years. Some articles and chapters from books having little bearing on Eliot are included because they were listed in Eliot bibliographies, and I wished to indicate to the user of this bibliography that he would find little in them on Eliot, saving him time and trouble. As the work progressed it became apparent that it would be a hopeless task to ferret out all that had been written in English on Eliot, and it seemed more important to get the bibliography into the hands of the students of Eliot than to pursue the ideal of completeness. I have read everything included here except for half a dozen items which I have been unable to see.

Items are arranged first chronologically and then alphabetically by names of authors, with items of especial value starred. Since the reading was done over many years, in the course of which my opinions changed, the stars should not be regarded as authoritative, especially in the case of omission of the star. Material in the appendix is of secondary importance for the student of purely literary criticism, but since most of the interviews with Eliot, information on his life, and theatrical history of his plays is to be found there, it will be useful to persons interested in those subjects.

Three indexes are provided: an author index, one of periodicals containing material on Eliot, and a subject-matter index. All items in the bibliography are numbered and each item in the indexes is numbered. The note "In the Eliot Collection" refers to the fine collection assembled by Henry Ware Eliot, the poet's elder brother, in the Houghton Library at Harvard. Comments for a few of the items were quoted from *American Literature,* abbreviated *AL.*

It is a pleasure to add my testimony that librarians are a generous and willing race. I am sincerely grateful to those of the following: The Boston Public, the British Museum, both the main reading room and the Newspaper Library; the Bucknell University Library (Mrs. Norine Blum, Mrs. Zoia Horn, Miss Gertrude Miles, Mrs. Robert Moser, Mrs. William C. Meyers, Mrs. Ernest M. Phillips, Miss Patricia Rom, Miss Mary Jane Stoneburg), Columbia University Library, Houghton Library (Miss Carolyn Jakeman), Widener Library, Harvard Undergraduate Library, University of Illinois (Miss Eva Benton), the New York Public Library, the Library of Congress, Penn State Library, University of Vermont Library, and Yale University Library.

The following persons have called articles to my attention, answered inquiries, provided me with copies of items, helped in checking and proofreading, and performed other services, for which I am more than grateful: Miss Cheryl Abbott, Mrs. Mozoyan Aladj, Mrs. Clarence Berdahl, Mrs. Robert Boulitrop, Mrs. Robert Calkins, Mr. James Carens, Miss Jacqueline Dildine, Mr. Ronald Dotterer, Mrs. Manuel Duque, Mrs. Theresa Garrett Eliot, Mr. William Eshleman, Mrs. Dorothy Goodman, Mr. Robert Gross, Mrs. Mathilde E. Finch, Mr. Hideo Funato, Mr. Donald Gallup, Mr. Harry Garvin, Mr. Mitsuaki Hasegawa, Mr. Mark McCullough, Miss Nancy Millichap, Mr. Richard Minton, Mr. Minoru Nishida, Mrs. Sherry Oreovicz, Mrs. William Rollins, Mrs. Florence Robbins, Mr. J. A. Smellie, Mr. Grover Smith, Mr. C. K. Stead, Mr. Peter Tasch, Mr. Harold Watts, Mother Mary Weining, Mr. John Wheatcroft, Mr. Philip Wheelwright, Miss Jean White, Miss Margaret Zerbe, and Miss Barbara Zeiders.

Bucknell University granted me a sabbatical leave to work on this project, as well as giving me travel grants and clerical assistance, for which I thank them.

LIST OF PUBLICATIONS

The abbreviations used here are those of PMLA where they exist. Titles of one word are not abbreviated. Newspapers are entered first under the place of publication, and except for the *New York Times, New York Herald Tribune, Christian Science Monitor, Times Literary Supplement,* and *Sunday Times* (London), are given in full.

JOURNALS

AB American Bookman
Accent
Adam
Adelphi
AF American Freeman
Agonia
AL American Literature
AM American Mercury
America America, a Catholic Review of the Week
AmP American Prefaces
AmR American Review
AN American Neptune
AN & Q American Notes and Queries
Anglia
AQ American Quarterly
AR Antioch Review
ArG Arts Gazette
Arion
ArQ Arizona Quarterly
ASch American Scholar
AsR Asiatic Review
Athenaeum
Atlantic Atlantic Monthly
AUMLA Journal of the Australasian Universities Language and Literature Association
AWR Anglo-Welsh Review (Pembroke Dock, Wales)

BA Books Abroad
BJA British Journal of Aesthetics
BJRL Bulletin of the John Rylands Library (Manchester)
Blackfriars
BNYPL Bulletin of the New York Public Library
BoC Book Collector
Booklist
Bookman
Bookman (English)
BR Bard Review
BrAL British Annual of Literature
BrW British Weekly, a Journal of Social and Christian Progress
BSJ Baker Street Journal
BSTCF Ball State Teachers College Forum
BT Britain Today
BuR Bucknell Review
BUSE Boston University Studies in English

CalR Calcutta Review
CamJ Cambridge Journal
CamR Cambridge Review
CanAB Canadian Author and Bookman

9

CanF Canadian Fiction
Canisian
CathR Catholic Review (Auckland)
CathW Catholic World
CE College English
CEA CEA Critic
CEKWJC Collected Essays, Kyoritsu Women's Junior College
Centaur
CentR Centennial Review of Arts and Sciences (Michigan State University)
CF Canadian Forum
Chapbook The Chapbook: a Monthly Miscellany
ChC Christian Century
Cherwell
ChiR Chicago Review
Chimera
ChrC Christianity and Crisis
Christendom
ChrNL Christian News Letter
ChrT Christianity Today
Chrysalis
ChS Christian Scholar
Cithara
CJ Classical Journal
CJR Contemporary Jewish Record
CL Comparative Literature
CM Call Magazine
CML Calendar of Modern Letters
Colos Coloseum, a Quarterly Review
ColQ Colorado Quarterly
Columbia
Commentary
ComR Communist Review
ComS Common Sense
ConI Contemporary Issues
ConR Contemporary Review
Contact
ConW Congress Weekly
CP Classical Philology
CrC Cross Currents
Cresset
Criterion

Criticism (Wayne State University)
CritQ Critical Quarterly
Crossroads
Cue
CurL Current Literature
Cweal Commonweal

DA Dissertation Abstracts
DarQ Dartmouth Quarterly
DD Double Dealer
Decachord
Dial
Diameter
Direction (Melbourne)
DownR Downside Review
DR Dalhousie Review
Drama
DramS Drama Survey
DubM Dublin Magazine
DubR Dublin Review
DUJ Durham University Journal

EA Études Anglaises
Échanges (Paris)
EdL Études de Lettres
Egoist
EIC Essays in Criticism
EIE English Institute Essays
EIHC Essex Institute Historical Collection
EJ English Journal
ELH English Literary History
ELN English Language Notes
EM English Miscellany
Encounter (London)
EngA English "A" Analyst (Northwestern University)
English (London)
EngR English Review
EngSW English Speaking World
ER Empire Review
ES English Studies
ESA English Studies in Africa (Johannesburg)
Esquire
Ethics
ETJ Educational Theatre Journal

European
Everyman
EWR East West Review
Expl Explicator

Fantasy
FJ Freeman's Journal
Fireside
Forum
FR Fortnightly
Freeman
Fresco
FrI Friends Intelligencer
Friend (London)
Fugative
Furioso

GaR Georgia Review
GL&L German Life and Letters
GR Germanic Review
GrR Grantite Review
Grad Graduate Student of English (Minneapolis)
Granta
Greyfriar
Griffin

HA Harvard Advocate
HAB Harvard Alumni Bulletin
HarB Harper's Bazaar
Harpers Harper's Magazine
HB House Beautiful
Here Here and Now
HH Hound and Horn
HIN History of Ideas Newsletter
HJ Hibbert Journal
HP Harvard Progressive
HR Hopkins Review
HSLL Hiroshima Studies in Language and Literature
Horizon
HudR Hudson Review
HumB Humanitas (Brescia)
HumM Humanitas (Manchester)
HumY Humanities (Yokohama)

IEY Iowa English Yearbook
IJES Indian Journal of English Studies

ILA International Literary Annual
ILN Illustrated London News
Independent
Indlander
Isis

JAAC Journal of Aesthetics and Art Criticism
JAL Journal of Arts and Letters
JAUMLA Journal of the Australasian Universities Language and Literature Association
JBR Journal of Bible and Religion
JEGP Journal of English and Germanic Philology
JF Jewish Frontier
JOW John O'London's Weekly

Kano S Kano Studies
KM Kansas Magazine
KR Kenyon Review

LA Living Age
LC Living Church
LCUT Library Chronicle of the University of Texas
Landfall Landfall, a New Zealand Quarterly
LanM Les Langues Modernes
Life
LitC Literary Criterion
LitD Literary Digest
LitDIBR Literary Digest International Book Review
LitHY Literary Half Yearly (Bangalore)
LitPsy Literature and Psychology
LitR Literary Review (Bombay)
LRev Little Review
LitW Literary World
LL Life and Letters and the London Mercury and Bookman (formerly Life and Letters)
Listener
LonA London Aphrodite
LonM London Magazine
LonMerc London Mercury

LQHR London Quarterly and Holborn Review
LS Life of the Spirit
LSUAL Louisiana State University Studies, Studies in American Literature
LuCQ Lutheran Church Quarterly

Mademoiselle
McMUQ McMaster University Quarterly
MD Modern Drama
Meanjin Meanjin Papers
Measure
MFS Modern Fiction Studies
MilB Milton Bulletin
Missionary (Washington, D.C.)
MissQ Mississippi Quarterly
MJ Menorah Journal
MLN Modern Language Notes
MLQ Modern Language Quarterly
MLR Modern Language Review
MM Modern Monthly
ModA Modern Age
ModR Modern Review
Monologue
Month
MP Modern Philology
MQ Modern Quarterly (London)
MR Massachusetts Review
MTL Methodist Times and Leader
MusQ Musical Quarterly

NaAt Nation and Athenaeum
N&Q Notes and Queries
NaR National Review
Nation
Nation (English)
NC Nineteenth Century
NE Near East
Neophilogus
NEQ New England Quarterly
NewA New Age
NewAd New Adelphi
NewCM New-Church Magazine

NewD New Democrat (Bombay)
NewEW New English Weekly
NewH New Humanist
NewL New Leader
NewM New Masses
NewOx New Oxford Outlook
NewP New Pearson's (New York)
NewR New Rambler
NewRev New Review (Calcutta)
NewT New Theatre
NewV New Verse
Nine
1924
NMQ New Mexico Quarterly Review
Newsweek
NorAR North American Review
NR New Republic
NS Die Neuren Sprachen
NSN New Statesman
NY New Yorker

Observer
Occidental
OL Orbis Litterarum
OC Open Court
OJES Osmania Journal of English Studies
Outlook
Outposts
OxM Oxford Magazine
OxO Oxford Outlook

PacW Pacific Weekly
Pagany
ParR Paris Review
PBSA Papers of the Bibliographical Society of America
Person Personalist
Perspective Perspective (a Quarterly Journal of Literature and the Arts)
PhilEW Philosophy East and West
PJ Poetry Journal
PMLA (Publications of the Modern Language Association)

PMLC Papers of the Manchester Literary Club

PNW Penguin New Writing

Poetry Poetry: a Magazine of Verse

PL Poetry (London)

Poetry L Poetry (London)

Poetry Q Poetry Quarterly

Poetry R Poetry Review

PP Picture Post: Hulton's National Weekly

PQ Philological Quarterly

PR Partisan Review

PrS Prairie Schooner

Psychoanalysis

PULC Princeton University Library Chronicle

Punch

PUP Publications of the University of Pretoria

Purpose

PW Publishers' Weekly

QJE Quarterly Journal of Economics

QQ Queen's Quarterly, a Canadian Review

QR Quarterly Review

QRL Quarterly Review of Literature

RBB Religious Book Bulletin

Renascence

REL Review of English Literature (Leeds)

Reporter

RES Review of English Studies

RevP Review of Politics

RL Religion in Life

RLC Revue de Littérature Comparée

RLM Rivista di Letterature Moderne

RLV Revue des Langues Vivantes

RMR Rocky Mountain Review

RR Rikkyo Review (Tokyo)

RUS La Revue de l'Université de Sherbrooke

Salmagundi

SAQ South Atlantic Quarterly

SaR Saturday Review

SatEP Saturday Evening Post

SatR Saturday Review of Literature (later Saturday Review)

SB Studies in Bibliography

Schoolmaster

Scotsman

Scribner's

Scrutiny

ScSo Science and Society

Secession

SELit Studies in English Literature and Language (Tokyo)

SenS Senior Scholastic

SGG Studia Germanica Gandensis

Shama'a Shama'a: a Magazine of Art, Literature and Philosophy

Shenandoah

Sign

Sketch

SocP Social Progress

SoR Southern Review

SoRA Southern Review: an Australian Journal of Literary Studies

SP Studies in Philology

Spirit Spirit: a Magazine of Poetry

SR Sewanee Review

Spectator

SS School and Society

Stage

Standpunte

Star (London)

StCL Studies in Comparative Literature

StLR St. Louis Review

Studies Studies, an Irish Quarterly Review (later, An Irish Literary Quarterly)

SWR Southwest Review

Sym Symposium

Tablet

TAr Theatre Arts

TC Twentieth Century

TCL Twentieth Century Literature

TCV Twentieth Century Verse

Theol Theology Today

Theology

Theoria

Thought

ThP Theatre Programme

ThW Theatre World

Time

Today

TP Terzo Programme

TQ Texas Quarterly

Trace

Traditio

Tri-Quarterly

TRSL Transactions of the Royal Society of Literature of the United Kingdom

TSE Tulane Studies in English

TSLL Texas Studies in Literature and Language

TT Time and Tide

TWA Transactions of the Wisconsin Academy of Sciences, Arts, and Letters

TxSE Texas Studies in English

UCSLL University of Colorado Studies in Language and Literature

UCSSA University of Colorado Studies, Series A

UDPSH University of Denver Publications, Studies in Humanities

UKCR University of Kansas City Review

Unity

UTQ University of Toronto Quarterly

Variety

Verse

VF Vanity Fair

Vice Versa

Vogue

Voices

VQR Virginia Quarterly Review

Wake

WeekER Week-end Review

WHR Western Humanities Review

Wind The Wind and the Rain

Wingover

WQ Windsor Quarterly

WorR World Review

WR Western Review

WSCL Wisconsin Studies in Contemporary Literature

WSCR Washington Square College Review

WT World Theatre

WUS Washington University Studies

WW Weekly Westminster

WWG Weekly Westminster Gazette (later, Weekly Westminster)

WWR Walt Whitman Review

X X, a Quarterly Review

XUS Xavier University Studies

YFS Yale French Studies

YR Yale Review

YWES Year's Work in English Studies

NEWSPAPERS

Atlanta Constitution
Aberdeen Press
Baltimore Evening Sun
Birmingham Post
(Bombay) *Times*
(Boston) *CSM* Christian Science Monitor
Boston Evening American
Boston Evening Post
Boston Sunday Post
Boston Evening Transcript
Boston Globe
Boston Herald
Boston Sunday Post
Boston Times and Mirror
Bristol Times and Mirror
Brooklyn Eagle
Cambridge (England) *Daily News*
Chicago Daily News
Chicago Daily Sun and Times
Chicago Tribune
Chicago Sunday Tribune
Dallas Morning News
Darlington, England—*Northern Echo*
Des Moines Register
(Dublin) *Irish Independent*
(Dublin) *Irish Times*
(Dublin) *Sunday Press*
Edinburgh Evening News
(Glasgow) *Evening News*
Glasgow Herald
Gloucester Daily Times
Inverness Courier
Liverpool Post
(London) *Catholic Herald*
(London) *Catholic Times*
(London) *Church of England Newspaper*
(London) *Church Times*
(London) *Daily Express*
(London) *Daily Herald*
(London) *Daily Mail*

(London) *Daily Telegraph and Morning Post*
(London) *Daily News*
(London) *Daily Sketch and Daily Graphic*
(London) *Evening News*
(London) *Evening Standard*
(London) *Methodist Times and Leader*
(London) *Morning Post*
(London) *News Chronicle*
(London) *Pall Mall Gazette*
(London) *Picture Post*
(London) *Reynolds News*
(London) *Sunday Chronicle*
(London) *Sunday Dispatch*
(London) *Sunday Observer*
(London) *Sun Times* Sunday Times
London Telegraph
(London) *Times*
(London) *Times Educational Supplement*
(London) *TLS* Times Literary Supplement
(London) *Times Magazine*
(London) *Times Weekly Edition*
(London) *Weekly Westminster Gazette*
(Los Angeles) *Daily News*
(Madison) *Daily Cardinal*
Manchester Guardian
Manchester Guardian Weekly
(New Haven) *Yale News*
New York American
(N.Y.) *Daily Compass*
(N.Y.) *Sunday Compass*
(N.Y.) *Daily Mirror*
New York Daily News
New York Evening Journal
New York Evening Post
New York Evening Post Literary Review

New York Globe and Commercial
 Advertiser
New York Herald
NYHT New York Herald
 Tribune
NYHTB New York Herald
 Tribune Books
New York Journal American
New York Journal of Commerce
New York Morning Telegraph
New York Post Magazine
New York Sun
 (N.Y.) Sun and New York
 Herald
NYT New York Times
NYTBR New York Times Book
 Review
NYTM New York Times
 Magazine
 (N.Y.) Town Topics
New York Tribune
 (N.Y.) Variety
 (N.Y.) Women's Wear Daily
New York World

New York World Telegram
Newark Evening News
Northern Whig (place of publica-
 tion not found)
Oakland Tribune
 (Portland) Oregonian
Oxford Times
 (Philadelphia) newspaper of title
 unknown to me
Philadelphia Record
Richmond Evening Journal
St. Louis Globe Democrat
St. Louis Post Dispatch
Sheffield Daily Telegraph
Southport Guardian
 (Springfield, Mass.) Springfield
 Republican
 (Stockton, Cal.) Record
 (Sydney) Sun
Washington Post
Wellesley College News
Yorkshire Post
 (York) Yorkshire Post and Leeds
 Mercury

A HALF-CENTURY OF ELIOT CRITICISM

An Annotated Bibliography
of Books and Articles
in English, 1916-1965

BIBLIOGRAPHY

1916

1. Aiken, Conrad. "Esoteric Catholicity." *PJ* 5 (April) : 127–29. [Prufrock; Portrait of a Lady]. Calls these poems "subtle to the verge of insoluble idiosyncrasy, introspective, self-gnawing."
2. Waugh, Arthur. "The New Poetry." *QR* 226 (October) : 386. [Prufrock]. Six lines are quoted and the poem dismissed as "the reduction to absurdity of literary license."

1917

3. Aiken, Conrad. "Divers Realists." *Dial* 63 (November 8) : 453–55. [Prufrock; Rhapsody on a Windy Night; Portrait of a Lady]. Calls Eliot a realist, praises his intuitions and technique. Reprinted in *Scepticisms*. New York: A. A. Knopf, Inc., 1919, pp. 203–5, partially reprinted in Unger, no. 1433.
4. Anon. "Recent Verse." *LitW* 83 (July 5) : 107. [Prufrock and Other Observations]. "We do not wish to appear patronising, but we feel certain Mr. Eliot could do finer work on traditional lines. With him it seems to be a case of missing the effect by too much cleverness."
5. ———. *LRev* 4, no. 4 (August) : 24–25. An unsigned letter that calls "Lune de Miel" "disgusting," and "The Hippopotamus" "satisfactory." The writer thinks that Pound and Eliot want to shock the reader.
6. ———. "Shorter Notices." *NSN* 9 (August 18) : 477. [Prufrock]. Eliot is no poet, but he is "decidedly amusing."
7. ———. *TLS*. Review of *Prufrock and Other Observations,* no. 805 (June 21), p. 299. The pieces "have no relation to poetry."
*8. Pound, Ezra. "T. S. Eliot." *Poetry* 10, (August) : 264–71. [Prufrock and Other Observations]. "I would praise the

work for its fine tone, its humanity, and its realism."
Pound compares Eliot to the best French writers and
praises his intelligence, which includes emotion. This is
an important early and subtle appreciation. Reprinted
in *Literary Essays of Ezra Pound*. New York: New Directions, 1954.

9. ———. "Drunken Helots and Mr. Eliot." *Egoist* 4, no. 5
(June) : 72–74. [Prufrock]. Pound announces a new
poet who has "no living betters."

10. Sinclair, May. "Prufrock: and Other Observations: a Criti-
cism." *LRev* 4 (December) : 8–14. A lively defense of
Eliot against his detractors in *Quarterly Review* and
New Statesman.

1918

11. Aiken, Conrad. "New Curiosity Shop—and a Poet." *Dial*
64 (January 31) : 112. [Preludes; Rhapsody on a Windy
Night]. Two paragraphs on Eliot's use of rhyme and
meter in the poems contributed to the anthology of
Imagist verse, *Others*.

12. B. D. [Babette Deutsch]. "Another Impressionist." *NR*
14 (February 16) : 89. [Prufrock and Other Observa-
tions]. Good brief appreciation, chiefly concerned with
meter.

13. Hartley, Marsden. "Breakfast Résumé." *LRev* 5, no. 7
(November) : 46–50. [Prufrock and Other Observa-
tions]. Objects to Eliot's learned words, but says "T.S.F.
[*sic*] has done far better things."

14. Jepson, Edgar. "Recent United States Poetry." *EngR* 26
(May) : 426–28. [Prufrock and Other Observations].
Contrasts Eliot favorably with Lindsay and Masters;
emphasizes his modernity and Americanism.

15. M. M. [Marianne Moore]. "A Note on T. S. Eliot's
Book." *Poetry* 12 (April) : 36–37. [Prufrock and Other
Observations]. Says the poems are disconcerting but
honest.

1919

16. Anon. "Is This Poetry?" *Athenaeum*, no. 4651 (June 20),
p. 491. [Poems]. The reviewer is confused. "We hope
that Mr. Eliot will quickly give us more and remove
our melancholy suspicion that he is a product of a
Silver Age."

17. ———. "Not Here, O Apollo." *TLS,* no. 908 (June 12),
p. 322. [Poems]. Eliot is clever, but says nothing.

18. ———. "Experiments in Poetry." *TLS,* no. 905 (May 22),
p. 274. [A Cooking Egg]. Eliot already has "some reputation." Praises the "elegant wit" and the "superior
Irony" of this poem.

19. Jepson, Edgar. "That International Episode." *LRev* 5,
no. 10–11 (February–March): 62–63. "I propose to go
right on asserting that the poetry of Mr. T. S. Eliot is
the fine flower of the United States spirit of today because that is just what it is."

20. Williams, William Carlos. "Prologue." *LRev* 6, no. 1
(May): 76–78. A slangy attack on Edgar Jepson, who
likes Eliot for being a "subtle conformist."

1920

21. Anon. review of *Poems, 1919. Booklist* 16 (June): 305.
This note comments on the "strangeness and freshness"
of the poems.

*22. ———. "The Sacred Wood." *ComS* (later incorporated
into the *Manchester Guardian Commercial*) (April
12). [So dated in the Eliot Collection, but the paper
did not appear on this date]. Eliot's "dry intellectual
tests" for literature are a "wholesome medicine." Good
early criticism.

23. ———. *Everyman* 16 (August 7): 356. [Sacred Wood].
A notice reading: "Eliot, T. S., An American who has
made his home in London. One of the cleverest critics
of modern English literature" has irritated the older
critics.

24. ———. "The Week's Books." *NE* 18 (December 23): 860.
[Sacred Wood]. Says that "his literary criticism is reasonably human."

25. ———. "English and American Poets—a Contrast."
NYTBR (June 27), p. 16. A reference to Eliot's fine use
of the "satiric vein."

26. ———. "A Wooden Rod." *Observer,* November 28. [Sa-
cred Wood]. Eliot's deficiencies as a literary critic are
that he does not enjoy literature, has no sense of humor,
and takes criticism too seriously.

27. ———. "A New Byronism." *TLS,* no. 948 (March 18),
p. 184. [Ara vos Prec]. "Mr. Eliot does not convince us

that his weariness is anything but a habit, . . . a new
Byronism."

28. ———. "The Criticism of Poetry." *TLS*, no. 952 (April
15), p. 236. [A Brief Treatise on the Criticism of
Poetry]. "Mr. Eliot, in attempting to prove that only a
poet can be a poetic critic, falls into a false analogy."
A long essay. See Eliot's reply, *TLS*, April 22, 1920.

29. ———. "The Function of Criticism." *TLS*, no. 956 (May
13), p. 289. [A Brief Treatise on the Criticism of Po-
etry]. A leading article treating Eliot seriously, but de-
ciding that he is wrong in saying the poet is the best
critic.

30. ———. "Poetry and Criticism." *TLS*, no. 985 (December
2), p. 795. [Sacred Wood]. Praises "Tradition and the
Individual Talent"; thinks Eliot takes a malicious
pleasure in showing up some of our old favorites.

31. Bettany, F. G. "The Bookshelf." *ArG* 2 (April 3) : 741–42.
[A Brief Treatise on the Criticism of Poetry]. Objects
to the criticism because it is too much the work of a
craftsman.

32. ———. *ArG* 3 (May 29) : 93. [Euripides and Professor
Murray]. He is shocked at Eliot's cavalier treatment of
Gilbert Murray's translation of Euripides.

33. Colum, Padraic. "Studies in the Sophisticated." *NR* 25
(December 8) : 52. [Poems]. This poetry marks the
end of the cycle of romantic poetry, if it does not begin
a cycle.

34. Cummings, E. E. "T. S. Eliot." *Dial* 68 (June) : 781–84.
[Poems]. Praises Eliot's technique, and is pleased that
"no however cautiously attempted dissection of Mr.
T. S. E's sensitivity begins to touch a few certain lines
whereby become big and blundering and totally un-
skilful our altogether unnecessary fingers."

35. Deutsch, Babette. "The Season for Song—A Page on the
Poets—T. S. Eliot's Weird and Brilliant Book." *New
York Evening Post* (May 29). [So dated in the Eliot
Collection, but the review was not found under this
date.] [Poems]. In the later poems the amateur ironist
has dismissed the more serious artist of "Prufrock."

36. Goldring, Douglas. "Modern Critical Prose." *Chapbook*
2, no. 8 (February) : 11. [Sacred Wood]. One paragraph in praise of Eliot's criticism. He has a "scientific,
analytical brain, . . . a standard of values, and he is
honest in applying them."

37. Hannay, A. H. "The Perfect Critic." *Athenaeum,* no. 4709 (July 30), p. 156. Raises good questions about "The Perfect Critic" in *The Sacred Wood.* Eliot's reply, August 6, 1920.

38. Hueffer, Ford Madox. "Thus to Revisit . . . Some Reminiscences." *EngR* 31 (September): 209–17. Eliot is mentioned as one of a group of writers whom Hueffer [Ford Madox Ford] and Arthur Marwood had set out to "encourage" in 1910–1914.

39. Lynd, Robert. "Buried Alive." *Nation* (English) 18 (December 4): supplement, 359–60. [Sacred Wood]. Chiefly occupied with criticism of the *Hamlet* essay. "Mr. Eliot fails as a critic because he brings the reader neither light nor delight." Reprinted in *Books and Authors,* London: Richard Cobden, 1922, pp. 248–55.

40. Murry, J. Middleton. "The Eternal Footman." *Athenaeum,* no. 4686 (February 20), p. 239. [Ara vos Prec]. A clever essay suggesting that Eliot's irony is the enemy of his deepest poetry.

41. Nichols, Robert. "An Ironist." *Observer* (London), (April 18), p. 7. [Ara vos Prec]. Wishes that Eliot would allow himself to express his taste for the more terrible realities, not merely for life's ironies.

42. Rickword, Edgell. "Weed Killing." *Daily Herald* (London) (November 24), p. 7. [Sacred Wood]. Good early review pointing out Eliot's significance for criticism.

43. A. de S. Review of *The Sacred Wood. Manchester Guardian,* (November 22), p. 5. Objects to his "over-compression."

44. Stroble, Marion. "Perilous Leaping." *Poetry* 16 (June): 157–59. [Poems]. Humorously protests against the obscurity of most of the poems, but heartily praises "Prufrock" and "The Portrait of a Lady."

45. Untermeyer, Louis. "Irony de Luxe." *Freeman* 1 (June 30): 381–82. [Poems]. Although admitting that Eliot's influence is "indisputable," he thinks that he fails because his irony is too cool; Untermeyer calls him a writer of *vers de société.*

46. Van Doren, Mark. "Anglo-Saxon Adventurer in Verse." *Nation* 110 (June 26): 856a–57a. [Poems]. Calls Eliot a "downright, diabolical genius." "Mr. Eliot will never be popular at this rate. But when will he not have readers?"

47. L. W. [Leonard Woolf?]. "Back to Aristotle." *Athenaeum,*

no. 4729 (Dec. 17) , pp. 834–35. [Sacred Wood]. Praises the solidity of Eliot's criticism.

48. Weaver, Raymond M. "What Ails Pegasus?" *Bookman* 52 (September) : 59. [Poems]. "He is usually intelligible only when he is nasty." One paragraph.

1921

49. W. J. A. "The Will to Value." *NewA* 29, n.s. (May 12) : 21. [Sacred Wood]. Says the essays are unilluminating because they draw no conclusions.

*50. Aiken, Conrad. "The Scientific Critic." *Freeman* 2 (March 2) : 593–94. [Sacred Wood]. Raises many of the questions concerning content and form to be discussed by later critics.

*51. Aldington, Richard. "A Critic of Poetry." *Poetry* 17 (March) : 345–48. [Sacred Wood]. A sensitive review praising Eliot in terms to be repeated endlessly by other critics.

52. ———. "The Sacred Wood." *Today* 8, no. 47 (September) : 191–93. Enthusiastic praise of Eliot's "right reason." "It *is* credible that readers and writers should disagree with what Mr. Eliot says, but it is perfectly incredible that any person above the ranks of the ignorant should affect to believe that Mr. Eliot's criticism is negligible."

53. Anon. "The Sacred Wood." *NSN* 16 (March 26) : 733–34. Analyzes suspiciously the reasons for the pleasure which Eliot's criticism gives the bookish, uncreative reader, and accuses Eliot of snobbery.

54. ———. "Detachment." *SaR* 131 (April 2) : 281–82. [Sacred Wood]. Eliot writes poetry without emotion and imagination, though he has "great ability."

55. ———. "The Razor of Croce." *TLS*, no. 1014 (June 23) , p. 393. [Hamlet and His Problems]. The reviewer suggests that Eliot's view of *Hamlet* results from making wrong demands on the play.

56. ———. "Critics and Criticism." *Weekly Westminster Gazette* 57 (February 5) : 16–17. [Sacred Wood]. Deplores the fact that Eliot does not apply his critical gifts to contemporary literature.

57. Bell, Clive. "Plus de Jazz." *NR* 28 (September 21) : 94–95. [Poems; Ara vos Prec]. "Mr. Eliot is about the best of our living poets, and like Stravinsky, he is as much a

product of the Jazz movement as so good an artist can be of any."

58. Birrell, Augustine. "The Reader—Lord Rosebery as Essayist." *Bookman* (English) 61 (November) : 80. [Sacred Wood]. He is uneasy about Eliot's insistence on impersonal criticism, but thinks he may be right.

59. Deutsch, Babette. "Orchestral Poetry." *Dial* 70 (March) : 343–46. She shows how Aiken echoes Eliot in phrasing and in an attitude of vague, somewhat amused disillusion.

60. Digby, Kenelm. "The Literary Lobby." *New York Evening Post Literary Review,* (February 19) , p. 16. Gossip reports that Eliot "is considered the best young poet in England."

61. MacCarthy, Desmond. "New Poets, T. S. Eliot." *NSN* 16 (January 8) : 418–20. [Ara vos Prec]. MacCarthy compares and contrasts Eliot with Browning and Laforgue. Reprinted under the title "T. S. Eliot (1921)" in *Criticism,* New York: Putnam, 1932, pp. 89–97.

62. McAlmon, Robert. "Modern Antiques." *Contact* (January) , unpaged, mimeographed. Protests that Eliot is a victim of "culture via ideas"; he has stopped writing good poetry and has turned to criticism; he will become a poor critic if he does not relate literature to reality rather than to literature.

63. Moore, Marianne. Review of *The Sacred Wood. Dial* 70 (March) : 336–39. "In his poetry, he seems to move troutlike through a multiplicity of foreign objects and in his instinctiveness and care as a critic, he appears as a complement to the sheen upon his poetry."

64. Moult, Thomas. "On Following One's Own Taste." *EngR* 32 (January) : 87–89. [Sacred Wood]. The essay begins with a reference to Eliot.

65. Murry, J. Middleton. Review of *The Sacred Wood. NR* 26 (April 13) : 194–95. Carefully explains Eliot's ideas, since so many critics have misunderstood them.

66. ———. "A Matter of Form." *NaAt* 29 (May 28) : 328–39. [Poetry in Prose]. Says of Pound, Eliot, H. D., and Aldington: "However good or bad as poets, they are at least intelligent."

67. Osborn, E. B. "Books of the Day." *ILN* 158 (January 8) : 48. [Sacred Wood]. Brief notice of "a collection of critical essays of varying merit."

68. Read, Herbert. "Readers and Writers." *NewA* 29, n.s. (September 8) : 222. [Poetry in Prose]. "Mr. Eliot's is not a very positive voice in the matter [of form in literature], but when we have applied all his negations, we are left with a very narrow field for positive errors."

69. ———. "Readers and Writers." *NewA* 29, n.s. (September 15) : 236. [Poetry in Prose]. A brief, complimentary reference.

70. E. S. "Literary History, Criticism." *LonMerc* 3 (February) : 447–50. [Sacred Wood]. Complains that Eliot's reasoning is elusive, although intelligent.

71. Van Doren, Mark. "England's Critical Compass." *Nation* 112 (May 4) : 669. [Sacred Wood]. "Mr. Eliot is not a perfect critic, because he does not write well enough in prose; but in the course of his essays he has drawn permanently valuable distinctions," and he says the critic must think.

1922

*72. Aldington, Richard. "The Poetry of T. S. Eliot." *Outlook* (London) 49 (January 7) : 12–13. On Eliot's literary antecedents, French and English metaphysical poets. Defends him against the charge of obscurity, and insists on the unity between his poetic theory and practice. Reprinted in *New York Evening Post Literary Review*, January 14, 1922, p. 350; in *Literary Studies and Reviews*, New York: Dial Press, and London: George Allen and Unwin, 1924, pp. 181–91; Unger, no. 1433.

73. Anon. "Comment." *Dial* 73 (December) : 685–87. [Waste Land; Sacred Wood]. Praises Eliot's invention, both in poetry and in prose, and presents the reason why *The Dial* gave him its $2,000 prize.

74. ———. "Books and Authors." *NYTBR* (November 26), p. 12. [Waste Land]. On the *Dial* award of $2,000 for *The Waste Land*. "Mr. Eliot's work is marked by an intense cerebral quality and a compact music that has practically established a movement among the younger men."

75. ———. "Justifying Hamlet." *Outlook* (London) 50 (September 2) : 196. [Hamlet and His Problems]. Praises Clutton-Brock for disposing of Eliot's judgment on *Hamlet*. Brief.

76. ———. Notice of *Andrew Marvell; Tercentenary Tributes by Various Contributors. Spectator* 129, no. 4916 (September 16) : 373. [Andrew Marvell]. "Mr. Massingham's and Mr. Eliot's essays are the most notable, for they most clearly discover the unique value of Marvell's poems."

77. ———. Notice of *The Criterion. TLS,* no. 1074 (August 17) , p. 525. A notice that the first issue of *The Criterion* will appear on October 15, a statement of policy, and a list of contributors.

78. ———. Notice of the first issue of *The Criterion* and review of *The Waste Land. TLS,* no. 1084 (October 26) , p. 690. Brief, but good. "Life [in the poem] is neither hellish nor heavenly: it has a purgatorial quality."

79. Bell, Clive. "The 'Difference' of Literature." *NR* 33 (November 29) : 19. An incidental reference: "About the best poet writing in England is, to my thinking, T. S. Eliot."

80. Clutton-Brock, Arthur. "The Case against 'Hamlet.' " *Shakespeare's 'Hamlet,'* pp. 14–32. London: Methuen and Co., 1922. [Hamlet and His Problems]. A scholarly essay objecting to Eliot's calling *Hamlet* an artistic failure. Eliot has treated the play as if it were the history of real persons.

81. Ely, Catherine B. "Whitman and the Radicals as Poets of Democracy." *Open Court* 36 (October) : 594–601. Deals briefly with Eliot.

82. [Lowell, Amy]. *A Critical Fable,* pp. 90–94. New York: Houghton Mifflin, 1922. Humorous doggerel, comparing Eliot and Pound.

83. H. J. M. "The World of Books." *NaAt* 31 (May 27) : 309. [Hamlet and His Problems]. Reviews Clutton-Brock's *Hamlet,* and dismisses Eliot's criticism of the play because his evidence is "flimsy."

84. Murry, J. Middleton. "The Dickens Revival." *Times Magazine* (May) . [This item has been seen only as a clipping] [Wilkie Collins and Dickens]. "Now that [Eliot] has granted his provisional imprimatur, the most advanced young man may carry a copy of Pickwick in his pocket."

85. Seldes, Gilbert. "T. S. Eliot." *Nation* 115 (December 6) : 614–16. [Waste Land; Sacred Wood]. As critic, Eliot's distinction is to be concerned with the aesthetic prob-

lem. As poet, he had found the right form, though seemingly disjointed, to express the present sterility of life.

86. A. T. [Allen Tate]. "Whose Ox." *Fugitive* 1 (December) : 100. [Waste Land]. Praises the unusual versification of *The Waste Land,* but remarks that the older forms "are not yet sapped." Brief.

87. Van Doorn, Willem. Review of *The Sacred Wood. ES* 4: 42–43. Chiefly quotation. "It will set one thinking. . . ." It is "without cant."

*88. Wilson, Edmund. "The Rag-bag of the Soul." *New York Evening Post Literary Review* (November 25) , pp. 237–38. An important article on modern consciousness as expressed by painters and men of letters. Places Eliot in his milieu.

*89. ———. "The Poetry of Drouth." *Dial* 73 (December) : 611–16. [Waste Land]. He considers the relation of the poem to Miss Weston's book, the vanity of the past but also its "heroic strains of unfading music," the complexity but also intelligibility of the poem, its lack of structure, but its power. A brilliant, rich essay.

1923

90. Aiken, Conrad. "An Anatomy of Melancholy." *NR* 33 (February 7) : 294–95. [Waste Land]. This review raises the main questions concerning *The Waste Land* to be discussed for the next twenty-five years. Aiken concludes that "the poem succeeds . . . by virtue of its incoherence . . . of its ambiguities."

91. Anon. "Shantih, Shantih, Shantih, Has the Reader any Rights before the Bar of Literature?" *Time* 1 (March 3) : 12. [Waste Land]. The poem is unintelligible.

92. ———. "A Fragmentary Poem." *TLS,* no. 1131 (September 20) , p. 616. [Waste Land]. Brings up the objections (too many quotations) and pays the compliments (his refinement and intensity) that were frequently repeated later. Brief, but good.

93. ———. "A Group of Poems by T. S. Eliot." *VF* 20 (June) : 67. Editorial comment on the early poems. Clear.

94. Bell, Clive. "T. S. Eliot." *NaAt* 33 (September 22) : 772– 73. [Waste Land]. Eliot lacks imagination, but he can write. Original, fresh criticism. Reprinted under the

title "The Elusive Art of T. S. Eliot" in *Vanity Fair*.
September 1923, p. 53.

95. Benét, William Rose. "Among the New Books. Poetry ad
Lib." *YR* 13 (October) : 161–62. [Waste Land]. A brief,
appreciative note. "I found it deeply emotional under-
neath all the attitudinizing."

96. Dawson, N. P. "Enjoying Poor Literature." *Forum* 69
(March) : 1371–79. [Waste Land]. Objects to its unintelligibility and pessimism. Facetious.

97. Gidlow, Elsa. "A Waste Land, Indeed." *NewP* 49 (July) :
57. [Waste Land]. "He has tried to swallow the modern
world but it sticks in his fastidious gullet."

98. Gorman, H. S. "The Waste Land of the Younger Generation." *LitDIBR* 1 (April) : 46, 48, 64. [Waste Land].
An objective summary of ten reviews of the poem, and
a defense of it.

99. Lucas, F. L. "The Waste Land." *NSN* 22 (November 3) :
116–18. The poem is unintelligible, the borrowings
cheap, and the notes useless.

100. MacCarthy, Desmond ["Affable Hawk"]. "Books in General." *NSN* 20 (March 10) : 660. Eliot is not a successor
of Donne because of Eliot's "emotional monotony."
Brief.

101. McAfee, Helen. "The Literature of Disillusion." *Atlantic*
132 (August) : 227. [Waste Land]. The unity of the
poem depends upon its black mood.

102. J. M. [John McClure?]. Review of *The Waste Land*. *DD*
5 (May) : 173–74. Objects to the poem as private and
discordant, but says, "Many of us have contended for
a long time that T. S. Eliot is one of the most exceptional
men of letters of his epoch. *The Waste Land* confirms
that belief."

103. Monro, Harold. "Notes for a Study of *The Waste Land:*
an Imaginary Dialogue with T. S. Eliot." *Chapbook*,
no. 34 (February) , pp. 20–24. Part I is a dialogue, with
Eliot saying "Possibly." Concludes, "This poem is at
the same time a representation, a criticism, and the
disgusted outcry of a heart turned cynical." Favorable
but puzzled.

104. Monroe, Harriet. "A Contrast." *Poetry* 21 (March) : 325–
30. [Waste Land]. Apparently tries to appreciate Eliot,
but prefers Lew Sarrett because he is a "man of faith."

Reprinted in *Poets and Their Art*. New York: Macmillan, 1926, pp. 100–108.

105. Munson, Gorham B. "Congratulations, and More 'Ill-Mannered References.'" *Secession,* no. 4 (January), pp. 31–32. The congratulations are to *The Dial* for its award to Eliot, "who deserves all the prizes in Christendom not only because he is a distinguished man of letters, but because he is besides a gentleman of letters." The second part of the title refers to Sherwood Anderson.

106. Murry, John Middleton. "More about Romanticism." *Adelphi* 1 (December): 557–69. A reasoned expression of his belief in romanticism as opposed to Eliot's classicism.

107. Ransom, John Crowe. "Waste Lands." *New York Evening Post Literary Review* 3 (July 14): 825–26. [Waste Land]. Taking Wordsworth as his standard, Ransom decides that the poem fails because it lacks unity. Interesting in the history of Eliot criticism. Reprinted in *Modern Essays, Second Series,* edited by Christopher Morley. New York: Harcourt, Brace, 1924, pp. 345–59.

108. Squire, J. C. "Poetry." *LonMerc* 8 (October): 655–56. [Waste Land]. A "grunt would serve equally well" as this poem.

109. Tate, Allen. "Waste Lands." *New York Evening Post Literary Review* 3 (August 4): 886. [Waste Land]. Reply to Ransom, no. 107. Tate defends the unity of the poem.

110. Untermeyer, Louis. "Disillusion vs. Dogma." *Freeman* 6 (January 17): 453. [Waste Land]. An outraged protest against the formlessness and obscurity of the poem.

111. ———. "T. S. Eliot." *American Poetry since 1900,* pp. 350–62. New York: Henry Holt, 1923. [Poems, 1920; Waste Land]. "As an analyst of psychic impotence, of dubious quiverings . . . , Eliot has created something whose value is, at least, documentary." Mr. Apollinax may be Bertrand Russell.

112. Wolfe, Humbert. "Waste Land and Waste Paper." *Weekly Westminster* 1, n.s. (November 17): 94. [Waste Land]. "I don't pretend to understand, but end with the sense that the five movements are knit together by some invulnerable strand. There remains in my mind a sound of high and desolate music." The "Waste Paper" refers to another book.

113. Wood, Clement. "The Tower of Drivel." *CM* (New York) (June 20), p. 11. [Waste Land.] "It is a farrago of nonsense."

*114. Wylie, Elinor. "Mr. Eliot's Slug Horn." *New York Evening Post Literary Review* (January 20), p. 396. [Waste Land]. A sensitive and witty appreciation.

1924

115. Anon. "The Ideal of Criticism." *TLS*, no. 1175 (July 24), pp. 453–54. The writer draws heavily on Eliot to support his own argument.

116. Blum, Walter C. "Journalist Critics." *Dial* 76 (June): 557–58. [Sacred Wood]. The essays are elegant, rigorously moral, and concerned primarily with the nature of the artistic process.

117. Muir, Edwin. "Recent Criticism." *NaAt* 36 (December 6): 370, 372. [Homage to John Dryden]. Admires Eliot's precision, but regrets that he is inconclusive.

118. Munson, Gorham B. "The Esotericism of T. S. Eliot." *1924*, no. 1 (July 1), pp. 3–10. [Waste Land]. Eliot chooses to mystify the reader in accordance with a theory of pessimism which America is right in rejecting.

119. Van Doren, Mark. "First Glance." *Nation* 119 (December 31): 732–33. [Homage to John Dryden]. A clear summary. Reprinted in *The Private Reader*. New York: Henry Holt, 1942, pp. 131–33.

120. Williams, Orlo. *Contemporary Criticism of Literature*, pp. 89–94, 143–54. London: Leonard Parsons, 1924. Eliot, a scientific critic, whose method is elucidation, is one of the few people who take criticism seriously, but "he goes too far in wishing to eliminate all expressions of opinion." Williams quotes largely from *The Sacred Wood*.

1925

*121. Aldington, Richard. "T. S. Eliot, Poet and Critic." *Vogue* (April) (British ed. only), pp. 70 ff. High praise for Eliot's classicism, his intellectualism, his reaching the bedrock of reality. Portrait. A good article.

122. Anon. "Life's Brass Medal." *Life* 85 (March 12): 24. [Waste Land]. *The Dial* is awarded a brass medal for giving its prize to Eliot.

123. ———. "A Parallel." *NSN* 25 (June 20): 290. [Waste Land]. On the similarity of Nancy Cunard's "Parallax" to *The Waste Land*.

124. ———. "We Nominate for the Hall of Fame." *VF* 24 (July): 55. A picture of Eliot and a paragraph concerning him.

125. Boyd, Ernest A. "Hyphenated Poets." *Studies from Ten Literatures*, pp. 315–17. New York: Scribner's, 1925. [Eliot's poems in French]. He corrects Eliot's French, and regards him as a buffoon.

126. Freeman, John. "Literary History and Criticism—II." *LonMerc* 11 (April): 662–64. [Homage to John Dryden]. A sympathetic summary of the book.

127. Kreymborg, Alfred. *Troubadour*, pp. 396–97. New York: Boni and Liveright, 1925. At a meeting with Eliot in London in 1922, Kreymborg was impressed with his suave intelligence and subtlety.

128. Mortimer, Raymond. "New Books from the Morning Room Table." *Vogue* (January) (British edition only) [Homage to John Dryden]. Eliot is the "most accomplished and much the most moving of contemporary poets." As a critic "he is always serious, always clear-headed, always independent."

*129. Muir, Edwin. "T. S. Eliot." *Nation* 121 (August 5): 162–64. As a poet, Eliot lacks seriousness, though he is "bitter, despairing, melancholy." But he deserves to be "ranked with the chief English critics." A good expression of an early attitude toward Eliot. Reprinted under the title "Contemporary Writers, III. Mr. T. S. Eliot," in *NaAt*, August 29, 1925, pp. 644–46, and in *Transition*, New York: Viking Press, 1926, pp. 131–44.

130. ———. "Mr. Eliot's Criticism." *CML* 1 (May): 242–44. [Homage to John Dryden]. "His criticism is more comprehensive and more sound than that of any other writer of this generation, but it would be infinitely better if it were compatible with an appreciation of the importance of Milton as well as of Marlowe, of Wordsworth as well as Dryden, in the English poetic tradition."

131. Rickword, Edgell. "The Modern Poet." *CML* 2 (December): 278–81 [Poems, 1909–1925]. The main stages in Eliot's technique are illustrated in "Prufrock," "Gerontion," and *The Waste Land*. Eliot's greatest gift is his sense of rhythm; his chief defect is the intermittent working of his verbal imagination.

132. "Tellalot, T. S." "Portrait of an Ex-Lady," and "Winkel-
     mann among the Teacups." *HA* 111 (April), parody
     number. [Prufrock; Portrait of a Lady].

133. Warren, C. Henry. "New Books. Three Poets." *Bookman*
     (English) 69 (February) : 263. [Poems 1909–1925]. He
     acknowledges the power of these poems, which he does
     not understand, but prefers more sentiment than they
     possess.

134. Wilson, Edmund. "T. S. Eliot and the Seventeenth Cen-
     tury." *NR* 41 (January 7) : 177–78. [Homage to John
     Dryden]. Chiefly quotation, little criticism.

135. ———. "Paul Valéry." *Dial* 78 (June) : 491–97. [Brief
     Introduction to the Method of Paul Valéry]. Says Eliot's
     preface is too difficult.

*136. Woolf, Leonard. " 'Jug Jug' to Dirty Ears." *NaAt* 38 (De-
     cember 5) : 354. [Poems, 1909–1925]. "I have admitted
     that Mr. Eliot's poetry is difficult, but I have admitted
     it with so many qualifications that the admission is
     valueless." Excellent brief appreciation.

1926

137. Anon. "Comment." *Dial* 80 (February) : 178. [Homage
     to John Dryden]. Eliot revives our enjoyment of Dry-
     den's satire and of Marvell's "precise taste."

138. ———. "The All-Star Literary Vaudeville." *NR* 47 (June
     30) : 162. A few lines praising Eliot's poetry and criti-
     cism.

139. ———. "Poetical Plays." *TLS,* no. 1295 (November 25) ,
     p. 848. [Introduction to *Savonarola*]. A discussion of
     Eliot's attitude toward the use of blank verse in drama.

140. Hood, Arthur. "Delicate Spirits and a Hunchback."
     Poetry R 17 (January–February) : 53–54. [Poems, 1909–
     1925]. Sees only squalor in the poems, and identifies the
     author with it.

141. Morgan, Louise. "The Poetry of Mr. Eliot." *Outlook*
     (London) 57 (February 20) , 135–36. [Poems, 1909–
     1925]. Sympathetic, fairly good.

*142. Murry, J. Middleton. "The 'Classical' Revival." *Adelphi*
     3 (February) : 585–95; (March) : 648–53. A subtle and
     penetrating statement of the contradictions between
     Eliot's desire for order and the "living emotional crea-
     tive part of him" which produced *The Waste Land.*

"He makes the impression of one who loves the prestige
and refuses the obligations of classicism."

*143. Richards, I. A. "Mr. Eliot's Poems." *NSN* 26 (February
20) : 584–85. [Poems, 1909–1925]. Eliot is not obscure.
The poetry is the "music of ideas," and must be read
emotionally. An influential review. Reprinted in *LA*
329 (April 10, 1926) : 112–15.

*144. ———. *Science and Poetry*, p. 76. New York: W. W. Norton, 1926. An important statement that Eliot has effected "a complete severance between his poetry and *all*
beliefs."

145. J. C. S[quire]. "Poems." *LonMerc* 13 (March) : 547–48.
[Poems, 1909–1925]. Complains of obscurity and lack
of content.

146. Stein, Gertrude. "The Fifteenth of November." *Criterion*
4 (January) : 71–75. A wry "portrait" of Eliot is a response to his request to see her "very latest" composition
for possible publication. The portrait (written the day
of the request, November 15, 1922) contains animad-
versions on grammatical minutiae and on Eliot's solemnity. Reprinted in *Portraits and Prayers*. New York:
Random House, 1934, pp. 71–75.

147. Stuart-Young, J. M. "A Leader of 'Modern' Verse—T. S.
Eliot." *PL* 9 (October–December) : 624–28. Eliot is not
a great poet because he does not write of Beauty, as
the Poet Laureate does.

148. Tate, Allen. "A Poetry of Ideas." *NR* 47 (June 30) : 172–
73. [Poems, 1909–1925]. Speaks of Elizabethan and
French influences on Eliot, and his poetic technique.
Defends his borrowings, and says he is at the end of
a phase.

149. Van Doorn, Willem. "How It Strikes a Contemporary,
New Series I. T. S. Eliot." *ES* 8, no. 5: 138–42. [Pru-
frock; Sweeney among the Nightingales; Waste Land].
Likes Eliot only when he writes as an impressionist.

150. Wilson, Edmund. "Stravinsky and Others." *NR* 46
(March 10) : 74 [Poems, 1909–1925]. Suggests that the
reason for Eliot's gloom is not the plight of Europe,
but the fact that he is a New England Puritan.

1927

151. Aiken, Conrad. "The Poetic Dilemma." *Dial* 82 (May) :
420–22. [Poems, 1909–1925]. On the search for a poetic

theme. "Why not—he says in effect—make a bitter sort of joke of one's nihilism and impotence?" Eliot's future as a poet is secure.

152. Aldington, Richard. "Mr. Eliot on Seneca." *NaAt* 42 (October 29) : 159. [Seneca in Elizabethan Translation]. A careful consideration of Eliot's scholarship, as well as of his critical method.

153. Anon. "Where the Poets Fail." *LitD* 95 (November 26) : 25. [Waste Land]. *The Waste Land* is not the hopeful poem praising our civilization which is needed today.

154. ———. "Literature and Tradition." *Nation* 125 (October 12) : 355. Eliot and the other critics emphasizing tradition are responsible for an increased interest in older literature.

155. ———. "New Subject." *Time* 10 (November 28) : 14. On Eliot's becoming a British subject.

156. ———. "Five Modern Poets." *TLS,* no. 1308 (February 24), p. 113. [Waste Land; A Cooking Egg]. An intelligent explanation of the difference between metaphysics in philosophy and in poetry clarifies the structure of Eliot's poetry. The reviewer also compares his poems with those of Herbert Read. Reprinted in *Living Age,* vol. 332, April 15, 1927, pp. 695–97.

*157. Belgion, Montgomery. "In Memory of T. E. Hulme." *SatR* 4, pt. I (October 1) : 154–55. An important article on the relation of Hulme's philosophy to that of Eliot.

158. A.Y.C. "Seneca and His Influence." *NSN* 30 (October 22) : 50, 52. [Seneca in Elizabethan Translation]. Patronizing approval.

159. Chambers, E. K. "Newton's Seneca." *Observer* (October 9), p. 7. [Seneca in Elizabethan Translation]. Says the introductory essay by Eliot "is full of good and suggestive critical points."

160. Fergusson, Francis. "T. S. Eliot and His Impersonal Theory of Art," *The American Caravan,* edited by Van Wyck Brooks *et al.,* pp. 446–53. New York: Macaulay Co., 1927. If Eliot's only value is aesthetic, freedom can be known only in the creative act, but there are recent indications that he is aware of moral problems, so that his position is ambiguous. Thoughtful.

*161. Fernandez, Ramon. "The Classicism of T. S. Eliot." *Messages,* translated by Montgomery Belgion, pp. 295–304. New York: Harcourt, Brace, 1927. First appeared in *La Nouvelle Revue Française* 24 (February 1925) : 246–51. Well organized, clear, and sympathetic.

162. Mirksy, D. S. "Literary History and Criticism." *LonMerc*, 17 (December) : 210. [Shakespeare and the Stoicism of Seneca]. "Certainly one of his best and most satisfactory critical essays."

*163. Morton, A. L. "Notes on the Poetry of Mr. Eliot." *Decachord* 2 (March–April) : 209–18. [Poems, 1909–1925]. Excellent on Eliot's spiritual sense, and his poetic technique.

164. Muir, Edwin. "Past and Present." *Atlantic* 140 (December) : 780–81. [Waste Land]. In a comparison of *The Waste Land* with *Ulysses,* Muir says that neither author had a valid plan, and that "the subconscious as shown . . . is never squared with the conscious."

165. Murry, J. M. "Towards a Synthesis." *Criterion* 5 (May) : 294–313. Eliot in the *Criterion* for October 1926 ranged himself on the side of "intelligence" as understood by Aquinas rather than on the side of intuition. Murry points out that if one accepts Aquinas's "intelligence," he will also have to accept his Christian faith, and Murry assumes that a modern man cannot do so.

166. Newbolt, Henry. *New Paths on Helicon,* pp. 401–3. London: Thomas Nelson and Sons, 1927 (?) , n.d. Eliot diminishes the effect of his irony by the triviality of his utterance. (See no. 249.)

167. Richards, I. A. "Nineteen Hundred and Now." *Atlantic* 140 (September) : 316–17. He greatly admires Eliot and Joyce without making his reasons clear.

168. Riding, Laura, and Graves, Robert. *A Survey of Modernist Poetry,* pp. 50–53, 165–74, 211–15, 235–42. London: W. Heinemann, 1927. [Waste Land; Burbank with a Baedeker]. Technique of *The Waste Land;* good analysis of "Burbank with a Baedeker." The entire book is good early criticism.

169. Vines, Sherard. *Movements in Modern English Poetry and Prose,* pp. 77–83, 181–87. (London: Oxford Press, 1927) . An introduction to Eliot's poetry and criticism for Japanese students. Brief, but suggestive. Reprinted in Tokyo, 1937.

*170. Williamson, George. "The Talent of T. S. Eliot." *SR* 35 (July) : 284–95. The original essay from which grew the book of the same title (no. 206) . Rich in discriminating criticism.

1928

171. Anon. "For Mr. T. S. Eliot." *NSN* 32 (December 29):
387–88. [For Lancelot Andrewes]. Thinks that this volume lacks unity, but praises Eliot for his lucidity and
force. (See Leavis's reply, no. 198.)

172. ———. "Modernist Poetry." *TLS*, no. 1355 (January 19),
p. 40. "In the best of Mr. Eliot's work we have a genuinely tragic bitterness whose effect is not hindered but
advanced by the deliberate triviality of its utterance."
An answer to Newbolt, no. 166.

173. ———. "Senecan Tragedy." *TLS*, no. 1358 (February 9),
p. 92. [Shakespeare and the Stoicism of Seneca]. A careful consideration of Eliot's introduction, especially his
scholarship.

174. ———. "Of Dramatick Poesie." *TLS*, no. 1376 (June
14), p. 447. [Dialogue on Dramatic Poetry]. Condescending toward Dryden, and a little less toward Eliot.

175. ———. "Mr. Eliot's New Essays." *TLS*, no. 1401 (December 6), p. 953. [For Lancelot Andrewes]. Eliot referred
to this as a "flattering obituary notice," in a manuscript
note in the Eliot Collection at Harvard.

176. Birrell, Francis. "The Poetic Drama Once More." *NaAt*,
43 (July 7): 470. [Dialogue on Dramatic Poetry]. Says
that the dialogue form makes confusion possible, and
suggests that some of the speakers had "made too free
with the port."

*177. Blackmur, R. P. "T. S. Eliot." Parts I and II. *HH* 1
(March): 187–213; (June): 291–319. The first essay
gives good analyses of five of Eliot's poems; the second
discusses him as a critic, emphasizing his intelligence
and the purity of his interest in literature.

178. Brownowski, J. Review of *For Lancelot Andrewes*. *CamR*
(November 30), p. 176. Reproaches Eliot for overem-
phasizing dogmatic Christianity at the expense of humanism, but calls most of the essays "important."

179. Campbell, Roy. "Contemporary Poetry." *Scrutinies*, edited
by Edgell Rickword, pp. 162–79. London: Wishart,
1928. [Waste Land]. A truculent assertion that *The
Waste Land* is the only "outstanding" contemporary
poem.

180. Lindsay, Jack. "Waste of Time, or, T. S. Eliot of Boston."
LonA, no. 3 (December), pp. 224–27. [Waste Land].
Eliot is the "tincan tied to the tail of the disillusioned

Nineties," and he is now dead. From the point of view of Nietzsche, Lindsay opposes Eliot's pessimism.

181. MacCarthy, Desmond. "The Bubble Reputation: a Lecture." *ER* 47 (February) : 114–22. The object of Eliot's poetry is "to express a spiritual state which mystics call 'dryness,' a sad consciousness of inability to respond gratefully and enthusiastically to life."

182. Moore, T. Sturge. "Mr. T. S. Eliot and Shelley's Skylark." *TLS*, no. 1402 (December 13), p. 991. A letter protesting Eliot's censure of lines in "The Skylark," and explaining them to him.

183. Munson, Gorham B. "The Embattled Humanists." *Bookman* 68 (December) : 404–10. Eliot is credited with having begun Act II of the humanist drama by "attacking humanism at one of its most vulnerable points—in its relation to religion."

*184. Murry, J. Middleton. "The 'Philosophy' of Shakespeare." *NewAd* 1, n.s. (March 1) : 253–56. [Shakespeare and the Stoicism of Seneca]. A stimulating essay in which Murry reproves Eliot for asserting that Shakespeare was influenced by Seneca.

185. Praz, Mario. Review of "Shakespeare and the Stoicism of Seneca." *ES* 10, no. 3: 79–87. Praise for the essay.

186. Seldes, Gilbert. "Mr. Eliot's Favorite." *Dial* 85 (November) : 437–40. [The Moonstone, introduction]. Praises the introduction, and uses it as the focus for his own criticism.

187. Shanks, Edward. "The Poetic Drama." *SaR* 145 (June 16) : 772–73. [A Dialogue on Poetic Drama]. "Dryden is interested in the subject under discussion and Mr. Eliot is not."

1929

188. Aiken, Conrad. "Retreat." *Dial* 86 (July) : 628–30. [For Lancelot Andrewes]. "Cautiously, jejunely, with an air of puritan acerbity [he] seeks a refuge from humanity in Grace, from personality in dogma, and from the present in the past."

189. D. W. B. "Book News and Reviews." *OxM* 47 (January 24) : 318–19. [For Lancelot Andrewes]. "It is hardly necessary at this time of day to point out the importance of Mr. Eliot as a symptom; it is still possible to acquire merit by asserting the intrinsic importance of Mr. Eliot's

criticism of life and letters," an assertion still paradoxical in England.

190. Chamberlain, John. "New Volumes of Essays by Aldous Huxley and T. S. Eliot." *NYTBR,* November 24, pp. 12–13. [For Lancelot Andrewes]. Eliot's mind is more subtle than Huxley's, and his art is greater; but "to those of us who are impelled to doubt the easy solution of perplexities by revealed religion, Huxley's feet must seem more firmly planted on what twentieth century multiplicity accepts as the ground."

191. Chesterton, G. K. "The Skeptic as a Critic." *Forum* 81 (February) : 65–69. [The Humanism of Irving Babbitt]. Eliot has led Babbitt so close to the door of the Catholic Church that they may both by accident fall into it.

192. Colton, Arthur. "A Significant Direction." *SatR* 5 (April 27) : 947. [For Lancelot Andrewes]. Emphasizes Eliot's love of order and his movement toward the seventeenth century.

*193. Dobrée, Bonamy. "T. S. Eliot." *The Lamp and the Lute,* pp. 107–33. (Oxford: Clarendon Press, 1929). Gives a brief analysis of *The Waste Land,* defends it against the charge of obscurity, explains Eliot's critical position. A good introduction.

194. Fergusson, Francis. "Golden Candlesticks." *HH* 2 (April-June) : 297–99. [For Lancelot Andrewes]. Traces the development of Eliot's thought from *The Sacred Wood* through *For Lancelot Andrewes.* Sympathetic, though not in agreement with Eliot's religious point of view.

195. Forster, E. M. "T. S. Eliot and His Difficulties." *LL* 2 (June) : 417–25. There are two kind of difficulties in reading Eliot: the reader's incompetence, and the fact that Eliot has had a vision of horror but declines to say so plainly. Reprinted in *Abinger Harvest,* New York: Harcourt, Brace, 1940, pp. 87–93, and in Unger, no. 1191.

196. Frost, A. C. "Donne and a Modern Poet." *CamR* 50 (May 17) : 499–50. There is no real comparison between Donne and Eliot; Eliot is Prufrock.

197. Kreymborg, Alfred. "T. S. Eliot and the Waste Land." *Our Singing Strength,* pp. 523–38. New York: Coward-McCann, 1929. Commonplace, favorable criticism of the whole of Eliot's poetry.

198. Leavis, F. R. "T. S. Eliot—a Reply to the Condescending." *CamR* 50 (February 8) : 254–56. [For Lancelot An-

drewes; Sacred Wood]. "Mr. Eliot's acquaintance with the past . . . has impressed us so much because it has illustrated for us both the past and the present."

199. Lucas, F. L. "Criticism." *LL* 3 (November) : 448–55. [For Lancelot Andrewes]. Quotes isolated sentences to condemn Eliot's critical dogmatism and "religious grimness."

200. MacCarthy, Desmond. "The World of Books: Anglo-Catholic Criticism." *Sun Times* (London), (February 3), p. 10. [For Lancelot Andrewes]. Sometimes Eliot's new religious point of view "leads him to exaggerate merits because they are connected with others to which he is now sensitive; sometimes it intensifies his penetration."

201. Munson, Gorham B. "An Analysis of T. S. Eliot's Style and Form." *Style and Form in American Prose,* pp. 37–40. Garden City, New York: Doubleday, Doran, 1929. A comparison of the prose styles of Poe and Eliot. Slight.

202. Murry, J. Middleton. "Notes and Comments. The Return of the 'Mayflower.' " *NewAd* 2, n.s. (March-May) : 195–98. [The Humanism of Irving Babbitt]. Eliot's criticism of humanism is that it is not feasible, whereas he ought to inquire only, "Is it true?" In rejecting humanism, Eliot "has become lonelier than ever. . . . He is not one of those enviable souls who can take Orthodoxy with a frolic welcome."

203. Quennell, Peter. "Mr. T. S. Eliot." *LL* 2 (March) : 179–90. [Waste Land]. Asserts the unity of Eliot's poetry and his criticism. Chiefly on *The Waste Land* and Eliot's indebtedness to the French symbolists.

204. Van Doren, Mark. "The Letter Giveth Life." *Nation* 128 (May 15) : 590. [For Lancelot Andrewes]. A brief but solid review saying that Eliot is not at the end but at the beginning of his critical career.

205. Vines, Sherard. "Intellectual Reaction." *NaAt* 44 (January 26) : 588–90. [For Lancelot Andrewes]. Dislikes Eliot's matter although he likes his manner.

*206. Williamson, George. *The Talent of T. S. Eliot,* 37 pp. Seattle: University of Washington Chapbooks, no. 32, 1929. The best early essays on Eliot's kinship to Donne and on the unity of his theory and practice. Important in the history of Eliot criticism.

207. Wilson, Edmund. "T. S. Eliot." *NR* 60 (November 13) : 341–49. An earlier and shorter version of the chapter in *Axel's Castle* (no. 270). Influential.

208. ———. "Correspondence: The Church and the Intellectuals." *NR* 58 (May 15) : 361–62. A letter to Cuthbert
Wright regarding Wilson's review of *For Lancelot Andrewes,* no. 209.

209. ———. "T. S. Eliot and the Church of England." *NR* 58
(April 24) : 283–84. [For Lancelot Andrewes]. Eliot's
religious position is unacceptable to a first-rate mind.

1930

210. Anon. "Johnson's Poetry." *TLS,* no. 29 (November 20),
p. 973. [Introduction to "London"]. The reviewer questions some of the statements in Eliot's introduction to
Johnson's "London."

211. Benét, William Rose. "Round about Parnassus." *SatR* 7
(October 18): 249–50. [Ash Wednesday]. Though Benét
does not like his point of view, he thinks Eliot is one of
the few modern poets who possess a "soul."

212. Birrell, Francis. "Mr. T. S. Eliot." *NaAt* 47 (May 31) :
292–93. [Ash Wednesday]. Birrell does not as yet understand the poem.

213. Blackmur, R. P. "The Discipline of Humanism." *The
Critique of Humanism,* edited by C. Hartley Grattan,
p. 251. New York: Brewer and Warren, 1930. Eliot undermines humanism.

214. Brown, E. K. "The New Writers. T. S. Eliot: Poet and
Critic." *CF* 10 (September) : 448. He is a minor poet
but great critic.

215. Burke, Kenneth. "The Allies of Humanism Abroad." *The
Critique of Humanism,* edited by C. Hartley Grattan,
pp. 183–87. New York: Brewer and Warren, 1930. Eliot
has been influenced by both Maurras and Babbitt and
has effected a synthesis between them by showing how
humanism hovers on the edge of religion, and how the
social utility of humanism and religion may differ. But
he has served to imperil American humanism as a "secular religion."

216. Canby, Henry Seidel. "New Humanists." *SatR* 6 (February 22) : 749–51. Eliot is out of place because he is the
only good humanist among the contributors to *Humanism in America.* Eliot is less dogmatic and is closer to
"Life."

217. Childs, M. W. "From a Distinguished Former St.
Louisan." *St. Louis Post Dispatch* (October 15), p. 3b.

Prints a letter from Eliot to the author, giving reminiscences of his first sixteen years in St. Louis.

218. [Collins, Seward]. "Chronicle and Comment." *Bookman* 71 (March) : 71–79. [Religion without Humanism]. He is troubled by Eliot's inclusion in the humanist symposium, interprets his differences from Babbitt on an entirely personal level, and concludes illogically, "Eliot remains a good humanist . . . but his present paper . . . is mainly irrelevant, because of his cramped use of the term humanism."

219. ———. "An Open Letter in Reply" (to Rebecca West, no. 244. *Bookman* 71 (August) : 522–27. A defense of humanism and of Eliot at a time when some considered him a humanist.

220. Eastman, Max. "The Swan Song of Humane Letters." *Scribner's* 88 (December) : 602–3. One of the papers in the humanist controversy, accusing Eliot of wanting the "right to talk loosely and yet be taken seriously in a scientific age."

*221. Empson, William. *Seven Types of Ambiguity*, pp. 98–101. London: Chatto and Windus, 1930. [Waste Land; Whispers of Immortality]. Detailed analyses of the desirable ambiguities in a passage from *The Waste Land* and from "Whispers of Immortality."

222. Gary, Franklin. Review of "Dante" and "Animula." *Sym* 1 (April) : 268–71. Eliot's classical ideal is that of "contemplation." He wishes sensibility and intellect to be in harmony. Eliot's style in his later poems is more contemplative than in his earlier ones. (See no. 226.)

*223. Gorman, William J. "Eliot's Ash-Wednesday." *Inlander* 11, no. 1 (November) : 5–10. A close reading of the text, helpful in understanding the poem.

224. Grattan, C. Hartley. "What Is This Humanism?" *Scribner's* 87 (April) : 423–32. He discovers with malicious delight that humanism is "merely a point of rest on the threshold of the church," and tells the humanists that they are in danger of being lured by Eliot or by Chesterton into their "respective ponds" of Anglicanism and Roman Catholicism.

225. Heard, Gerald. "T. S. Eliot." *WeekER* 1 (May 3) : 268–69. [Ash Wednesday]. Places Eliot in the main (Protestant) stream of English religious poetry.

226. Heyl, Bernard C. Letter. *Sym*. 1: 387–89. Apropos of no. 222, objecting to Eliot's and Gary's implications that

classicism must be associated with religion and morals, Heyl says that the connection is illogical.

227. Howard, Brian. "Mr. Eliot's Poetry." *NSN* 36 (November 8) : 146. [Ash Wednesday]. On Eliot's poetic influence in the early 1920s, with a brief but thoughtful comment on the style of "Ash Wednesday."

228. Leighton, Lawrence, "Eliot on Dante," *HH* 3 (April) : 442–44. A competent review, adding that the book shows Eliot as "more definitely anti-romantic in his tastes than before."

229. Mangan, Sherry. "A Note: On the Somewhat Premature Apotheosis of T. S. Eliot." *Pagany* 1 (Spring) : 23–36. Deplores Eliot's defeatism in its effect on young American writers.

230. McKenzie, Orgill. "Recent Books." *NewAd* 3, n.s. (June-August) , 336–38. [Ash Wednesday; Waste Land]. Shows the similarity between Eliot's attitude toward life and that of the author of *Ecclesiastes*. "Mr. Eliot's poetry is greater than his cleverness." Objects to the too great erudition of *The Waste Land*.

231. Morrow, Felix. "The Serpent's Enemy: Mr. More as Social Thinker." *Sym* 1 (April) : 168–93. An attack on Paul Elmer More's conservatism, incidentally bracketing Eliot with More as believing in the same values.

232. Moult, Thomas, "Contrasts in Current Poetry," *Bookman* (English) 78 (September) : 354–55. [Ash Wednesday; Anabasis]. " 'Ash Wednesday' is for those who are willing to follow the drift of a cultured uncommonly sensitive philosopher's thought in poetry." Praises the translation of *Anabasis*.

233. Olivero, Federico. "An English Poet-Critic and an Italian Reviewer." *Poetry R* 21 (January-February) : 68–69. [Dante]. Praises Eliot's analysis of Dante's symbolism, but cannot agree that Dante uses few metaphors. Chiefly summary.

234. Rascoe, Burton. "Pupils of Polonius." *The Critique of Humanism,* edited by C. Hartley Grattan, pp. 115–27. New York: Brewer and Warren, 1930. [Waste Land; Humanism and America]. Attacks Eliot for being a humanist, but thinks *The Waste Land* is a great poem.

*235. Richards, I. A. "The Poetry of T. S. Eliot." *Principles of Literary Criticism,* pp. 289–94. New York: Harcourt, Brace, 1930. Eliot's poetry is a "music of ideas." The ideas are arranged, not that they may tell us something, but "that their effects in us may combine into a coherent whole of feeling and attitudes and produce a peculiar liberation of the will." A significant essay. Reprinted in Unger, no. 1191.

236. Roberts, Michael. "Others as Well as Mr. Eliot." *Poetry R* 21 (March-April) : 122-32. The Cambridge poets represented in *Songs for Sixpence* show Eliot's influence on almost every page, but "others as well as Mr. Eliot are adding something to the range and scope of English poetry."

237. Roberts, R. Ellis. "Two Poets." *Bookman* (English) 77 (March) : 359-60. [Dante]. The essay should help non-Catholics appreciate Dante.

238. Seldes, Gilbert. "Finding the Lost Generation." *SatEP* 203 (August 30) : 69. [Waste Land]. A passage on what the ordinary reading of *The Waste Land* was, that "from now on the world was a desolate waste."

239. Twitchett, E. G. Review of "Ash Wednesday." *LonMerc* 22 (October) : 557. "'Ash Wednesday' contains some gratifying Swinburnean passages, but chiefly agitates to a new and original music, composed out of erudite little rhythmical tricks."

240. Walton, Eda Lou. "T. S. Eliot Turns to Religious Verse." *NYTBR* (July 20), p. 9. [Ash Wednesday]. "Any one who cares to analyze 'The Waste Land' will find in it the seeds of the religious poetry to which Eliot has of late given himself." Brief, but good.

241. ———. "Desire for Oblivion." *Nation* 131 (August 6) : 155. [Ash Wednesday]. A brief analysis of the meaning of the poem, repeating some of the points made in no. 240.

242. Wells, H. G. *The Autocracy of Mr. Parham,* 370 pp. London: Heinemann, 1930. "The hero is a sort of composite of T. S. Eliot, Middleton Murry, and perhaps of J. C. Squire." (Manuscript note by H. W. Eliot, Jr. in the Eliot Collection.)

243. West, Rebecca. "The Weaker Image." *NYHTB* (January 5), p. 8. [Dante]. Eliot fears reality. Most of the essay concerns Aldous Huxley, whom she prefers to Eliot.

244. ———. "A Last London Letter: A counterblast to Humanism." *Bookman* 71 (August) : 513-22. An open letter to Seward Collins, no. 219, attacking humanism at a time when Eliot was considered a humanist.

245. Williams, Charles Walter S. "T. S. Eliot." *Poetry at Pres-*

ent, pp. 163–74. Oxford: Clarendon Press, 1930. Suggests that Eliot may mean something important, though Williams does not understand him. Reprinted in *Selected Modern English Essays,* second series, edited by H. S. Milford, Oxford: Clarendon Press, 1932, pp. 278–87.

246. Wilson, Edmund. Review of "Ash Wednesday." *NR* 64 (August 20) : 24–25. Chiefly quotations from the poem. Is made tired by hearing Eliot refer to himself as an "agéd eagle."

247. Zabel, Morton D. "T. S. Eliot in Mid-Career." *Poetry* 36 (September) : 330–37. [Ash Wednesday; Journey of the Magi; A Song for Simeon; Dante]. Traces Eliot's spiritual career and its effect on his poetry, which Zabel thinks "deprives his art of its once incomparable distinction in style and tone."

1931

248. Aldington, Richard. *Stepping Heavenward,* 63 pp. London: Chatto and Windus, 1931. The imaginary biography of Jeremy Pratt Sybba, an amusing and ironic portrait of Eliot.

249. Anon. "Book Reviews." *DubM* 6 (April -June) : 73. [Ash Wednesday]. Finds the poem obscure, but having "the unmistakable touch of poetry." Brief.

250. ———. "Thoughts after Lambeth." *TLS,* no. 1523 (April 9) , p. 280. Summary of contents; little criticism.

251. Brown, Alec. "The Lyric Impulse in the Poetry of T. S. Eliot." *Scrutinies,* edited by Edgell Rickword, vol. 2, pp. 1–52. London: Wishart, 1931. Eliot has a poetic, Shellyan impulse, which sometimes fortunately breaks through in spite of his resistant sophistication.

252. Collin, W. E. "T. S. Eliot." *SR* 39 (January-March) : 13–24. Points out his indebtedness to French symbolists, and concludes that his "importance as a poet consists in this: that by his enigmatic and mystic lines he has brought us into . . . a seriously spiritual mood" like that desired by the symbolist poets.

253. ———. "T. S. Eliot the Critic." *SR* 39 (October-December) : 419–24. An essay on Eliot's analytical method which Collin likes as a corrective of aesthetic and impressionistic criticism.

254. Eastman, Max. *The Literary Mind,* pp. 20–23, 110–12. New York: Scribner's, 1931. [Ash Wednesday; Waste

Land]. Eliot, as one of the New Humanists, has igno-
rantly tried to resist the advance of science. "Ash
Wednesday" is "an oily puddle of emotional noises."

255. Gregory, Horace. "Eliot Inward." *NYHTB* (January 25),
p. 14. [Ash Wednesday]. "For all his ability to write
poetry of great distinction, Eliot seems to be directing
his talents into very narrow channels indeed." This
statement is not explained.

*256. Higgins, Bertram. "The Critical Method of T. S. Eliot."
Scrutinies, vol. 2, edited by Edgell Rickword, pp. 54–71.
London: Wishart, 1931. A thoughtful and intelligent
essay; assumes a knowledge of Eliot's work.

257. Hilton, Charles. "The Poetry of T. S. Eliot." *EJ* 20, college ed. (November): 749–61. Hilton relies on Eliot's
other critics, giving them credit, for a simple explanation.

258. Hughes, Glenn. *Imagism and the Imagists.* Stanford, Cal.:
University Press, 1931. An objective summary of Eliot's
views on *vers libre* and on the differences between poetry
and prose.

259. Jameson, Raymond de Loy. *Poetry and Plain Sense (A
note on the poetic method of T. S. Eliot),* 25 pp. Peiping:
National Tsing Hua University, 1931. Reprinted from
the *Tsing Hua Review,* November 1931. Based upon
I. A. Richards's criticism. Concentrates on Eliot's disre-
gard for plain sense, and defends him.

260. Jay, Douglas. "Mr. T. S. Eliot: after Lambeth." *OxO* 11
(June): 78–85 [Thoughts after Lambeth]. "Humanity
flows past Mr. Eliot as the tide flows past a limpet, that
consoles itself for passivity with its supermarine eleva-
tion."

261. Leavis, F. R. "The Influence of Donne on Modern Poetry." *Bookman* (English) 79 (March): 346–47. Eliot
has made a fresh start in poetry, inspired by Donne,
though "except in exhibiting a complex sensibility . . .
Mr. Eliot's poetry is not like Donne's."

262. McGreevy, Thomas. *Thomas Stearns Eliot,* 71 pp. London: Chatto and Windus, 1931. Interprets the poems in
terms of their presumed approach to Catholicism; depre-
cates the earlier ones. Reviewed in *Poetry* 42 (April):
44–45.

263. Moore, Marianne. "A Machinery of Satisfaction." *Poetry*

38 (September): 337–39. [Marina]. On the technique of the poem.

264. Murry, J. Middleton. "Mr. Eliot at Lambeth." *Adelphi* 2, n.s. (April): 70–73. [Thoughts after Lambeth]. Disagrees politely and eloquently with Eliot's opinion that the Christian church is needed to save the world, preferring unofficial Christianity.

265. Nimr, Amy. "Introduction to the Poety [*sic*] of Mr. T. S. Eliot." *Échanges* (Paris), no. 4 (March), pp. 35–57. Abundant quotation with a running commentary.

266. Powell, Dilys. "The Poetry of T. S. Eliot." *LL* 7 (December): 386–419. A competent and sympathetic survey of Eliot's poetic development to 1931. Uses his prose for understanding his poetry.

*267. Tate, Allen. "Irony and Humility." *HH* 4 (January-March), 290–97. [Ash Wednesday]. For an appreciation of the poetry, the question of our own acceptance or rejection of Eliot's doctrine is irrelevant. An intelligent critical essay. Reprinted under the title "T. S. Eliot," in *The Limits of Poetry,* New York: Swallow Press, 1948; in *Reactionary Essays,* New York: Scribner's, 1936; also in Unger, no. 1191.

268. ———. "Taste and Dr. Johnson." *NR* 68 (August 19): 23–24. A few lines in praise of Eliot's introduction to "London" and "The Vanity of Human Wishes"; most of the essay concerns the superficiality of modern taste.

269. Williamson, Hugh Ross. "T. S. Eliot and His Conception of Poetry." *Bookman* (English) 79 (March): 347–50. Chiefly concerned with Eliot's poetic technique, ending with a belated note of alarm lest he accept a religious creed.

*270. Wilson, Edmund. "T. S. Eliot." *Axel's Castle,* pp. 93–131. New York: Scribner's, 1931. [Prufrock; Waste Land; Ash Wednesday]. Still a good survey, in broad outline, of the whole of Eliot's prose and poetry up to 1931. Influential criticism, much quoted. Reprinted in Unger, no. 1191; also in *Literary Opinion in America,* edited by Morton D. Zabel, New York: Harper, 1951, pp. 213–16, 226–27.

1932

271. Anon. "Chronicle and Comment: T. S. Eliot Comes

Home." *Bookman* 75 (September) : 449–51. Repeats well-known facts and opinions on Eliot's reputation and influence.

272. ———. "The Writer's Personality." *Everyman* 8 (September 15) : 240. [Tradition and the Individual Talent]. Sympathetic summary of the essay, which the reviewer has just discovered.

273. ———. "From Humanism to Anglo-Catholicism." *Glasgow Herald* (September 15). [Selected Essays 1917–1932]. Eliot's prose "deals passionately with fundamental issues," but as he has moved toward Catholicism, his outlook has become less catholic.

274. ———. "T. S. Eliot Goes Home." *LA* 342 (May) : 234–36. Reprint of an article from *The Manchester Guardian* concerning Eliot's return to the United States.

275. ———. "A Critic of Poets." *Punch* 183 (October 5) : 391. [Selected Essays 1917–1932]. Eliot's best essays are on poets and poetry. Very complimentary.

276. ———. "Poet and Critic." *SaR* 154 (October 8) : 370. [Selected Essays 1917–1932]. As a critic, Eliot "stands on an eminence that is unassailable," but his poetry is "uncouth."

277. ———. "Mr. T. S. Eliot." *TLS*, no. 1602 (October 13), p. 728. [Selected Essays 1917–1932]. "In practical criticism, focused on actual work, Mr. Eliot's method is successful and assured." But in general discussion, he misleads through being too brief.

278. B. "Ye Agéd Eagle." *Granta* 42 (October 14) : 18. [Selected Essays]. Is concerned with the "blemishes" of the volume.

279. Barker, George. "Reviews," of F. R. Leavis's *New Bearings in English Poetry. Adelphi* 4, n.s. (June) : 641–42. Eliot is not a contemporary. Mr. Leavis assigns him greater modernity than he actually possesses.

280. Bullett, Gerald. "The Challenge of T. S. Eliot." *Observer* (September 25), p. 10. Values his literary criticism highly, but finds that in ethics and religion Eliot keeps his "distance from the subject."

281. Burnet, W. Hodgson. "A Joint Affair." *SaR* 154 (December 17) : 639. A parody of the styles of Eliot and Joyce, called "Sweeney's Shemi-Shaunties."

282. Caldwell, James Ralston. "An Explorer in Poetic Fields." *SatR* 8 (January 9) : 437–39. Examines the meaning of

Eliot's expression, "sensuous thought" and applies this analysis to his poetry.

283. Cantwell, Robert. "Mr. Eliot's Sunday Afternoon." *NR* 72 (September 14), 132–33. [Introduction to Charles-Louis Philippe's *Bubu of Montparnasse*]. In this introduction, Eliot shows his weakness as a Tory.

284. Chew, Samuel C. "Essays in Criticism." *YR* 22 (December): 386–88. [Selected Essays 1917–1932]. Brief, but competent. Says the essays are an "intellectual feast."

285. Dobrée, Bonamy. "A Major Critic." *Listener* 8, (October 5): supplement, xi. [Selected Essays]. "Mr. Eliot, though detached, is never aloof." Prefers his literary to his religious and moral essays.

286. Frank, Waldo. "The 'Universe' of T. S. Eliot." *NR* 72 October 26): 294–95. [Selected Essays 1917–1932]. Frank dislikes Eliot's world because it is static. Reprinted in *Adelphi* 5, n.s. (February 1933): 321–26, and in *In the American Jungle,* New York: Farrar and Rinehart, 1937, pp. 220–27.

287. Friend, Albert C. "T. S. Eliot—an Appreciation," *StLR* 2 (December 31): 6–8. A much simplified but sound explanation of "the direction of Eliot's poems," through "Ash Wednesday."

288. Garrison, W. E. "Humanism Criticizes Itself." *ChC* 49 (October 12): 1243. [Selected Essays 1917–1932]. A good essay on whether or not Eliot is a humanist.

289. Gary, Franklin. Review of F. R. Leavis's *New Bearings in English Poetry. Sym* 3 (October): 521–34. (See Leavis, no. 298, for summary of Gary's review.) In addition to the review, Gary has an essay defining Eliot's "reordering" of the poetic tradition as a technique of giving the illusion of thought by spoken words.

290. George, R. E. Gordon. "The Return of the Native." *Bookman* 75 (September): 423–31. A pretentious discussion of Eliot's life and work. "He has New England's best in his blood and bones."

291. Grudin, Louis. *Mr. Eliot among the Nightingales,* 71 pp. London: Joiner and Stelle, 1932. Examines three or four of Eliot's sentences in his poems, and finds that he, as well as other modern poets, is insufficiently aware of the linguistic aspects of his problems; Grudin's own theory of language is not expressed clearly. Reviewed in *Poetry* 42 (April 1933): 44–45.

292. Hare, Joseph Crosland, *The Literary Criticism of T. S. Eliot and I. A. Richards, The University of Colorado Studies, Series A.* 20, no. 1 (November) : 40–41. Very brief abstract of a master's thesis.

293. Hazlitt, Henry. "The Mind of T. S. Eliot." *Nation* 135 (October 5) : 312–13. [Selected Essays 1917–1932]. A refusal to comprehend Eliot's basic assumptions weakens the criticism.

294. ———. "Our Greatest Authors: How Great Are They?" *Forum* 88 (October) : 248. One paragraph on Eliot. "The contemporary poet who seems to have much the greatest chance of long survival is T. S. Eliot."

295. Jury, C. R. *T. S. Eliot's "The Waste Land": Some Annotations.* Pamphlet No. 1 of the English Association, Adelaide branch, 24 pp. F. W. Preece and Sons, 1932. Explanation of the symbols of the poem, one by one, with no attempt to weave them together. In general, the explanations are sound.

296. Knight, Grant C. *American Literature and Culture,* pp. 474–76. New York: Ray Long and Richard R. Smith, Inc., 1932. [Waste Land]. On the obscurity of the poem.

297. N.A.M.L. Review of *Selected Essays. Isis,* no. 854 (October 19) , p. 14. The essays are dry and over-scholarly.

*298. Leavis, F. R. "T. S. Eliot." *New Bearings in English Poetry,* pp. 75–132. London: Chatto and Windus, 1932. [Waste Land; Gerontion; Hollow Men; Burbank; Ash Wednesday; Ariel Poems; Marina]. Leavis's thesis: "Mr. Eliot has shown up the English poetry of the nineteenth century . . . and has . . . effected a revolution comparable to what is sometimes called the Romantic 'revolt.' " Summary by F. Gary, *Sym* 3 (1932) : 523; reprinted in Unger, no. 1191.

299. Macaulay, Rose. "Miss West, Mr. Eliot, and Mr. Parsons." *Spectator* 149, no. 5443 (October 22) : 534–35. Deplores the fact that the "calm Mr. Eliot" has been made the occasion for a literary wrangle. See nos. 304, 305, 323, 324.

300. Mitchison, Naomi. "Two Moderns: Virginia Woolf and T. S. Eliot." *WeekER* 6 (October 15) : 447–48. Reproaches Eliot for saving his own soul and neglecting the souls of others.

301. More, Paul Elmer. "The Cleft Eliot." *SatR* 9 (November 12) : 233, 235. [Selected Essays, 1917–1932]. There is a cleavage between the poet of chaos in *The Waste*

Land and the critic who judges the world as a classicist, royalist, and Anglo-Catholic. Reprinted in Unger, no. 1191, also in *Designed for Reading, an Anthology Drawn from The Saturday Review of Literature, 1924–1934*, New York: Macmillan, 1934, pp. 333–38.

*302. Oras, Ants. *Critical Ideas of T. S. Eliot*. vol. B xxciii, 118 pp. Tartu, Estonia: Acta et commentationes Universitatis tartuensis, 1932. A well-informed and intelligent account of Eliot's criticism through 1932. The last section considers his relations with Santayana, Babbitt, the writers of the French anti-romantic movement, and Remy de Gourmont.

303. Parkes, Henry Bamford. "T. S. Eliot." *The Pragmatic Test*, pp. 178–86. (Essay written in 1932.) San Francisco: Colt Press, 1941. On Communism versus Catholicism, using Eliot as the spokesman for the latter.

304. Parsons, I. M. "Mr. Eliot's Authority." *Spectator* 149, no. 5441 (October 8): 450–52. [Selected Essays 1917–1932]. Chiefly an attack on Rebecca West, who reviewed Eliot unfavorably. Eliot's new volume "confirms his claims to be regarded as the most important contemporary critic of English letters." (See nos. 323, 324.)

305. ———. "Miss West, Mr. Eliot, and Mr. Parsons." *Spectator* 149, no. 5443 (October 22): 534. A continuation of the controversy having as its occasion Eliot's merits as a critic. Contains little on Eliot himself.

306. Porteus, Hugh Gordon. *Wyndham Lewis,* pp. 144–50. London: Desmond Harmsworth, 1932. Throughout the book, Porteus uses Eliot's critical dicta in judging Lewis.

307. Pryce-Jones, Alan. "Chronicles, Poetry." *LonMerc* 26 (September): 455–56. [Poems 1909–1925]. Eliot has little to say.

308. Quennell, Peter. "T. S. Eliot the Critic." *NSN* 4, n.s. (October 1): 377–78. [Selected Essays 1917–1932]. A good review, chiefly on Eliot's prose style. Compares him as a critic to Charles Whibley.

309. Rahv, Philip. "T. S. Eliot." *Fantasy* 2 (Winter): 17–20. Condemns all of the poems since "Prufrock" because "a poetry of aristocratic moods and ascetic ideas is neither possible nor desirable in an era of plebeian revolt and materialistic dynamics."

310. Rice, Philip Blair. "Out of the Waste Land." *Sym* 3 (October) : 422–42. The first six pages concern Eliot's solution for leading mankind out of despair; Rice prefers the solutions of Thomas Mann and D. H. Lawrence.

311. Roberts, Michael. "Reviews: Selected Essays." *Adelphi* 5, n.s. (November) : 141–44. [Selected Essays 1917–1932]. Unfavorable criticism from the liberal point of view. "We find in Mr. Eliot's essays too much wisdom, too little human sympathy."

312. ———. "T. S. Eliot." *Poetry R* 23 (November–December) : 465–70. A review of Williamson's and Grudin's books on Eliot. Eliot is unpopular because his culture is only for the upper classes.

313. Sackville-West, V. "Books of Week." *Listener* 8 (September 28) : 461. [Selected Essays 1917–1932]. Tries to persuade readers of *The Listener* to attempt the difficult reading of *The Essays*.

314. Scott-James, R. A. "A Critic's Critic." *Sun Times* (London) (October 2) , p. 8. [Selected Essays 1917–1932]. A friendly review, expressing surprise that Eliot does not see that both romantic and classical tendencies are necessary.

315. Shuster, George N. "Mr. Eliot Returns." *Cweal* 16 (October 19) : 581–83. [Selected Essays 1917–1932]. Eliot's insistence on autonomy in art might unfortunately result in its not mattering what a poet believes.

316. Sitwell, Osbert. "A Great Critic." *WeekER* 6 (September 17) : 318. [Selected Essays 1917–1932]. Brief but excellent criticism.

317. Stonier, George W. "Eliot and the Plain Reader." *FR* 132, n.s. (November 1) : 620–29. A dialogue using Williamson's *The Poetry of T. S. Eliot* as a starting point; reluctant praise. Reprinted in *Gog Magog and Other Critical Essays*, London: Dent and Sons, 1933, pp. 140–55.

318. Sunne, Richard. "Men and Books." *TT* 13 (October 15) : 1110–11. [Selected Essays 1917–1932]. An interesting comparison of Eliot and Dr. Johnson. Eliot has insufficient sympathy with the purely poetic, "which comes from imagination, not thought."

319. E. R. T. "Mr. Eliot's Essays." *Manchester Guardian* (October 24) , p. 5 [Selected Essays 1917–1932]. These essays "for precision of thought, economy of diction,

and solidity of scholarship have hardly been equalled in our time."

320. Tate, Allen. "A Note on Donne." *NR* 70 (April 6) : 212–13. [Donne in Our Time]. Questions Eliot's statement that Donne's new reputation will speedily decline. Part of a longer review of *A Garland for John Donne,* edited by Theodore Spencer.

*321. Taupin, René. "The Classicism of T. S. Eliot." *Sym* 3 (January) : 64–82. Eliot's relation to the French symbolists. Good. See Laboulle's review of Taupin in *Revue de Littérature Comparée* (no. 588).

322. Van Doren, Mark. "Mr. Eliot and His Critic." *NYHTB* December 11), p. 4. [John Dryden; Grudin's *Mr. Eliot among the Nightingales*]. Dislikes Grudin's snobbery; is pleased with Eliot's "normal" criticism.

323. West, Rebecca. "What Is Mr. T. S. Eliot's Authority as a Critic?" *Daily Morning Post and Telegraph* (London) (September 30). [Selected Essays 1917–1932]. An attack that gave rise to Charles Powell's article in *The Manchester Guardian* (no. 2347) and to letters in *The Spectator* (nos. 299, 324). Part of the humanist controversy.

324. ———. "Miss West, Mr. Eliot, and Mr. Parsons." *Spectator* 149, no. 5442 (October 15) : 480. Attacks Eliot's criticism as dull, authoritarian, and tradition-laden. See nos. 299, 304, 305.

*325. Williamson, Hugh Ross. *The Poetry of T. S. Eliot,* 185 pp. London: Hodder and Stoughton, 1932. A useful early manual of relevant explanation. Reviewed in *Poetry* 42 (April, 1933) : 44–45.

326. ———. "Notes at Random: Is Communism Inevitable?" *Bookman* (English) 82 (April) : 1–3. On Middleton Murry's and Eliot's radio talks on Communism. "Both men are offering a form of religion as an alternative to chaos and Russian Communism—Mr. Eliot, a return to the authority of the Catholic Church, Mr. Murry, a national act of self-abnegation."

327. ———. "T. S. Eliot's 'The Waste Land.'" *Bookman* (English) 82 (July) : 185. "I believe that 'The Waste Land' is comparable from the point of view of importance and far-reaching influence with the famous 'Lyrical Ballads' of Wordsworth and Coleridge."

328. ———. "A Commentary on T. S. Eliot's 'The Waste Land.'" *Bookman* (English) 82 (July, August, Septem-

ber): 192–95, 244–48, 289–91. An excellent, if limited, interpretation of *The Waste Land* in terms of its literary allusions.

329. ———. "Notes at Random. Lawrence and Eliot." *Bookman* (English) 83 (October): 4–6. [Selected Essays 1917–1932]. "When a colony of Lawrences start to construct rather than revolt, they will have to begin with Eliot."

330. Zabel, Morton D. "The Still Point." *Poetry* 41 (December): 152–58. [Triumphal March; Difficulties of a Statesman]. The reviewer is puzzled; he is not sure that the style fits the content.

1933

331. Anon. "Poetry and Criticism." *Independent* 1 (November 25): 21–22. [The Use of Poetry and the Use of Criticism]. Eliot's "discourses are only fitfully satisfactory in print," because of faults of style and of "two fundamental misapprehensions" of his task.

332. ———. "Book Reviews." *StLR* 2 (January 14): 18 [John Dryden]. A brief summary.

333. ———. "Thomas Stearns Eliot." *StLR* 2 (January 14): 12–13. Two paragraphs of biography, and some attempt to explain Eliot's position in poetry and prose.

334. ———. "Reassurance to the Spirit." *StLR* 2 (January 28): 3. A note on Eliot's lecture in St. Louis, "The Study of Shakespearean Criticism."

335. ———. Review of *The Use of Poetry and the Use of Criticism. Schoolmaster* (London), in supplement, p. iii, entitled "Christmas Books for Young and Old" (November 23). A paragraph of summary, and one of brief favorable comment.

336. ———. "Poetry and Criticism: Mr. Eliot's Harvard Lectures." *Scotsman* (November 23), p. 2. [The Use of Poetry and the Use of Criticism]. An excellent critical summary of the lectures.

337. ———. "The Use of Poetry." *TLS*, no. 1663 (December 14), p. 892. [The Use of Poetry and the Use of Criticism]. These essays are inconclusive. Likes Eliot's "intuitive discussions" of poetry, but not his theology.

338. Barker, George. Review of "Sweeney Agonistes." *Adelphi* 5 (January): 310–11. "Eliot has contrived as deathly an

elegy of his poetic decease, as he composed a triumphal ode of his birth, The Waste Land." However, Barker calls "Sweeney" "exquisite," "lucid," and *easily* admirable."

339. Bates, Ernest S. "T. S. Eliot; Leisure Class Laureate." *MM* 7 (February) : 17–24. Sees Eliot as a member of an impotent and degenerate leisure class which oppresses the workers.

340. Benét, William Rose. "T. S. Eliot Again." *SatR* 9 (January 21) : 393. [Review of H. R. Williamson's *The Poetry of T. S. Eliot*]. Does not like Eliot, but thinks Williamson's book is good for an introduction.

341. Bennett, Arnold. *The Journal of Arnold Bennett*. vol. 3, pp. 64–65, 78, 127, 240, 275. New York: Viking Press, 1933. [Waste Land; Sweeney Agonistes]. Reports conversations with Eliot.

342. Bennett, Joan. Review of *The Use of Poetry and the Use of Criticism, CamR* 55 (November 24) : 132–33. The value of the book lies in its incidental remarks and asides.

343. Blackmur, R. P. "T. S. Eliot in Prose." *Poetry* 42 (April) : 44–49. [John Dryden; Selected Essays 1917–1932]. Defends Eliot against the charge of writing worse for being a Christian.

*344. Boynton, Grace M. "Without a Parable: An Encounter with the Poetry of T. S. Eliot." *WQ* 1 (Summer) : 102–10. A readable narrative of a slowly growing understanding of Eliot's poetry.

345. Bridson, D. G. "Views and Reviews: Sweeney Agonistes." *NewEW* 2 (January 12) : 304. That the fragments "give a fair picture of banality is the most that can be said for them."

346. ———. "Poetry and Criticism." *NewEW* 4 (December 28) : 256–57. [The Use of Poetry and the Use of Criticism]. Eliot has failed to make clear the use of either poetry or criticism, but he was sure to fail in the attempt.

347. Brown, Leonard S. "Our Contemporary Poetry." *SR* 41 (January–March) : 59–63. [Prufrock; Waste Land]. Shows how Eliot has made contact with the "modern world," which believes in nothing.

348. F.C. "The Use of Mr. Eliot." *Granta* 43 (November 15) : 103. [The Use of Poetry and the Use of Criticism]. A

brief but thoughtful essay taking issue with Eliot's remarks on education and on Coleridge.

349. Cunliffe, J. W. "Masefield and the New Georgian Poets." *English Literature in the Twentieth Century*, pp. 323–29. New York: Macmillan, 1933. He is baffled, but quotes from Eliot's admirers and lets Aldington sum him up.

*350. Daniells, J. R. "T. S. Eliot and His Relation to T. E. Hulme." *UTQ* 2 (April) : 380–96. A lucid statement of the identity of Eliot's position and Hulme's.

351. Davies, Hugh Sykes. "Criticism and Controversy." *Listener* (November 29). [So dated in the Eliot Collection, but article was not found under this date.] [The Use of Poetry and the Use of Criticism]. Summary.

352. Deutsch, Babette. "Fine Insights." *New York Sun* (December 16), p. 27. [The Use of Poetry and the Use of Criticism]. She finds the book disappointing because of Eliot's own lack of poetic theory.

353. Drew, Elizabeth. *Discovering Poetry*, pp. 111–21 and *passim*. New York: Norton, 1933. [A Cooking Egg; Waste Land]. Good analyses.

354. "Gaffer Peeslake." *Bromo Bombastes, a Fragment from a Laconic Drama*, 6 pp. London: The Caduceus Press, 1933. A parody of *Sweeney Agonistes*.

355. Gorman, William J. "The Taste for Purity." *NR* 75 (May 31) : 80. [John Dryden the Poet the Dramatist the Critic]. Eliot does not show what Dryden can teach a modern poet: "He merely states the indisputable things about Dryden."

*356. Harding, D. W. "Mr. Eliot at Harvard." *Scrutiny* 2 (December) : 289–92. [The Use of Poetry and the Use of Criticism]. An excellent review and criticism of Eliot's attitude toward the "significance of the poet's motives and beliefs."

357. Hawkins, Desmond. "Mr. Eliot's Criticism." *WeekER* 8 (December 9) : 636. [The Use of Poetry and the Use of Criticism]. Calls Eliot's criticism the "finest . . . of the century." Brief.

358. Hicks, Granville. "Trumpet Call." *The Great Tradition*, pp. 268–70. New York: Macmillan, 1933. A brief sketch of Eliot's poetic career. "Mr. Eliot's principles seem to be strangling his poetic gifts; he can now speak neither as a poet of faith nor as a poet of doubt," but as a repre-

sentative of a decadent tradition. Partially reprinted in Unger, no. 1191.

359. Hillyer, Robert. "Book Reviews." *NEQ* 6 (June) : 402–4. [Selected Essays 1917–1932]. Indiscriminate attack on Eliot's poetry and prose.

360. House, Humphrey. "Mr. Eliot as a Critic." *NewOx* 1 (May) : 95–105. A well-reasoned analysis of Eliot's condemnation of Milton's poetry.

361. Jack, Peter Monro. "The Cream of T. S. Eliot's Literary Criticism." *NYTBR* (January 29), p. 2. [Selected Essays 1917–1932]. Points out the healthful influence that Eliot's opinions might have on conduct.

362. ———. "Mr. Eliot's New Essays in the Field of Poetry." *NYTBR* (December 3), p. 2. [The Use of Poetry and the Use of Criticism]. A labored and rather obscure review.

363. Kingsmill, Hugh. "Goethe, Wordsworth, and Mr. Eliot." *EngR* 57 (December) : 667–70. [The Use of Poetry and the Use of Criticism]. Eliot "misrepresents and disparages" Goethe, and he is wrong in supposing that Wordsworth did not feel the "horror in nature."

*364. Knickerbocker, William S. "Bellwether: an exercise in dissimulation." *SR* 41 (January–March) : 64–79. An excellent comparison of the criticism and prose styles of Eliot and Matthew Arnold.

*365. Knight, G. Wilson. *The Christian Renaissance, with Interpretations of Dante, Shakespeare, and Goethe, and a Note on T. S. Eliot,* pp. 370–74. Toronto: Macmillan, 1933. One of the good "middle period" criticisms; an explanation of Eliot's technique in regard to his alleged obscurity, and an analysis of his advance from cynicism to hope.

366. Krutch, Joseph Wood. "A Poem Is a Poem." *Nation* 137 (December 13) : 679–80. [The Use of Poetry and the Use of Criticism]. Deplores that in Eliot's criticism "one will look in vain . . . [for] a complete, original, definite, and logically formulated body of doctrine."

367. MacCarthy, Desmond. "Poetry as Criticism of Life." *Sun Times* (London) (December 3), p. 8. [The Use of Poetry and the Use of Criticism]. MacCarthy considers the question of what poetry is. He values Eliot's lectures for their sincerity.

368. Mégroz, Rodolphe Louis. *Modern English Poetry 1882–1932,* pp. 199–204. London: Ivor Nicholson and Wat-

son, 1933. [Prufrock; Waste Land; Hollow Men]. "As a thinker Eliot is as unsubtle as Tennyson, which is perhaps why he similarly became the voice of his age." Mégroz likes Eliot's poems of decadence, but not his later ones.

*369. Moore, Marianne. "Reviews, Sweeney Agonistes." *Poetry* 42 (May) : 106–9. Written in an allusive and poetic style, Miss Moore's essay says that this is an "Aristophanic melodrama" set in a London flat from which Sweeney flees. He is superior to the other characters.

370. Muir, Edwin. "The Use of Poetry." *Spectator* 151, no. 5499 (November 17) : 703. [The Use of Poetry and the Use of Criticism]. Summary and brief favorable comment.

371. Palmer, Herbert Edward. "The Hoax and Earnest of The Waste Land." *DubM* 8 (April–June) : 11–19. "The serious way in which this sardonic jest and frightfully clever literary medley has been received and treated, is proof enough to me that the desiccation and disintegration of poetry have definitely begun."

*372. Phare, Elsie Elizabeth. *The Poetry of Gerard Manley Hopkins,* pp. 102–6. Cambridge: Cambridge University Press, 1933. The influence of Hopkins on Eliot. A thoughtful and sensitive study.

373. Phillips, William. "Categories for Criticism." *Sym* 4 (January) : 44–45. A philosophical essay, condemning the application of inadequate "metaphors" such as "Freudianism" or "Humanism" to the criticism of literature; Eliot usually avoids such an error.

*374. Pound, Ezra. "Praefatio aut tumulus cimicium." *Active Anthology,* pp. 9–27. London: Faber and Faber, 1933. [Selected Essays]. Pays Eliot gay compliments, combined with disparaging remarks on publishers. Lively criticism. Reprinted in *Polite Essays,* London: Faber and Faber, 1937, pp. 135–52, and in Unger, no. 1191.

375. Powys, Llewelyn. "T. S. Eliot: the Tutor-Poet." *WeekER* 7 (May 20) : 556–57. Takes Eliot severely to task for not being "life-infatuated," and for being aware of poetic theory. A review consisting chiefly of quotations.

376. Rickword, Edgell. "The Modern Poet." *Towards Standards of Criticism,* edited by F. R. Leavis, pp. 100–106. London: Wishart, 1933. [Poems, 1909–1925]. Devoted chiefly to *The Waste Land,* which he praises with many reservations.

377. ———. "Selected Essays." *Scrutiny* 1 (March) : 390–93. "The intelligence displayed in the later essays might be matched by several of his contemporaries; the literary sensibility of the earlier essays is not matched in any of them." Discriminating analyses. Reprinted in *The Importance of Scrutiny,* edited by Eric Bentley. New York: George W. Stewart, 1948, pp. 273–376.

378. Schappes, Morris U. "T. S. Eliot Moves Right." *MM* 7 (August) : 405–8. [Selected Essays 1917–1932; John Dryden; Criterion]. Suggests that Eliot's earlier fascism came from ignorance of communism, and that since he has read Marx, and only religion stands in his way, he should reconsider the matter.

379. Sélincourt, Basil de. "The Diety of Dryness—Mr. Eliot's Harvard Lectures." *Observer* (November 12) , p. 4. [The Use of Poetry and the Use of Criticism]. A criticism of Eliot's theory that poetry should not be expected to provide "supersubstantial nourishment." A well-written essay.

380. Siegel, Eli. "Literary Sign Posts." *Scribner's* 93 (January) : 7–8. [Selected Essays 1917–1932; John Dryden]. He dislikes both the prose and the poetry because they are prim and bleak.

*381. Spencer, Theodore. "The Poetry of T. S. Eliot." *Atlantic* 151 (January) : 60–68. An excellent introduction to the poetry through "Ash Wednesday."

382. Spender, Stephen. "The Use of Poetry." *NSN* 6, n.s. (November 18) : 637–38. [The Use of Poetry and the Use of Criticism]. A review criticizing Eliot's personality rather than his essay.

383. Strachey, John. *The Coming Struggle for Power,* pp. 218–21. New York: Covici Friede, 1933. A Marxist interpretation of *The Waste Land;* the poem expresses despair at capitalistic society.

384. Strong, Robert. "The Critical Attitude of T. S. Eliot." *LQHR* 158 (October) : 513–19. [Selected Essays 1917–1932]. Chiefly on "Tradition and the Individual Talent." Repeats well what has often been said.

385. Van Doren, Mark. "Shall We Be Saved by Poetry?" *NYHTB* (December 17) , p. 5. [The Use of Poetry and the Use of Criticism]. Brings out clearly the central theme of the lectures: that poetry is one of the valuable things of which we shall never know the price or the exact use, but which cannot take the place of religion.

386. Walton, Eda Lou. "Death in the Desert." *SatR* 10 (August 26) : 61–63. A survey of English and American poetry since 1920, with Eliot playing the part of the over-intellectual villain.

*387. Wheelwright, Philip. "A Contemporary Classicist." *VQR* 9 (January) : 155–60. [Waste Land; Gerontion]. Eliot's classicism consists in his emphasis on the objectivity of the poetic enterprise and on precision in poetry. "Gerontion" is the portrayal of a mood such as an old man might feel, whereas *The Waste Land* gives a combination of moods. It is a diagnosis of our spiritual impotence.

388. Zabel, Morton D. "A Modern Purgatorio." *Cweal* 17 (April 19) : 696–97. [Sweeney Agonistes]. The publication of this dull book is a "tactical error."

1934

389. Aiken, Conrad. "The Use of Poetry." *YR* 23 (March) : 643–46. [The Use of Poetry and the Use of Criticism]. Criticizes Eliot's theories from the point of view of I. A. Richards, who holds that poetry is a sufficient source of "belief."

390. ———. "After Ash Wednesday." *Poetry* 45 (December) : 161–65. [After Strange Gods; The Rock]. The essay and the pageant make Aiken "uneasy about Mr. Eliot's future." Since *The Waste Land* his circle has narrowed.

391. Anon. Review of *The Rock*. *Everyman*, no. 47 (August 17) , p. 189. "The trappings of a doctrinal humility do not at all become a poet of Mr. Eliot's standard."

392. ———. Review of *After Strange Gods*. *LL* 10 (April) : 111–13. A good review stressing the religious insight of the lectures.

393. ———. Review of *The Rock*. *Listener* 11 (June 6) : 945. A brief discussion of Eliot's theory of the poetic drama.

394. ———. "Mr. Eliot's Criticism." *Manchester Guardian* (April 3) , p. 5. [After Strange Gods]. Protests against being lectured to "from an Anglican pulpit"; Eliot's attitude is to be avoided by a creative writer.

395. ———. Review of *The Rock*. *Sun Times* (London) (September 30) , p. 12. The choruses are still "haunted by the whimper already familiar."

396. ———. *Tablet* 164 (August 4) : 138. [The Rock]. "Un-

happily, there is little freshness and beauty of thought to mollify the exacerbating diction."

397. ———. "The Rock, Ecclesiastical Revue." *TAr* 18 (December) : 926–29. Does not think that the play reads well, but its success as acted indicates that "it is scaled for the theatre."

398. ———. Editorial on *The Rock. Theology* 29 (July) : 4–5. Likes the play because the words have bite, are satiric, witty, and poetic.

399. ———. "Mr. Eliot's Pageant Play." *TLS*, no. 1688 (June 7) , p. 404. [The Rock]. A generalized account of Eliot's debt to his predecessors and contemporaries.

400. ———. Review of *After Strange Gods. TLS*, no. 1681 (April 19) , p. 278. Finds Eliot's opinions "eccentric."

401. Beevers, John. "Mr. Eliot, Moralist." *TT* 15 (March 17) : 350–51. [After Strange Gods]. Calls Eliot an "anaemic Fascist." (See no. 2397.)

402. Belgion, Montgomery. "Some Recent Books," *DubR* 194 (January) : 151–53. [The Use of Poetry and the Use of Criticism]. The lectures are unsatisfactory because Eliot does not define poetry.

403. ———. "Some Recent Books." *DubR* 194 (April) : 320–24. [After Strange Gods]. An unfavorable review, from the Roman Catholic standpoint.

404. Benét, William Rose. "T. S. Eliot and Original Sin." *SatR* 10 (May 5) : 673, 678. [After Strange Gods]. Thinks Eliot has lost contact with reality since he entered the Anglican Church. A good summary, with many quotations.

405. ———. "The Rock." *SatR* 11 (September 22) : 129. One paragraph. "It has not very much to do with literature." Compares Eliot with Coventry Patmore.

406. Birrell, Francis. "Mr. Eliot's Revue." *NSN* 7 (June 2) : 847. [The Rock]. A light review, dividing attention equally between the poetry and the spectacle.

407. Blackmur, R. P. "The Dangers of Authorship." *HH* 7: 719–26. [After Strange Gods]. Cannot accept Eliot's idea of evaluating literature by the criterion of Christian orthodoxy because "the greater part of us have lost, surrendered, or denied—if indeed we ever had it." Reprinted in *The Double Agent*, New York: Arrow editions, 1935, pp. 172–83.

408. Bodkin, Maud. *Archetypal Patterns in Poetry*, pp. 308–

14. London: Oxford Press, 1934. [Waste Land]. The poem exemplifies the Jungian pattern of rebirth. (See nos. 503, 990, 1012, and 1016.)

409. Brickell, Herschel. "The Use of Poetry." *NorAR* 237 (February) : 192. [The Use of Poetry and the Use of Criticism]. Praises the clarity of the prose, though he says that he does not understand the poetry.

410. Bridson, D. G. "Mr. Eliot Again." *NewEW* 5 (July 5) : 285–86. [The Rock]. The play is imitative and hastily written.

411. Brooks, Cleanth. "Eliot's Harvard Lectures." *SWR* 19, Supplements 1–2 (January) : 1–2. [The Use of Poetry and the Use of Criticism]. The unity of Eliot's criticism lies in his "reordering the poets of the English tradition. His prose style has been condemned as over-exact because critics have not understood his general thesis, or seen that he has one."

412. Bullough, Geoffrey. "Herbert Read; D. H. Lawrence; T. S. Eliot." *The Trend of Modern Poetry*, pp. 133–54. Edinburgh: Oliver and Boyd, 1934. [Prufrock; Waste Land; Gerontion; Mr. Eliot's Sunday Morning Service; Ash Wednesday]. A survey of Eliot's work. The 3rd ed., 1948, pp. 153–82, brings the survey to date, through the *Four Quartets*.

413. Burdett, Osbert. "Literary History and Criticism." *Lon-Merc* 29 (April) : 567. [After Strange Gods]. One paragraph, saying that the book suffers from Eliot's failure to define Orthodoxy, from which vantage point Eliot criticizes heretical living writers.

414. Calverton, V. F. "T. S. Eliot: an Inverted Marxian." *MM* 8 (July) : 372–73. [After Strange Gods]. Eliot employs "tradition to stand for what the Marxians call ideology." The book is full of "inverted psychology and perverted sociology."

415. Catlin, George. "A Daniel Come to Judgment?" *Sun Times* (London) (March 18), p. 12. [After Strange Gods]. Raises a pertinent question concerning the relation to rationalism to traditionalism. He thinks Eliot pays too little attention to the former.

416. Common, Jack. Review of *After Strange Gods*. *Adelphi* 8 (April) : 68–69. An attempt to be clever at Eliot's expense, calling him "Auntie Eliot," and saying that he "writes in mittens."

417. Cowley, Malcolm. "The Religion of Art. I: Readings from

the Lives of the Saints." *NR* 77 (January 3) : 216–18.
[Waste Land]. On the publication of *The Waste Land*
with its preference of the past to the present, most
younger writers began to move away from Eliot. Reprinted in *Exile's Return*, New York: W. W. Norton,
1934, pp. 123–28, and in Unger, no. 1191.

*418. Dawson, Christopher. "Mr. Eliot's Heresy Hunt." *Listener*
11 (March 7) : supplement, xi. [After Strange Gods].
An excellent objective summary.

*419. Day-Lewis, C. *A Hope for Poetry*. Oxford: Basil Black-
wood, 1934. [Prufrock; Waste Land]. Lively criticism.
Discusses Eliot's influence on Auden, Spender, and himself. Rev. ed., 1939, pp. 181–88.

420. Dobrée, Bonamy. "Views and Reviews: the Elizabethans."
NewEW 4 (November 8) : 91–92. [Elizabethan Essays].
Says these essays are provocative.

421. J. E. "Books to Interest the Workers." *NewL* (London)
(March 23). [After Strange Gods]. The reviewer is
astonished at the religious assumptions on which this
book rests.

422. Every, Brother George. Review of *After Strange Gods*.
Theology 29 (July) : 56–57. Brief but intelligent.

423. Fergusson, Francis. "Eliot's Norton Lectures." *HH* 7
(January–March) : 356–58. [The Use of Poetry and the
Use of Criticism]. A defense of Eliot against an attack
by Waldo Frank in *NR*. (See no. 286.)

424. J.G. Review of *After Strange Gods*. *Isis* (Oxford), no.
890 (February 22), p. 8. A brief review, saying that
Eliot fails as a prophet, but is good as a critic.

425. Gohdes, Clarence. "Poetry and Criticism." *SAQ* 33
(April) : 205–7. [The Use of Poetry and the Use of
Criticism]. Eliot is prejudiced.

426. Gregory, Horace. "The Man of Feeling." *NR* 79 (May
16) : 23–24. [After Strange Gods; The Use of Poetry
and the Use of Criticism]. A vague essay saying that
Eliot has become an "uneasy composite of poet and
public figure," and the latter has been revealed as an
"unhappy, persecuted, lonely man."

*427. Harding, D. W. "The Rock." *Scrutiny* 3 (September) :
180–83. The poetry here "forms a transition to a stage
of Mr. Eliot's work that has not yet fully defined itself."
Good criticism.

428. Hayakawa, S. Ichiye. "Mr. Eliot's Auto da Fé." *SR* 42

(July–September) : 365–71. [After Strange Gods]. An essay by a disappointed admirer who regrets Eliot's narrowness and coldness of moral outlook, especially on racial purity and tradition.

429. Heppenstall, Rayner. Review of *The Use of Poetry and the Use of Criticism*. *Adelphi* 7 (March) : 460–62. A labored detraction, apparently from the Marxist point of view.

430. Irvine, Lyn. "Mr. T. S. Eliot Annoys the Critics." *Monologue* (London) (March 15), pp. 1–8. [This is a mimeographed magazine.] Defense of *After Strange Gods* against Mrs. K. John's criticism (no. 431). Good but highly personal criticism.

431. John, K. (Mrs.) "The Grand Inquisitor." *NSN* 7 (February 24) : 274. [After Strange Gods]. A bad-mannered attack on Eliot's attitude.

432. Knights, L. C. "Shakespere and Shakesperians." *Scrutiny* 3 (December) : 311–14. [Elizabethan Essays]. Is especially interested in Eliot's excellence as a critic of Shakespeare. Reprinted in *Explorations*, London: Chatto and Windus, 1946, pp. 82–85.

433. Lattimore, Richmond. Review of *The Use of Poetry and the Use of Criticism*. *JEGP* 33 (July) : 482–84. An earnest but immature review.

434. Leavis, F. R. "Mr. Eliot, Mr. Wyndham Lewis and Lawrence." *Scrutiny* 3 (September) : 184–91. [After Strange Gods]. Leavis regrets the lessening of Eliot's critical ability and analyzes his essay on Lawrence to substantiate this opinion. Reprinted in *The Importance of Scrutiny*, edited by Eric Bentley, New York: George W. Stewart, 1948, pp. 276–83, also in *The Common Pursuit*, London: Chatto, 1952, pp. 240–47.

435. Lewis, Wyndham. "T. S. Eliot (Pseudoist)." *Men without Art*. London: Cassel and Co., 1934, pp. 65–100. Examines Eliot's theory of the impersonality of the artist, and the difficulties to which it leads, from the point of view of one to whom moral beliefs are the enemy of art. (See no. 434).

436. A.M. Review of *The Use of Poetry and the Use of Criticism*. *Blackfriars* 15, no. 166 (January) : 70–72. Ordinary criticism, favorable.

437. ———. Review of *After Strange Gods*. *Blackfriars* 15, no. 170 (May) : 359–60. "We are convinced by his argument, but disagree with his examples." Brief.

438. ———. Review of *The Rock. Blackfriars* 15, no. 174 (September) : 642–43. The reviewer's chief interest is that "Mr. Eliot has come out of the Waste Land a Christian."

439. Mirsky, D. S. "T. S. Eliot and the End of Bourgeois Poetry." *NewM* 13 (November 13) : 17–19. Eliot is the last and greatest of the bourgeois poets, whose theme, Death, is the only possible one.

440. Moore, Harry Thornton. Review of *The Rock. Adelphi* 9 (December) : 188–89. The critic says, "There it is, not so big as Gibraltar, but apparently as big as an act of faith can be these days."

441. Muir, Edwin. "Mr. Eliot on Evil." *Spectator* 152, no. 5515 (March 9) : 378–79. [After Strange Gods]. The book is excellent in matter but it is not full enough.

442. Nicoll, Allardyce. "Mr. T. S. Eliot and the Revival of Classicism." *EJ* 23. College ed. (April) : 269–78. Good analysis of the likenesses between this age and the seventeenth century; less illuminating for Eliot's poetry.

443. O'Casey, Sean. "Notes on the Way." *TT* 15 (February 10) : 168. [The Use of Poetry and the Use of Criticism]. He is too much annoyed to consider Eliot's criticisms of Shelley clearly.

444. Passmore, John Arthur. *T. S. Eliot,* 19 pp. Sydney University Literary Society, September 1934. "His greatness . . . rests in his power to present feelings thinking, to present thought tossed and inverted by desires,—in short, in his power to present situations of psychological intricacy; his weakness in his inability to 'think straight,' to develop the problems he raises with coherence and clarity."

445. Peel, Robert. "T. S. Eliot and the Classic-Romantic Yardstick." *CSM, Weekly Magazine Section* (June 6) , p. 11. [After Strange Gods]. "It is possible to sympathize profoundly with his general thesis while disagreeing in nearly every respect with his dogmatic beliefs, which he holds as a Tory and an Anglo-Catholic."

446. ———. "A Classical Contemporary Pageant from Mr. T. S. Eliot." *CSM, Weekly Magazine Section* (November 14) , p. 12. [The Rock]. "Judged as a drama, or even as a pageant, the play is very uneven in its merits." But in the best of the choruses, "Mr. Eliot overtops Dryden in majesty, while preserving the simplicity . . . of modern speech." Good criticism.

447. Pound, Ezra. "Mr. Eliot's Mare's Nest." *NewEW* 4 (March

8) : 500. [After Strange Gods]. An attack on Eliot because he does not see that organized Christianity is weak in ignoring economics. Written from a highly specialized point of view.

448. ———. "Mr. Eliot's Quandaries." *NewEW* 4 (March 29) : 558–59. [After Strange Gods]. Pound answers questions raised in a letter to him from Eliot on March 15, 1934, in *NewEW* 4, and continues his attack on Eliot's religion and lack of interest in economics.

449. ———. "Mr. T. S. Eliot's Quandaries." *NewEW* 5 (April 26) : 48. A continuation of the controversy concerning Eliot's religion and economics.

450. ———. "Mr. Eliot's Looseness." *NewEW* 5 (May 10) : 95–96. A continuation of the controversy; see above.

*451. ———. "What Price the Muses Now." *NewEW* 5 (May 24) : 130–33. [The Use of Poetry and the Use of Criticism]. Thinks one would do well to read the first part of the book and "chuck the rest into the waste basket." Refreshing criticism, aside from the economic bias.

*452. ———. "Mr. Eliot's Solid Merit." *NewEW* 5 (June 12) : 297–99. Defends Eliot's criticism in impolite, and vigorous language. Significant criticism. Reprinted in *Polite Essays,* London: Faber and Faber, 1937, pp. 98–105.

453. Powell, Dilys. "T. S. Eliot." *Descent from Parnassus,* pp. 57–100. New York: Macmillan, 1934. A good, simple survey of Eliot's career to 1934.

454. Quiller-Couch, Arthur T. "Tradition and Orthodoxy." *The Poet as Citizen and Other Papers,* pp. 44–61. Cambridge: Cambridge University Press, 1934. [After Strange Gods]. A criticism of Eliot's phrase, "a society like ours, worm-eaten with liberalism," saying that liberalism is tradition itself, and Eliot's alternative is brute force. Reprinted in *Q. Anthology,* edited by F. Brittain, London: Dent, 1948.

*455. Ransom, John Crowe. "T. S. Eliot on Criticism." *SatR* 10 (March 24) : 574. [The Use of Poetry and the Use of Criticism]. An important article assessing Eliot's strength, his devotion to literature as literature; and his weakness—a refusal to formulate a critical theory.

456. Roberts, Michael. *Critique of Poetry,* pp. 16–17, 209–12, 216–19. London: Jonathan Cape, 1934. He praises Eliot's tragic sense and elegance, but is somewhat disturbed that his poetry does not rouse to action. Written from a moderate socialist point of view.

457. Salmon, Christopher V. "Critics and Criticism." *NC* 115 (March): 359–69. [The Use of Poetry and the Use of Criticism]. Salmon is interested only in Eliot's view of the relation between the critic and society.

458. Sampson, Ashley. "In Pursuit of Psyche." *SaR* 157 (February 17): 190. [The Use of Poetry and the Use of Criticism]. A discrepancy between Eliot's criticism and his poetry. He excels "as a critic of critics."

459. Sayers, Michael. "The Drama: Mr. T. S. Eliot's 'The Rock.'" *NewEW* 5 (June 21): 230–31. Fails as drama because it confines its subject matter to abstractions and does not deal with individual experience. Objects to the language. Moderate in tone.

460. Sélincourt, Basil de. "A New Cure for the Times." *Observer* (March 4), p. 5. [After Strange Gods]. In the name of British freedom protests against Eliot's demand for orthodoxy.

461. Sengupta, S. K. "T. S. Eliot: A New Force in English Poetry." *CalR* 50 (March): 307–16. Probably valuable to English-speaking Indians as an introduction to Eliot; surveys his entire poetic career, with some biographical details and plentiful quotations.

462. Shillito, Edward. "The Faith of T. S. Eliot." *ChC* 51 (August 1): 994–95. [The Rock]. Summary of the pageant.

463. Short, John. "A Provocative Critic." *Friend* (London) (September 7). [After Strange Gods]. Brief summary. "This is a book with which many will violently disagree: it is a book few can afford to ignore."

*464. Sitwell, Edith. "T. S. Eliot." *Aspects of Modern Poetry*. London: Duckworth, 1934, pp. 99–140. Excellent analysis by a poet of the adjustment of diction and rhythm to meaning.

465. Sparrow, John. *Sense and Poetry*. New Haven: Yale University Press, 1934, pp. 46–50, 67–70, 143, *passim*. F. O. Matthiessen says Sparrow "combines considerable knowledge of the past, a certain amount of common sense in pointing out the excesses of certain minor figures in modern art, and an almost complete lack of taste or ability to discriminate between Eliot and Edith Sitwell."

466. Spender, Stephen. "The Artistic Future of Poetry." *NR* 78 (April 18): 269. He praises Eliot for having broken

away from the "decaying tradition of post-Victorian or Georgian poetry."

467. Stone, Geoffrey. "Indirect Affirmations." *Cweal* 19 (February 9) : 418–19. [The Use of Poetry and the Use of Criticism]. A rather confused summary.

468. Strong, L. A. G. Review of *The Rock. Observer* (July 22) , p. 8. Short review, chiefly descriptive. Says it is good drama.

469. Sunne, Richard. "Men and Books." *TT* 15 (June 16) : 774. [The Rock]. Good criticism, setting this play against the background of Eliot's earlier thought. "Mr. Eliot believes, as firmly as any Communist or Fascist, in a whole of which individuals are a part; but the needs of that whole can only be gained by the voluntary transcendence . . . of the individual."

470. Swinnerton, Frank A. "Later Visions: T. S. Eliot and the New Academicism." *The Georgian Scene: a Literary Panorama*, pp. 491–95. New York: Farrar and Rinehart, 1934. Thinks Eliot has done more harm than good by encouraging a "tribe of arid sciolists."

471. K.S.T. Review of *After Strange Gods. Cherwell* 40 (March 10) : 190. The reviewer says "his statement of his case should be read with care; although it will provoke many into furious denunciations, I am not sure that it is not salutary chastisement." Brief.

472. Thompson, T. H. "The Bloody Wood." *LonMerc* 29 (January) : 233–39. A delightful parody on over-subtle critics, in the form of the story of Sweeney's murder of Mrs. Porter's daughter. Reprinted in Unger, no. 1191.

473. Tillyard, E. M. W. *Poetry Direct and Oblique*. London: Chatto and Windus, 1934. Scattered paragraphs on Eliot's use of allusions.

474. ———. "The Personal Heresy in Criticism: a Rejoinder." *Essays and Studies by the Members of the English Association* 20. Oxford: Clarendon Press, 1935, 11. [The Rock]. The most successful passages are those in which Eliot's normal personality is most perceptible in the style.

475. Troy, William. "T. S. Eliot, Grand Inquisitor." *Nation* 138 (April 25) : 478–79. [After Strange Gods]. Says Eliot is a Fascist.

476. Turnell, G. Martin. "Tradition and T. S. Eliot." *Colos* 1 (June) : 44–54. [After Strange Gods]. A carefully

developed objection to Eliot's advocating an European tradition when he is actually speaking for an Anglican tradition.

477. Verschoyle, Derek. "The Theatre." Review of *The Rock. Spectator* 152, no. 5527 (June 1): 851. Reproaches Eliot for not justifying the existence of the Church.

478. C.H.W. "Mr. Eliot Shuts the Door." *Everyman,* no. 27 (March 29), p. 167. [After Strange Gods]. C.H.W. cannot accept Eliot's doctrine because he does not believe in original sin.

479. Wecter, Dixon. "The Harvard Exiles." *VQR* 10 (April): 244–57. A clear, graceful essay on the attraction of Europe and the past for three Harvard men: Henry Adams, Santayana, and Eliot.

480. Williamson, Hugh Ross. "Notes at Random, T. S. Eliot's 'Primer of Modern Heresy.'" *Bookman* (London) 85 (March): 468–71. [After Strange Gods]. A lucid statement of the case for individualism, politely disagreeing with Eliot.

481. Wilson, James Southall. "The Faculty of Poets." *VQR* 10 (July): 477–78. [The Use of Poetry and the Use of Criticism]. Part of an omnibus review; he finds this a provocative and irritating book.

482. Zabel, Morton D. "The Use of the Poet." *Poetry* 44 (April): 32–37. [The Use of Poetry and the Use of Criticism]. The worth of this volume "lies in what it tells of Eliot's career and his importance to an age which his work has both enlightened and perplexed."

483. ———. "Poetry for the Theatre." *Poetry* 45 (December): 152–58. [The Rock]. Eliot's pageant is used merely as an example in this essay.

1935

484. Aiken, Conrad [pseud., Samuel Jeake, Jr.]. "London Letter." *NY* 11 (July 13): 53–55. [Murder in the Cathedral]. A chatty letter, expressing surprise that Eliot here shows himself to be very human.

485. Anon. Review of *The Rock. PoetryR* 26 (January–February): 78–79. Likes only the choruses.

486. ———. "Mr. Eliot's New Play." *TLS,* no. 1741 (June 13), 376. [Murder in the Cathedral]. The danger to Eliot's dramatic writing is in "his rhymes, and . . . its merits most movingly appear in the prose sermon and in those

passages of verse that are direct in their attack and not twisted to irony or humor." Reprinted in A. C. Ward. *Specimens of English Dramatic Criticism XVII–XX Centuries,* London: Oxford University Press, 1945, pp. 326–38.

487. Barnes, T. R. "Poets and the Drama." *Scrutiny* 4, no. 2 (September) : 189–91. [Murder in the Cathedral]. Summary.

*488. Blackmur, R. P. "T. S. Eliot. From Ash Wednesday to Murder in the Cathedral." *The Double Agent,* pp. 184–218. New York: Arrow editions, 1935. ". . . the modern reader is not fitted to appreciate either a mind or its works conceived in relation to Christianity as a living discipline. . . . If I have shown to what degree the reader must perform an imaginative resurrection, I have so far done enough." There has been no growth in Eliot's subject matter, but only in technique in attempting to reach a wider audience. Reprinted in Unger, no. 1191.

489. Blake, Howard. "Thoughts on Modern Poetry." *SR* 43 (April–June) : 187–96. Eliot's poetry, along with that of MacLeish, Stevens, and Crane, lacks catholicity.

490. Bogan, Louise. "The Season's Verse." *NY* 11 (November 9) : 85. [Murder in the Cathedral]. Finds the verse monotonous.

491. Brophy, John. "Letters to the Editor: T. S. Eliot's 'Notes on the Way.' " *TT* 16 (January 19) : 95–96. Eliot's views on war are confused. (See nos. 494, 500, 519, 522, 533, 535, 537, 538, 539, 540.)

492. Brown, Ivor. "Criticism in Cameo. The Stage." *Sketch* (London) , 172 (October 9) : 84 [Sweeney Agonistes]. Expresses disapproval of a performance by the Group Theatre at Westminster Theatre.

493. Brown, Wallace Cable. "T. S. Eliot and the Demon of the Ego." *NewH* 8 (Summer) : 81–85. A restatement of Eliot's attitude toward tradition and the individual.

494. Butts, Mary. "Letters to the Editor: Mr. T. S. Eliot's 'Notes on the Way.' " *TT,* 16 (January 26) : 124. Agrees with the religious assumptions behind Eliot's January 12 article in *TT* 16 on war and pacifism.

495. Cajetan, Brother. "The Pendulum Starts Back." *CathW* 140 (March) : 654–55. [Ash Wednesday]. Predicts that Eliot's religious quest will end in the Catholic Church.

496. Damon, S. Foster. *Amy Lowell, a Chronicle.* Boston: Houghton Mifflin, 1935. Miss Lowell is quoted as saying, "I do not think that Eliot was intended by nature for a poet." All her references to Eliot are unflattering.

497. Deutsch, Babette. "Heirs of the Symbolists." *This Modern Poetry,* pp. 117–32. New York: Norton, 1935. Repeats what other critics have said.

498. Dobson, E. J. "The Hollow Men, and the Work of T. S. Eliot." *Some Recent Developments in English Literature,* pp. 33–52. Sydney: Sydney University extension lectures, 1935. (Also in *Some Modern Writers,* with a postscript on *The Family Reunion,* pp. 96–117, Sydney, 1940.) *The Waste Land* is the "nightmare of a man who is at once a student of anthropology and comparative religion and a lover of literature, who has an abiding sense of religion, and an equally abiding sense of the unworthiness of humanity."

499. Donnelly, Ian. "T. S. Eliot Himself." *The Joyous Pilgrimage,* pp. 177–79. London: Dent, 1935. An account of a conversation with Eliot.

500. Edwards, F. M. "Letters to the Editor. T. S. Eliot's 'Notes on the Way.'" *TT* 16 (February 2) : 156. Eliot is obscure and sophistical in his controversial writing.

501. I.F. "Literary Fascism. Book News of the Day." *CSM* (September 25), p. 18. [Murder in the Cathedral]. The riches of the classical spirit displayed here are a delight, but Eliot has forgotten that a poet must understand the "contemporary main current of thought" also.

502. Gordon, George Stuart. *Poetry and the Moderns,* 33 pp. (Oxford, Clarendon Press, 1935). So condescending as to be one of the curiosities of Eliot criticism.

503. Harding, M. Esther. *Woman's Mysteries Ancient and Modern,* pp. 297–99. London: Longmans, Green and Co., 1935. A Jungian interpretation of *The Waste Land.* Brief. Rev. ed., 1955, pp. 204–9.

504. Humphries, Rolfe. "Eliot, Auden, Isherwood, and Cummings." *NewM* 18 (December 31) : 23–24. [Murder in the Cathedral]. An adverse criticism from the moderate leftist point of view. Eliot "may . . . still be an artist more honest than he prefers to admit."

505. Hutchison, Percy. "T. S. Eliot's Pageant Play of Faith." *NYTBR* (July 14), p. 8. [The Rock]. The spirit of the greatest English poetry is revived in this play, which has at the same time a modern touch.

506. Jack, Peter Monro. "T. S. Eliot's Drama of Beauty and Momentous Decision." *NYTBR* (October 27), p. 11. [Murder in the Cathedral]. A summary of the plot.

507. Jennings, Humphrey. "Eliot and Auden and Shakespeare." *NewV*, no. 18 (December), pp. 4–7. States that Shakespeare is superior to the two modern dramatists. Thin in content.

508. Kronenberger, Louis. "T. S. Eliot as Critic." *Nation* 140 (April 17): 452–53. Dismisses him by saying: "He is not acute about the things that interest us most [social-political questions] but *is* acute about the things that interest us somewhat." He has "begun to fade from the scene."

*509. Laughlin, James. "Mr. Eliot on Holy Ground." *NewEW* 7 (July 11): 250–51. [Murder in the Cathedral]. Eliot has attempted a fusion of the classical and medieval dramatic formulas. Informal, intelligent criticism. Appeared also in *New Democracy* 5, nos. 9, 10 (January 1–15): 159–60.

510. Loring, M. L. S. "T. S. Eliot on Matthew Arnold." *SR* 43 (October-December): 479–88. The fundamental difference between Eliot and Arnold is that the latter found generalization very easy, the former, very difficult.

511. H.M. "Book Parade." *Stage* 13 (November): 97. [Murder in the Cathedral]. Admits that the verse is good for drama, but says there is little dramatic feeling.

512. MacCarthy, Desmond. "Sweeney Agonistes." *Listener* 13 (January 9): 80–81. Account of a production given by the Group Theatre. He did not understand the play, but found it impressive.

513. MacNeice, Louis. "Poetry Today." *The Arts Today,* edited by Geoffrey Grigson, pp. 25–67. London: John Lane, The Bodley Head, 1935. An essay on the modern poets, using Eliot as the central figure. A good survey.

514. P.M. [Philip Mairet]. "Belief and Criticism," *NewEW* 7 (May 9): 71–72. [Religion and Literature]. A defense of Eliot against Spender's attack in *The Destructive Element* (no. 531) and a criticism of "Religion and Literature." Gets at fundamental issues.

515. Mason, H. A. "Tradition and the Academic Critic." *Scrutiny* 4 (December): 311–12. [Review of Matthiessen's *The Achievement of T. S. Eliot*]. Shows the characteristic preference of *Scrutiny* for Eliot's earlier work.

*516. Matthiessen, F. O. *The Achievement of T. S. Eliot: an Essay on the Nature of Poetry*, 160 pp. New York: Houghton Mifflin, 1935. Rev. ed., 1947, Oxford University Press, 202 pp. One of the best studies of Eliot's poetry—sympathetic, clear, scholarly. The first six chapters are an "estimate not so much of particular poems as of Eliot's poetic method." Chapters 7 and 8, added to the 1947 edition, are on the plays, and the *Four Quartets*. Reviews: *TLS*, November 16, 1935; *NYHTB*, January 12, 1936; G. S. Fraser in *The PoetryR* 40 (1949) : 52–54. Chapter 6, "The Sense of His Own Age" reprinted in Unger, no. 1191; chapter 8, "The Four Quartets" reprinted in *Literary Opinion in America*, edited by Morton D. Zabel, New York: Harper, 1951, pp. 282–95.

517. ———. "T. S. Eliot's Drama of Becket." *SatR* 12 (October 12) : 10–11. [Murder in the Cathedral]. More summary here than in the *Achievement* (no. 516) and less criticism.

518. Meagher, Margaret C. Review of *The Use of Poetry and the Use of Criticism. CathW* 140 (January) : 498–99. Summary.

519. Milne, A. A. "Letters to the Editor: T. S. Eliot's 'Notes on the Way.' " *TT* 16 (January 19) : 94. Combats Eliot's criticism (*TT*, January 12, 1935) of Milne's attack on war. He accuses Eliot of confusion.

520. ———. "Letters to the Editor: T. S. Eliot's 'Notes on the Way.' " *TT* 16 (February 2) : 154.

521. ———. "New Literature." *LonMerc* 32 (July) : 281–83. [Murder in the Cathedral]. Helpful for anyone who has read the play.

522. Murdock, James. "Letters to the Editor: T. S. Eliot's 'Notes on the Way.' " *TT* 16 (February 2) : 155. Eliot is the only person in the controversy who is aware what the Pope's encyclical on war means. (See nos. 494, 500, 519, 530, 535, 537, 538, 539, 540.)

523. Oliphant, E. H. C. "Tourneur and Mr. T. S. Eliot." *SP* 32 (October) : 546–52. [Cyril Tourneur]. A scholarly attack on Eliot's ascription of *The Revenger's Tragedy* to Tourneur.

524. Parsons, I. M. "Poetry, Drama, and Satire." *Spectator* 154, no. 5583 (June 28) : 1112–14. [Murder in the Cathedral]. "He has reanimated a literary form which in England has been dead or dormant for nearly three hundred years, and in so doing he has found himself anew

as a poet, only with an added ease, lucidity and objectiveness."

525. Pottle, Frederick A. "Drama of Action." *YR* 25 (December) : 426–29. [The Rock; Murder in the Cathedral]. A clear account of the two plays, resting on considered critical principles.

526. Rees, Richard. Review of *Murder in the Cathedral*. *Adelphi* 11 (October) : 60–61. The reviewer is chiefly interested in Eliot's political opinions, of which he does not approve.

527. Richards, I. A. *Coleridge on Imagination*, pp. 216–19, and *passim*. New York: Harcourt, Brace and Co., 1935. [Ash Wednesday]. On the reading of "because I do not hope to turn again" and "Although I do not hope to turn again," in relation to the problem of meaning in poetry.

528. Scarfe, Francis. "The Achievement of T. S. Eliot." *CamR* 57 (November 15) : 108. Purporting to be a review of Matthiessen (no. 516), this is a breezy essay on Eliot's differences from, and superiorities to, his predecessors.

529. Shillito, Edward. "Murder in the Cathedral." *ChC* 52 (December 18) : 1636. A "noble" play, raising questions of deep spiritual significance.

530. Smith, N. A. "Letters to the Editor: T. S. Eliot's 'Notes on the Way.'" *TT* 16 (January 19) : 96. Eliot's controversy with Milne (see nos. 519, 520) is confusing at a time when reasonable thinking is needed.

*531. Spender, Stephen. "T. S. Eliot in His Poetry"; "T. S. Eliot in His Criticism." *The Destructive Element*, pp. 132–52, 153–75. London: Jonathan Cape, 1935. Expresses cautious disapproval of Eliot's poetic and critical beliefs. Eliot's characters lack life because they are symbols of his own spiritual individuality. Reprinted in Unger, no. 1191.

532. Stone, Geoffrey. "Plays by Eliot and Auden." *AmR* 6 (November) : 121–28. [Murder in the Cathedral]. Glances at Eliot's criticism and earlier poetry, praises the idea of the play, but Stone's best criticism is of the abstractness of Eliot's characters.

533. Tomlin, E. W. F. "Letters to the Editor: T. S. Eliot's 'Notes on the Way.'" *TT* 16 (February 2) : 156. An attack on Rebecca West's January 26 article on Eliot. Tomlin defends Eliot's logic.

534. Van Doren, Mark. "The Holy Blisful Martir." *Nation* 141 (October 9) : 417. [Murder in the Cathedral]. Eliot

leaves the question of Becket's holiness unanswered, since he may have become a martyr for the wrong reason. Reprinted in *The Private Reader,* New York: Henry Holt, 1942, pp. 210–12.

535. Van Raalte, George. "Letters to the Editor: T. S. Eliot's 'Notes on the Way.'" *TT* 16 (January 19) : 96. Attacks Eliot's assumptions on war.

536. D.W. "At the Play." *Punch* 189 (October 9) : 412. [Sweeney Agonistes]. Clear account of the production by the Group Theatre and of the meaning of the fragment.

537. West, Rebecca. "Letters to the Editor: Mr. T. S. Eliot's 'Notes on the Way.'" *TT* 16 (January 12) : 43–44. She objects to Eliot's reasoning in an article in *TT* 16 on January 5.

538. ———. "Letters to the Editor: T. S. Eliot's 'Notes on the Way.'" *TT* 16 (January 19) : 94–95. Eliot's article on war is "a tissue of confusions, and his thinking is not only insufficient: it is merely a feeble groping at the threshold of thought."

539. ———. "Letters to the Editor: Mr. T. S. Eliot's 'Notes on the Way.'" *TT* 16 (January 26) : 123–24. Attacks Eliot for misunderstanding her letter of January 12 (no. 537) and for foggy thinking and bad writing on the question of liberty.

540. ———. "Letters to the Editor: T. S. Eliot's 'Notes on the Way.'" *TT* 16 (February 2) : 155. A continuation of previous attacks on Eliot.

1936

541. Admur, Alice Steiner. *The Poetry of Ezra Pound,* pp. 60–64. Cambridge: Harvard University Press, 1936. Comparison of Eliot and Pound's *Hugh Selwyn Mauberley:* Pound "has not Eliot's creative imagination, Eliot's fusing intellect, nor Eliot's sense of values."

542. Aiken, Conrad. "Mr. Eliot in the Wilderness." *NR* 88 (October 21) : 326–37. [Essays Ancient and Modern]. The essays are dull, and show a retrogression of mind as astonishing as it is melancholy. Aiken objects to Eliot's religion.

543. Anon. "Temptation." *Cweal* 23 (March 13) : 560. [Murder in the Cathedral]. One paragraph of good comment on the London production.

544. ——. "Reviews." *NewEW* 9 (July 23) : 297. [The Crite-
rion]. Review of the July, 1936 issue, with a few lines
of praise for Eliot's editorial, and his review of Murry's
Shakespeare.

545. ——. "Stage: Thoughtful and Moving Drama of a Martyr's Murder." *Newsweek* 7 (March 28) : 26. [Murder
in the Cathedral]. Says that "Eliot's beautifully resonant
and melodious abstractions make difficult material for
inexperienced actors."

546. ——. "Royalist, Classicist, Anglo-Catholic." *Time* 27, pt.
2 (May 25) : 90–91. [Collected Poems 1909–1935]. Is
interested to note that in this collection Eliot has re-
tained some of his earlier, non-Christian verse, which
the reviewer prefers.

547. ——. "Mr. Eliot's New Essays." *TLS*, no. 1779 (March
7), p. 192. [Essays Ancient and Modern]. Mainly a fair
and detailed summary of the essays on Pascal and Tennyson.

548. Arvin, Newton. "About T. S. Eliot." *NR* 85 (January 15) :
290. [Murder in the Cathedral]. The play "impresses
much less the glory of martyrdom than the dreamlike
unreality . . . of all temporal things, the guilty vileness
of mankind and the monstrousness of nature."

*549. Atkinson, Brooks. "Strange Images of Death." *NYT*
(March 29), sec. 9, p. 1. [Murder in the Cathedral].
A long, carefully written review. Without "creative di-
rection Mr. Eliot's play would be only a literary rite.
Resourcefully directed, it becomes a liturgical drama
of exalted beauty."

550. C.E.B. "Books of the Day." *ILN* 189 (September 12) : 428.
[Collected Poems 1909–1935]. The reviewer objects to
Eliot's obscurity but nevertheless enjoys his verse. Slight.

551. Beach, Joseph Warren. "The Vanishing Point: T. S.
Eliot." *The Concept of Nature in Nineteenth-Century
English Poetry*, pp. 554–55. New York: Macmillan, 1936.
Eliot's interest in nature is nonexistent.

552. Bell, Bernard Iddings. "Mr. T. S. Eliot's Essays." *LC* 95
(October 17) : 433. [Essays Ancient and Modern]. A
summary of the book by a fellow Anglo-Catholic. "Nothing more sane has been written on religion and society
for a long time."

553. Benchley, Robert. "The Government Takes a Hand." *NY*
12 (March 28) : 32. [Murder in the Cathedral]. Praises

the Federal Theatre for producing the play; he enjoyed especially the satire of the knight's speeches.

554. Black, Ivan. "A Note on T. S. Eliot." *Verse* (June). [I have seen this only as a clipping.] [Collected Poems 1909–1935]. A bitter attack, unsupported by evidence.

555. Bovey, John A. "The Literary Criticism of T. S. Eliot." *AmP* 1 no. 5 (February): 67–71. A wandering essay praising the prose doctrines at the expense of the poems.

*556. Brooks, Cleanth. "Three Revolutions in Poetry: III. Metaphysical Poetry and the Ivory Tower." *SoR* 1 (Winter): 568–83. Evaluates Eliot's poetry and criticism from the point of view which defines poetry as the reconciliation of opposites.

557. F.C. "Gods True and False." *Granta* 43 (February 28): 292. [After Strange Gods]. Religious differences between Eliot and the reviewer prevent him from understanding the book.

558. Carter, Barbara B. "Modern English Poetry." *CathW* 143 (June): 292–97. [Waste Land; Ash Wednesday; After Strange Gods]. Repeats commonplaces of criticism from a Roman Catholic, sympathetic point of view.

559. Colum, Mary M. "Life and Literature: Revival in the Theater." *Forum* 95 (June): 344–45. [Murder in the Cathedral]. On the production in New York by the WPA; admires the poetry but says that the scene with the tempters breaks the mood.

560. ———. "Life and Literature: Studies of the American Mind." *Forum* 96 (October): 175. [Essays Ancient and Modern]. Says that Eliot is a first-class critic, though she does not agree with his view of Baudelaire. Considers also the essay on Pascal.

561. Connolly, Cyril. "Major Poet. The Influence of Mr. Eliot." *Sun Times* (May 3), p. 8. [Collected Poems 1909–1935]. Without Eliot, English poetry "would have advanced no further from the Georgian poets than they had progressed from the 'nineties.' "

562. Cowley, Malcolm. "Afterthoughts on T. S. Eliot." *NR* 87 (May 20): 49. [Collected Poems 1909–1935]. Dislikes his religious poetry; implies that the subject makes for their "indifferent quality as verse."

563. Daniells, Roy. "The Christian Drama of T. S. Eliot." *CF* 16 (August): 20–21. [The Rock; Murder in the Cathe-

dral; The Use of Poetry and the Use of Criticism]. He can accept the Christian dogma as presented in the plays, but not in the criticism.

564. Deutsch, Babette. "The Most Influential Poet of Our Time." *NYHT* (May 31), p. 7. [Collected Poems 1909–1935]. A clear statement of her conviction that Eliot's poetry of disillusionment was better than his more affirmative poetry.

565. ———. "The Orthodox Mr. Eliot." *NYHTB* (September 13), p. 14. [Essays Ancient and Modern]. She says that "one is repeatedly overcome by a feeling that the author is living in a time remote from our own and forming his judgments on a basis of doctrines that carry no weight with men of skeptical intelligence today."

*566. Dodds, A. E. Review of *The Use of Poetry and the Use of Criticism*. *MLN* 51 (January): 49–52. A thoughtful and well-informed essay. Compares Eliot with Croce.

567. Downey, Harris. "T. S. Eliot—Poet as Playwright." *VQR* 12 (January): 142–45. [Murder in the Cathedral; The Rock]. He says that the "pageant and the play incorporate predilections of the earlier poetry and tenets of the criticism."

568. Drew, Elizabeth. "The Trouble with Modern Poetry." *SatR* 14 (May 23): 3, 4, 14. [Waste Land]. Using *The Waste Land* as an example, Miss Drew says that modern poets render communication difficult.

569. Dukes, Ashley. "The English Scene: Listener's Theatre." *TAr* 20 (January): 25–26. [Murder in the Cathedral]. Good criticism by the English producer of the play; he says that Eliot is a "natural dramatist."

570. Elliott, George R. "T. S. Eliot and Irving Babbitt." AmR 7 (September): 442–54. Defends Babbitt against Eliot's charge that his religion is a "by-product of Protestant theology in its last agonies."

571. Fieling, Keith. "Set in Authority: Mr. T. S. Eliot's Essays." *Observer* (May 3), p. 9. [Essays Ancient and Modern]. Good summary of contents; little criticism.

572. Gassner, John W. "Perspectives—Past and Present." *NewT* 3 (May): 10–12; 36–37. [Murder in the Cathedral]. Really two plays: "an undramatic formal confession of faith and a real, if fleeting, drama of pessimism and hatred of the world." Also a criticism of the WPA production, which is "ingenious."

573. Gilmore, William. "The Service of T. S. Eliot to Contemporary Criticism." *Brooklyn Daily Eagle* (August 30), col. 9. A long and careful explanation of the relation of Eliot's religious beliefs to his critical beliefs, especially in relation to "personality."

574. Gregory, Horace. "The Mixed Role of T. S. Eliot." *NYHTB* (January 12), p. 4. [Murder in the Cathedral; Matthiessen's *Achievement of T. S. Eliot*]. A good rapid summary of Eliot's career, based on Matthiessen. Competent criticism of the play.

*575. Harding, D. W. "T. S. Eliot, 1925–1936." *Scrutiny* 5 (September): 171–76. [Collected Poems 1909–1935]. An excellent review, emphasizing Eliot's later attitude toward suffering compared with his earlier one. Reprinted in *The Importance of Scrutiny,* edited by Eric Bentley, New York: George W. Stewart, 1948, pp. 262–66.

576. Hawkins, Ann. "An Enduring Poem." *PacW* 4 (March 30): 174–75. [Murder in the Cathedral]. "What can be said of a man whom you have no right to condemn, but cannot praise?" She thinks he is too pessimistic.

577. Hayward, John. "London Letter." *New York Sun* (March 28), p. 19. [Collected Poems 1909–1935]. He remarks how easy it is now to understand Eliot's poetry.

578. Holmes, John Haynes. "Eliot Poet and Playwright." *Unity* 117 (August 3): 218. The reviewer is surprised that he understood *Murder in the Cathedral,* for in the *Poems,* "most of the stuff . . . is as unintelligible to me as so much Choctaw."

579. Humphries, Rolfe. "Eliot's Poetry." *NewM* 20 (August 18): 25–26. [Collected Poems 1909–1935]. Humphries speaking as a poet admires Eliot; speaking as a leftist, he disapproves.

580. ———. "Anima Naturaliter Marxiana?" *NewM* 20 (September 8): 24–26. [Essays Ancient and Modern]. As a poet who has also written good prose, Eliot must be admired. Says that Eliot "has approximated many Marxist conclusions."

581. "Ibee." "Murder in the Cathedral." *Variety* (March 25). The "play is far from commercial."

582. Isaacs, Edith J. R. "Saints and Lawmakers: Broadway in Review." *TAr* 20 (May): 341–43. [Murder in the Cathedral]. A favorable review of the Federal Theatre Project's production. Pen and ink sketch of one scene.

583. Jack, Peter Monro. "T. S. Eliot, Poet of Our Time." *NYTBR* (June 14), pp. 1, 14. [Collected Poems 1909–1935]. A popular but careful review of the poems to 1936.

584. ———. "The World of T. S. Eliot." *NYTBR* (September 13), pp. 5, 26. [Essays Ancient and Modern]. Deplores his forsaking purely literary for religious criticism.

585. Jones, Howard Mumford. "The Legend of T. S. Eliot." *SatR* 14 (September 19): 13–14. [Essays Ancient and Modern]. Takes Eliot to task for introducing moral and religious questions into literature.

586. Krutch, Joseph Wood. "The Holy Blissful Martyr." *Nation* 142 (April 8): 459–60. [Murder in the Cathedral]. Emphasizes the medieval quality of the play.

587. ———. "How Dead Is Liberalism?" *Nation* 143 (September 19): 334. Krutch calls Eliot a liberal democrat, since he does not regard Lambeth Palace as a final authority.

588. Laboulle, M. J. J. "T. S. Eliot and Some French Poets." *RLC* 16 (April-June): 389–99. Deals with the influence of the Symbolist poets on Eliot, correcting Taupin at one point. (See no. 321.)

589. Laws, Frederick. "Mr. Eliot's Sunday Evening Service." *NSN* 11 (June 20): 973. An amusing parody.

590. Leavis, F. R. "Eliot and Education." *Scrutiny* 5 (June): 84–89. [Essays Ancient and Modern]. Leavis is very much annoyed with the Eliot of these essays, although he makes his annoyance sound like literary criticism. Reprinted in *The Importance of Scrutiny*, edited by Eric Bentley, New York: George W. Stewart, 1948, pp. 283–87.

591. P.M. [Philip Mairet]. "Views and Reviews: The Inevitability of Eliot." *NewEW* 8 (March 26): 472–73. [Essays Ancient and Modern]. The unity of these essays is that of religious faith. "Far from having 'fallen back' on something safe and certain, the position he has taken is vulnerable, precarious, and hard to defend in the modern world; and on that, I think, depends its value to this generation."

592. Meter, W. J. "Eliot, Morals, and Censorship." *SatR* 14 (October 3): 9. [Essays Ancient and Modern]. A defense of Eliot against the criticism leveled at him by Howard Mumford Jones. (See no. 585.)

*593. Mizener, Arthur. "Letter from Yale." *SR* 44 (January-

March) : 94–98. A well-reasoned examination of Matthiessen's statement that "for an appreciation of Eliot's poetry the question of our own acceptance or rejection of his doctrine remains irrelevant."

594. Moore, Marianne. "If I Am Worthy, There Is No Danger." *Poetry* 47 (February) : 279–81. [Murder in the Cathedral]. A brief explanation of Becket's saintliness and praise of "the appropriateness of verse to subject matter and the consequent varying rhythms."

595. ———. "It Is Not Forbidden to Think." *Nation* 142 (May 27) : 680–81. [Collected Poems 1909–1935]. Two main tendencies mark these poems: a desire for order and certitude, and contempt for sham.

596. Muir, Edwin. "Mr. Eliot's Poetry." *Spectator* 156, no. 5623 (April 3) : 622 [Collected Poems 1909–1935]. Finds a dichotomy of attitude between the poems after "The Hollow Men" and the poetry preceding them. Considers also his influence.

597. Munson, Gorham B. "Book Reviews." *NorAR* 242 (Winter) : 394–400. [Essays Ancient and Modern]. Little criticism; chiefly a competent summary of Eliot's position as expressed in the essays.

598. Otake, Masaru. "T. S. Eliot: the Lyric Prophet of Chaos." *SELit* 16 (Tokyo) (October) : 542–54. A thoughtful essay on the possible genesis of *The Waste Land*.

599. Putt, S. Gorley. "This Modern Poetry." *Voices,* no. 85 (Spring) , pp. 58–61. [Murder in the Cathedral].

600. Quennell, Peter. "Mr. T. S. Eliot." *NSN* 11 (April 18) : 603–4. [Collected Poems 1909–1935; Essays Ancient and Modern]. A swift review of Eliot's entire poetic development and a briefer note on his prose. Fairly good.

601. Quinn, Kerker. "Out of the Slough of Despond." *VQR* 12 (October) : 621–22. [Collected Poems 1909–1935]. Thinks highly of Eliot's earlier poems, but deplores the loss in later ones of "inevitableness of phrase and rhythm."

602. Rahv, Philip. "A Season in Heaven." *PR* 3, no. 5 (June) : 11–14. [Murder in the Cathedral]. Praise of the poetry, while lamenting the "distortion" of the perdition it records, by a left-wing liberal. Defends the play against a charge of fascism brought by Marxist critics.

603. Ransom, John Crowe. "Autumn of Poetry." *SoR* 1 (Winter) : 619–23. [Murder in the Cathedral]. Compares

this play with *Samson Agonistes* and finds Eliot lacking in unity of tone. "This is a striking assemblage of poetic ingredients, at the best, and short of the highest poetry." But it is superior to the work of any other modern author. Reprinted 1938 in *The World's Body,* pp. 166–72.

604. Rees, Garnet. "A French Influence on T. S. Eliot: Remy de Gourmont." *RLC* 16 (October-December) : 764–67. Eliot found in de Gourmont the right mean for a criticism between impressionism and pseudo-scientific dogmatism, but Eliot has gone far beyond de Gourmont.

605. Roberts, Michael. "The Poetry of T. S. Eliot." *LonMerc* 34 (May) : 38–44. An essay briefly considering various aspects of Eliot's poetic theory and practice.

606. Ross, Hugh. "Mediaeval Drama Redivivus." *ASch* 5 (Winter) : 49–63. [Murder in the Cathedral]. Eliot is the father-philosopher of the movement that finds in medieval themes material for modern drama. Appreciative.

607. Sayers, Michael. "A Year in the Theatre." *Criterion* 15 (July) : 653–55, 657. [Murder in the Cathedral]. Though the play is incisive, mordant, and original, it is a bore, untheatrical.

608. Smith, H. Jeffrey. "Along the Bookshelf." *Person* 17 (Summer) : 330–32. [Collected Poems 1909–1935]. Tries to cover Eliot's entire poetic career.

609. Tate, Allen. "The Function of the Critical Quarterly." *SoR* 1 (Winter) : 558–59. [Criterion]. Two pages in a longer article, calling *The Criterion* "the best critical quarterly of our time."

610. Taylor, Walter F. "Divergent Trends. I. The Survival of Classicism." *A History of American Letters,* pp. 433–36; bibliography, pp. 593–95. Boston: American Book Company, 1936. In poetry, Eliot insists on the barrenness of modern life when unillumined by the traditions of the past. In criticism, he is a true classicist.

611. Turnell, G. Martin. "The Poetry of Jules Laforgue." *Scrutiny* 5 (September) : 128–49. Suggests that in *The Waste Land* Eliot had learned a good deal about versification from Laforgue, but the point is not developed.

612. Untermeyer, Louis. "New Books in Review: New Poetry." *YR* 26 (September) : 165–66. [Collected Poems 1909–1935]. "Eliot is . . . a minor poet in the grand manner."

613. Van Doren, Mark. "Mr. Eliot Glances Up." *Nation* 143

(September 19) : 340–42. [Essays Ancient and Modern]. The play seems simple, but the question of Becket's holiness is unanswered. Reprinted in *The Private Reader,* New York: Henry Holt, 1942, pp. 212–16, also in Unger, no. 1191.

614. Vernon, Grenville. "The Play and Screen: Murder in the Cathedral." *Cweal* 23 (April 3) : 636. Eliot "has written his play in verse of a flexibility and power which is on a plane with his subject."

615. Voight, Gilbert P. "Has the Pendulum Started Back?" *LuCQ* 9 (April) : 149–55. Rejoices that Eliot "no longer mocks at religion."

616. Wolff, Charlotte. "T. S. Eliot." *Studies in Hand-Reading,* pp. 93–94. London: Chatto and Windus, 1936. What Eliot's hand reveals about his character, with a photograph.

617. Wyatt, Euphemia V. Review of *Murder in the Cathedral. CathW,* 142 (March) : 760–61. A partial summary of the play.

618. Yeats, W. B. "Introduction." *The Oxford Book of Modern Verse, 1892–1935,* pp. xxi–xxiii. New York: Oxford University Press, 1936. Eliot's art seems gray, cold, and dry. It has the rhythmical flatness of *The Essay on Man.* Reprinted in Unger, no. 1191.

619. Young, Stark. "Government and Guild." *NR* 86 (April 8) : 253. [Murder in the Cathedral]. Chiefly on the presentation of the play, which he praises. As theater, the play is an astonishing combination of the simple and the difficult.

620. Zabel, Morton D. "Poets of Five Decades." *SoR* 2 (Summer) : 168–71. [Collected Poems 1909–1935]. On the change in style in these poems. Very general.

1937

621. Anon. *TAr* 21: (Feb.) : 161. [Murder in the Cathedral]. Picture of a scene from the play, and a paragraph on its success.

622. Blackmur, R. P. "The Whole Poet." *Poetry* 50 (April) : 48–51. [Collected Poems 1909–1935]. *"Burnt Norton* makes the earlier poems grow and diminish, as it illuminates them or shows them up. Yet it is not easy to say what the poem is about."

623. Botkin, B. A. "Regionalism and Culture." *The Writer in*

a *Changing World,* edited by Henry Hart, pp. 151, 153. Equinox Cooperative Press, 1937. Eliot is a "wistful, though not uncritical fellow-traveller of the Agrarians." A brief reference.

*624. Brooks, Cleanth. "The Waste Land: an Analysis." *SoR* 3 (Summer) : 106–36. An excellent complete analysis of the poem, using quotations from Eliot's other works, examination of sources, and Brooks's favorite critical device, attention to irony and paradox. Reprinted in *Modern Poetry and the Tradition,* Chapel Hill: University of North Carolina Press, 1939; pp. 136–72, also in Unger, no. 1191.

*625. ———, and Warren, Robert Penn. "The Reading of Modern Poetry." *AmR* 8 (February) : 442–49. [Rhapsody on a Windy Night; Ash Wednesday]. A defense against the charge of unintelligibility leveled at these poems by Sparrow and Eastman.

626. Burke, Kenneth. "Acceptance and Rejection." *SoR* 2 (Winter) : 627–29. Two pages on *Murder in the Cathedral* to illustrate Burke's thesis that a poet works by "overt or covert acts of 'transcendence.'"

*627. Bush, Douglas. "American Poets." *Mythology and the Romantic Tradition in English Poetry,* pp. 506–18. Cambridge: Harvard University Press, 1937. [Prufrock; Sweeney Erect; Sweeney among the Nightingales; Waste Land]. A consideration of Eliot's use of classical mythology which broadens out into a wider appreciation of his poetry.

628. Butler, John F. "Tragedy, Salvation, and the Ordinary Man." *LQHR* 162 (October) : 489–97. [Murder in the Cathedral]. Chiefly concerned with the relation of the tragic hero to the concept of salvation, but touches briefly on the relation of the ordinary man as exemplified by the chorus to the tragic saint as exemplified by Thomas.

629. Dukes, Ashley. "The English Scene." *TAr* 21 (February) : 103–4. [Murder in the Cathedral]. Generalized criticism of this play and of Archibald MacLeish's *Panic* as representatives of a new dramatic movement led by the poets, a movement distasteful to the established critics.

630. Fletcher, John Gould. *Life Is My Song.* New York: Farrar and Rinehart, 1937. Recalls Eliot's personal charm, his brilliance, and his tolerance as editor of the *Criterion,* but deplores his Anglicanism.

631. Fox, Arthur W. "Collected Poems of T. S. Eliot." *PMLC*
     63: 23–40. Gives most space to the Choruses in *The
     Rock,* because "I understand them more clearly and
     because . . . they contain a distinct and noble message
     to his time."

632. Gielgud, Val. "Radio Play: In the Age of Television."
     TAr 21 (February) : 108–11. [Murder in the Cathedral].
     References to the success of the broadcast.

633. Gilkes, Martin. "The Years of Disillusion. T. S. Eliot."
     A Key to Modern English Poetry, pp. 71–90 and *passim.*
     London: Blackie and Son, 1937. [Waste Land; Geron-
     tion]. *The Waste Land* is the document *par excellence*
     of the generation which suffered postwar disillusion-
     ment, not entirely successful but very important "as a
     landmark in poetry's progress." Explanation of the
     method behind two lines of "Gerontion," that of giving
     "under-surface meanings."

634. Grierson, Herbert J. C. *Milton and Wordsworth, Poets
     and Prophets,* pp. 125–27. London: Chatto and Windus,
     1937. Eliot is unjust in his criticism of Milton because
     he dislikes the spirit and tone of *Paradise Lost;* he ig-
     nores the total purpose of Milton's poems; and he lays
     too much stress on the predominance of auditory im-
     pressions in Milton.

635. Hawkins, Desmond. "Views and Reviews; Anne to Vic-
     toria." *NewEW* 9 (April 22) : 31–32. A brief comment
     on Eliot's "Byron" in Bonamy Dobrée's anthology, *Anne
     to Victoria.*

636. Higgins, J. Review of Djuna Barnes's *Nightwood,* with
     an introduction by Eliot. *HA* 123 (April) : 28–29. The
     review contains one paragraph summarizing Eliot's in-
     troduction.

637. Horton, Philip. *Hart Crane.* New York: W. W. Norton,
     1937. Horton quotes brief comments on *The Waste
     Land* and "The Hollow Men" and makes an analysis of
     the metaphors in "The Love Song of J. Alfred Pruf-
     rock" and "Rhapsody on a Windy Night."

638. Kelly, Blanche May. Review of *Collected Poems 1909–
     1935. CathW* 145 (May) : 245–46. Dislikes the later Eliot
     because he has settled down "into the quagmire of com-
     promise."

639. Kenmare, Dallas. "Story of a Pilgrimage." *Poetry R* 18
     (January-February) : 23–27. [Collected Poems 1909–
     1935]. "The progress from *The Waste Land* to the

final poems is not wholly surprising; in a poem so stark
with horror a realization of the Kingdom of God is in-
herent. . . . It seems that the pilgrimage is ended, and
there is peace."

640. Lewis, Wyndham. "First Meeting with Eliot." *Blasting and
Bombardiering,* pp. 283–85. London: Eyre and Spottis-
woode, 1937. Reminiscences of Eliot and Joyce, and the
difficulties of Lewis and Eliot in trying to pay for entertainment before Joyce could do so.

641. Loggins, Vernon. "Intellectuals and Experiment." *I Hear
America . . . ,* pp. 315–23. New York: Crowell, 1937.
Biography, and a survey of Eliot's prose and poetry.

642. Morrow, Betty. "The Waste Land (with Humblest Apolo-
gies to T. S. Eliot)." *NY* 13 (October 16) : 27. Parody.

643. Olson, Elder. "A Defense of Poetry." *Poetry* 50 (April) :
54–56. [Matthiessen's The Achievement of T. S. Eliot].
Mattheissen's criticism, like Eliot's, is insufficiently occupied with the poetry itself. Mattheissen's concern is
chiefly with the poet, Eliot's with ethics.

644. Partridge, A. C. "T. S. Eliot." *PUP,* series 3, no. 4, pp. 3–
22. Written for the person who knows nothing of Eliot;
covers his entire career to 1937.

645. Porteus, Hugh Gordon. "Observatory." *NewEW* 11 (April
22) : 32–33. Brief comment on Eliot's attitude toward
Fascism as shown in *The Criterion.*

*646. Praz, Mario. "T. S. Eliot and Dante." *SoR* 2, no. 3 (Winter) : 525–48. Dante's influence—coming to Eliot
through Pound, Santayana, and Grandgent—exhibiting
itself in the love of the clear visual image and clear
luminous language is most apparent in "Ash Wednesday," but appears also in "Gerontion," "La Figlia," and
in his prose doctrine. An excellent essay. Reprinted in
Unger, no. 1191, and in Praz's *The Flaming Heart,*
New York, 1958.

647. Rice, Philip Blair. "The Critic as Prophet." *Poetry* 50
(April) : 51–54. [Essays Ancient and Modern]. Prefers
Eliot's essays on Pascal and Tennyson to those dealing
with religion.

648. Stone, Geoffrey. "Morals and Poetry." *AmR* 9 (April) :
58–63. On Eliot's and I. A. Richards's critical principles.

649. Trueblood, D. Elton. "Are Literary Standards Merely
Literary?" *Christendom* 2 (Winter) : 129–31. [Essays

Ancient and Modern]. Is concerned with the importance of Eliot's criticism for Christian readers.

650. West, Alick. "The Waste Land" and "Mr. Eliot as Critic."
Crisis and Criticism, pp. 26–34, 35–49, *passim.* London:
Lawrence and Wishart, 1937. Through the figure of
Tiresias, Eliot expresses the "bourgeois desire to escape
from individualism and to remain within the social
order that created it." He was a potential Marxist, but
chose to defend capitalism.

651. Wilson, Edmund. "Mr. More and the Mithraic Bull." *NR*
91 (May 26) : 64–68. A report of a conversation with
Paul Elmer More about Eliot in 1929. Reprinted in
The Triple Thinkers, New York: Harcourt, Brace,
1938, pp. 5–6.

652. Winters, Yvor. *Primitivism and Decadence, a Study of
American Experimental Poetry.* New York: Arrow editions, 1937. Judged by Winters's criterion for poetry,
that it must be capable of a complete prose paraphrase,
Eliot's poetry as well as most of that of the twentieth
century is poor.

653. Wolfe, Thomas. "Mr. Malone." *NY* (May 29) , pp. 23–24.
A satire on an imaginary author's bitter, envious attack
on all American authors including Eliot, who is accused
of being incomprehensible and a Royalist.

1938

654. Aiken, Conrad. "Homage to T. S. Eliot." *HA* 125, no. 3
(December) : 17. Tells of his efforts to get "Prufrock"
published. Praises Eliot's "wholeness."

655. Anon. "Verse." *NY* 14 (March 12) : 63–64. [Translation
of St.-J. Perse's *Anabasis*]. Eliot's translation sometimes
flattens the sonority and ecstasy of the original.

656. ———. "New and Old Plays in Manhattan: Murder in the
Cathedral." *Time* 31 (February 28) : 34. A routine review, praising the second half of the play, and giving
a brief summary of Eliot's life. (See the letter in *Time,*
March 21, 1938, pp. 2, 4, 6, from H. W. Eliot, Jr., pointing out errors in the biography.)

657. ———. "Mortal Blow." *Time* 31 (May 9) : 35. Brief
article on the rejection by the Royal Academy of Wyndham Lewis's portrait of Eliot.

658. Atkinson, Brooks. "Note on Poetic Drama." *NYT* (May

1), sec. 10, p. 1. [Murder in the Cathedral]. Eliot is a great poet but a poor dramatist because 1) the play is physically monotonous, 2) the speech is studied rather than spontaneous, and 3) it lacks power to differentiate characters.

659. Baker, Howard. "Homage to T. S. Eliot." *HA* 125, no. 3 (December) : 46–47. Twenty-five years ago, Eliot showed new poets how to write serious poetry.

660. Blackmur, R. P. "Homage to T. S. Eliot." *HA* 125, no. 3 (December) : 20. "What is most remarkable about Eliot's mind is its seminal quality."

661. Bogan, Louise. "Poetry." *America Now*, edited by H. E. Stearns, pp. 51–54. New York: Scribners, 1938.

*662. Brooks, Cleanth, and Warren, Robert Penn. Analysis of "The Love Song of J. Alfred Prufrock." In *Understanding Poetry*, pp. 589–96. New York: Henry Holt, 1938. A well-known detailed examination of the poem; useful. Reprinted in 1950 ed., pp. 433–44.

663. Brown, Calvin S., Jr. "T. S. Eliot and 'Die Droste.' " *SR* 46 (October–December) : 492–500. [Rhapsody on a Windy Night]. Holds that Eliot is indebted to Annette von Droste Hülshoff's "Durchwachte Nacht." Grover Smith (no. 1412) states that in a letter to him, Eliot says he has never read this German poem.

664. Brown, E. K. "Mr. Eliot and Some Enemies." *UTQ* 8 (October) : 69–84. Repeats what Eliot's attackers say, defends him, and outlines his ideas.

*665. Chakravarty, Amiya. *The Dynasts and the Post-War Age Poetry: a Study in Modern Ideas*, pp. 92–106. London: Oxford University Press, 1938. [Murder in the Cathedral]. A suggestive comparison of the religious and philosophical ideas in this play and Hardy's *The Dynasts*.

666. Church, Ralph W. "Eliot on Bradley's Metaphysic." *HA* 125, no. 3 (December) : 24–26. A summary of Eliot's Ph.D. dissertation, entitled *Experience and the Objects of Knowledge in the Philosophy of F. H. Bradley*.

667. Clark, John Abbot. "Our Literary Intellectuals." *Cweal* 27 (January 21) : 345. An emotional attack on Eliot for his "The Humanism of Irving Babbitt." (See Phillips's reply, no. 693.)

668. Dasgupta, Rabindrakumar. "T. S. Eliot's 'Murder in the

Cathedral.'" *CalR* 69 (December) : 296–306. A labored essay on Eliot's indebtedness to Greek tragedy.

*669. Dukes, Ashley. "A Poet Turns Dramatist." *NYT* (February 20) , sec. 11, pp. 1, 3. [Murder in the Cathedral]. The best account of the acting history of the play from its first performance at Canterbury to the second New York production.

670. ———. "Re-enter the Chorus." *TAr* 22 (May) : 340. [Sweeney Agonistes; The Rock]. On the use of the chorus in these two plays.

671. Eberhart, Richard. "Homage to T. S. Eliot." *HA* 125, no. 3 (December) : 18–19. A poem by Longfellow resembles Eliot's "Animula."

672. Funaroff, S. "What the Thunder Said: a Fire Sermon." *The Spider and the Clock,* pp. 25–32. New York: International Publishers, 1938. The author says that the Marxist poem by this title challenges the attitudes of negation expressed in *The Waste Land.*

673. Goldie, Grace Wyndham. "J'Accuse." *Listener* 19 (January 19) : 134. [Waste Land]. A favorable review of the radio dramatization of the poem.

674. Harvey-Jellie, W. "T. S. Eliot among the Prophets?" *DR* 18 (April) : 83–90. Enthusiastic, but naïve.

675. Kenmare, Dallas. "The Christian Renaissance in Contemporary Literature." *PoetryR* 29 (September–October) : 353–57. Treats Eliot along with Aldous Huxley, Dorothy Sayers, and Christopher Hassall as evidence of a development of interest in religion.

676. Lawrence, T. E. *The Letters of T. E. Lawrence,* edited by David Garnett, pp. 488, 542, 748, 752, 756. New York: Doubleday Doran, 1938. Lawrence thinks Eliot is a great poet, but a poor critic because "he has a confused and knotty mind."

677. Leighton, Lawrence. "A Note on the Poems." *HA* 125, no. 3 (December) : 10, 48. [Early *Advocate* poems]. Attempts to find adumbrations of Eliot's later poems in the earlier ones.

678. Lind, L. Robert. "Sonnet." *SR* 46 (January–March) : 24. Parody.

679. Lowell, R. T. S. "Homage to T. S. Eliot." *HA* 125, no. 3 (December) : 20, 41. A short note, praising Eliot for opposing democracy.

680. MacLeish, Archibald. "Homage to T. S. Eliot." *HA* 125, no. 3 (December) : 18. One paragraph. "No one has taught us more."

681. ———. "Public Speech and Private Speech in Poetry." *YR* 27 (March) : 536–47. Pound, Eliot, and Yeats have recovered the use of the living language for poetry and enable poetry again to occupy the living world of political, social, and economic change.

682. MacNeice, Louis. *Modern Poetry, a Personal Essay*. London: Oxford University Press, 1938. Eliot is "first and foremost an American tourist."

683. Madge, Charles. "In Memoriam, T. S. E." *NewV* 31–32 (Autumn) : 18–21. Mr. Madge is witty on the subject of Eliot's being a King of the Dead.

*684. Matthiessen, F. O. "For an Unwritten Chapter." *HA* 125, no. 3 (December) : 22–24. Concerning *Murder in the Cathedral* and Eliot's earlier interest in the drama.

685. McAlmon, Robert. *Being Geniuses Together, an Autobiography*, pp. 8–12, 130–31. London: Secker and Warburg, 1938. A gossipy account of an evening with Eliot.

686. Monroe, Harriet. *A Poet's Life*, p. 394. New York: The Macmillan Company, 1938. Quotation *re* Eliot in a letter from Pound.

687. Moore, Merrill. "Homage to T. S. Eliot." *HA* 125, no. 3 (December) : 42, 45. A brief essay on the part played by the unconscious in the composition of *The Waste Land*.

*688. Morgan, Roberta, and Wohlstetter, Albert. "Observations on 'Prufrock.'" *HA* 125, no. 3 (December) : 27–30, 33–40. Good, detailed analysis.

*689. Morrison, Theodore. "Ash Wednesday: A Religious History." *NEQ* 11 (June) : 266–86. A sensitive and honest interpretation of the poem, clearly expressed.

690. O'Donnell, George M. "Homage to T. S. Eliot." *HA* 125, no. 3 (December) : 17–18. Testifies to the continuing influence of Eliot on young poets.

691. Ould, Herman. *The Art of the Play*, pp. 124–28, 138. London: Pitman's Theatre and Stage Series: Pitman, 1938. [Murder in the Cathedral]. Praises the handling of the chorus, but finds the epilogue undramatic.

692. Palmer, Herbert Edward. "Eliot's Waste Land." *Post-Victorian Poetry*, pp. 312–22, and *passim*. London: Dent, 1938. Eliot at his best is a "poet in a cellar."

693. Phillips, Charles W. "Communication: Our Literary In-
     tellectuals." *Cweal* 27 (February 18) : 470. In defense
     of Eliot against Clark (no. 667) Phillips points out
     exactly what Eliot says about Babbitt.

*694. Power, Sister Mary J. "T. S. Eliot Emerges from the Waste
     Land." *Poets at Prayer,* pp. 125–36. New York: Sheed
     and Ward, 1938. Reproduces an important letter from
     Eliot on his religious history. The essay, written from
     a Roman Catholic point of view, overemphasizes Eliot's
     religiosity.

695. Prokosch, Frederic. "Homage to T. S. Eliot." *HA* 125,
     no. 3 (December) : 41. A brief note, saying that Eliot
     is a minor poet, but a fine one.

696. Sitwell, Edith. "Three Eras of Modern Poetry, Second
     Lecture." *Trio,* pp. 107–18, 141–58. London: Macmil-
     lan, 1938. Sensitive analysis of rhythm and sound of
     several passages of Eliot's poems.

*697. Spencer, Theodore. "On 'Murder in the Cathedral.'" *HA*
     125, no. 3 (December) : 21–22. A fresh analysis of the
     structure of the play, placed against its Christian back-
     ground.

698. Stevens, Wallace. "Homage to T. S. Eliot." *HA* 125, no.
     3 (December) : 41. Eliot's great reputation presents a
     difficulty in reading him.

699. Stonier, G. W. "The Mystery of Ezra Pound." *Purpose* 10
     (January–March) : 21–26. Eliot was Pound's pupil, but
     has outrun his master.

700. Tate, Allen. "The Reading of Modern Poetry." *Purpose*
     10 (January–March) : 31–41. [Rhapsody on a Windy
     Night; Ash Wednesday]. A defense of the intelligibility
     of passages from these poems against the attacks made
     on them in Sparrow's *Sense and Poetry* (no. 465) and
     Eastman's *The Literary Mind* (no. 254) . Clear explana-
     tion of the passages in dispute.

701. ———. "Homage to T. S. Eliot." *HA* 125, no. 3 (Decem-
     ber) : 41–42. More about Tate than about Eliot.

702. Tillyard, E. M. W. "Milton's Visual Imagination." *The
     Miltonic Setting, Past and Present,* pp. 90–104. New
     York: Macmillan, 1938. A temperate, thoughtful refu-
     tation of Eliot's early strictures on Milton's style.

703. Tinckom-Fernandez, W. G. "T. S. Eliot '10; an Advocate
     Friendship." *HA* 125, no. 3 (December) : 5–10, 47–48.
     Reminiscences of Eliot. Reprinted in *The Harvard*

Advocate Anthology, edited by Donald Hall, New York: Twayne Publishers, 1950, pp. 317–27.

704. Van der Vat, D. G. "The Poetry of T. S. Eliot." *ES* 20, no. 3: 107–18. Eliot has no more poetry in him.

705. Vernon, Grenville. "The Play and the Screen." *Cweal* 27 (March 4) : 524. [Murder in the Cathedral]. Favorable notice of the presentation of the play at the Ritz Theatre, comparing it with the Federal Theatre Project production of 1936.

706. Walton, Eda Lou. "T. S. Eliot's Translation of Perse." *NYTBR* (April 24) , p. 3. [Translation of St.-J. Perse's *Anabasis*]. Brief. Praises the translation.

707. Warren, Robert Penn. "Homage to T. S. Eliot." *HA* 125, no. 3 (December) : 46. Eliot's work does not indicate a withdrawal from society.

708. Williams, William Carlos. "Homage to T. S. Eliot." *HA* 125, no. 3 (December) : 42. Eliot has deteriorated since leaving America.

709. Young, Stark. "Mr. Miller's Importations." *NR* 94 (March 2) : 101–2. [Murder in the Cathedral]. A comparison of this production with that of 1936.

1939

710. Agate, James. "The Eumenides at Home, Audience at Sea." *Sun Times* (London) (March 26) , p. 4. [Family Reunion]. Verse review.

711. Anon. "The Listener's Book Chronicle: The Family Reunion. A Play by T. S. Eliot." *Listener* 21 (April 6) : 750. The play is narrative rather than dramatic. Eliot's moral sensitivity is as great as that of Henry James.

712. ———. Review of *The Idea of a Christian Society. Listener* 22 (November 30) : 1086. Two-paragraph summary, concluding, "whether or not we accept his assumption that new wine can be poured effectively into old bottles, he has stated succinctly the essential values which any re-integrated society must embody."

713. ———. "Our London Correspondence. The Criterion Passes." *Manchester Guardian* (January 3) , p. 10. "There is no other periodical with the same high . . . interest in scholarship and imaginative writing. . . ." The *Criterion* parties will also be missed.

714. ———. "The Last Criterion." *NewEW* 14 (January 5) :

184. Expresses regret for the disappearance of the quarterly and reviews its policy.

715. ——. "Between Ourselves. An Announcement and Some Observations." *NewEW* 14 (February 16) : 285–86. Announces that Eliot will become a regular contributor to *NewEW*.

716. ——. "A Poet's Play." *PP* 3 (April 8) : 34. [Family Reunion].

717. ——. "The Idea of a Christian Society." *Tablet* 174 (November 18) : 576–77. An independent essay on the difficulties encountered by a national church such as Eliot advocates, written from the Roman Catholic point of view.

718. ——. "Tom to T. S." *Time* 33, pt. 1 (January 2) : 35. A review of Eliot's career, occasioned by the publication of *The Harvard Advocate* devoted to him.

719. ——. "Last Words." *Time* 33, pt. 1 (January 30) : 65. [Criterion]. A useful short summary of the history of *The Criterion*.

720. ——. "Cat Book." *Time* 34, pt. 2 (November 20) : 87–88. [Old Possum's Book of Practical Cats]. Points out that it is like Edward Lear and Lewis Carroll in spirit.

721. ——. "Mr. Eliot in Search of the Present." *TLS,* no. 1938 (March 25) , p. 176. [Family Reunion]. The characters "are the statues of an intellectual commentary." The play is a failure.

722. ——. "Mr. T. S. Eliot's Cats." *TLS,* no. 1966 (October 7) , p. 578. [Old Possum's Book of Practical Cats]. An appropriately facetious little review.

723. ——. "A Christian Society. Mr. Eliot on Ideals and Methods. Democracy's Spiritual Problem." *TLS,* no. 1970 (November 4) , pp. 640, 642. [Idea of a Christian Society]. An extended, sympathetic summary of the book.

724. ——. "The Spirit and the Crisis." *TLS,* no. 1970 (November 4) , p. 641. [Idea of a Christian Society]. An editorial defending the democratic ideal against Eliot.

725. Anthony, George. "Myth and Psychosis." *SR* 47 (October–December) : 599–604. [Family Reunion]. It is suggested that Freudian analysis will help in the interpretation of the play, but the suggestion is not well developed.

726. T.F.B. "Men and Books. Mr. T. S. Eliot's New Play." *Tablet* 173 (April 1) : 424. [Family Reunion]. A sum-

mary of the play, largely through quotation. "Never before on a modern stage has poetry been so interfused into such a prosy existence, and religion so truly operative in a grossly material world."

*727. Bailey, Ruth. *A Dialogue on Modern Poetry,* pp. 9–31, 38–39, *passim.* London: Oxford University Press, 1939. [Gerontion]. An excellent and interesting analysis of "Gerontion," and a justification of modern poetry largely in terms of Eliot.

728. Bodkin, Maud. "The Eumenides and Present-Day Consciousness." *Adelphi* 15 (May): 411–13. [Family Reunion]. "At a time like the present, in a world where . . . the air around us is dark with the wings of curses coming home to roost, surely the myth of the Eumenides—dread pursuers that avenge not private but communal crime—far from being academic, has dreadful relevance."

729. Bogan, Louise. "Verse." *NY* 15 (April 15): 83. [Family Reunion]. "The new play presents an integrated Eliot, completely in control of himself and so filled with insight that the old Eliot comes in for some pretty close dissection."

730. Brégy, Katherine. "T. S. Eliot: a Study in Transition." *America* 61 (July 15): 331–32. Emphasizes the transition from "Prufrock" to *The Family Reunion,* and predicts that "the end of his journey is not yet reached."

731. Brooks, Cleanth. "Sin and Expiation." *PR* 6 (Summer): 114–16. [Family Reunion]. Eliot has faced the problem of saying something to people who are not able to accept the author's metaphysic and he has solved it.

732. Brown, Ivor. "The Family Reunion." *Observer* (March 26), p. 15. The actors assist in sending the play "on its strange, uneven passage to the mind and heart."

733. Cane, Melville. "Mr. Eliot's Cat Book." *SatR* 21 (November 11): 4. [Old Possum's Book of Practical Cats]. Humorous verse.

734. Connolly, Cyril. *Enemies of Promise,* pp. 50–52. Boston: Little, Brown and Co., 1939. Says that Eliot's influence is bad because his background is unlike that of other people, but he praises him for having created a world.

735. Conrad, Sherman. "T. S. Eliot's New Play." *SatR* 19 (April 1): 12. [Family Reunion]. With this play, Eliot

is an "accomplished poet dramatist." The form is "identical with the values it elucidates," which are the planes of spiritual blindness and insight.

736. L. G. D. "Theatre: The Family Reunion." *PL* 1, no. 2 (April): unpaged. Complimentary, based on a performance of the play.

737. Darlington, W. A. "Benign Note on T. S. Eliot and the Highbrows." *NYT* (April 9), sec. 10, p. 1. [Family Reunion]. "The few who will have the patience to overlook its obvious theatrical ineptitudes will find much to admire in its language."

738. Deutsch, Babette. "Ghosts of Mr. Eliot." *NYHTB* (June 4), p. 6. [Family Reunion]. Says that plays about original sin and damnation have no relevance for a modern audience.

739. ———. "T. S. Eliot and the Laodiceans." *ASch* 9 (Winter): 19–30. Eliot's work has always been concerned with evil, but "his interest fastens with peculiar horror" upon the men and women "who have a fatal incapacity for life."

740. Garrett, John. "Drama." *EngSW* 21 (June): 278–79. [Family Reunion]. Easy-going criticism; emphasizes Eliot's humor.

741. Gaye, Phoebe F. "Expiation Becomes Orestes." *TT* 20 (March 25): 388–89. [Family Reunion]. Intelligent summary and criticism. Says the Monchensey family never becomes quite alive.

742. Gregory, Horace. "The Unities and Eliot." *LL* 23 (October): 53–60. [Family Reunion]. One of Eliot's successful failures, chiefly because of the Eumenides.

*743. Harding, D. W. "Christian or Liberal?" *Scrutiny* 8 (December): 309–13. [Idea of a Christian Society]. He protests, from the liberal point of view, against the oppression and gloom of Eliot's Christian society. Reprinted in *The Importance of Scrutiny*, edited by Eric Bentley, New York: George W. Stewart, 1948, pp. 287–90.

744. Hawkins, Desmond. "Hamlet and T. S. Eliot." *NewEW* 15 (July 20): 221–22 [Family Reunion]. Comparing Harry to Hamlet, Hawkins sees both characters seeking to achieve the objective correlative and failing in their desire. A highly favorable review.

745. ———. "London Letter." *PR* 6 (Summer) : 89. Two paragraphs on the demise of *The Criterion*. The periodical commanded respect if not enthusiasm.

746. ———. "Views and Reviews; Hamlet and T. S. Eliot." *NewEW* 15 (July 20) : 221–22. [Family Reunion]. Chiefly on the character of Harry. A serious review, assuming a knowledge of the play. The hero is a "myth-figure, a protagonist of the age."

747. Henderson, Philip. "The Agony of Mr. Eliot." *The Poet and Society*, pp. 154–71. London: Secker and Warburg, 1939. Reads all of Eliot's poems as autobiography, and his "agony" is interpreted as his inability to love.

*748. Horton, Philip. "Speculations on Sin." *KR* 1 (Summer) : 330–33. [Family Reunion]. The weakness of the play is that it does not offer adequate motivation for the action. A thoughtful review.

749. Howarth, R. G. "T. S. Eliot's Literary Reminiscences." *N&Q* 176 (June 24) : 436–37. [Whispers of Immortality]. Identification of the source of two phrases from the poem.

750. Jack, Peter Monro. "T. S. Eliot's Modern Variation on the Eumenides Myth." *NYTBR* (April 9), pp. 2, 20. [Family Reunion]. Summary of the play, and unqualified praise.

751. Kelley, Bernard. Review of *The Family Reunion. Blackfriars* 20 (June) : 469–71. Deals with the symbolism of the play from the Roman Catholic point of view; says it lacks the "Christian sense of the profundity of evil."

752. Knowlton, Edgar C. "A Playwright Preoccupied with Sin." *SAQ* 38 (October) : 467–68. [Family Reunion]. Suggests that Eliot is interested not in crime, but in sin. Too short to develop the idea.

753. Lewis, Clive Staples. "Shelley, Dryden, and Mr. Eliot." *Rehabilitations and Other Essays*, pp. 3–34. London: Oxford University Press, 1939. "I will now maintain that Shelley is to be regarded, on grounds which Mr. Eliot himself will allow, as a . . . more *classical* poet than Dryden." Lewis overstates his case.

754. MacCarthy, Desmond. "Some Notes on Mr. Eliot's New Play." *NSN* 17 (March 25) : 455–56. [Family Reunion]. In spite of fine passages, the play fails because the device of the Eumenides is not convincing to a modern audience.

755. MacNeice, Louis. "Original Sin." *NR* 98 (May 3): 384–85. [Family Reunion]. Says apologetically that this is a good play.

*756. Muir, Edwin. *The Present Age from 1914. Introductions to English Literature,* edited by Bonamy Dobrée. vol. 5, pp. 73–87, *passim.* London: Cresset Press, 1939. A brilliant short introduction to Eliot's poetry through "Ash Wednesday."

757. D. O'K. "Politics." *Studies* 28 (December): 695–97. [Idea of a Christian Society]. A noncommital summary, chiefly by means of quotations.

*758. Pottle, Frederick A. "A Modern Verse Play." *YR* 28 (June): 836–39. [Family Reunion]. Praise of the verse form and a fine analysis of reasons for the failure of the play as drama.

759. Ransom, John Crowe. "T. S. Eliot as Dramatist." *Poetry* 54 (August): 264–71. [Family Reunion]. Ransom thinks poorly of most popular dramas, but says that Eliot's success here is "unquestionable."

760. Rascoe, Burton. "Shreds and Tatters." *Newsweek* 13 (April 3): 40. [Family Reunion]. Says "he is simply vulgar in the cheap, snob way. And besides he is dull."

*761. Reckitt, Maurice B. "Views and Reviews: A Sub-Christian Society." *NewEW* 16 (December 7): 115–16 [Idea of a Christian Society]. Mr. Reckitt thinks that the society advocated by Eliot would not be religious enough to be called a truly Christian society. See also December 14, "A Sub-Pagan Society," a reply by T. S. Eliot: and letters, December 21 (by Every); January 4 (by Peck); January 11 (by Demant); January 18 (by Reckitt); and February 1 (by Eliot). The entire correspondence is interesting.

762. Roberts, Michael. "Mr. Eliot's New Play." *LonMerc* 39, no. 234 (April): 641–42. [Family Reunion]. Praises the flexibility of the verse form and the reality of the characters, but is dubious about the plot.

*763. Schwartz, Delmore. "The Criterion, 1922–39." *KR* 1 (Autumn): 437–49. A broad and intelligent survey of the magazine which Eliot edited for seventeen years. (Appears also in *Purpose* 11 (October): 225–37.)

764. ———. "Orestes in England." *Nation* 148 (June 10): 676–77. [Family Reunion]. An attempt at impartial analysis.

765. Smith, Bernard. *Forces in American Criticism,* pp. 358–59, 382–88. New York: Harcourt, Brace, 1939. In the 1920s Eliot employed only aesthetic standards for criticism; by the 1930s he had been forced to recognize that non-aesthetic standards are the ultimate tests of value.

766. Smyth, Charles. "Church, Community, and State." *Spectator* 163, no. 5812 (November 17) : 687. [Idea of a Christian Society]. Summary and criticism. He repeats what Reckitt (no. 761) and one or two others have said.

767. Spender, Stephen. "Cats and Dog." *Listener* 22 (October 26) : supplement, viii. [Old Possum's Book of Practical Cats]. "This is a charming book, charmingly produced."

768. Sullivan, A. M. "A Note on Left Wing Poetry that Strives to Save the World." *America* 62 (December 9) : 243–44. Notes that the young radical poets are in rebellion against Eliot "on whose early cynicism they were weaned" for having "taken refuge in the shadow of Westminster—and the monarchical coat-of-arms."

769. Symons, Julian. "The Family Reunion." *TCV,* no. 18 (June–July) , pp. 44, 46, 48. The play is a failure because it was written only for Mr. Eliot and a few people like him. "I wait with interest and respect to see what he will do next."

770. P.T. [Pamela Travers]. "Drama, The Family Reunion." *NewEW* 14 (April 6) : 397–98. Extravagant praise. "He is a spirit moving on the face of the waters when most of the world is content to be uncreated."

771. Turnell, G. Martin. "Mr. Eliot's New Play." *Scrutiny* 8 (June) : 108–14. [Family Reunion]. The play marks a further stage in the decline of Eliot's power, which began with *The Rock* and continued through *Burnt Norton.*

*772. Unger, Leonard. "Notes on Ash Wednesday." *SoR* 4 (Spring) : 745–70. A careful, extended study of the literary sources of the poem, emphasizing St. John of the Cross's *Dark Night of the Soul.* Reprinted in Unger, no. 1191.

773. Van Doren, Mark. "Seventeenth-Century Poetry and Twentieth-Century Critics." *Studies in Metaphysical Poetry,* with Theodore Spencer, pp. 21–29. New York: Columbia University Press, 1939. [Metaphysical Poets]. Eliot's analysis of seventeenth-century sensibility, influencing such critics as George Williamson and Basil

Wiley, is still the best explanation of the fineness of seventeenth-century poetry.

774. Verschoyle, Derek. "Stage and Screen: The Theatre." *Spectator* 162, no. 5778 (March 24) : 484. [Family Reunion].

775. "Watchman." "Things in General: T. S. Eliot's 'The Family Reunion.' " *BrW* 105 (March 30) : 466. He has not seen the play, but the memory of reading it haunts him.

1940

776. Anon. Review of *The Idea of a Christian Society. CJR* 3 (March–April) : 217. Regards the volume as a vicious attack on democracy.

777. ———. "Shorter Notices." *Nation* 150 (March 16) : 370–71. [Idea of a Christian Society]. The reviewer is fearful of fascism like that of Franco's Spain in this book.

778. ———. *RBB* (March), pp. 3–4. [Idea of a Christian Society]. Summary.

779. ———. "Recent and Readable." *Time* 25, pt. 1 (January 15) : 67. [Idea of a Christian Society]. A highly condensed but clear summary.

*780. Barber, C. L. "T. S. Eliot after Strange Gods." *SoR* 6 (Autumn) : 387–416. [Family Reunion]. This play is a failure because what Eliot wants to express is "inacceptable. . . . As the play stands . . . the unintelligibility of the curse and the Furies who convey it forces us to look for unconscious symbolic meanings, and these reveal the Eumenides to be elements in a fantasy that supports contradictory social impulses." Eliot does not know that the Eumenides are false gods. Reprinted in Unger, no 1191.

781. Bell, Bernard Iddings. "T. S. Eliot Examines the Spiritual State of Society Today." *NYTBR* (January 7), pp. 3, 19. [Idea of a Christian Society]. The reviewer says that "somehow this calm, dispassionate poet-philosopher has a way of making even a rebellious Liberal-Democrat begin to reexamine his customary assumptions."

782. Binsse, Harry L. "About a Possible Future." *Cweal* 31 (January 19) : 288. [Idea of a Christian Society]. Praises the style, isolates Eliot's definitions of democ-

racy and liberalism for study; calls his analyses "brilliant."

783. Bishop, Virginia Curry. "Letters to the Editor. Humble Rebuttal." *SatR* 21 (March 2) : 9. [Idea of a Christian Society]. A defence of Eliot against Joseph Ratner's criticism. (See nos. 816, 817.)

784. Bixler, J. S. "The Doubtful Value of Imposed Unity." *Christendom* 5 (Spring) : 278–79. [Idea of a Christian Society]. Condemns the book, apparently from the Protestant point of view.

785. Blackmur, R. P. "It Is Later than He Thinks." *The Expense of Greatness,* pp. 239–44. New York: Arrow editions, 1940. [Idea of a Christian Society]. Says he cannot accept Eliot's idea of a Christian society because he cannot accept Christianity. (Appears also in *KR* 2, Spring: 235–38.)

786. Brightman, Edgar Sheffield. "Christianity Today." *JBR* 8 (May) : 91. [Idea of a Christian Society]. Written from the Roman Catholic point of view, condemns Eliot's proposals, but admires his courage in raising and facing the fundamental question—"What is a Christian society?"

787. H. B. [Harry Brown]. "The Foggy Foggy Dew." *Vice Versa* 1 (November–December) : 26–27. A rather clever but bad-mannered defense of Eliot against Carl Sandburg's strictures on a speech, as reported in the *NYHT*.

788. Burgum, E. B. "The Road to Rome." *NewM* 34 (February 6) : 27 [Idea of a Christian Society]. Condemnation from the political left.

789. Clayton, Robert L. "T. S. Eliot's vision of a Christian Society." *LC* 102 (March 13) : 10. [Idea of a Christian Society]. He notes that most of the reviews of the book have been unfavorable. But "we may be witnessing a revival of political thought which takes into account the deeper facts of life as well as the more superficial and pressing needs."

790. Colum, Mary M. "Religion and the Modern World." *Forum* 103 (April) : 199. [Idea of a Christian Society]. Points out that the book is a contribution to a serious intellectual debate that is being carried on by Dawson, Maritain, Berdyaev, and others.

791. Cowley, Malcolm. "Tract for the Times." *NR* 102 (June 17) : 829–30. [Idea of a Christian Society]. "Once you

have granted Mr. Eliot his doubtful premises, the rest of his argument moves toward wholly logical conclusions." Thinks he is confusing religion in general with Christianity.

792. Daiches, David. "T. E. Hulme and T. S. Eliot." and "T. S. Eliot." *Poetry and the Modern World*, pp. 90–105, 106–27. Chicago: University of Chicago, 1940. The first chapter is an excellent essay on Eliot's relations with the Imagist poets. The latter is too general to be of much value.

793. Dobson, Charles A. "Three of T. S. Eliot's Poems." *New-Rev* (Calcutta) 12 (November) : 361–72. [Aunt Helen; La Figlia Che Piange; Hollow Men]. Paraphrases of the poems to show that Eliot has more of reason "than any of his followers."

*794. Drew, Elizabeth, and Sweeney, John L. *Directions in Modern Poetry*, pp. 37–55, 133–47. New York: Norton, 1940. [Waste Land; Hollow Men; Burnt Norton; Murder in the Cathedral; Family Reunion]. Good comparison and contrast with Pound and a sketch of Eliot's development.

*795. Dur, Philip. "A Church for All and a Job for Each." *HP* 4 (February) : 19. [Idea of a Christian Society]. A judicious review, pointing out likenesses of Eliot's structure to that of the Middle Ages.

796. Evans, B. Ifor. "Towards the Twentieth Century: Gerard Manley Hopkins and T. S. Eliot." *Tradition and Romanticism*, pp. 192–200. London: Methuen, 1940. Calls Eliot a romanticist.

797. Every, Brother George. "Christian Polity." *Purpose* 12 (January–March) : 31–37. [Idea of a Christian Society]. A comparison of Eliot's book with J. Middleton Murry's *The Defence of Democracy*.

*798. Fergusson, Francis. "Notes on the Theatre." *SoR* 5, no. 3: 562–64. [Family Reunion]. An examination of the dramatic structure of the play and the reasons for its failure.

799. Fleming, Edward Vandemere. "Feet of Clay." *Poetry R* 31 (April) : 166–69. A letter reproving Eliot for having praised Ezra Pound's "Homage to Sextus Propertius" because Eliot does not see that the poetry is doggerel, and he is not aware of the badness of Pound's Latin.

800. Gallup, Donald C. "Our Society Is a Negative One, T. S. Eliot Declares in Essay." *Dallas Morning News* (Janu-

ary 14), sec. 5, p. 4. [Idea of a Christian Society]. A summary of the book. Gallup notes the similarity of Eliot's thesis to that of Matthew Arnold.

801. C. P. H. "The Idea of a Christian Society." *SocP* (Crawfordsville, Ind.) 30 (February) : 26. [Idea of a Christian Society]. A clear summary and praise of the brilliant insight and the unity of the volume.

802. Holmes, John Haynes. "The World and the Faith." *NYHTB* (February 18), p. 16 [Idea of a Christian Society]. "This book is all too esoteric for any comfort."

803. Jones, Howard Mumford. "Shadow Boxing." *Boston Evening Transcript* (January 20), sec. 6, p. 1. [Idea of a Christian Society]. Accuses Eliot of muddled thinking because he has not defined "Christian."

804. Lehmann, John. "The Background of the Twenties," *New Writing in Europe,* pp. 16–18. London: Penguin Books, 1940. [Waste Land]. Speaks briefly and approvingly of the "disillusioned cynicism" of *The Waste Land.*

805. Leo, Brother. "God in Government." *Missionary* (Washington, D.C.) 54 (May) : 130. [Idea of a Christian Society]. Summary.

806. ———. "Books and Bookman." *Columbia* 19 (June) : 14. [Idea of a Christian Society].

807. Mellers, W. H. "Cats in Air-Pumps (or Poets in 1940) ." *Scrutiny* 9 (December) : 298–300. [East Coker]. Mellers's review suffers from the fact that it was written before the last two *Quartets* had appeared. He says that the poem is gloomy. Reprinted in *The Importance of Scrutiny,* edited by Eric Bentley, New York: George W. Stewart, 1948, pp. 267–69.

808. Millar, Moorhouse F. X. "Society, Law." *Thought* 15 (December) : 720–22. [Idea of a Christian Society]. Brief summary.

809. Moore, Harry Thornton. "Poetry on Records." *Poetry* 57 (October) : 55. [Gerontion; Hollow Men]. Eliot's "nerve-weary, neutral voice, . . . is exactly the right one for projecting the substance of these poems."

810. Niebuhr, Reinhold. "Can Church Restrain State?" *ComS* 9 (February) : 26–27. [Idea of a Christian Society]. Agrees with Eliot's criticism of present-day culture, but as a Protestant is afraid the Catholic principle which Eliot advocates would lead to "religious pretension."

*811. Oldham, J. H. Review of *The Idea of a Christian Society*. *ChrNL*, no. 18, supplement (February 28). Eliot replied to this review in an article entitled "Education in a Christian Society," *ChrNL*, no. 20, supplement, (March 13).

812. ——. "Professor Clarke and Mr. Eliot." *ChrNL*, no. 22 (March 27).

813. ——. "Can Education Survive Organization?" *ChrNL*, no. 23, supplement (April 3). An article continuing the previous discussion.

814. O'Malley, Francis J. "A Christian Society." *RevP* 2 (October): 488–90. [Idea of a Christian Society]. Sympathetic but critical summary from the Roman Catholic point of view.

815. Pound, Ezra. "T. S. Eliot." *We Moderns* (Gotham Book Mart, catalogue no. 42, 1940), pp. 24–25. An ungrammatical and racy survey of Eliot's career, saying "he is a damn'd good poet."

816. Ratner, Joseph. "T. S. Eliot and Totalitarianism." *SatR* 21 (January 6): 7. [Idea of a Christian Society]. An irresponsible and vicious attack. (See Virginia C. Bishop's letter to the editor, no. 783.)

817. ——. "Letters to the Editor. Mr. Ratner Replies." *SatR* 21 (March 2): 9, 18. [Idea of a Christian Society]. A continuation of his previous assertions that Eliot's book is fascistic.

818. Shain, Charles Edward. "The Idea of a Christian Society." *MilB* 3 (May): 8–9. A simplified summary and criticism.

819. Shapiro, Leo. "The Medievalism of T. S. Eliot." *Poetry* 56 (July): 202–21. Notes on Eliot's medieval sources.

820. Smith, Logan Pearsall. *Milton and His Modern Critics*. London: Oxford University Press, 1940. Smith seems to dislike Eliot's criticism of Milton mainly because Eliot is an American.

821. Southworth, James G. "The Poetry of T. S. Eliot." *Sowing the Spring*, edited by Basil Blackwell, pp. 76–91. London: Oxford University Press, 1940. Accuses Eliot of snobbishness, oversimplification, lack of humanity and of imagination.

*822. Spencer, Theodore. "Mr. Eliot's Orestes." *Boston Evening Transcript* (November 9), sec. 3, p. 6. [Family Reunion]. States Eliot's problems in writing this play and evaluates his success in solving them. The Eumenides do not function adequately; the last act is static. But the verse is excellent, and this is a better play than *Murder in the Cathedral*. Excellent criticism.

823. Spender, Stephen. "How Shall We Be Saved?" *Horizon* 1 (January) : 51–56. [Idea of a Christian Society]. Eliot is confused about tradition. "His own best poetry, and his admiration for James Joyce, tell him that tradition is something outrageous and even revolutionary"; but at the same time, he is looking for it "in the chapel among the ruins" rather than in the Waste Land itself.

824. Stonier, G. W. "The Gaiety of Mr. Eliot." *NSN* 19 (May 11) : 627–28. [Old Possum's Book of Practical Cats]. Chiefly quotation; pleasant indication of the contents of the book.

825. ———. "Mr. Eliot's New Poem." *NSN* 20 (September 14) : 267–68. [East Coker]. An expert indication of the themes of the poem, a note on its blemishes, and a conclusion that it is his "best and most mature poem."

*826. Trilling, Lionel. "Elements That Are Wanted." *PR* 7 September-October) : 367–79. [Idea of a Christian Society]. An honest and searching essay on materialism and supernaturalism by a liberal in politics. He concludes that Eliot's book "suggests elements which a rational and naturalistic philosophy, to be adequate, must encompass."

827. Vann, Gerald. "Mr. Eliot's Idea of a Christian Society." *Blackfriars* 21 (February) : 119–22. A criticism of Eliot from the Roman Catholic point of view, suggesting three points on which he wishes Eliot had elaborated.

828. Weinstein, Jacob J. "Religion and the Wasteland." *JF* 7, no. 3 (March) : 25–26. [Idea of a Christian Society]. "It will supply the more subtle of the Fascists with fine-spun rationalizations to justify their un-Christian intentions."

829. Wells, Henry W. *New Poets from Old: a Study in Literary Genetics.* New York: Columbia University Press, 1940. On Eliot's indebtedness for his colloquial tone to the Renaissance poets. The scope of Wells's subject causes his treatment to be sketchy.

830. Wilder, Amos N. "Mr. T. S. Eliot and the Anglo-Catholic Options." *The Spiritual Aspects of the New Poetry,* pp. 205–16. New York: Harpers, 1940. [Waste Land; Murder in the Cathedral]. A sympathetic and critical study of Eliot's theology in his poetry, from the Protestant point of view.

831. Zabel, Morton D. "Two Years of Poetry: 1937–1939." *SoR* 5, no. 3: 590–92. [Family Reunion]. It is superior to the other verse plays of this period because it has a genuinely human hero and a significant moral theme.

1941

832. Aldington, Richard. *Life for Life's Sake,* New York: Viking Press, 1941. Friendly reminiscences of Eliot in the late teens and early twenties, with anecdotes illustrating his social charm.

833. Anon. "Mr. T. S. Eliot's Progress. Search for Tradition. From Revolution to Orthodoxy." *TLS* 40, no. 2075 (November 8), pp. 554–58. [Points of View; Dry Salvages]. Patronizing essay on Eliot's thought.

834. ———. "Camp of Dejection." *TLS* 40, no. 2075 (November 8), 555. Deplores the fact that Eliot's influence has made writers more critical.

835. Barker, George. "To T. S. Eliot." *Poetry L,* 1, no. 5 (March-April): 138. A Sonnet on Eliot's religious doubts.

836. Bodkin, Maud. *The Quest for Salvation in an Ancient and a Modern Play,* 54 pp. London: Oxford University Press, 1941. A detailed examination of the relationship between *The Family Reunion* and the *Eumenides* of Aeschylus.

*837. Brenner, Rica. "Thomas Stearns Eliot." *Poets of Our Time,* pp. 161–205. New York: Harcourt Brace, 1941. A useful introduction to all aspects of Eliot's life and work.

838. Brooks, Van Wyck. "What Is Primary Literature?" *Opinions of Oliver Allston,* pp. 218–27. New York: Dutton, 1941. A cursory attack on Eliot's critical judgments. Reprinted in Unger, no. 1191.

839. Cargill, Oscar. "The Decadents." *Intellectual America,* pp. 235, 258–74. New York: Macmillan, 1941. Approves the poems of Eliot's "decadent" period, but not those after his conversion to Anglicanism.

840. Church, Richard. "T. S. Eliot: a Search for Foundations." *Eight for Immortality,* pp. 183–97. London: Dent, 1941. He points out the likenesses between Eliot and Shelley.

841. Coxe, Louis O. "Winters on Eliot." *KR* 3 (Autumn): 498–500. A spirited defense of Eliot against Winters's criticism (no. 866).

842. Daniels, Earl. *The Art of Reading Poetry,* pp. 404–9. New York: 1941. [Rhapsody on a Windy Night; Triumphal March]. Paraphrases of the poems, for the beginning student.

843. Deutsch, Babette. "Religious Elements in Modern Poetry." *MJ* 29 (Winter) : 30–36. She says, "Eliot seems to be one contemporary poet whose sense of guilt demands belief in God and in a soul capable of damnation."

844. DeVoto, Bernard. "Under Which King, Bezonian?" *Harper's* 183 (September) : 447. DeVoto says that Eliot's distaste for the typist and the "young man carbuncular" of *The Waste Land* had been proved wrong by their wartime heroism. Reprinted in *The Literary Fallacy,* Boston: Little, Brown, 1944, pp. 108–11.

*845. Haüsermann, H. W. "East Coker by T. S. Eliot." *ES* 23, no. 4 (August) : 108–10. Contains a letter from Eliot identifying some of the sources of the poem.

846. Hodgson, R. A. "Tradition and Mr. Eliot." *NewEW* 19 (September 25) : 221–22. A simple sketch of Eliot's poetry and criticism.

847. Jackson, Elizabeth. "Poetry and Poppycock." *SatR* 23 (January 25) : 13–14. Objects as a Plain Reader to quotations as used by Eliot and Yeats.

848. Kirkup, James. "Eliot." *Poetry L,* 1, no. 4 (January 15) : 115–16. [East Coker]. "Humility is the keynote of the poem," which is also notable for its beauty of language.

*849. MacNeice, Louis. *The Poetry of W. B. Yeats.* London: Oxford University Press, 1941. A subtle comparison of Eliot and Yeats in regard to democracy, religion, the modern waste land, use of images, and diction and rhythm.

850. Masters, Charlie. "Some Observations on 'Burnt Norton.'" *AmP* 6 (Winter and Spring) : 99–112, 212–31. A determined but not altogether successful attempt to understand the poem in the light of Eliot's earlier work.

851. Matthiessen, F. O. *American Renaissance.* New York: Oxford University Press, 1941. Eliot is quoted here only to illuminate Matthiessen's study of American authors.

852. Montgomerie, William. "Harry, Meet Mr. Prufrock: T. S. Eliot's Dilemma." *LL* 31 (November) : 115–28. [Family Reunion]. A psychoanalytic study of the play.

*853. Pottle, Frederick A. *The Idiom of Poetry,* pp. 86–92.

Ithaca: Cornell University Press, 1941. [Ash Wednesday]. An excellent paraphrase of the first, second, and fifth stanzas of the poem.

854. Ransom, John Crowe. "Eliot and the Metaphysicals." *Accent* 1 (Spring) : 148–56. Ransom translates Eliot's terms "thoughts" and "feelings" into his own terms of "structure" and "texture." Partially reprinted in *New Criticism*, Norfolk, Conn.: New Directions, 1941.

*855. ———. "T. S. Eliot: the Historical Critic." *New Criticism*, pp. 135–208. Norfolk, Conn.: New Directions, 1941. Section 4 of the volume is an extended discussion of Eliot's essay on Jonson; section 5 is a discussion (no. 854) of Eliot's essay on the metaphysical poets. An influential essay. Reprinted in Unger, no. 1191.

856. Speaight, Robert. "Two Famous Plays." *Sign* (New Jersey) 20 (February) : 398–99. [Murder in the Cathedral]. Interesting reminiscences by the actor who created the role of Thomas à Becket.

857. Spender, Stephen. "The Year's Poetry." *Horizon* 3 (February) : 138–41. [East Coker]. Praises Eliot for being aware that the poetic task is "to describe the situation of that part of humanity which happens to be living at a particular time, struggling with the circumstances of its environment. . . . Throughout 'East Coker' Eliot makes use of religious experience to insist on eternal and universal truths . . . which exist like shining and rather terrible jewels in the somber contemporary setting which he can convey with greater ease than any other of the moderns."

858. ———. "Books and the War—VII." *PNW*, no. 18, edited by John Lehmann, pp. 125–32. New York: Penguin Books, 1941. [Family Reunion]. A contrast between the poetic language of Synge's dramas, springing from the Irish peasants, and the "deliberate flatness and lack of poetry" of *The Family Reunion*, language which is a criticism of the lives of the speakers.

859. Stephenson, Ethel M. "T. S. Eliot and the Lay Reader." *Poetry R* 32 (October) : 289–94. [Burnt Norton]. "Eliot has not swept a rainbow paintbrush across an exotic heaven; he has used the ingredient of concentrated thought."

*860. Sweeney, James Johnson. "East Coker: a Reading." *SoR* 6 (Spring) : 771–91. In an unpublished letter to H. W.

Eliot, Jr., Eliot says: "There is an excellent detective article on East Coker by J. J. Sweeney in *The Southern Review*. He has followed up every clue, and attributes to me a good deal more than I was conscious of, as well as a knowledge of minor works of Thomas Elyot which I have not read. He does not appear to know Charles Williams's The Greater Trumps, which stimulated the figure of 'dancing' which first appeared in 'Burnt Norton.' " Reprinted in Unger, no. 1191.

861. Tate, Allen. "What Is a Traditional Society?" *Reason in Madness*, pp. 224–27. New York: G. P. Putnam's Sons, 1941. [Waste Land]. An interpretation of a passage in *The Waste Land* to support Tate's thesis that we are living in an untraditional society.

862. Thomas, Wright, and Brown, Stuart Gerry. *Reading Poems; an Introduction to Critical Study*, pp. 716–31, 749–52. New York: Oxford University Press, 1941. [Waste Land]. Notes to *The Waste Land* identifying many literary references. A useful compilation.

863. Voight, F. A. "Milton, Thou Shouldst Be Living." *NC* 130 (October) : 211–21. A defense of Milton against his detractors, especially Eliot.

864. Wanning, Andrews. "Criticism and Principles: Poetry of the Quarter." *SoR* 6 (Spring) : 796–98 [Burnt Norton; East Coker]. The review suffers from having been written before the two final "Quartets" appeared.

865. Winkler, R. O. C. "Crumbs from the Banquet." *Scrutiny* 10 (October) : 194–98. [Points of View]. Agrees with Leavis that Eliot's criticism has deteriorated since his conversion. Reprinted in *The Importance of Scrutiny*, edited by Eric Bentley, New York: George W. Stewart, 1948, pp. 291–94.

866. Winters, Yvor. "T. S. Eliot, the Illusion of Reaction." *KR* 3 (Winter) : 7–30; (Spring) : 221–39. Accuses Eliot of contradicting himself on five points in his criticism, of being unaware of his own contradictions, of having a bad influence on both modern criticism and poetic practice, and of being under the influence of Ezra Pound. Reprinted in *The Anatomy of Nonsense*, pp. 120–67. Norfolk, Conn.: New Directions, 1943, in Unger, no. 1191, and in *Yvor Winters on Modern Poets*, World Publishing Co., 1959.

1942

867. Ali, Ahmed. *Mr. Eliot's Penny World of Dreams; an essay in the Interpretation of T. S. Eliot's Poetry.* 138 pp. Bombay: Published for the Lucknow University by the New Book Company, 1942. Writing from the Communist point of view, and using an irresponsible Freudian technique for the interpretation of Eliot's poems, the author indulges in contradictions.

868. Anand, Mulk Raj. "Mr. Eliot's Kipling." *LL* 32 (March) : 167–70. [A Choice of Kipling's Verse]. Believes Eliot overpraises Kipling's thought.

*869. Bradbrook, M. C. "The Liturgical Tradition in English Verse; Herbert and T. S. Eliot." *Theology* 44 (January) : 13–23. Whereas the emblem-writers provided Herbert with his methods and material, Dante supplies them for Eliot.

*870. ———. "The Lyric and Dramatic in the Latest Verse of T. S. Eliot." *Theology* 44 (February) : 81–90. In *Murder in the Cathedral* and *Four Quartets* Eliot is attempting to picture the vision of eternity with its results in time—the miracle of incarnation.

*871. Buck, Philo M. Jr. "Faith of Our Fathers—T. S. Eliot." *Directions in Contemporary Literature,* pp. 261–90. New York: Oxford University Press, 1942. A well-unified essay on Eliot's religion as it appears in his prose and poetry; a sustained comparison with Dante. Excellent criticism.

872. Eliot, Henry Ware, Jr. Letter to the *Gloucester Daily Times* (February 27) , p. 4. [Dry Salvages]. Speaks of the youthful associations of the poet with these reefs, the Dry Salvages.

*873. Gardner, Helen Louise. "The Recent Poetry of T. S. Eliot." *New Writing and Daylight,* pp. 84–96. London: Hogarth Press, 1942. [Four Quartets]. For description, see no. 1063, which is an expansion of this essay.

874. "Gens." "Views and Reviews: Eliot on Kipling." *NewEW* 21 (May 7) : 25–26. [A Choice of Kipling's Verse]. "Mr. Eliot offers an important defense of Kipling's imperialism."

875. Godolphin, F. R. B. Review of *The Classics and the Man of Letters. Chimera* 1, no. 2 (Autumn) : 43. A brief, competent summary of the book.

876. Haüsermann, H. W. "T. S. Eliot's Conception of Poetry." *EdL*, no. 51 (Lausanne) (October), pp. 165–78. [Waste Land]. Haüsermann regards *The Waste Land* as an artistic failure because it is an attempt to write a Christian poem without a Christian terminology.

877. Hogan, J. P. "Eliot's Later Verse." *Adelphi* 18 (January-March): 54–58. [East Coker; Dry Salvages]. *"East Coker* is about experience; it is about the meaning of experience; about the meaninglessness of giving experience a fixed meaning; and about the struggle with words. . . . *The Dry Salvages* teaches the lesson of humility, which means getting rid of one's personality."

878. Humphries, Rolfe. "Salvation from Sand in Salt." *Poetry* 59 (March): 338–39. [Dry Salvages]. The poem "moves, and is moving and beautiful." Most of the review deplores Eliot's despair.

*879. Leavis, F. R. "Eliot's Later Poetry." *Scrutiny* 11 (Summer): 60–71. [Four Quartets; Marina; Coriolan poems]. Eliot tries to present Christian views "without invoking Christian dogma." Subtle analysis of the poems from "Marina" onward. Reprinted in *Education and the University,* London: Chatto and Windus, 1943, pp. 87–104.

880. Liceaga, Elvira J. *Emotion in Poetry,* pp. 7–16. English pamphlet series no. 1. Buenos Aires: Argentine Association of English Culture, 1942. A good undergraduate paper on Eliot's poetic technique.

881. MacCarthy, Desmond. "A Religious Poem." *TLS* (December 19), p. 622. [Little Gidding]. Admits he has fallen under the spell of "Little Gidding."

882. Martinez Diaz (de Vivar), Dora. *The Auditory Imagination,* pp. 17–30. English Pamphlet Series no. 1. Buenos Aires: Argentine Association of English Culture, 1942. Well-intentioned appreciation.

883. Nuhn, Ferner. "Orpheus in Hell: T. S. Eliot." *The Wind Blew from the East,* pp. 195–255. New York: Harpers, 1942. Does not try to develop a thesis about Eliot, but presents a series of observations on the essays and poems, contrasting them. Some good points. Reprinted in Unger, no. 1191.

884. Orwell, George. "Rudyard Kipling." *Horizon* 5 (February): 111–25. [A Choice of Kipling's Verse]. A small amount of adverse comment on Eliot's introduction to the Kipling anthology, saying that "whenever an aesthetic judgment on Kipling's verse seems to be called

for, Mr. Eliot is too much on the defensive to be able to speak plainly." (See no. 889.)

*885. ———. "Points of View. T. S. Eliot." *Poetry* L 2, no. 7 (October-November): 56–59. [Burnt Norton, East Coker, Dry Salvages, Prufrock]. The weakness of the later poems compared with those of the 1920s springs from the fact that Eliot does not really feel his faith. Says that "the later poems express a melancholy faith and the earlier ones a glowing despair."

886. Pollock, Thomas Clark. *The Nature of Literature*, pp. 130–31. Princeton: Princeton University Press, 1942. [Animula]. Brief analysis of the line, "Pray for us now and at the hour of our birth."

887. Powell, Dilys. "T. S. Eliot." *BT*, no. 69 (January), pp 25–26. [Points of View; Dry Salvages]. Miss Powell shows how the two books represent the stages of a pilgrimage.

888. Prince, Frank. "Some Recent Books." *DubR* 210 (January): 92–94. [Dry Salvages]. Eliot is trying to express an experience which he has not had.

*889. Raine, Kathleen. "Points of View: Another Reading." *Poetry* L 2, no. 7 (October-November): 59–62. [Burnt Norton, East Coker, Dry Salvages]. Defends Eliot's Christian point of view against Orwell (See no. 885). Both the essays are good.

890. Rowland, John. "The Spiritual Background of T. S. Eliot." *NewCM* 61 (January-March): 52–55. An oversimplified comment dividing Eliot's work into anti-religious (1909–1925) and religious (1925–   ). He approves of the later period.

891. Scarfe, Francis. *Auden and After: the liberation of poetry, 1930-1941*, pp. 54–55, 62–67. London: George Routledge & Sons, 1942. A brief comparison of a passage of Louis MacNeice's poetry with that of Eliot.

892. Shewring, Walter. "Some Recent Books." *DubR* 211 (October): 184–85. [The Classics and the Man of Letters]. Suggests that a knowledge of the Bible and the chief theological and devotional classics is as necessary as the knowledge of the Greek and Roman classics which Eliot advocates.

893. Speaight, Robert. "Little Gidding." *Tablet* 180 (December 19): 302–3. It is a fine poem, but "only those who are prepared to accept the fundamental doctrine of Christian asceticism . . . will receive the profound thought to which the poetry so rigorously conforms."

894. Stephenson, Ethel M. "T. S. Eliot and the Lay Reader, II." *Poetry R* 33 (March-April) : 80–83. [East Coker].

895. ———. "T. S. Eliot and the Lay Reader, III." *Poetry R* 33 (September-October) , 306–8. [Waste Land].

896. M. T. "Classics." *Studies* 31 (December) : 527. [The Classics and the Man of Letters]. One paragraph of favorable summary.

*897. Unger, Leonard. "T. S. Eliot's Rose Garden: a Persistent Theme." *SoR* 7 (Spring) : 667–69. Usually in the rose-garden theme is the experience of sexual-religious ecstasy, along with the idea of an inadequate response to the situation, and the "self-conscious effort for its recreation." Reprinted in Unger, no. 1191.

*898. Untermeyer, Louis. "T. S. Eliot." *Modern American Poetry*, pp. 420–24. New York: Harcourt, Brace and Company, 1942. [Prufrock, Portrait of a Lady, Waste Land, Hollow Men, Ash Wednesday, Murder in the Cathedral, Idea of a Christian Society]. A skillful account of Eliot's themes and technique, relying on Untermeyer's own reading and the criticism of Edmund Wilson, F. O. Matthiessen, Edwin Muir, Malcolm Cowley, and Horace Gregory.

*899. Wheelwright, Philip. "The Burnt Norton Trilogy." *Chimera* 1, no. 2 (Autumn) : 7–18. A study of the philosophical themes and imagery of the first three *Quartets*. The essay raises interesting questions. Revised as no. 1095.

1943

900. Anon. "Mr. Eliot." *Cweal* 38 (May 28) : 148. [Four Quartets]. "Mr. Eliot's poetry is exacting; it has the right to be so."

901. ———. "The Family Reunion at the A. D. C., Cambridge." *NSN* 25 (February 20) : 124. A short notice of a performance of the play in Cambridge, England.

902. ———. "At the Still Point." *Time* 41, pt. 2 (June 7) : 96–101. [Four Quartets]. The *Quartets* "are capable of charming and teaching many thousands of the great general reading public." A factually correct summary of Eliot's life follows the criticism.

903. ———. "Restoration." *Time* 42, pt. 2 (October 25) : 98, 101. [A Choice of Kipling's Verse]. A good summary of Eliot's preface.

904. Auden, W. H. "The Poet of the Encirclement." *NR* 109

(October 25) : 579–81. [A Choice of Kipling's Verse]. Little on Eliot, chiefly praise of Kipling. See also an exchange of letters between Auden and William Rose Benét, *NR* 110 (January 10) : 55–56, apropos of Auden's review.

905. Becker, May Lamberton. "T. S. Eliot in the Yukon." *NYHTB* (September 5) , sec. 8, p. 13. A short list of critical books and articles on Eliot for an aviator in Alaska.

906. Benét, William Rose. "Phoenix Nest." *SatR* 26 (October 9) : 20. [A Choice of Kipling's Verse]. Benét makes a few comparisons between Eliot and Kipling. "He is not a genius, like Kipling, but his is a subtle and interesting mind."

907. Bogan, Louise. "Verse." *NY* 19 (May 22) : 72–74. [Four Quartets]. Superficial. The meaning of the poem escapes her.

908. ———. Review of *A Choice of Kipling's Verse, NY* 19 (October 2) : 76–78. "It is . . . strange to see him bending the subtle resources of his intelligence in a hopeless cause," that of rehabilitating Kipling.

*909. Bradbrook, M. C. "Little Gidding." *Theology* 46 (March) : 58–62. A fine interpretation of the poem, taking into account expression as well as meaning.

910. Browne, Irene. "Correspondence. Mr. Eliot, Mr. Orwell, and Miss Raine." *Poetry L* 2, no. 9: 61. Attacks Miss Raine. (See no. 889.) Miss Browne says Eliot's approach to religion is "too gloomy and sectarian."

911. Chaning-Pearce, Melville. "Little Gidding." *NC* 133 (February) : 74–78. Gives much superficial attention to verse form.

912. Collier, K. G. "Correspondence. Eliot on Elites." *NewEW* 22 (February 18) : 156. [Notes towards a Definition of Culture]. He suggests that culture can be achieved more easily than Eliot thinks it can, and proposes to do it by giving special education to the most gifted one or two percent of children. Eliot replies to Collier on March 4, 1943.

913. Cowley, Malcolm. "Beyond Poetry." *NR* 108 (June 7) : 767–68. [Four Quartets]. Grudging admiration. He is afraid that Eliot is intent on the contemplative process that leads to "the total destruction of all the world where poetry is accustomed to dwell."

914. Deutsch, Babette. "The Enduring Music of the Past." *NYHTB* (July 18), p. 6. [Four Quartets]. She is interested chiefly in the musical virtuosity of the poems.

915. Farber, Marjorie. "The Apostle of an Empire." *NYTBR* (September 26), pp. 1, 22. [A Choice of Kipling's Verse]. Praises Eliot's "valuable distinction between ballad-makers and poetry-makers," and his clearing away some of the prejudice surrounding Kipling, but regrets that Eliot ignores Kipling's pleasure in hating.

916. Fletcher, John Gould. "Poems in Counterpoint." *Poetry* 63 (October): 44–48. [Four Quartets]. A brief and inconclusive essay on analogies with music in the *Quartets*.

917. Garrison, W. E. "The Cult of the Irrational." *ChC* 60 (May 19): 609–10. [Four Quartets]. Compares Eliot and Dali as great artists who are both addicted to "the cult of incongruity and irrationality."

*918. Goodman, Paul. "T. S. Eliot: the Poet of Purgatory." *NewL* (August 14), pp. 3, 7. [Four Quartets]. A troubled, serious essay on Eliot's concepts of time and morality.

*919. Gregory, Horace. "Fare Forward, Voyagers." *NYTBR* (May 16), p. 2. [Four Quartets]. The best of the American newspaper reviews of the *Quartets*. Gregory reads them in the light of all Eliot's previous poetry; compares them with Wordsworth's *Prelude*. He says that Eliot writes with "newly awakened insight," and protests against the view that Eliot has nothing further to say.

*920. Harding, D. W. "We Have Not Reached Conclusion." *Scrutiny* 11 (Spring): 216–19. [Little Gidding]. A fine explanation and criticism of the poem, taking no previous acquaintance for granted. Brief. Reprinted in *The Importance of Scrutiny*, edited by Eric Bentley, New York: George W. Stewart, 1948, pp. 269–73.

921. Higinbotham, R. N. "Objections to a Review of 'Little Gidding.'" *Scrutiny* 11 Summer), 259–61. Objects to Harding's review (no. 920) as too favorable.

922. Holden, Raymond. "The Dark Night of the Soul." *SatR* 26 (July 24): 11. [Four Quartets]. He believes there is something in the poem to be understood, but does not know what it is.

923. Hughes, Josephine. "The Unfamiliar Name." *America* 69 (August 28): 577–78. [Four Quartets]. Praise from the Roman Catholic point of view, emphasizing the Christian content of the poems.

924. Kirkup, James. "Eliot," *Poetry L* 2, no. 9: 52–55. [Little Gidding]. Summary, with many quotations, and praise of the musicality of the poem.

925. Kirschbaum, Leo, and Basler, Roy P. "Eliot's Sweeney among the Nightingales." *Expl* 2, no. 3 (December): item 18. Two replies to the query, "What is the meaning of the line, 'And Sweeney guards the hornéd gate?' " (See no. 977).

926. Larrabee, Ankey. "Three Studies in Modern Poetry, . . . Prufrock and Joseph Wood Krutch." *Accent* 3 (Winter): 120–21. [Prufrock]. "Prufrock" is explained by a quotation from Krutch.

927. Lasky, Melvin, "On T. S. Eliot's New Poetry." *NewL* (June 19), p. 3. [Four Quartets]. Chiefly references to reviews of the poem; competent.

928. Leavis, F. R. *Education and the University*, 140 pp. London: Chatto and Windus, 1943; Toronto: The Macmillan Company, 1943. Eliot's influence is apparent throughout the volume, in Leavis's insistence that education should develop the "sensibility" as well as the intellect, in the use of Eliot's prose and poetry as central classics for study, and in the general critical method proposed. For comments on "T. S. Eliot's Later Poetry," pp. 87–104, see no. 879.

929. ———. "Reflections on the Above." *Scrutiny* 11 (Summer): 261–67. (Concerns nos. 1137 and 1138.) [Little Gidding, Four Quartets]. Much more than an answer to Higinbotham, this deals with the relation between intellect and feeling in poetry, and the demands made on the reader by Eliot's later poetry.

930. Lebowitz, Martin. "Thought and Sensibility." *KR* 5 (Spring): 219–27. Considers the fallacy of supposing that thought and sensibility are separate, and uses Eliot's poetry as an illustration of "sensibility as the correlate of intelligence."

*931. Matthiessen, F. O. "Eliot's Quartet's." *KR* 5 (Spring): 161–78. He analyzes the structure of the poems, considers their themes, the symbol of fire, the religious thought, and the relative artistic value of the four poems. Rich and condensed. Reprinted as the last chapter in the 1947 revision of *The Achievement of T. S. Eliot*. Appears also in *Literary Opinion in America*, edited by Morton D. Zabel, New York: Harper, 1951, pp. 282–95.

932. Maugham, Somerset. *Introduction to Modern English and American Literature,* pp. 321–23. New York: New Home Library, 1943. Without mentioning his obscurity, introduces Eliot to a "larger audience."

933. Mesterton, Eric. *The Waste Land, Some Commentaries.* Translated by Llewellyn Jones, 22 pp. Chicago: Argus Bookshop, 1943. The essay is disorganized, but for a reader who has some knowledge of the poem, is enlightening.

934. Muir, Edwin. "Little Gidding." *NSN* 25, n.s. (February 20) : 128. This is the "most essential and intimate poetry that Mr. Eliot has written." Brief. Appeared also in *NewL* (New York) , May 1, 1943, p. 3.

*935. ———. "T. S. Eliot and His Time: the Homeless Generation." *BT,* no. 86 (June) , pp. 21–24. The intention here is to "try to see him historically, in relation to the generation to which he belongs."

936. Naumburg, Carl T. "A Package of Kiplingiana." *SatR* 26 (November 6) : 8–9. [A Choice of Kipling's Verse]. A Kipling enthusiast praises Eliot's thorough and erudite preface.

937. Nicholson, Norman. "T. S. Eliot." *Man and Literature,* pp. 193–203. London: S.C.M. Press, 1943. [Waste Land, Triumphal March, Family Reunion, Murder in the Cathedral, Four Quartets]. Eliot's chief poems and a play are considered in the light of Christian doctrine. He approaches God by the Negative Way, which if pursued "to the logical end would demand the rejection of poetry."

938. Ransom, John Crowe. "The Inorganic Muses." *KR* 5 (Spring) : 294–300. A hesitating and elaborate criticism of the lack of architecture in Eliot's poetry, through "Burnt Norton."

939. Rosenfeld, Paul. "What Has Happened to the Prose Poem?" *SatR* 26 (July 24) : 9–11. Accuses Eliot's article, "The Borderline of Prose" (1917) , of having been influential in discouraging the prose poem.

940. Schwartz, Delmore. "Anywhere out of the World." *Nation* 157 (July 24) : 102–3. [Four Quartets]. Discusses versification, compares the poems briefly with the late Quartets of Beethoven, suggests that Eliot's religion of renunciation is close to Buddhism.

941. Sitwell, Edith. "Lecture on Poetry since 1920." *LL* 39

(October): 86–93. [Sweeney among the Nightingales, Waste Land]. An interpretation of the emotional and musical effects in Eliot's early poetry, especially *The Waste Land.*

942. Spender, Stephen. "Sensuousness in Modern Poetry." *PNW*, no. 16, edited by John Lehmann, pp. 118–26. New York: Penguin Books, March, 1943. Spender uses Eliot's critics to illustrate the errors of modern criticism, and discusses "Prufrock," and the *Four Quartets* briefly to illustrate his own critical principle that poetry should be sensuous.

*943. Sweeney, James Johnson. "Little Gidding: Introductory to a Reading." *Poetry* 62 (July): 214–23. An illuminating essay on the religious and philosophical sources of the poem.

944. Trilling, Lionel. "Mr. Eliot's Kipling." *Nation* 157 (October 16): 436, 440, 442. Dislikes Eliot's admiration for Kipling and draws analogies between the two poets; accuses Eliot of anti-Semitism, which he denied. (See *Nation,* January 15, 1944, p. 83.)

945. L. T. [Luke Turner]. Review of "Little Gidding." *Black-friars,* 24 (February): supplement, xii–xiv. Says that "Little Gidding is a magnificent completion of a task that might have been thought beyond the powers of a community of poets."

946. Untermeyer, Louis. "Eight Poets." *YR* 33 (December): 348–49. [Four Quartets]. " 'Four Quartets' is both simpler and subtler than anything Eliot has written since 'The Waste Land.' "

*947. Waggoner, H. H. "T. S. Eliot and the Hollow Men." *AL* 15 (May): 101–26. Bergson, Bradley, Hulme, and Babbitt have been the philosophic influences leading Eliot to the conclusion that science alone produces hollow men and a waste land.

948. Wells, Henry W. *The American Way of Poetry,* pp. 194 ff. and *passim.* New York: Columbia University Press, 1943. The optimism and Americanism of Hart Crane's *The Bridge* are a reply to Eliot's pessimism and Anglophilism.

*949. Williams, Charles. "A Dialogue on Mr. Eliot's Poem." *DubR,* 212 (April): 114–22. [Four Quartets]. A dialogue between two men and two women, written in the mood of good talk, containing excellent criticism.

1944

950. Blackmur, R. P. "Mr. Eliot and Notions of Culture: a Discussion." *PR* 11, no. 3 (Summer, 1944) : 302–4. [Notes towards the Definition of Culture]. An attack on the book (See also Greenberg, no. 958, Phillips, no. 965, and Richards, no. 966.)

951. Bradford, Curtis B. "Footnotes to East Coker; a Reading." *SR* 52 (Winter) : 169–75. Untrustworthy additions to Sweeney's interpretation. (See no. *860.)

952. Campbell, Harry M. "An Examination of Modern Critics; T. S. Eliot." *RMR* 8 (Summer) : 128–38. Answers Winters's and Ransom's objections to Eliot's critical principles (nos. 854 and 866), and adds his own, and concludes that Eliot's essays on religion and the relation of literature to religion may prove to be the greatest of his accomplishments. Brief bibliography.

953. Connelly, Francis X. Review of *Four Quartets. Spirit* 10 (January) : 185–87. An appreciative review.

954. Cotten, Lyman A. "Wasted Commentary." *QRL* 2, no. 1 (Fall) : 80–81. [On Eric Mesterton's *The Waste Land: Some Commentaries*]. Says that Mesterton's book is confused.

*955. Diggle, Margaret. "The Ancient Mariner and the Waste Land: Two Types of Imaginative Creation." *Poetry L* 2, no. 10: 195, 205–8. Although the themes of these two poems are the same, man's guilt, his punishment, and need for redemption, the poems differ in that the conflict is expressed unconsciously in "The Ancient Mariner"; in Eliot, it is analyzed.

956. P. O. D. [Patrick Orpen Dudgeon]. "Murder in the Cathedral." *Agonia* 12 (Primavera) : 72–74. On the production of the play, which was a success, in Buenos Aires.

957. Gardner, W. H. *Gerard Manley Hopkins.* London: Martin Secker and Warburg, 1944. Eliot has not been greatly influenced by Hopkins, but there are certain likenesses of theme and expression.

958. Greenberg, Clement. "Mr. Eliot and Notions of Culture: a discussion." *PR* 11, no. 3 (Summer) : 305–7. [Notes towards the Definition of Culture]. Attacks the book. (See also nos. 950, 965, and 966.)

959. Grierson, Herbert J. C. and Smith, J. C. "Twentieth Century Poetry: between the Wars, 1919–1939." *A Critical*

History of English Poetry, pp. 500–501, 511–13. London: Chatto and Windus, 1944. Condemns Eliot for obscurity coming from the use of private associations and too many allusions.

960. Jack, Peter Monro. "A Review of Reviews; T. S. Eliot's *Four Quartets.*" *AB* 1 (Winter) : 91–99. [Four Quartets]. "This is not a review of Eliot's poems but a review of some of the reviews about them." But there is excellent criticism of the *Quartets* as well as of ten reviews, of which all but two were favorable.

*961. Laski, Harold J. *Faith, Reason, and Civilization,* pp. 96–100, 180–82. New York: Viking Press, 1944. A criticism of Eliot's political and economic position from the point of view of a liberal wholly opposed to it. Clear and eloquent. Reprinted in Unger, no. 1191.

*962. McLuhan, Herbert Marshall. "Eliot's 'The Hippopotamus.'" *Expl* 2, no. 7 (May) : item 50. A sound explanation of the intent of the entire poem.

*963. O'Brien, Bernard. "More Reflections on 'Murder in the Cathedral.'" *Canisian* (Corpus Christi College, Werribee, Australia) 8 (November) : 4–8. A penetrating essay on the spiritual meaning of the play. Eliot wrote on the copy of the review in the Eliot Collection at Harvard: "I think this is a very intelligent review."

964. O'Brien, R. D. "I Am Not Prince Hamlet." *MilB* 7 (February) : 13–14. [Four Quartets]. A brief introduction to all of Eliot's poetry.

965. Phillips, William. "Mr. Eliot and Notions of Culture: a Discussion." *PR* 11, no. 3 (Summer) : 307–9. [Notes towards the Definition of Culture]. Attacks the book. (See also nos. 950, 958, and 966.)

966. Richards, L. A. "Mr. Eliot and Notions of Culture: a Discussion." *PR* 11 (Summer) : 310–12. [Notes towards the Definition of Culture]. An attack with special reference to education. (See also nos. 950, 870, and 965.)

*967. Savage, D. S. "The Orthodoxy of T. S. Eliot." *The Personal Principle,* pp. 91–112. London: Routledge, 1944. Considers Eliot's poetry and criticism; a clear statement of the anti-religious position. Reprinted in Unger, no. 1191.

968. Scarfe, Francis. "Two Lectures: the Classics and the Man of Letters, and the Music of Poetry." *Poetry L* 10 (December) : 239–42. Excellent criticism of these two lectures by Eliot.

*969. Shand, John. "Around 'Little Gidding.'" *NC* 136 (September): 120–32. A man who modestly claims to be a common reader gives a record of his triumphs and defeats in reading "Little Gidding," and in so doing provides a fresh view of the poem.

*970. Snell, Reginald. "T. S. Eliot and the English Poetic Tradition." *NewEW* 26 (December 14): 77–78. [Four Quartets]. A rich and thoughtful review; much is said in short space.

971. Stephenson, Ethel M. *T. S. Eliot and the Lay Reader,* 56 pp. London, Fortune Press, 1944. "The book is not, in any real sense, written at all; it is an uncoordinated series of note-book jottings." (From a review in *NewEW,* January 11, 1945, pp. 95–96.) 2nd ed., 1946, 94 pp.

*972. Storman, E. J. "Time and Mr. Eliot." *Meanjin* 3 (Winter): 103–10. [Four Quartets]. An illuminating and concise account of the central meaning of the poem, that an eternal reality is present in various events of time.

973. Sypher, Wylie. "The Metaphysicals and the Baroque." *PR* 11 (Winter): 3–17. Eliot, as a classicist, should appreciate the baroque rhetoric of Milton, since rhetoric is a kind of liturgy in verse.

974. Tate, Allen. "The State of Letters." *SR* 52 (Autumn): 610–11. Quotes an attack made by Sandburg on Eliot. (See no. 2486.)

*975. Utley, Francis L. "Eliot's 'The Hippopotamus.'" *Expl* 3, no. 2 (November): item 10. A well-rounded explication of the poem.

976. Vivas, Eliseo. "The Objective Correlative of T. S. Eliot." *AB* 1 (Winter): 7–18. Vivas objects, on aesthetic and psychological grounds, to the expression theory contained in the doctrine of the objective correlative; he says it is unintelligible.

977. Walcutt, Charles C. "Eliot's 'Sweeney among the Nightingales.'" *Expl* 2, no. 6 (April): item 48. An explanation of the line, "And Sweeney guards the hornéd gate." (See no. 925.)

978. Weiss, T. "The Nonsense of Winters' *Anatomy,* Part II. T. S. Eliot." *QRL* 1, no. 4 (Summer): 300–307. [Function of Criticism]. Analyzes Yvor Winters's criticism of Eliot, explaining Winters's irritation by saying that Eliot "beat him to the draw of ideas Winters would claim as his own."

979. Williams, William Carlos. "The Fatal Blunder." *QRL* 2 (Winter) : 125–26. [Ash Wednesday]. Objects to two lines in Part I as being untrue, philosophically and religiously.

1945

980. Anon. "Results of Competition No. 780." *NSN* 29 (February 3) : 82–83. [Waste Land]. Four prize-winning paragraphs are printed, giving Samuel Johnson's supposed opinion of the poem. He is shown disliking it but admitting its permanent values.

981. Arms, George W., Kirby, J. P., and others. "Eliot's 'Burbank with a Baedeker; Bleisstein with a Cigar.' " *Expl* 3, no. 7 (May) : item 53. A clear explanation of the allusions in the poem.

982. Battenhouse, Roy W. "Eliot's 'The Family Reunion' as Christian Prophecy." *Christendom* 10 (Summer) : 307–21. A long explanation of the play.

983. Bickersteth, G. L. "A Classic." *NaR* 124 (June) : 519–22. [What Is a Classic?]. In a detailed analysis, Mr. Bickersteth takes Eliot to task for concerning himself with Virgil's "maturity" of language instead of with his historical "centrality." He suggests that Eliot is insufficiently acquainted with Latin.

984. Bodgener, J. Henry. "Spiritual Life and Literary Trends." *LQHR* 170 (July) : 324–36. [Four Quartets]. Emphasizes the spiritual helpfulness of the poems.

985. Bush, Douglas. *Paradise Lost in Our Time: Some Comments,* pp. 4, 8–23, 26. Ithaca: Cornell University Press, 1945. Quotes or summarizes all of Eliot's strictures against Milton and answers them.

986. Chase, Richard. "The Sense of the Present." *KR* 7 (Spring) : 218–31. Chiefly on Eliot's use of mythology. The essay raises interesting questions.

987. Dillon, George. "Correspondence." *Poetry* 67 (October) : 50–52. An informal account of Eliot's lecture in Paris, "Le Rôle Social du Poète."

988. Dupee, F. W. "Difficulty as Style." *ASch* 14 (Summer) : 355–57. The difficulty of modern poetry is not a failure on the part of either poet or reader, but is a regular feature of modern poetic style.

989. Every, Brother George. "Mr. Eliot and the Classics." *NewEW,* 26 (March 29) : 191. [What Is a Classic?]. A short review.

990. Foster, Genevieve W. "The Archetypal Imagery of T. S. Eliot." *PMLA* 60 (June) : 567–85. Miss Foster says: "I am merely attempting what I believe to be an ordinary Jungian interpretation of certain of Eliot's images" up to the *Four Quartets*. (These ideas are further developed by Elizabeth Drew, no. 1231.)

991. Fowlie, Wallace. "Eliot and Tchelitchew." *Accent* 5 (Spring) : 166–70. [Four Quartets]. Draws an analogy between the children in the apple tree of *Four Quartets* and the painting "Cache-Cache" of Pavel Tchelitchew.

*992. Gilbert, Katherine. "A Spatial Configuration in Five Recent Poets." *SAQ* 44 (October) : 422–31. [Four Quartets]. Images of the crossroads or door, pathway or stair, and mountaintop or garden as used by Eliot, Auden, Spender, Yeats, and Day-Lewis to sketch out a moral landscape. This is a suggestive essay.

*993. Haüsermann, H. W. " 'East Coker' and 'The Family Reunion.' " *LL* 47 (October) : 32–38. A comparison of the theme and structure of these two works clarifies each.

994. Hayward, John. "New Literature: the Classic Ideal." *BT*, no. 110 (June), pp. 39–40. [What Is a Classic?]. A skillful summary of the essay.

995. Hodin, J. P. "T. S. Eliot on the Condition of Man Today." *Horizon* 12 (August) : 83–89. Report of an interview with Eliot concerning the future of Europe and of mankind.

996. Hook, Sidney. "The Dilemma of T. S. Eliot." *Nation* 160 (January 20) : 69–71. [Notes towards the Definition of Culture]. Eliot is "unwilling to embrace current forms of totalitarianism, but his diagnosis of the causes of their rise leads him to proposals which, if enforced, would result in some kind of ecclesiastical fascism."

997. James, Bruno S. "What Is a Classic?" *Blackfriars* 26 (June) : 236–37. A good summary. Eliot "has argued his thesis so enchantingly and so clearly that it is hard not to believe that it will take its place among the few . . . masterpieces of our time."

998. King, Alec. " 'Obscurity' in Modern Poetry." *Meanjin* 4 (Spring) : 202–3. A defense of Eliot against the charge of obscurity; he has deliberately written for a small audience who can understand him.

999. Lea, Richard. "T. S. Eliot's Four Quartets." *Adelphi* 21

(July–September) : 186–87. Inarticulate admiration.

1000. Muir, Edwin. "New Literature: Later Poetry of T. S. Eliot." *BT*, no. 105 (January) , pp. 37–38. [Four Quartets].The review is concerned chiefly with the unity of the *Quartets*.

1001. Paul, David. "Views and Reviews: Structure in Some Modern Poets." *NewEW*, 27 (July 26) : 131. One paragraph on Eliot, suggesting that music offers the best parallel to his poetic structure.

1002. Peschmann, Hermann. "The Later Poetry of T. S. Eliot; the Four Quartets and Their Relationship to His Earlier Work." *English 5* (Autumn) : 180–88. Quotations with a thin thread of comment.

1003. Pope, John C. "Prufrock and Raskolnikov." *AL* 17 (November) : 213–30. Offers the theory that Eliot's reading of *Crime and Punishment* played a crucial part in the germination of "The Love Song of J. Alfred Prufrock." (See no. 1080.)

1004. Rezanno (de Martini) , Maria Clotilde. *The Gerontion of T. S. Eliot,* 27 pp. English Pamphlet no. 10. With a preface by P. O. Dudgeon. Buenos Aires: Argentine Association of English Culture, 1945. A line-by-line examination of the poem, identifying the allusions. This essay is intended for a reader indifferent to or hostile toward the poem.

1005. Schwartz, Delmore. "T. S. Eliot as the International Hero." *PR* 12, no. 2 (Spring) : 199–206. Leonard Unger says: "Eliot . . . becomes a strange god in Schwartz's presentation of him as an international culture hero, one of the heroic and international hallmarks being Eliot's concern with the related difficulties of making love and having religious beliefs." Reprinted in Unger, no. 1191.

1006. Shapiro, Karl. *Essay on Rime.* New York: Reynal and Hitchcock, 1945) , pp. 16–17, 22, 40, 60–61. Part of a long poem. Eliot's great influence on poets, the beauty of the music of *Ash Wednesday* and *The Waste Land,* and Eliot's early poetic career. Reprinted in Unger, no. 1191.

1007. Speaight, Robert. "The Later Poetry of T. S. Eliot." *DubR* 216 (April) : 152–59. [Four Quartets]. Treats the main theme of the *Quartets,* the soul's pilgrimage and purgation. "These poems will remain."

1946

1008. Arms, George W., Kirby, J. P., and others. "Eliot's Gerontion." *Expl* 4, no. 8 (June) : item 55. F. A. Pottle suggests that "Gerontion" is classical Greek for "little old
man." (See no. 1282.)

1009. Basler, Roy P. "Psychological Pattern in 'The Love Song
of J. Alfred Prufrock.'" *Twentieth Century English,*
edited by W. S. Knickerbocker, pp. 384–400. New York:
Philosophical Library, 1946. An ingenious interpretation of the poem as a dialogue between Prufrock's self-
love, speaking as "I"; and "You," belonging to the
world of matter. Reprinted in Basler's *Sex, Symbolism,
and Psychology in Literature.* New Brunswick, N.J.:
Rutgers University Press, 1948.

1010. Blisset, William. "The Argument of T. S. Eliot's Four
Quartets." *UTQ* 15 (January) : 115–26. The primary
argument deals with time and its redemption, and the
secondary argument with the poet's task.

*1011. Coats, R. H. "An Anchor for the Soul: a Study of T. S.
Eliot's Later Verse." *HJ* 44: 112–18. [Four Quartets].
A study of the *Quartets* under four aspects: philsophical,
psychological, religious, and poetical. Brief, but full.

1012. Coomaraswamy, Ananda K. "Primordial Images." *PMLA*
61 (June) : 601–2. Comment on G. W. Foster's "Archetypal Imagery of T. S. Eliot" (no. 990) , with respect to
references to Jung and to the distinction between *le
symbolisme qui sait et le symbolisme qui cherche;* with
her reply (no. 1016) .

*1013. D'Apice, Anthony. "Mr. T. S. Eliot's 'Murder in the
Cathedral.'" *CathR* (Auckland) 1 (February) : 641–56.
Intelligent explanation and criticism of the play, which
he thinks is one of the "really great plays of the language."

*1014. Dobrée, Bonamy. "The Present Century." *English Es-
sayists,* pp. 44–46. London: Collins, 1946. Eliot's essay
style represents the fusion of the Baconian method with
that of Montaigne. Watercolor of Eliot by Katherina
Wilczinski facing p. 41.

1015. Eshelman, William R. "Eliot's Gerontion." *Expl* 4, no. 6
(April) : item 44. Identifies references and interprets the
entire poem.

1016. Foster, Genevieve W. Reply to A. K. Coomaraswamy (no.
1012) . *PMLA* 61 (June) : 602–3.

1017. Gregory, Horace, and Zaturenska, Marya. "T. S. Eliot, the Twentieth Century 'Man of Feeling,' in American Poetry." *A History of American Poetry 1900–1940*, pp. 413–28. New York: Harcourt, Brace, 1946. A quick survey of Eliot's reputation, a short biography, and a poorly organized survey of the poetry.

1018. Hall, Vernon, Jr. "Eliot's La Figlia Che Piange." *Expl* 5, no. 2 (November) : item 16. The theme of the poem is the struggle between the poet as an artist and as a moral being.

1019. Julian, Constance. "T. S. Eliot and the Anglo-Catholics." *Fireside* (Sydney) 12 (February 1) : 11–14. Deplores the fact that Eliot has not become a Roman Catholic.

1020. Knights, L. C. "Four Quartets Rehearsed." *HumB* 1 (Summer) : 41–42. [Preston's *Four Quartets Rehearsed*]. Praises the book, and insists that those who "express their sense of living values" in forms other than Christian can profit by reading *Four Quartets*.

1021. Marnau, Fred. "Mr. Eliot's Music." *Centaur* (Amsterdam) 1 (February) : 210–18. [Four Quartets].

1022. Mason, H. A. "Elucidating Eliot." *Scrutiny* 14 (Summer) : 67–71. A review of Preston's *Four Quartets Rehearsed* (no. 1029). Says the book shows how the theological approach handicaps the critic.

1023. Moloney, Michael F. "Mr. Eliot and Critical Tradition." *Thought* 21 (September) : 455–74. Overemphasizes the Catholic element in Eliot's criticism.

1024. ———. "Eliot and Maritain." *America* 75 (June 29) : 277–79. He points out that Eliot and Maritain agree on the desirable kind of Christian literature, on unified sensibility, and on Baudelaire.

*1025. Moore, Dom Sebastian. "East Coker: the Place and the Poem." *Focus Two,* edited by B. Rajan and A. Pearse, pp. 91–103. London: Dennis Dobson, 1946. A sensitive and illuminating interpretation of the poem.

1026. Nicholson, Norman. "T. S. Eliot." *Writers of To-day,* edited by Denys Val Baker, pp. 139–52. London: Sidgwick Jackson, 1946. An examination of Eliot's work "in the light of Christian doctrine." Draws only on Eliot's poetry for information.

*1027. Peacock, Ronald. "T. S. Eliot." *The Poet in the Theatre,* pp. 3–25. New York: Harcourt, Brace, 1946. A rich essay on the theme, "There is a direct line of development from Eliot's criticism and earlier verse to *Murder in the Cathedral* and *The Family Reunion*."

1028. Peschmann, Hermann. Review of "What Is a Classic?" *Adelphi* 22 (January–March) : 90–91. "What Mr. Eliot seems to be implying is that the classic is the true norm of literary expression of a fully mature society; that it does not necessarily occur—that it is even unlikely to, for example, in our own country; that when it does occur it is the penultimate moment of that civilization flowering that has produced it."

*1029. Preston, Raymond. *Four Quartets Rehearsed*, 64 pp. New York: Sheed and Ward, 1946. Valuable suggestions for understanding the poems are scattered throughout this small book, which emphasizes the religious aspect of the poetry without overlooking the poetic. Written in a difficult style.

1030. Reed, Henry. "Chard Witlow: (Mr. Eliot's Sunday Evening Postscript) ." *A Map of Verona and Other Poems*, pp. 33–34. London: J. Cape, 1946. Parody.

1031. Routh, H. V. "Leading Interpreters of the Interwar Period: Thomas Stearns Eliot." *English Literature and Ideas in the Twentieth Century*, pp. 12, 112, 113, 140, 160–67. London: Methuen & Co., 1946. [Prufrock and Other Observations; Gerontion; Waste Land; Hollow Men; Ash Wednesday; Four Quartets]. There is a section on Eliot's literary and cultural antecedents, and a brief consideration of his poems. Emphasizes the difficulty of his work and his haughtiness. But "Eliot will surpass them all if and when he works his way out of the maze."

1032. Shahani, Ranjee G. "Some British I Admire: Mr. T. S. Eliot." *AsR* (London) 42, n.s. (October) : 378–82. On Eliot's relation to French poetry and an account of a brief interview; much quotation from the *Quartets*.

1033. Smith, Francis J. "A Reading of 'East Coker.'" *Thought* 21 (June) : 272–86. An extremely Catholic interpretation of the poem.

1034. Smith, Grover. "Observations on Eliot's 'Death by Water.'" *Accent* 6 (Summer) : 257–63. [Waste Land]. An argument for the thesis that the death referred to in the passage is spiritual death.

*1035. Spender, Stephen. "Poetry for Poetry's Sake and Poetry beyond Poetry." *Horizon* 13 (April) : 221–38. [Four Quartets; Waste Land]. A complex but rewarding discussion of the techniques of half a dozen minor poets; Spender is most interested in the two levels of Eliot's language, the creative level of poetry and the level of philosophic thought.

*1036. ———. "Three English Poets and the War." *Meanjin* 5 (Autumn) : 19–21. The three poets are Eliot, Auden, and MacNeice. Spender praises Eliot's integrity and poetic sensibility discriminatingly, especially in the *Quartets,* but deplores his indifference to social justice.

1037. Stauffer, Donald A. *The Nature of Poetry.* New York: W. W. Norton, 1946. Stauffer analyzes briefly some of Eliot's poetic techniques to illustrate his own views on poetry.

1038. M. T. "Miscellaneous." *Studies* 35 (March) : 143–44. [What Is a Classic?]. Accuses Eliot of performing a logical sleight-of-hand trick in this essay, since he has defined a classic so that only Virgil fits the description.

1039. Treece, Henry. "The 'Four Quartets' of Mr. Eliot." *How I See Apocalypse,* pp. 108–22. London: L. Drummond, 1946.

1040. Wall, Bernard. "Mr. Eliot's Four Quartets." *Tablet* 187 (May 11) : 238–39. Wall says that the "tensions in a poet who belongs to the twentieth century and is theological as the century is not, are the key to Eliot's work." Stresses his relationship to Dante.

1041. Watts, Harold H. "T. S. Eliot and the Still Point." *ChiR* 1 (Spring) : 52–66. [Four Quartets]. The still point is a "certain moment in time: the present, a moment when . . . time comes in contact with something that is distinctly not time," but eternity. A thoughtful essay, worth careful reading.

1042. Weiss, T. "T. S. Eliot and the Courtyard Revolution." *SR* 54, no. 3: 289–307. A reply to Ransom's (no. 855) and Vivas' (no. 976) objections to Eliot's critical principles.

1947

1043. Anon. "People Who Read and Write: Men of Art." *NYTBR* (May 18) , p. 8. [Milton]. Appreciation of Eliot's manner in his Milton lecture and of his modesty.

1044. ———. "Milton is O.K." *Time* 49, pt. 2 May 19) : 108. Chiefly quotation from Eliot's lecture on Milton at the Frick Museum.

1045. ———. "Milton Lost and Regained." *TLS,* no. 2356

(March 29), p. 140. A clear, useful summary of Eliot's attitude toward Milton in 1936 and as revised in 1947.

1046. ———. "T. S. Eliot 'the literary conscience of an era.'" *Vogue* (August 1). Photograph of Eliot and a paragraph on his recent honors.

1047. Blyth, Ion (pseud. of David Page). *The Redeemed Realm, a Satire on T. S. Eliot and the Hollywood Hindus*, 19 pp. Boston: David Page, 1947). A parody of *The Waste Land* and its notes.

*1048. Bradbrook, M. C. "Eliot's Critical Method." *T. S. Eliot, A Study of His Writings by Several Hands, Focus Three*, edited by B. Rajan, pp. 119–28. London: Dennis Dobson, 1947. A masterly view of twenty-five years of Eliot's critical activity.

*1049. Brooks, Cleanth. "The Waste Land: An Analysis." *T. S. Eliot, A Study of His Writings by Several Hands, Focus Three*, edited by B. Rajan, pp. 7–36. London: Dennis Dobson, 1947. Same as no. 640. Reprinted in *Modern Poetry and the Tradition*, Chapel Hill, 1939, also in Unger, no. 1191.

1050. Brown, Ivor. "Can There Be a Revival of Poetic Drama in the Modern Theatre?" *TRSL* 23, n.s.: 75. His answer to his question is "I doubt it." The only reference to Eliot is "his High Church hocus-pocus manner."

1051. Brown, Wallace Cable. "Mr. Eliot without the Nightingales." *UKCR* 14 (Autumn): 31–38. [Sacred Wood]. Restudies *The Sacred Wood* in the light of recent attacks upon Eliot's criticism.

1052. Browne, E. Martin. "The Poet and the Stage." *The Penguin New Writing*, edited by John Lehmann, no. 31, pp. 87–92. London, 1947. Includes passing remarks on Eliot's use of poetry for the stage. Brief, but excellent.

1053. Chapin, Katherine Garrison. "T. S. Eliot at the National Gallery." *Poetry* 70 (September): 328–29. A description of Eliot's public reading of his poetry in Washington, D. C.

1054. Chase, Richard. "T. S. Eliot in Concord." *ASch* 16 (Autumn): 438–43. An ironically sympathetic account of a commencement exercise at a girls' school where Eliot spoke.

1055. Cleophas, Sister Mary. *Between Fixity and Flux; a study of the concept of poetry in the criticism of T. S. Eliot*, 122 pp. Washington: Catholic University of America

Press, 1947. [The author's name appears on the dissertation as "Sister Mary Cleophas Costello"]. An attempt to discover what Eliot means by "poetry."

1056. Daiches, David. "Some Aspects of T. S. Eliot." *CE* 9 (December) : 115–22. [Waste Land; Gerontion; Four Quartets]. A guide to Eliot's poems, better for the early ones, especially "Gerontion," than for the later ones. Appears also in *EJ* 36 (December 1947) : 501–8.

1057. Davies, Leila. "Views and Reviews, 'Family Reunion' Revisited." *NewEW* 30 (January 30) : 149–50. A competent analysis of her reasons for liking the play better the second time she saw it.

1058. ———. "Views and Reviews: Eliot and the Poetic Drama." *NewEW* 30 (March 20) : 199–200. [Murder in the Cathedral; Family Reunion]. Explains and defends Eliot's use of verse when it is close to prose, but questions the effectiveness of the chorus.

*1059. Duncan-Jones, Elsie E. "Ash Wednesday." *T. S. Eliot, A Study of His Writings by Several Hands, Focus Three,* edited by B. Rajan, pp. 37–56. London: Dennis Dobson, 1947. A very satisfactory *explication de texte* from the religious point of view.

*1060. Fergusson, Francis. "Action as Passion: *Tristran* and *Murder in the Cathedal.*" *KR* 9 (Spring) : 201–21. Two essays, one on Wagner and one on Eliot; demands careful reading, but illuminating. Reprinted in *The Idea of a Theatre.* Princeton, N.J.: Princeton University Press, 1949.

1061. Frank, Joseph. "Force and Form: a Study of John Peale Bishop." *SR* 55 (Winter) : 102–3. [Four Quartets]. A brief comparison of Bishop with Eliot.

*1062. Gallup, Donald. *A Bibliographical Check-List of the Writings of T. S. Eliot, including his contributions to periodicals and translations of his work into foreign languages,* 128 pp. New Haven: Yale University Library, 1947. The authoritative bibliography, indispensable. New ed., London: Faber and Faber, 1952, 177 pp.

*1063. Gardner, Helen Louise. "Four Quartets: a Commentary." *T. S. Eliot, A Study of His Writings by Several Hands, Focus Three,* edited by B. Rajan, pp. 57–77. London: Dennis Dobson, 1947. "This commentary will try to interpret the *Quartets* by the earlier works and by the reading that lies behind them, in order to help readers to that moment when they share with the poet the joy of apprehending significant relations." Excellent. Also appeared in *Penguin New Writing,* no. 29, edited by John Lehmann, London, 1947, pp. 123–47.

1064. J. J. H. "Milton." *Studies* 36 (December) : 504–6. A summary of the controversy concerning Milton. An unexplained annoyance pervades this essay.

*1065. Hagstrum, J. H. "La Figlia Che Piange." *EngA* (Department of English, Northwestern University, Evanston, Illinois, no. 3) (October) , 7 pp. An excellent and detailed analysis of the poem in mimeographed form, prepared for the use of classes at Northwestern University.

1066. Hayward, John. *Prose Literature since 1939,* pp. 32–33, 38. Published for the British Council. London: Longmans, Green and Co., 1947. [The Idea of a Christian Society]. Eliot's criticism since 1939 has been fragmentary, but it deserves special attention because of his great influence. *The Idea of a Christian Society* is "coldly intellectual."

1067. Leavis, F. R. "Approaches to T. S. Eliot." *Scrutiny* 15 (December) : 56–67. [Review of *T. S. Eliot, a Study of His Writings by Several Hands,* edited by B. Rajan]. Mingled with discriminating appraisal of the contributors to Rajan, there is much personal acidity. Important for a study of the attitude of Leavis and the *Scrutiny* group toward Eliot. Reprinted in *The Common Pursuit,* London: Chatto and Windus, 1952, pp. 278–92.

1068. Lehmann, John. "The Search for the Myth." *Penguin New Writing,* no. 30, edited by John Lehmann, pp. 152–54. New York: Penguin Books, 1947. [Four Quartets]. A few sentences on the *Four Quartets* as possessing "an elaborate system of symbols" which Lehmann admires, but in which "one cannot live."

1069. Liddell, Robert. *A Treatise on the Novel.* London: J. Cape, 1947, p. 159. On the novels of Ivy Compton-Burnett as an influence on *The Family Reunion.*

*1070. MacCallum, H. Reid. "The Waste Land after Twenty-five Years." *Here* 1 (Toronto) (December) : 16–24. A subtle reading of the poem.

1071. MacCarthy, Desmond. "Milton and Mr. Eliot." *Sun Times* (London) (November 9) , p. 3. An examination of Eliot's attitude toward Milton. Eliot answers McCarthy in the same paper on November 16, 1947, p. 6.

1072. Mankowitz, Wolf. "Notes on 'Gerontion.'" *T. S. Eliot, A Study of His Writings by Several Hands, Focus Three,* edited by B. Rajan, pp. 129-38. London: Dennis Dobson, 1947. A line-by-line analysis of the poem, treating it as specifically Christian.

*1073. Martz, Louis L. "Wheel and the Point; aspects of imagery and theme in Eliot's later poetry." *SR* 55 (January-March): 126-47. [Poems, Murder in the Cathedral]. The "rose garden" represents the "still point" in the life of the individual. Part of Martz's material is based on a conversation with Eliot. Reprinted in Unger, no. 1191.

*1074. Matthiessen, F. O. "American Poetry, 1920-1940." *SR* 55 (January-March): 31-36. An authoritative survey of Eliot's poetry and of the criticism illuminating it. He first contrasts Pound's and Eliot's poetry, to the advantage of the latter. He apologizes for Eliot's political views. Reprinted in *Literary History of the United States,* edited by Robert E. Spiller and others, New York: Macmillan, 1948, pp. 1340-43, 1355-57.

1075. Maxwell, Ian R. *Three Modern Poets. Selections from Gerard Manley Hopkins, William Butler Yeats, Thomas Stearns Eliot.* Issued by the Department of English, Melbourne, Australia, 1947. Two pages outlining Eliot's life and work, with a brief bibliography.

1076. Millen, D. J. "Tribute to 'East Coker.'" *Poetry R* 38 (December): 413. A conventional sonnet in praise of "East Coker."

1077. Moloney, Michael F. "The Critical Faith of Mr. T. S. Eliot." *Thought* 22 (June): 297-314. A summary of Eliot's critical principles.

1078. Moore, Dom Sebastian. "The Desire of God." *DownR* 65 (July): 251, 256. [Four Quartets]. On the Christian mysticism of the *Four Quartets.*

1079. O'Connor, William Van. *"Gerontion* & the *Dream of Gerontius." Furioso* 3 (Winter): 53-56. Cautiously points out parallels between John Henry Newman's poem and Eliot's.

1080. Pope, John C. "Prufrock and Raskolnikov again: a letter from Eliot." *AL* 18 (January): 319-21. Quotes a letter from Eliot correcting a detail in a theory offered (in no. 1003) and giving a comment on the growth of the poem.

1081. Porteus, Hugh Gordon. "Four Quartets." *Poetry L* 3, no. 11 (September-October) : 66–68. Slight suggestions on the relation of the poem to Taoism, to Auden, and to modern art.

1082. Rajan, B. "The Unity of the Quartets." *T. S. Eliot, A Study of His Writings by Several Hands, Focus Three,* edited by B. Rajan, pp. 78–95. London: Dennis Dobson, 1947. Valuable for hints and flashes of insight, but not as showing the unity of the *Quartets.* Most space is given to "The Dry Salvages" and "Little Gidding."

*1083. ———. ed. *T. S. Eliot, A Study of His Writings by Several Hands, Focus Three,* 153 pp. London: Dennis Dobson; New York: Funk and Wagnalls, 1947. Contents: Cleanth Brooks, "The Wasteland: An Analysis" (no. 1049) ; E. E. Duncan-Jones, "Ash Wednesday" (no. 1059) ; H. L. Gardner, "Four Quartets: a Commentary" (no. 1063) ; B. Rajan, "The Unity of the Quartets" (no. 1082) ; P. Wheelwright, "Eliot's Philosophical Themes" (no. 1095) ; Anne Ridler, "A Question of Speech" (no. 1084) ; M. C. Bradbrook, "Eliot's Critical Method" (no. 1048) ; W. Mankowitz, "Notes on Gerontion" (no. 1272) ; and a check-list of Eliot's work.

*1084. Ridler, Anne. "A Question of Speech." *T. S. Eliot: A Study of His Writings by Several Hands, Focus Three,* edited by B. Rajan, pp. 107–18. London: Dennis Dobson, 1947. A brief, good analysis by a poet of Eliot's poetic technique.

1085. Routh, H. V. Review of F. O. Matthiessen's *Achievement of T. S. Eliot. YWES, 1947* 28 (London: Oxford University Press, 1949) : 255–56. "Is not our generation taking Eliot too seriously?"

*1086. Sansom, Clive. *The Poetry of T. S. Eliot:* text of a lecture delivered to the Speech Fellowship 18 May 1946. 31 pp. London: Oxford University Press, 1947. A distinguished address on the technique of Eliot's poetry. Reviewed in *NewEW,* May 15, 1947, p. 43.

1087. Schenk, W. "The Experience and the Meaning, A Note on Eliot's 'Burnt Norton.' " *HumM* 1 (June) : 23–27. [Burnt Norton; Family Reunion]. He interprets the first five lines of the poem as a statement that will be rejected later. Schenk thinks that Eliot means that time is redeemable through religious experience.

1088. Smith, R. Gregor. "Mr. Eliot's *The Family Reunion* in the Light of Martin Buber's *I and Thou.*" *Theology* 50

(February): 59–64. A suggestive analysis of the play pointing out similar ideas in a modern theologian.

1089. Speaight, Robert. *Drama since 1939*. London: Longmans, Green & Co., for the British Council, 1947): 35–37. [Family Reunion]. Reasons why the play was successful.

*1090. Thorp, Willard. "The Poetry of T. S. Eliot." McGregor Room Seminars in Contemporary Poetry and Prose, Sponsored by the Schools of English, University of Virginia (March 21, 1947). Mimeographed, in the Eliot Collection, Houghton Library. [Gerontion; Journey of the Magi; Waste Land; Four Quartets; Hollow Men]. An excellent analysis of Eliot's poetry, centering on "Gerontion," but using the other poems also. Eliot likes to speak through a mask, to use clear visual images having symbolic meaning, and one of his characteristic themes is experience, "which has undergone a profound transformation in his later work."

1091. Tindall, William York. "The Forest of Symbols." *Forces in Modern British Literature 1885–1946*, pp. 224–82 and *passim*. New York: Knopf, 1947. Tindall is patronizing.

1092. ———. "The Recantation of T. S. Eliot." *ASch* 16 (Autumn): 431–37. [Milton]. Defends Eliot's consistency in his poetry and prose, using his attitude toward Milton as his example. He thinks that Eliot's recantation is limited.

1093. Tuve, Rosemond. *Elizabethan and Metaphysical Imagery*. Chicago: University of Chicago Press, 1947. A number of incidental comparisons of Eliot's metaphysical imagery with that of the sixteenth and seventeenth centuries. A good note (p. 414) on the luminosity of some of Eliot's later images.

1094. Waters, Leonard Adrian. *Coleridge and Eliot: a Comparative Study of Their Theories of Poetic Composition*, 390 pp. Ann Arbor, Mich.: Microfilm, no. 1081, 1948. This dissertation concludes that humanistic principles uniting Eliot and Coleridge are more important than their differences.

*1095. Wheelwright, Philip. "Eliot's Philosophical Themes." *T. S. Eliot: a Study of His Writings by Several Hands, Focus Three*, edited by B. Rajan, pp. 96–106. London: Dennis Dobson, 1947. [Four Quartets]. The themes of the *Quartets* are to be found in the Heracletian paradox that the way up and the way down are one and the same, fused with the idea of the Hindu philosophy of Krishna concerning rebirth through discipline and concentration. The essay raises interesting questions.

1096. Wilson, Edmund. "The Essays of V. S. Pritchett—The Journals of Baudelaire." *NY* 23 (November 1) : 93–96. Disagrees with Auden and Eliot, who emphasize Baudelaire's Christianity.

1948

1097. Aiken, Conrad. "King Bolo and Others." *T. S. Eliot: a Symposium,* edited by R. March and Tambimuttu, pp. 20–23. London: Editions Poetry, 1948. Personal reminiscences of Eliot's early years at Harvard and in London.

1098. Anceschi, Luciano. "T. S. Eliot and Philosophical Poetry." *T. S. Eliot: a Symposium,* edited by R. March and Tambimuttu, pp. 154–66. London: Editions Poetry, 1948. A restatement of the truisms about Eliot's poetry.

1099. Angioletti, G. B. "Encounters with Mr. Eliot," translated by G. S. Fraser. *T. S. Eliot: a Symposium,* edited by R. March and Tambimuttu, pp. 138–40. London: Editions Poetry, 1948. On Eliot's influence in Italy.

1100. Anon. Editorial, *HAB* 51 (December 4) : 258. On the occasion of the announcement of the Nobel Prize to Eliot; an appreciation.

1101. ———. "1,000 Lost Golf Balls." *Time* 52, pt. 2 (November 15) : 32. Condensed summary of Eliot's career, on the occasion of his receiving the Nobel Prize. Refers to him as the "greatest living poet."

1102. ———. "The Year in Books." *Time* 52, pt. 2 (December 20) : 101. A short paragraph saying that he deserves the Nobel Prize.

1103. ———. "Time and Tide Diary." *TT* 29 (January 10) : 37. Praise for Eliot on his being awarded the Order of Merit.

1104. ———. "A Vision of Humanity." *TLS,* no. 2445 (December 11) , p. 691. [Notes towards the Definition of Culture]. A long article lacking in clarity.

1105. ———. "Leisure and Culture." *TLS,* no. 2445 (December 11) , p. 697. [Notes towards the Definition of Culture]. An editorial reflecting the writer's doubt and confusion.

1106. Auden, W. H. "For T. S. Eliot." *T. S. Eliot: a Symposium,* edited by R. March and Tambimuttu, p. 43. London:

Editions Poetry, 1948. A poem praising Eliot for expressing the "thirst and fear" of a generation.

1107. Barker, George. "Verses for the Sixtieth Birthday of
Thomas Stearns Eliot." *T. S. Eliot: a Symposium*, edited
by R. March and Tambimuttu, pp. 136–37. London:
Editions Poetry, 1948. Four stanzas of verse.

1108. Barry, Sister Mary Martin. *An Analysis of the Prosodic
Structure of Selected Poems of T. S. Eliot*, 135 pp.
Washington, D.C.: Catholic University of America,
1948. An elaborate statistical analysis of the prosody.

1109. Belgion, Montgomery. "Irving Babbitt and the Conti-
nent." *T. S. Eliot: a Symposium*, edited by R. March
and Tambimuttu, pp. 51–59. London: Editions Poetry,
1948. A roundabout essay on Babbitt's relations with
French authors and with Eliot; also on Eliot's relations
with the French symbolists.

1110. Bell, Clive. "How Pleasant to Know Mr. Eliot." *T. S.
Eliot: a Symposium*, edited by R. March and Tambimuttu, pp. 15–19. London: Editions Poetry, 1948. Anecdotes about Eliot's clothes, his wit, and his versified
addresses on letters.

1111. Berryman, John. "Poetry Chronicle: Waiting for the End,
Boys." *PR* 15, no. 2 (February) : 254–67. The essay includes some short passages on Eliot's influence on the
younger poets, which he says is diminishing.

1112. ———. "A Peine ma Piste." *PR* 15, no. 7 (July) : 826–28.
A lively review, suggesting that in the end Eliot's poetry
may prove to be personal.

1113. Betjeman, John. "The Usher of Highgate Junior School."
T. S. Eliot: a Symposium, edited by R. March and Tam-
bimuttu, pp. 89–92. London: Editions Poetry, 1948.
Thin reminiscences of Eliot as a schoolmaster.

1114. Blisset, William. "T. S. Eliot." *CF* 28 (July) : 86–87. A
good, brief introduction telling what Eliot's poetry has
meant to the writer. The excitement of reading Eliot is
first that of recognition and then of dread.

1115. Bose, Amalendu. "T. S. Eliot and Bengali Poetry." *T. S.
Eliot: a Symposium*, edited by R. March and Tambimuttu, pp. 225–30. London: Editions Poetry, 1948.
"Since 1930, the archetypal influences on Bengali poetry
are those of Eliot and Tagore . . . and it is a nice question as to whose influence cuts deeper."

1116. Bottrall, Ronald. "Dead Ends." *T. S. Eliot: a Symposium*, edited by R. March and Tambimuttu, pp. 71–72. London: Editions Poetry, 1948. An imitation of Eliot's earlier poetic style.

1117. Brace, Marjorie. "Dying into Life." *SatR* 31 (June 19): 17. [Review of Unger, *T. S. Eliot: a Selected Critique*]. Eliot has critics who regard him as merely weak or deluded; others, more intelligent, who regard him as a propagandist who puts more emphasis on dying than on living; others see him as a man "disciplined, rather than defeated, by the knowledge of good and evil," and his most sensitive critics "realize that his theme is a basic pattern of guilt, remorse, and redemption, which cannot be intellectually legislated out of existence."

1118. Breit, Harvey. "An Interview with T. S. Eliot—and Excerpts from His Birthday Book." *NYTBR* (November 21), p. 3. The interview quotes Eliot on his reputation for obscurity, on Gide, American football, and his work with Faber and Faber.

1119. Brotman, D. Bosley. "T. S. Eliot: 'The Music of Ideas.'" *UTQ* 18 (October): 20–29. The basic musical structure of "East Coker" is analyzed in general terms. Suggestive, but not entirely satisfactory.

1120. Brown, Wallace Cable. "A Poem Should Not Mean But Be." *UKCR* 15 (Autumn): 61–62. [Boston Evening Transcript]. An elucidation of the poem.

*1121. Browne, E. Martin. "The Dramatic Verse of T. S. Eliot." *T. S. Eliot: a Symposium,* edited by R. March and Tambimuttu, pp. 196–207. London: Editions Poetry, 1948. The producer of Eliot's plays presents a good technical analysis of the dramatic verse from *The Rock* through *The Family Reunion.*

1122. Cecchi, Emilio. "A Meeting with Eliot," translated by Bernard Wall. *T. S. Eliot: a Symposium,* edited by R. March and Tambimuttu, pp. 73–76. London: Editions Poetry, 1948.

1123. Chew, Samuel C. "Poetry in the Twentieth Century." *A Literary History of England,* edited by A. C. Baugh, pp. 1585–87. New York: Appleton-Century Crofts, 1948. Two-and-a-half pages of textbook criticism, grudging in tone.

1124. Coghill, Nevill. "Sweeney Agonistes (an Anecdote or Two)." *T. S. Eliot: a Symposium,* edited by R. March and Tambimuttu, pp. 82–87. London: Editions Poetry,

1948. Report of a conversation with Eliot concerning a London production of *Sweeney*.

1125. Curtius, Ernst Robert. "T. S. Eliot and Germany," translated by Richard March. *T. S. Eliot: a Symposium*, edited by R. March and Tambimuttu, pp. 119–25. London: Editions Poetry, 1948. Deplores the fact that in the 1940s Eliot and Germany did not understand one another.

1126. Dey, Bishnu. "Mr. Eliot among the Arjunas." *T. S. Eliot: a Symposium*, edited by R. March and Tambimuttu, pp. 96–102. London: Editions Poetry, 1948. An essay on Eliot's influence in India.

1127. Dukes, Ashley. "T. S. Eliot in the Theatre." *T. S. Eliot: a Symposium*, edited by R. March and Tambimuttu, pp. 111–18. London: Editions Poetry, 1948. Concerning the conditions of first production of *Murder in the Cathedral*, with some literary criticism of *The Family Reunion*.

1128. Dupee, F. W. "Surveying T. S. Eliot." *Nation* 166 (June 19) : 696–97. [Unger's *T. S. Eliot: a Selected Critique*].

1129. Durrell, Lawrence. "Anniversary." *T. S. Eliot: a Symposium*, edited by R. March and Tambimuttu, p. 88. London: Editions Poetry, 1948. A poem in honor of Eliot.

1130. Empsom, William. "The Style of the Master." *T. S. Eliot: a Symposium*, edited by R. March and Tambimuttu, pp. 35–37. London: Editions Poetry, 1948. Four or five anecdotes of Eliot's conversation.

*1131. Evans, B. Ifor. "T. S. Eliot." *English Literature between the Wars*, pp. 91–101. London: Methuen and Co., 1948. [Prufrock; Waste Land; Journey of the Magi; The Rock; Murder in the Cathedral]. An excellent essay on Eliot's relations to Hulme and I. A. Richards; on his influence in the 1920s; on his attitude toward romanticism and religion.

1132. Every, Brother George. "The Way of Rejections." *T. S. Eliot: a Symposium*, edited by R. March and Tambimuttu, pp. 181–88. London: Editions Poetry, 1948. A discussion of Eliot's political and religious point of view by an Anglican priest.

1133. Flint, R. W. "The Four Quartets Reconsidered." *SR* 56 (Winter) : 69–81. "I hope . . . to clarify somewhat Eliot's position in the religious and philosophical controversies which have become more real to us since the *Quartets* first appeared." Useful explanation.

*1134. Fluchère, Henri. "Défense de la Lucidité." *T. S. Eliot: a Symposium,* edited by R. March and Tambimuttu, pp. 141–45. London: Editions Poetry, 1948. A sensitive and well-balanced appreciation of Eliot's critical method.

1135. "Four Winds," "Time and Tide Diary." *TT* 29 (December 4) : 1227. [After Strange Gods; Notes towards the Definition of Culture]. Refers to the argument between Eliot and Quiller-Couch on tradition and orthodoxy, and suggests that they are not really opposed.

1136. Fowlie, Wallace. "The Child: Eliot and Tchelitchew." *The Clown's Grail. A Study of Love in Its Literary Expression,* pp. 146–54. Denver: Alan Swallow, 1948. [Four Quartets]. Written in poetic prose, this highly personal, subjective study contains flashes of clear insight.

1137. Fraser, G. S. "A Language by Itself." *T. S. Eliot: a Symposium,* edited by R. March and Tambimuttu, pp. 167–77. London: Editions Poetry, 1948. [Ash Wednesday; Four Quartets]. An analysis of the conversational language of the earlier poetry and the "language by itself" of "Ash Wednesday" and *Four Quartets.*

1138. ———. "Mr. Eliot and the Great Cats." *Adam* (London) 16 (May) : 10–14. On tigers as symbolizing the destructive human instincts in Eliot's poetry.

1139. Fry, Edith. "The Poetic Work of T. S. Eliot." *BrAL* 5 (London: British Authors' Press, 1948) :8–14. An attempt without any central point of view to cover Eliot's entire career.

1140. Glicksberg, Charles I. "T. S. Eliot as Critic." *ArQ* 4 (Autumn) : 225–36. "Religion gained a powerful advocate and literary criticism lost a great critic when Eliot embraced Anglo-Catholicism." Typical of many essays presenting this point of view.

1141. Hamburger, Michael. "T. S. Eliot." *T. S. Eliot: a Symposium,* edited by R. March and Tambimuttu, p. 178. London: Editions Poetry, 1948. A poem.

1142. Hawkins, Desmond. "The Pope of Russell Square." *T. S. Eliot: a Symposium,* edited by R. March and Tambimuttu, pp. 44–47. London: Editions Poetry, 1948. Superficial personal reminiscences.

1143. Heath-Stubbs, John. "We Have Heard the Key Turn." *T. S. Eliot: a Symposium,* edited by R. March and Tambimuttu, pp. 236–42. London: Editions Poetry, 1948. Eliot's poetry is unified from the earliest to the latest by the presence of "the abyss," "making men more real by compelling them to face nothingness." The thesis is not well developed.

1144. Hernigman, Bernard. "Two Worlds and Epiphany." *BR* 2 (May) : 156–59. [Four Quartets]. A comparison with Wallace Stevens's *Ideas of Order, Parts of a World,* and *Transport to Summer.*

1145. Hyman, Stanley Edgar. "T. S. Eliot and Tradition in Criticism." *The Armed Vision,* pp. 73–91, 97–105. New York: Knopf, 1948. Announces that his intention is to study the method of the criticism, and not the critic. Hyman's point of view is that of the political left. "The doctrine of tradition in Eliot's criticism seems primarily a weapon for achieving an unattractive society."

*1146. Iyengar, K. R. Srinivasa. "The Crystal Vase." *NewD* (Bombay) (November 26) , pp. 11–13. A clear and lively review of Eliot's work from the beginning.

1147. Lewis, Wyndham. "Early London Environment." *T. S. Eliot: a Symposium,* edited by R. March and Tambimuttu, pp. 24–32. London: Editions Poetry, 1948. Tells of Ezra Pound's friendship for Eliot in 1914 and later.

1148. Ludowyk, E. F. C. "T. S. Eliot in Ceylon." *T. S. Eliot: a Symposium,* edited by R. March and Tambimuttu, pp. 103–5. London: Editions Poetry, 1948. Says that "though the influence was not considerable, it was important."

1149. MacCallum, H. Reid. *Time Lost and Regained. The Theme of Eliot's 'Four Quartets.'* 26 pp. (mimeographed) . Toronto: Convent Book Room, 1948. Reprinted in *Imitation and Design and Other Essays,* edited by W. Blisset, Toronto,1953. A provocative analysis which becomes needlessly complicated.

1150. MacNeice, Louis. "Eliot and the Adolescent." *T. S. Eliot: a Symposium,* edited by R. March and Tambimuttu, pp. 146–51. London: Editions Poetry, 1948. What Eliot meant to eighteen-year-old readers in 1926. "The Waste Land . . . was the poem . . . which most altered our conception of poetry and, I think one can add, of life."

1151. Magny, Claude E. "A Double Note on T. S. Eliot and James Joyce," translated by Sonia Brownell. *T. S. Eliot: a Symposium,* edited by R. March and Tambimuttu, pp. 208–17. London: Editions Poetry, 1948. In spite of some misconceptions, Magny is suggestive and provocative.

1152. March, Richard. "A Journey to the Center of the Earth." *T. S. Eliot: a Symposium,* edited by R. March and Tambimuttu, pp. 249–59. London: Editions Poetry, 1948. [Little Gidding]. An allegory relating how Eliot tries to teach Stetson something about God.

1153. ——, and Tambimuttu, eds., *T. S. Eliot: a Symposium from Conrad Aiken and Others,* 259 pp. London: Editions Poetry, 1948; Chicago: Regnery, 1949. This collection of forty-seven essays and poems consists of "reminiscences from those who were intimately associated with Mr. Eliot at various times," and of essays describing the influence which Eliot had on the writers. They are very unequal in value. Each is entered separately in this bibliography.

1154. Meyerhoff, Hans. "Mr. Eliot's Evening Service." PR 15 (January) : 131–38. An account by a non-Anglican of Eliot's report on English Church affairs at a parish-house meeting in Washington, D. C.

1155. Mims, Edwin. "Contemporary Poets: T. S. Eliot." *The Christ of the Poets,* pp. 212–16. New York: Abingdon-Cokesbury Press, 1948. Finds that Eliot is more interested in the Church than in Christ; his belief is an affair of the intellect, not of the emotions.

1156. Montale, Eugenio. "Eliot and Ourselves," translated by Bernard Wall. *T. S. Eliot: a Symposium,* edited by R. March and Tambimuttu, pp. 190–95. London: Editions Poetry, 1948. A difficult essay on Eliot's international reputation.

1157. Moore, Marianne. "A Virtuoso of Make-Believe." *T. S. Eliot: a Symposium,* edited by R. March and Tambimuttu, pp. 179–80. London: Editions Poetry, 1948. Suggests half humorously that Eliot might have become a short-story writer.

1158. Moore, Nicholas. "Three Poems for Mr. Eliot: Muse as Bicyclist; Bathcubes; Portrait of Mr. Eliot à la Mode." *T. S. Eliot: a Symposium,* edited by R. March and Tambimuttu, pp. 48–50. London: Editions Poetry, 1948.

1159. Morley, F. V. "T. S. Eliot as a Publisher." *T. S. Eliot: a Symposium,* edited by R. March and Tambimuttu, pp. 60–70. London: Editions Poetry, 1948. Written in the style of a detective story, this article contains some interesting anecdotes of Eliot's days with the firm of Faber and Gwyer.

1160. Muir, Edwin. "A Tribute." *T. S. Eliot: a Symposium,* edited by R. March and Tambimuttu, pp. 152–53. London: Editions Poetry, 1948. A guarded tribute.

1161. Nicholson, Norman. "Words and Imagery." *T. S. Eliot: a Symposium,* edited by R. March and Tambimuttu, pp. 231–34. London: Editions Poetry, 1948. When, at the age of twenty, he first encountered Eliot's poems, "the modern world came into focus for the first time."

1162. O'Connor, William Van. *Sense and Sensibility in Modern Poetry.* Chicago: University of Chicago Press, 1948. This study attempts to follow out the results of the "dissociation of sensibility" in modern poetry which came about through the influence of science. O'Connor considers Eliot's successful use of myth, prose idiom, French symbolism, the metaphysical poets, irony, and obscurity.

1163. Orwell, George. "Culture and Classes." *Observer* (London) (November 28), p. 4 [Notes towards the Definition of Culture]. Suggests that Eliot may be too pessimistic about the future.

1164. Osterling, Anders. "The 1948 Nobel Prize for Literature." *Les Prix Nobel en 1948* (Stockholm, 1949), pp. 48–51; Gustof Hellstrom, "Toast to Eliot," pp. 55–56. Solemn eulogies of Eliot's achievements, on the occasion of his receiving the Nobel Prize.

1165. Pope, Myrtle. "Eliot's Gerontion." *Expl* 6, no. 7 (May): Q 16. A question concerning the proper names, showing confusion as to the meaning of the poem.

1166. Porteus, Hugh Gordon. "Resurrection in the Crypt." *T. S. Eliot: a Symposium,* edited by R. March and Tambimuttu, pp. 218–24. London: Editions Poetry, 1948. Eliot as a member of a "Quartet" composed of W. Lewis, Joyce, Pound, and himself.

1167. Praz, Mario. "T. S. Eliot and Eugenio Montale." *T. S. Eliot: a Symposium,* edited by R. March and Tambimuttu, pp. 244–48. London: Editions Poetry, 1948. Points out an affinity between the two poets.

1168. Raine, Kathleen. "The Poet of Our Time." *T. S. Eliot: a Symposium,* edited by R. March and Tambimuttu, pp. 78–81. London: Editions Poetry, 1948. On Eliot's influence as a poet, critic, and person. Good.

1169. Rees, Goronwy. "Modest Proposal." *Spectator* 181, no. 6282 (November 19) : 666. [Notes towards the Definition of Culture]. A cautious and noncommittal review. Points out that Eliot has often had the most influence on his antagonists.

1170. Reeves, James. "Cambridge Twenty Years Ago." *T. S. Eliot: a Symposium,* edited by R. March and Tambimuttu, pp. 38–42. London: Editions Poetry, 1948. Concerning the powerful effect of Eliot on Cambridge undergraduates of the late 1920s.

1171. Ribalow, Harold U. "T. S. Eliot—Poet and Prejudice." *ConW* 15 (November 15) : 7–8. "For the second year in succession the Nobel Prize for Literature has been awarded to a man . . . known for anti-democratic and anti-Semitic tendencies."

1172. Ridler, Anne. "I Who am Here Dissembled." *T. S. Eliot: a Symposium,* edited by R. March and Tambimuttu, p. 189. London: Editions Poetry, 1948. Says poetically that Eliot's poems can give comfort.

1173. Schoeck, R. J. "T. S. Eliot, Mary Queen of Scots, and Guillaume de Machaut." MLN 63 (March) : 187–88. [East Coker]. On the sources of the opening phrase of "East Coker."

1174. Seferis, George. "T. S. Eliot in Greece," translated by Nanos Valaoritis. *T. S. Eliot: a Symposium,* edited by R. March and Tambimuttu, pp. 126–35. London: Editions Poetry, 1948. A fine essay, distinguished in thought and expression; assumes a knowledge of Eliot's poetry.

1175. Severs, Kenneth. "Imagery and Drama." *DUJ* 41 (December) : 24–33. [Waste Land]. In an essay primarily on imagery as used by the dramatist, there is an extended section on the imagery of *The Waste Land,* especially the literary allusions drawn from mythology.

1176. Sickels, Eleanor M. "Eliot's Wasteland." *Expl* 7, no. 3 (December) : item 20. An explanation of the levels of meaning in the line "Hurry up please its time."

1177. Sisson, C. H. "Views and Reviews. What Is Culture?" *NewEW* 34 (December 2) : 91–92. [Notes towards the Definition of Culture]. Suggests that he still sees English society from the outside.

1178. Sitwell, Edith. "For T. S. Eliot." *T. S. Eliot: a Symposium,* edited by R. March and Tambimuttu, pp. 33–34.

London: Editions Poetry, 1948. A poem comparing Eliot to Prometheus.

*1179. Sitwell, Osbert. *Laughter in the Next Room,* pp. 32–33. London: Macmillan, 1949; Boston: Little, Brown, 1948. A vivid and interesting picture of Eliot's appearance and manners in 1917, stressing his courtesy and the rhythm of his movements.

*1180. Smith, Francis J. "Eliot—out of the 'Waste Land.'" *America* 80 (December 11): 265–66. [Waste Land; Four Quartets]. He emphasizes the continuity of mood in the two poems; popular but sound.

1181. Smith, Grover. "T. S. Eliot and Sherlock Holmes." *N&Q* 193 (October 2): 431–32. Identifies a passage in *Murder in the Cathedral* as having its source in A. Conan Doyle's *The Musgrave Ritual.*

1182. Speaight, Robert. "Mr. Eliot's Birthday Party; a Tribute from His Friends." *Tablet* 192 (October 30): 279–80. Review of March and Tambimuttu's *T. S. Eliot: a Symposium.* "There are reminiscences to surprise and delight on every page. . . . It is, however, much more than this, for it contains a good deal of acute criticism as well as affectionate homage." Mr. Speaight adds interesting reminiscences and anecdotes.

1183. Spender, Stephen. "Speaking to the Dead in the Language of the Dead." *T. S. Eliot: a Symposium,* edited by R. March and Tambimuttu, pp. 106–10. London: Editions Poetry, 1948. A poem of artistic integrity. (Appeared also in *HAB,* June 26, 1948.)

1184. Spiller, Robert E., ed. "Bibliographies: Individual Authors." *Literary History of the United States.* vol. 3, pp. 488–92. New York: Macmillan Company, 1948. Bibliography of Eliot's separate works, collections and reprints, and biography and criticism.

1185. Stanford, Derek. "The Example of T. S. Eliot." *Poetry R* 39 (February): 71–77. "The regeneration of English verse which Eliot undertook at this juncture [1914] demanded three significant changes: a change of subject matter, a change of attitude, and . . . a change of style." "Eliot's earlier verse, since we live in a . . . climate of negation, has more meaning for us than Yeats'."

1186. Tambimuttu. "O What a Beautiful Morning." from "Natarajah: a poem for Mr. T. S. Eliot." *T. S. Eliot: a Symposium,* edited by R. March and Tambimuttu, p.

77. London: Editions Poetry, 1948. The poem begins "Life is the address between awning and yawning."

1187. Todd, Ruthven. "A Garland for Mr. Eliot." *T. S. Eliot: a Symposium,* edited by R. March and Tambimuttu, p. 235. London: Editions Poetry, September. A poem.

1188. Toynbee, Philip. "The Flight of the Eagle." *NSN* 36 October 9) : 308. [Review of March and Tambimuttu's *T. S. Eliot: a Symposium*]. Dwells on the irony of Eliot's great reputation now in comparison with the first twenty-five years, when he was a "literary outlaw."

*1189. Traversi, Derek. " 'The Waste Land' Revisited: a Critical Analysis of Mr. Eliot's Work." *DubR,* no. 443 (Second Quarter) , 106–23. [Waste Land]. A close analysis, section by section, of the meaning of the poem. Excellently digests and presents the modern criticisms.

1190. Turner, E. S. *Boys Will Be Boys,* pp. 37–47. London: M. Joseph, 1948. On the identity of Sweeney.

*1191. Unger, Leonard, ed. *T. S. Eliot: a Selected Critique,* 478 pp. New York: Rinehart and Company, 1948. Contains thirty-one articles, reprinted in whole or in part, well selected and with an interesting preface on the main critical attitudes toward Eliot. Each article is listed separately in this bibliography, under date of first publication. The volume contains a bibliography of 268 items. See reviews of Unger in *PR* 15: 826–28; *ArQ* 4: 374; *HudR* 2: 146–47; *Nation* 166 (June 19) : 696–97; *SatR* 31 (June 19) : 17.

1192. Walcutt, Charles Child. "Eliot's 'Whispers of Immortality.' " *Expl* 7, no. 2 (November) : Q 11. A tentative explanation of the poem; sensible. (See no. 1212.)

1193. Watkins, Vernon. "To T. S. Eliot." *T. S. Eliot: a Symposium,* edited by R. March and Tambimuttu, p. 243. London: Editions Poetry, 1948. A calm and lucid tribute.

1194. Weber, Brom. *Hart Crane.* (New York: The Bodley Press, 1948) . Shows that although by 1922 Eliot's overpowering influence on Crane is over, Crane had a continuing interest in Eliot's criticism.

1195. Wedgwood, C. V. "Culture Defined." *TT* 29 (November 6) : 128. [Notes towards the Definition of Culture]. A friendly summary of the volume.

*1196. Wilson, Francis A. C. C. *Six Essays on the Development of T. S. Eliot,* 65 pp. London: Fortune Press, 1948. Short critical bibliography. The function of these essays is "to provide a brief introduction to Eliot's poetry and to the plays." Scholarly, well-balanced criticism.

1197. Wyndham, S. J. "Outline for a Critical Approach to T. S. Eliot as Critic." *ConI* 1 (Winter) : 106–16. "In developing backwards towards the Middle Ages as the source of his ideas—dogmatic, irrational, authoritarian, and having their material source in serfdom, Eliot is supplying in advance the ideological needs of capitalism, the retrogressive movement toward totalitarianism." This essay is one of the most extended statements of the point of view that Eliot is a fascist.

1198. Yarros, Victor S. "Phoenix Nest." *SatR* 31 (August 7) : 40. A letter, with a reply by W. R. Benét. Yarros protests that Eliot is not concerned with "our crucial problems." Yarros prefers humanism to Christianity. Benét defends Eliot.

1199. ———. "Debunking Poet Eliot." *AF,* no. 2114 (November), p. 7. A superficial attack on Eliot for asserting that a non-Christian civilization will fail, and for saying that while prose may deal with ideals, poetry must deal with the actual.

1200. Zabel, Morton D. "Summary in Criticism." *Literary History of the United States,* edited by Robert E. Spiller, Willard Thorp, and others, pp. 1368–69. New York: Macmillan, 1948. Eliot is the dominating figure in aesthetic analysis in the United States since 1925.

1949

1201. Anon. "Eliot on Lambeth." *Isis,* no. 1096 (February 2), p. 14. An account of Eliot's criticism of the weaknesses in the Report of the Lambeth Conference.

1202. ———. Letters to the editor regarding the Bollingen Award. *PR* 16 (July) 764–66. Two of the letters, from Henry A. Woodfin, Jr., and Robert Fitzgerald, contain references to Eliot's supposed anti-Semitism.

1203. ———. "T. S. Eliot and Posterity." *SatR* 32 (April 16) : 31. Letters from A. E. Johnson and Henry Taylor regarding Ben Ray Redman's article. (See no. 1274.)

1204. ———. "Back to the Waste Land." *Time* 53 (March 21) : 104 ff. [Notes towards the Definition of Culture]. "What makes this book so valuable is the fact that there is enough meat in it to keep thoughtful readers growling over it indefinitely."

1205. ———. "White Fire." *Time* 53 (May 30): 60. On the newest portrait of Eliot, by Wyndham Lewis.

1206. ———. "New Play in Edinburgh." *Time* 54 (September 5): 58. [Cocktail Party]. A factual account of the revision of the play and a summary of criticisms.

1207. Auden, W. H. "Port and Nuts with the Eliots." *NY* 25 (April 23): 92–97. [Notes towards the Definition of Culture]. A hurried review, written apparently against the grain.

1208. Bantock, G. H. "Mr. Eliot and Education." *Scrutiny* 16 (March): 64–70. [Notes towards the Definition of Culture]. A rambling essay objecting to Eliot's implication that the achievement of culture should be without self-consciousness. (See no. 1401.)

*1209. Barrett, William. "Aristocracy and/or Christianity." *KR* 11 (Summer): 489–96. [Notes towards the Definition of Culture]. Examines the assumptions behind Eliot's argument, and finds that he has not been thoroughgoing in considering them. Compares him unfavorably with Nietzsche and Ortega y Gasset. A thoughtful review. Reprinted in *The Kenyon Critics,* edited by John Crowe Ransom, 1951, pp. 324–33.

1210. Baum, Bernard. "Willa Cather's Waste Land." *SAQ* 48 (October): 589–601. "There is . . . a remarkably close similarity of ideological web in her most significant fiction and Eliot's poetry."

1211. Benét, William Rose. "Correspondence: Ezra Pound, Continued." *NR* 121 (October 17): 4. In answer to Malcolm Cowley's (no. 1225) defense of Eliot in the Bollingen Prize controversy, Benét points that Eliot and Pound are old friends.

1212. Bernardete, José A. "Eliot's Water Imagery; an adventure in symbolism." *Occidental,* no. 7 (September), pp. 1–6. Traces the use of water imagery in six of the poems; suggestive for the serious student.

1213. Blackmur, R. P. "T. S. Eliot on Culture." *Nation* 168 (April 23): 475–76. [Notes towards the Definition of Culture]. An ardent defense of Eliot's ideas, particularly that "culture is the incarnation of the religion of a people."

1214. Bowra, C. M. "T. S. Eliot, 'The Waste Land.'" *The Creative Experiment,* pp. 159–88. London: Macmillan, 1949. Admires the poem, but brings no fresh understanding to it.

1215. Bradford, Curtis B. "Journeys to Byzantium." *VQR* 25 (Spring) : 214–25. [Waste Land; Four Quartets]. The Eliot portion of this essay, which includes Yeats, is chiefly a much simplified summary of the *Four Quartets*.

1216. Breit, Harvey. "Talk with Mr. Hanford." *NYTBR* (November 6) , p. 12. A brief, acid comment by J. H. Hanford on Eliot's attitude toward Milton.

*1217. Brombert, Victor H. *The Criticism of T. S. Eliot: Problems of an 'Impersonal Theory' of Poetry,* 42 pp. New Haven: Yale University Press, 1949. Traces the changes in Eliot's theory from his early insistence that the question of belief should not enter into the reading of a poem to his admission that the view of life presented may influence the reader's judgment. A clear statement of Eliot's views and the aesthetic difficulty in which they involve him.

*1218. Bush, Douglas. "No Small Program." *VQR* 25 (Spring) : 287–90. [Notes towards the Definition of Culture]. A brief but lucid analysis of the content of the book, with some sympathetic criticism.

1219. H. C. [Hayden Carruth]. "A Few Notes on the Recent Essays of Mr. Robert Hillyer." *Poetry* 74 (August) : 283–85. A general defense of modern poets and critics against Hillyer's attack in *SatR*.

1220. Catlin, George. "T. S. Eliot and the Moral Issue." *SatR* 32 (July 2) : 7–8, 36–38. [Notes towards the Definition of Culture]. A temperate and careful analysis of Eliot's attitude toward democracy.

1221. Clark, John Abbot. "On First Looking into Benson's *Fitzgerald*." *SAQ* 48 (April) : 258–69. He exaggerates the influence of Benson's biography of Fitzgerald on Eliot's earlier poems.

1222. Cleophas, Sister Mary. "Eliot's Whispers of Immortality." *Expl* 8, no. 3 (December) : item 22. A philosophical interpretation. (See also no. 1192.)

1223. Colby, Reginald. "Murder in the Cathedral. Mr. Eliot's Reception in Berlin." *Tablet* 194 (November 12) : 311. Quotes the article in the Berlin Soviet sector magazine *Roland von Berlin,* by Walter Kaul, abusing Eliot, the play, and the church.

1224. Cowley, Malcolm. "T. S. Eliot's Ardent Critics—and Mr. Eliot." *NYHTB* (March 13) , pp. 1–2. "His production is slender, but he keeps the scholars busy."

1225. ———. "The Battle over Ezra Pound." *NR* 121 (October 3) : 18. A brief defense of Eliot against Robert Hillyer's attack on his politics. (See nos. 1249, 1250.)

1226. Daiches, David. "T. S. Eliot." *YR* 38 (March) : 460–70. Eliot is a social snob in his prose, but in his poetry has achieved fine effects in representing the mood of the Waste Land and the "note of quiet hope" suggested by contemplative inward emotion.

1227. Davis, Robert Gorham. "Culture, Religion, and Mr. Eliot." *PR* 16 (July) : 750–53. [Notes towards the Definition of Culture]. A rather confused though earnest discussion of some of the issues raised by this volume.

1228. ———. "The New Criticism and the Democratic Tradition." *ASch* 19 (Winter, 1949–50) : 9–19. A highly controversial article identifying the New Criticism with the anti-democratic movement, and Eliot with the New Criticism.

1229. Dawson, Christopher. "Mr. T. S. Eliot on the Meaning of Culture." *Month* 1, n.s. (March) : 151–57. [Notes towards the Definition of Culture]. Agrees with Eliot's point of view except that Eliot does not give enough weight to the "necessary transcendence of the religious faith" over the cultural. Also in a precise analysis he distinguishes Eliot's "defense of culture" from Matthew Arnold's.

1230. Douglas, Wallace, Lamson, Roy, and Smith, Hallett. *The Critical Reader*, pp. 125–30. New York: W. W. Norton and Co., 1949. [Gerontion]. An elementary, clear explanation of the poem.

*1231. Drew, Elizabeth. *T. S. Eliot: the Design of His Poetry,* 216 pp. New York: Scribner's, 1949. A well-controlled Jungian analysis, sometimes over-subtle, but always suggestive. One of the major works of criticism of Eliot. Reviewed in *Nation* 169 (July 9, 1949) : 42–43; *HudR* 2: 473–77; *WR* 14 (1949) : 71–72; *Poetry* 75 (November 1949) : 112–13.

1232. Duffey, Bernard. "Eliot's Complete Concert and Related Matters." *WR* 14 (Fall) : 71–72. [Drew's *T. S. Eliot: the Design of His Poetry*]. He is interested chiefly in Miss Drew's method.

1233. Edman, Irwin. "T. S. Eliot's Sociology." *NYTBR* (March 6) , pp. 3, 22. [Notes towards the Definition of Culture]. He is annoyed by Eliot's conservatism.

*1234. Fergusson, Francis. "Hamlet as an Artistic Failure." *HudR*

2 (Summer) : 166–70. A thoughtful objection to Eliot's assertion that *Hamlet* is an artistic failure.

*1235. ———. "Murder in the Cathedral: The Theological Scene." *The Idea of a Theater,* pp. 210–22. Princeton, N.J.: Princeton University Press, 1949. A specialized and suggestive study of the dramatic structure of the play. It "is unique in our time, and it is therefore more important to investigate what kind of thing it is (and is not) than to reach any judgment of its ultimate value as drama."

1236. Fiedler, Leslie A. "Understanding Eliot." *Nation* 169 (July 9) : 42–43. [Drew's *T. S. Eliot: the Design of His Poetry*]. The book is clear, but "as an application of Jungian concepts to the body of Eliot's work it marks merely a beginning."

1237. Forster, E. M. "The Three T. S. Eliots." *Listener* 41 (January 20) : 111. [Notes towards the Definition of Culture]. Eliot's definition of culture suffers from inconclusiveness and religious dogmatism.

*1238. Frankenberg, Lloyd. "Time and Mr. Eliot." *Pleasure Dome,* pp. 39–117. Boston: Houghton-Mifflin, 1949. [The early poems; Waste Land; Four Quartets; the plays]. A suggestive and penetrating essay.

*1239. Gardner, Helen Louise. *The Art of T. S. Eliot,* 186 pp. London: Cresset Press, 1949. A serious and illuminating study, worth the patient reading which it demands. Reviewed in *Britain Today,* no. 164, December, pp. 14–18; *Poetry,* October, 41–47.

*1240. Graves, Robert. *The Common Asphodel, Collected Essays on Poetry, 1922–1949.* London: Hamish Hamilton, 1949. A good explanation of "Burbank with a Baedeker," pp. 154–58; comment on *Murder in the Cathedral,* pp. 286–88; *The Rock,* pp. 288–89. Technical notes by a poet.

1241. I. H. "Mr. T. S. Eliot's New Play." *Manchester Guardian* (August 23) , p. 3. [Cocktail Party]. The provenance of this play is in the *Four Quartets.* "Eliot's difficult, extremely precise, and stoical thought has never been expressed with more clarity."

1242. Haldeman-Julius, E. "T. S. Eliot—Bigot." *AF,* no. 2118 (March), p. 1. A violent attack on Eliot, whom he accuses of fascism.

1243. ———. "Eliot and the Critics." *AF,* no. 2126 (November) , p. 9. [Notes towards the Definition of Culture]. Condemns the critics of the book for being too courteous toward it.

1244. ———. "Eliot's Christian Society." *AF*, no. 2127 (December), p. 5. [Idea of a Christian Society]. He likes the essay because it "condemns usury" but dislikes its Christianity.

1245. Hamilton, Fyfe. "Analysis of Culture." *John O'London's Weekly* (January 21), p. 49. [Notes towards the Definition of Culture].

*1246. Hamilton, George Rostrevor. "Tradition and the Sense of Man's Greatness: the Work of T. S. Eliot." *The Telltale Article: a Critical Approach to Modern Poetry*, pp. 63–94. London: W. Heinemann, 1949. Eliot's poetry suffers from his failure to see that man, in spite of original sin, is essentially and tragically great. Suggestive.

1247. Hamilton, Iain. "Comments on *The Cocktail Party* (An Interview and Criticism)." *WorR* (November), pp. 19–22. Eliot answers fourteen questions on the play in a sibylline fashion.

1248. Highet, Gilbert. "The Symbolist Poets and James Joyce." *The Classical Tradition*, pp. 513–16. New York and London: Oxford University Press, 1949. [Sweeney Erect; Sweeney among the Nightingales; Waste Land]. Highet concludes that Eliot personifies himself as Prufrock, then as Tiresias. There is also material on Eliot's use of the classics.

1249. Hillyer, Robert. "Treason's Strange Fruit: The Case of Ezra Pound and the Bollingen Award." *SatR* 32 (June 11): 9–11; 28. A virulent attack on Eliot in the course of an article on Pound. (See no. 1225.)

1250. ———. "Poetry's New Priesthood." *SatR* 32 (June 18): 7–9, 38. A continuation of the preceding article, accusing Eliot of being a fascist. (See no. 1225.)

1251. Hoffman, Frederick J. "The Rhetoric of Evasion." *SR* 57 (Spring): 246–47. [Prufrock]. A paragraph on the meaningful ambiguity of the poem.

*1252. Hyman, Stanley Edgar. "Five Books in Search of an Author." *HudR* 2 (Spring): 146–47. [Unger's *T. S. Eliot: a Selected Critique*]. An excellent review.

1253. Johnson, Maurice. "The Ghost of Swift in *Four Quartets*." *MLN* 64 (April): 273. A letter from Eliot confirms the theory that he is thinking of Swift in "Little Gidding," pt. 2, the "ghost" passage.

1254. Kemp, Lysander. "Eliot's The Waste Land, I, 49–50." *Expl* 7, no. 8 (June): item 60. Explanation of the symbolism of "Belladonna, the Lady of the Rocks." (See also no. 1283.)

1255. Kenner, Hugh. "Mr. Eliot's New Book." *HudR* 2 (Summer): 289–94. [Notes towards the Definition of Culture]. "It is a meditation on order, not a program for action." His apology for the book is not entirely convincing.

1256. ———. "Eliot's Moral Dialectic." *HudR* 2 (Autumn): 421–48. [Gerontion; Ash Wednesday; Murder in the Cathedral]. A detailed analysis of the relation between Eliot's moral and religious meaning and the manner in which that meaning is expressed.

1257. Koch, Vivienne. "Programme Notes on The Cocktail Party." *Poetry* Q 2 (Winter): 248–51. A naïve account of the play.

*1258. Leavis, F. R. "Mr. Eliot and Milton." *SR* 57 (January–March): 1–30. [Milton]. Eliot's recantation of his earlier strictures against Milton shows a decline in his critical power. A close and careful examination of some of Eliot's points. Reprinted in *The Common Pursuit*, London: Chatto and Windus, 1952.

1259. Lerner, Max. "Toward a Definition of T. S. Eliot." *NR* 120 (May 9): 22–23. [Notes towards the Definition of Culture]. "Eliot's curious notion is that you can hold a society together by invoking the sanction of a church that once was central to that society but is so no longer."

1260. Lewis, Arthur O., Jr. "Eliot's Four Quartets, Burnt Norton, IV." *Expl* 8, no. 2 (November): item 9. An interpretation of a ten-line passage on four levels: literal, allegorical, moral, and anagogical.

1261. Meredith, William. "Every Poem an Epitaph." *HudR* 2 (Autumn): 473–77. [Drew's *T. S. Eliot*]. Grudging praise of the book. Meredith thinks Eliot's poems are "useless" just now, and that he has failed to communicate his symbols because of a "deficiency of sensibility."

1262. Meyer, Christine. "Eliot's The Hippopotamus." *Expl* 8, no. 1 (October): item 6. The mango, the pomegranate, and the peach all have the same value, being symbols of spiritual truth.

*1263. Moore, Harry Thornton. "Poetry on Records." *Poetry* 74 (September): 367–70. Analysis of Eliot's reading of

The Waste Land, "Ash Wednesday," "The Love Song of J. Alfred Prufrock," and the Ariel poems.

1264. Nathan, Paul S. "Books into Films." PW 156 (October 1): 1586. [Murder in the Cathedral; Cocktail Party]. Concerning George Hoellering's adaptation of Murder in the Cathedral for the screen and the publication of The Cocktail Party.

1265. Nicoll, Allardyce. "T. S. Eliot and the Revival of the Poetic Play in England." World Drama from Aeschylus to Anouilh, pp. 871–73. London: George G. Harrap & Co., 1949. [Murder in the Cathedral; Family Reunion]. A summary of Murder in the Cathedral and comment on the use of the chorus. The Family Reunion shows that a poetic style cannot be harmonized with contemporary dramatic characters.

1266. Palmer, Winthrop. "Why Eliot?" Spirit 16 (May): 61–63. The reviewer can see no reason why Eliot should have been awarded the Nobel Prize; he likes Eliot's earlier "vaudeville" manner.

*1267. Pellegrini, A. "Arts and Letters: London Conversation with T. S. Eliot," translated by Joseph Frank. SR 57 (Spring): 287–92. An important conversation on religious and literary topics, centering on the loss of faith and its effect upon Eliot's work, especially his dramas.

1268. Peschmann, Hermann. "The Significance of T. S. Eliot." Wind (London) 6 (Autumn): 108–23. Peschmann asks: "What is the significance of Eliot for literature, religion, politics, and morals?" He does not answer the question clearly.

1269. ———. Review of Notes towards the Definition of Culture. Adelphi 25 (July–September): 331–32. "Mr. Eliot is conservative in the exact sense in which all his prose writing from Tradition and the Individual Talent (1917) to The Idea of a Christian Society (1939) is conservative; and all valuable writing about culture must be of this nature."

1270. Peter, John. "The Family Reunion." Scrutiny 16 (September): 219–30. A good analysis of the strength and weakness of the play; feels that the protagonist's remorse is too great to be explained by the facts.

*1271. Rago, Henry. "T. S. Eliot on Culture." Cweal 50 (May 13): 122–25. [Notes towards the Definition of Culture]. Honest, intelligent examination of Eliot's book; temperate.

1272. Raine, Kathleen. "The Art of T. S. Eliot." *BT*, no. 164
       (December), pp. 14–18. [Gardner's *The Art of T. S.
       Eliot*]. An independent essay. "It is because he inter-
       prets the actual and imaginative world into which the
       more conscious and imaginative members of our genera-
       tion have been born that he is perhaps the most potent
       and influential poet in the world today."

1273. Read, Herbert. "Mr. Eliot's New Book." *HudR* 2 (Sum-
       mer) : 285–89. [Notes towards the Definition of Cul-
       ture]. Expresses well the egalitarian as opposed to the
       aristocratic point of view; raises the question of the
       dangers inherent in Eliot's doctrine of *élites*.

1274. Redman, Ben Ray. "T. S. Eliot: in Sight of Posterity."
       SatR 32 (March 12) : 9–11, 30–31. Tries to anticipate
       Eliot's future reputation; thinks posterity will like indi-
       vidual lines of his poetry.

1275. Reinsberg, Mark. "Footnote to Four Quartets." *AL* 21
       (November) : 342–44. [Burnt Norton]. Identifies the
       source of "Time and the bell have buried the day," as a
       pre-Elizabethan lyric. Also a note on Eliot's thrush.

1276. Russell, Peter. "A Note on T. S. Eliot's New Play." *Nine* 1
       (Autumn) : 28–29. [Cocktail Party]. People were baffled
       by "the contrast between its apparently frivolous humor
       and its earnest contemplative philosophy." But Eliot is
       wiser than his academic critics in choosing to retain not
       only "novitas" in his poetry, but also "diversitas." He
       has produced a play "very near to life as we suffer it
       today."

1277. Schwartz, Delmore. "Literary Dictatorship of T. S. Eliot."
       PR 16 (February) : 119–37. An interesting and con-
       scientious attempt to systematize Eliot's critical prin-
       ciples.

1278. Shahani, Ranjee G. "T. S. Eliot Answers Questions." *John
       O'London's Weekly* (August 19) : 497. Eliot answers
       intelligent questions about his work.

1279. Shawe-Taylor, Desmond. "The Edinburgh Festival—I."
       NSN 38 (September 3) : 243. [Cocktail Party]. Says that
       the "whole play is a superbly contrived conversation
       piece—lively, often cynical, sometimes profound."

1280. Simon, Brian. "The Defence of Culture." *ComR* 4 (De-
       cember) : 763–68. [Notes towards the Definition of Cul-
       ture]. "Under the tattered banner of the defence of
       culture is concealed a contempt and fear of the masses,
       and a complacent egoism, which aims to keep the people

in darkness while the 'privileged few,' the 'superior individuals' enjoy their 'rewards and emoluments' and bask in the warmth of the prevailing 'respect for learning.'"

*1281. Smidt, Kristian. *Poetry and Belief in the Work of T. S. Eliot,* 228 pp. Oslo: I. Kommisjon Hos Jacob Dybwad, 1949. 2nd ed., completely revised, New York: Humanities Press, 1961. George Williamson (*AL* 22 (1950): 363-65) says: "This book is concerned primarily with the philosophical background of Eliot's poetry, or with the current of ideas to which he may be related, and on that subject it is our most comprehensive study."

1282. Smith, Grover. "Eliot's Gerontion." *Expl* 7, no. 4 (February): item 26. An explanation of the names in the poem. (See no. 1008.)

1283. ———. "T. S. Eliot's Lady of the Rocks." *N&Q* 194 (March 19): 123-25. [Waste Land; Ash Wednesday; Family Reunion]. A scholarly study of the myth and symbolism contained in the figure of the sibyl who appears in the poems and the play. (See also no. 1254.)

1284. Spark, Muriel. "The Poet in Mr. Eliot's Ideal State." *Outposts,* no. 14 (Summer), pp. 26-28. [Notes towards the Definition of Culture]. The poet in Eliot's ideal state will need a patron, but will be encouraged by the lack of uniformity in culture and language. Noncontroversial in tone.

*1285. Speaight, Robert. "The Cocktail Party." *Tablet* 194 (September 3): 154-55. An excellent review of the poetry, the meaning, and the acting of the play by the actor who created the part of Becket in *Murder in the Cathedral.* Suggests that Edward Chamberlayne is J. Alfred Prufrock.

1286. Stamm, Rudolf. "The Orestes Theme in Three Plays by Eugene O'Neill, T. S. Eliot and Jean-Paul Sartre." *ES* 30, special number (October): 244-55. [Family Reunion]. An interesting comparison of the three dramatists to bring out the philosophical content of the plays.

1287. Stauffer, Donald A. "Mr. Eliot: Two Studies." *NYTBR* (March 27), p. 27. [Rajan's *T. S. Eliot: a Study of His Writings by Various Hands;* Drew's *T. S. Eliot: the Design of His Poetry*]. A careful and enlightened review.

1288. Stern, John. "Book News, Poet T. S. Eliot's Defense against Menacing Fear" (Spring), p. A-2. [This has been seen as a clipping; I have not been able to identify its source.] If Eliot is remote from ordinary people, as Laski said, it is a remoteness which is a "magnificent defense against an awful fear."

1289. Vinograd, Sherna S. "The Accidental: a Clue to Structure in Eliot's Poetry." *Accent* 9 (Summer) : 231–38. A difference in tone between the early and the later poems is explained by a difference in imagery.

*1290. Ward, Anne. "Speculations on Eliot's Time-World: an analysis of *The Family Reunion* in Relation to Hulme and Bergson." *AL* 21 (March) : 18–34. "It is the purpose of this paper to analyze the time-world created by Eliot in *The Family Reunion* with reference 1) to the Bergsonian metaphysic of time as explained by Hulme, and 2) to Hulme's insistence upon concreteness in poetic diction." Includes bibliography.

1291. Weaver, Richard M. "Culture and Construction." *SR* 57 (Autumn) : 714–18. [Notes towards the Definition of Culture]. A sympathetic summary of the book. Weaver emphasizes Eliot's praise of regionalism.

1292. Williamson, George. Letter to *SatR* 32 (July 2) : 26. A cleverly ironic reply to Hillyer. (See nos. 1249 and 1250.)

1293. ———. "A Design upon Design." *Poetry* 75 (November) : 112–13. [Drew's *T. S. Eliot: the Design of His Poetry*]. Miss Drew's method, a combination of the mythic and the structural, leads her to overlook some elements or to distort them. Her analyses are often derivative.

1294. Wormhoudt, Arthur. "A Psychoanalytical Interpretation of 'The Love Song of J. Alfred Prufrock.'" *Perspective* 2 (Winter) : 109–17. ". . . an analysis of the psychological content of the poem shows it to be concerned with the masochistic attachment of the child to the pre-oedipal image."

*1295. Worthington, Janet. "Epigraphs to the Poetry of T. S. Eliot." *AL* 21 (March) : 1–17. Bibliography. Indicates specifically the sources for the epigraphs of the fifteen poems in *Collected Poems 1909–1935*.

1296. Young, Charlotte. "The Definition of Culture." *Adam* (London), 17 (March) : 20. [Notes towards the Definition of Culture]. A brief summary.

1950

*1297. Acton, H. B. "Discussion: Religion, Culture, and Class."
Ethics 60 (January) : 120–30. [Notes towards the Definition of Culture]. A careful, scholarly examination
of the presuppositions and consequences of Eliot's
theory of society, pointing out inconsistencies.

*1298. Adair, Patricia M. "Mr. Eliot's 'Murder in the Cathedral.' "
CamJ (England) 4 (November) : 83–95. A full and
penetrating study, pointing out, among other things,
the reasons why this play is not a tragedy.

1299. Adrian, Brother. "Two Poles of Thought in T. S. Eliot."
JAL 2 (Autumn) : 213–21. The two poles are classicism
and Catholicism; most space in the discussion is given
to the second. Finds Eliot's Catholicism unsatisfactory
because it is Anglican, and so lacks "the authentic tradition."

1300. Anon. "Theater: New Plays." *Newsweek* 35 (January 30) :
66. [Cocktail Party]. Chiefly summary; photograph.

1301. ———. "New Plays in Manhattan: the Cocktail Party."
Time 55 (January 30) : 37. Sympathetic summary, although the reviewer thinks the last scene is too long
and is weak.

1302. ———. "Screw-eyed Success." *Time* 55 (February 13) : 52.
[Cocktail Party]. On the financial success of the play.

*1303. ———. "Reflections, Mr. Eliot." *Time* 55 (March 6) : 22–
26. An extended, accurate introduction to Eliot's life
and poetry, drama, and prose.

1304. ———. "The Laurels." *Time* 55 (April 17) : 80. On the
Drama Critics' Circle award to *The Cocktail Party*.

1305. ———. "People: The Calloused Hand." *Time* 56 (October
23) : 42. [Cocktail Party]. Quotations from an interview with Eliot.

1306. ———. "A Boy & a River." *Time* 56 (October 23) : 106.
On Eliot's introduction to *Adventures of Huckleberry
Finn*.

1307. ———. "Find Your Own Answers." *Time* 56 (November
13) : 53–54. A news story on a seminar conducted by
Eliot at the University of Chicago.

1308. ———. "The Year in Books." *Time* 56 (December 18) :
107. Picture of Eliot and Christopher Fry; paragraph on
the success of *The Cocktail Party*.

1309. ———. "Poetry and Theater." *TLS,* no. 2505 (February

3), p. 73. The reviewer fears that the success of Fry's and Eliot's poetic dramas will not help increase the sales of other kinds of poetry. But Eliot's play "is the work of a dramatist who, without compromising his own truth, is acutely aware of the theatre's present necessity," that of breaking away from realism.

*1310. ———. "Entertainment and Reality." *TLS*, no. 2513 (March 31), p. 198. [Cocktail Party]. Good criticism, taking account of the dramatic structure, verse, and meaning.

1311. ———. "Writing for the Theatre." *TLS*, no. 2534 (August 25), p. viii. [Cocktail Party]. A good survey of Eliot's relation to the contemporary British theatre.

1312. Arms, George W., and Kuntz, Joseph M. *Poetry Explication: a checklist of interpretation since 1925 of British and American poems, past and present,* pp. 64–73. New York: Swallow Press and William Morrow Co., 1950. A useful bibliography, arranged by poems, of articles of *explication de texte*.

*1313. Arrowsmith, William. "Notes on English Verse Drama, Christopher Fry." *HudR* 3 (Summer): 203–5. The first three pages of this excellent article are devoted to Eliot as an expert craftsman in the theatre; also considers his influence on younger dramatists.

*1314. ———. "Notes on English Verse Drama, II: The Cocktail Party." *HudR* 3 (Autumn): 411–30. A scholarly and illuminating analysis of the Christian meaning of the play.

*1315. Atkinson, Brooks. "T. S. Eliot's Party." *NYT* (January 29), sec. 2, p. 1. [Cocktail Party]. "Mr. Eliot is writing about things that cannot be adequately expressed in the earthbound, cerebral style he has deliberately chosen for his experiment." Good newspaper review.

1316. Bain, Donald. "The Cocktail Party." *Nine* 2 (January): 16–22. An extended, sympathetic study of the play; he thinks that Eliot has enlarged the scope of poetic drama by using it for nonromantic subject matter.

1317. Barnes, Howard. "The Theatres; Modern Morality Play." *NYHT* (January 23), p. 12. [Cocktail Party]. "The Cocktail Party is an eventful piece of theatre, if somewhat disappointing."

1318. ———. "Eliot Brings Poetry to the Stage." *NYHT* (January 29), sec. 5, p. 1. [Cocktail Party]. "In the final scene there is a let-down from genuine emotion," for "faith and drama are at odds in 'The Cocktail Party.' "

*1319. Barrett, William. "Dry Land, Dry Martini." *PR* 17 (April) : 354–59. [Cocktail Party]. A thoughtful review, expressing the opinion that this is "the weakest poetry that Eliot has yet written."

1320. Bateson, F. W. *English Poetry: a Critical Introduction.* (London: Longmans, Green & Co., 1950. [Waste Land]. Approves of Eliot's insistence on meaning in poetry, and his emphasis on reason, points out an injustice to Milton on Eliot's part, comments on the characters in *The Waste Land.*

1321. Beyer, William Henry. "The State of the Theatre: Seasonal High Lights." *SS* 72 (September 16) : 180–82. [Cocktail Party]. A thoughtless review chiding Eliot for not knowing what he is doing in the play.

1322. Bland, D. S. "The Tragic Hero in Modern Literature." *CamJ* 3 (January) : 214–23. [Family Reunion]. "Harry emerges as an individual," contrary to the usual situation of the modern tragic hero, who becomes an allegorical figure or a type. One-and-a-half-pages on this play.

*1323. Bradbrook, M. C. *T. S. Eliot,* 62 pp. London, New York: Longmans, Green & Co., 1950. An authoritative survey of Eliot's career to 1950; sensitive and intelligent.

1324. Breit, Harvey. "Repeat Performances." *NYTBR* (November 5) , p. 36. [Selected Essays; Introduction to Adventures of Huckleberry Finn]. A slight, favorable review.

1325. Brooks, Cleanth. "The Crisis in Culture." *HAB* 52, no. 18 (1950) : 768–72. [Notes towards the Definition of Culture]. Brooks's interest in Eliot is secondary to his displeasure with the daily world's "numbing paralysis."

*1326. ———. "T. S. Eliot: 'The Waste Land.' " In Brooks and Robert Penn Warren, *Understanding Poetry,* pp. 645–67. New York: Holt, 1950. A simplified version of Brooks's analysis of the poem which appeared in *The Southern Review,* 1937 (no. 624) . Useful, clear.

1327. Brown, Ivor. "Gin and Falernian." *Observer* (May 7) . [Cocktail Party]. The critic does not like the religion in the play, especially the psychiatrist.

1328. Brown, John Mason. "Honorable Intentions." *SatR* 33 (February 4) : 28–30. [Cocktail Party]. He does not understand the play. Reprinted in *Still Seeing Things*, New York: McGraw-Hill, 1950, pp. 167–74.

1329. Burke, Kenneth. "Eliot: Early Poems and Quartets." *A Rhetoric of Motives*, pp. 265 ff. New York: Prentice-Hall, 1950. The essay is so integrally implicated with Burke's philosophy that it is almost unintelligible without understanding the larger whole. He is concerned with "down-turning" and "up-turning" moods in the poems and with the poet's "kinds of dialectical resources."

1330. Burnham, Philip. "Communications: The Cocktail Party." *Cweal* 51 (February 17): 507–8. A reply to Kappo Phelan's review of the play (no. 1399). Clear explanation of what the play meant to one spectator.

1331. Carne-Ross, Donald. "The Position of 'The Family Reunion' in the Work of T. S. Eliot." *RLM* (Florence) 2 (October): 125–39. A unified essay drawing on all of Eliot's work to support the thesis that this play shows the necessity of finding a position "somewhere on the other side of despair."

1332. Cleophas, Sister Mary. "Notes on Levels of Meaning in 'Four Quartets.'" *Renascence* 2 (Spring): 102–16. An analysis of the poem on the historical, allegorical, moral, and anagogical levels. The author admits that the first three levels are not well defined.

1333. Clurman, Harold. "Theatre: Cocktail Poetry." *NR* 122 (February 13): 30. [Cocktail Party]. Attacks the play as a "pessimistic and devitalized defense of the *status quo*."

*1334. Cohen, S. Marshall. "Music and Structure in Eliot's Quartets." *DarQ* 5 (Summer): 3–8. The main object of the essay is to "explore the effect which Eliot obtains by forcing the reader to juxtapose parallel movements in the various quartets." This essay adds new interpretations to those of Rajan, Drew, and others.

1335. Cookman, A. V. "The Verse Play." *The Year's Work in the Theatre 1949–50*, pp. 24–28. Published for the British Council. London: Longmans, Green & Co., 1950. [Cocktail Party]. Eliot's triumph in this play is that "he alone has kept clearly in view the only terms on which poetry can be received back into the theatre," that is, it must entertain better than prose could do.

1336. Cormican, L. A. "Mr. Eliot and Social Biology." *Scrutiny* 17 (Spring): 2–13. [Notes towards the Definition of

Culture]. Objects to Eliot's failure to define his terms and to offer concrete instances. He does not accept Eliot's premise that the church is necessary.

1337. Cotten, Lyman A. "T. S. Eliot's The Waste Land, I, 43–46." *Expl* 9, no. 1 (October) : item 7. Offers an explanation for the name *Sosostris*. (See also no. 1374.)

1338. A. D. "Some Notes on the Waste Land." *N&Q* 195 (August 19) : 365–69. An excellent piece of source-hunting for allusions in nine passages of the poem, frequently taking issue with Cleanth Brooks (no. 624).

1339. Daiches, David, and Charvat, William. *Poems in English 1530–1940.* New York: Ronald Press, 1950. Notes to "Gerontion," pp. 738–40; "Journey of the Magi," p. 740; "Marina," p. 741; "Burnt Norton," pp. 741–42. A routine explanation of the poems. That for "Burnt Norton" depends chiefly on Gardner (no. 1063).

*1340. Dobrée, Bonamy. "Books and Writers." *Spectator* 184, no. 6356 (April 21) : 541. [Cocktail Party]. A good essay on the four levels of the play: amoral, metaphysical, moral, and transcendental. (See nos. 1348 and 1391.)

1341. Dunkel, Wilbur Dwight. "T. S. Eliot's Quest for Certitude." *Theol* 7 (July) : 228–36. [Cocktail Party]. "The stoical acceptance of the *status quo* by the Chamberlaynes, the psychiatrist's inability to recognize an ethical standard of good and evil, and Celia's involvement in a cause, fortunately Christian, are interesting but scarcely definitive Christian answers to mankind's problem."

1342. Dutton, Geoffrey. "London Letter: a Measure for a Cocktail." *Meanjin* 9 (Spring) : 204–6. [Cocktail Party]. A comparison of *The Cocktail Party* with *Measure for Measure,* to the disparagement of the former. Dutton dislikes Eliot's play because it is Christian.

1343. Dwyer, Daniel N. "Eliot's Ash Wednesday, IV. 1–4." *Expl* 9, no. 1 (October) : item 5. An explanation of the color symbolism.

*1344. Edman, Irwin. "Incantations by Eliot." *SatR* 33 (June 24) : 56–57. [Cocktail Party]. A competent criticism of the play as recorded by the English cast.

1345. Fern, Dale E. "Knowing How and Learning How." *LC,* 121 (September 24) : 16–17. A short comparison of Eliot and Emily Dickinson.

1346. Fish, Clifford J. "Eliot's The Love Song of J. Alfred Prufrock." *Expl* 8, no. 8 (June) : item 62. Proposes the identification of Lazarus in the poem with the beggar of Luke 16:19. (See no. 1453.)

1347. Fleming, Peter. "Contemporary Arts. Theatre." *Spectator* 184, no. 6359. (May 12) : 645. [Cocktail Party]. Seeing the play was "altogether quite a memorable evening," perhaps because the play has the rare quality of compassion.

*1348. Flint, R. W. Review of Gardner's *The Art of T. S. Eliot*. *Poetry* 77 (October) : 41–47. A long and careful criticism, suggesting that Miss Gardner should have analyzed the *Four Quartets* on the levels of four meanings: literal, moral, metaphysical, and religious.

1349. Forster, E. M. "Mr. Eliot's 'Comedy.' " *Listener* 43 (March 23) : 533. [Cocktail Party]. He thinks the idea of the play is unconvincing, but that "Mr. Eliot can do whatever he likes with the English language."

1350. Fox, John J. "Communications: The Cocktail Party." *Cweal* 51 (February 17) : 508. An answer to Kappo Phelan's unfavorable review of the play (no. 1399).

1351. Frankenberg, Lloyd. "The Poets, Their Spoken Words Attract a New Audience." *HarB*, no. 2865 (August) : pp. 139, 196. A few sentences on Eliot's recordings, with a portrait. "Eliot has had perhaps the most pervasive influence on our poetic climate."

1352. Freimarck, Vincent. "Eliot's Ash Wednesday, III-V." *Expl* 9, no. 1 (October) : item 6. An explanation of the "figure dressed in blue and green."

1353. Fussell, Paul, Jr. "A Note on 'The Hollow Men.' " *MLN* 65 (April) : 254–55. Points out a similarity between a passage in *Julius Caesar* and one in "The Hollow Men."

1354. Fyvel, T. R. "Letter from London." *NewL* (July 22) , pp. 16–17. [Cocktail Party]. The play confirmed his view that Eliot "has flashes of genius into the human situation and has no insight into the current social situation."

1355. H. C. G. [Gardiner, Harold]. "Hors-d'oeuvre for the 'Party.' " *America* 82 (March 25) : 725. [Cocktail Party]. "I believe that Mr. Eliot is hinting at the fact that God's grace is distributed at various levels, that holiness . . . can be won by all sorts of people in all conditions of life."

1356. Gibbs, Wolcott. "Eliot and Others." *NY* 25 (January 28) : 47–48. [Cocktail Party]. He does not understand the mystical part of the play, but gives a fairly competent journalistic summary of it.

1357. Glazier, Lyle. "Eliot's The Waste Land, I, 24–30." *Expl* 8, no. 4 (February) : item 26. An extended explanation of the symbolism of the "rock."

*1358. Greenberg, Clement. "T. S. Eliot: the Criticism, the Poetry." *Nation* 171 (December 9) : 531–33. Thinks that Eliot is the greatest of all critics, but that his poetry lacks organization.

1359. "T. E. Greenleaf" [T. G. Eliot]. Letter to *Time. Time* 55 (March 27) : 8. On the relationship between T. S. Eliot and President C. W. Eliot of Harvard.

1360. Greenwood, Ormerod. "The House of Atreus." *The Playwright: A Study of Form, Method, and Tradition in the Theatre,* pp. 103–9. London: Theatre and Stage Series, Pitman, 1950. [Family Reunion]. An interpretive summary of the play, including brief comparisons with O'Neill's *Mourning Becomes Electra* and *Eumenides.*

1361. Hamalian, Leo. "Mr. Eliot's Saturday Evening Service." *Accent* 10 (Autumn) : 195–206. [Family Reunion; Cocktail Party]. "In this paper, my aim is to illuminate the text of *The Cocktail Party* by showing how it is related to, and grows out of, ideas contained in his poems, essays, and other plays."

*1362. Hamilton, George Rostrevor. "Reviews of Books." *English* 8, no. 44 (Summer) : 95–96. [Gardner, *The Art of T. S. Eliot*]. Fears that commentaries on Eliot's work will multiply so that its study will become a whole-time job. Balanced criticism of Miss Gardner's book.

1363. Heimann, Heidi. "A God in Three Disguises." *WorR* (June), pp. 66–69. [Cocktail Party]. Hermes is the archetypal figure for Alex, who appears also in Cocteau's *Orphée* and Mann's *Young Joseph.*

1364. Heywood, Robert. "Everybody's Cocktail Party." *Renascence* 3 (Autumn) : 28–30. Suggests that there are many valid interpretations of the play; thin in content.

1365. Hillyer, Robert. "The Crisis in American Poetry." *AM* 70 (January) : 65–71. Thinks that the New Critics, whom he calls the School of Eliot, have almost ruined American poetry. Eliot is an interesting dead-end.

1366. Hobson, Harold. "Eliot." *Sun Times* (London) (January 8), p. 2. [Cocktail Party]. On changes in the play from the first performance in Edinburgh through Brighton to New York. Informative.

1367. ———. "Poetic Drama Ascendant." *CSM* (March 25), p. 4. [Cocktail Party]. Compares Christopher Fry and Eliot; finds *The Cocktail Party* as a whole difficult to understand.

1368. ———. "Mr. Eliot's Play." *Sun Times* (London) (May 7), p. 4. [Cocktail Party]. The play "comes from a mind as acute as Sir Isaac Newton's, that wishes to write like Dostoevsky, and succeeds at its best but not its most ambitious in doing as well as Jane Austen."

1369. ———. "The Theatre in Paris and London." *Sun Times* (London) (May 21), p. 6. Speaks of the success of *Murder in the Cathedral* in Paris and says that a French version of *The Cocktail Party* would be a success.

1370. Hope-Wallace, Philip. "Theatre: The Cocktail Party." *TT* 31 (May 13): 466. The scene at the psychiatrist's with the husband, wife, and mistress is "one of the finest things the theatre has given us."

*1371. Hutchins, Robert Maynard. "T. S. Eliot on Education." *Measure* 1 (Winter): 1–8. [Notes towards the Definition of Culture]. Eliot says this is the best criticism anyone has written of his book; it raises fundamental questions.

1372. Iglesias, Antonio. "Style Makes the Man." *SatR* 33 (August 12): 13. Eliot's style in the 1920s prophesied that he would eventually turn from the world of human degradation to the world of human values.

1373. Inge, W. Motter. "Bookshelf." Review of *The Cocktail Party*. *TAr* 34 (May): 8–9. He says it is religious propaganda, and not good drama.

1374. Kemp, Lysander. "Eliot's The Waste Land, I, 43–59." *Expl* 8, no. 4 (February): item 27. A suggestion for the origin of the name *Sosostris*. (See also no. 1352.)

1375. Keown, Eric. "At the Play." *Punch* 218 (May 10): 524. [Cocktail Party]. He likes this play less than he did *The Family Reunion* "because of its obscurity."

1376. Kinsman, Robert S. "Eliot's The Hollow Men." *Expl* 8, no. 6 (April): item 48. An interesting parallel exists between the underworld allusions in this poem and those in Virgil and Dante.

1377. Koch, Vivienne. *William Carlos Williams*. Norfolk, Conn.:

New Directions Books, 1950. The volume contains incidental references to Eliot and a quotation from an unfavorable comment on Eliot written by Williams in
1918. (See no. 20.)

1378. Kramer, Hilton. "T. S. Eliot in New York (Notes on the
End of Something)." *WR* 14 (Summer) : 303–5. [Cock-
tail Party]. On the continuity of this play with Eliot's
earlier work, and the social significance of Eliot's picture being on the cover page of *Time*.

1379. Krutch, Joseph Wood. "T. S. Eliot on Broadway."
NYHTB (March 19) , p. 7. [Cocktail Party]. A well-
written review, reporting some of the strained allegorical interpretations of the play.

1380. Lal, P. "T. S. Eliot Survives the Attack." *LitR* 1 (Bombay) (April) : 7–8. A popular discussion of the three
major attacks on Eliot: 1) against *The Waste Land*
2) for his conversion to Anglicanism 3) that led by
Hillyer apropos of awarding the Bollingen Prize to
Pound.

1381. Lawrence, Seymour. "Reviews." *Wake* 9: 120–22. [Cock-
tail Party]. "This is not a play."

1382. Lobb, Kenneth Martyn. *T. S. Eliot: Murder in the Cathedral (Notes on Chosen English Texts)*, 27 pp. London:
J. Brodie Ltd., 1950. Notes only, not the text of the play.
Intended for young students, a short account of Eliot's
life, the background of the play, and useful notes on
the text.

1383. MacLeish, Archibald. *Poetry and Opinion: the pisan cantos of ezra pound*, 52 pp. Urbana: University of Illinois
Press, 1950. Points out the danger of Eliot's statement
that a poem need not be "bad" because its opinions are
"bad." This discussion is apropos of the Bollingen
award to Pound.

1384. Marshall, Margaret. "Drama." *Nation* 170 (January 28) :
94–95. [Cocktail Party]. A hurried review saying that
the play "scores its greatest success as sophisticated
comedy."

1385. Matthiessen, F. O. Introduction to *The Oxford Book of
American Verse*, pp. xv–xvi; xxv; xxx–xxxiii. New
York: Oxford University Press, 1950. Matthiessen considers Eliot's Americanism, his importance in American
poetry, his views on diction, and his likenesses to Robert
Frost. (Pts. 3 and 4 appear also in *Poetry* 77: 38–40, October, 1950.)

1386. Maxwell, J. C. "Reflections on 'Four Quartets.' " *Month* 4, n.s. (July) : 59–68. A detailed analysis of the rose imagery and the theme of time. Takes issue with the interpretations of Schenk (no. 1087) and Preston (no. 1029).

*1387. McLaughlin, John J. "A Daring Metaphysic: the Cocktail Party." *Renascence* 3 (Autumn) : 15–28. The leading idea of the play, that there are "degrees of perfection which vary according to the spiritual capacity of the individual," is best explained by the Thomistic doctrine of Act and Potency. This essay deepens comprehension of the play.

1388. Miles, George. "Books: The Cocktail Party." *Cweal* 52 (May 5) : 106–8. Favorable on the whole, but raises questions both about the expression of certain passages and about the placing of the "dull, implacable mediocrities . . . on the same level with the sacrificial figure."

1389. Morgan, Frederick. "Notes on the Theater." *HudR* 3 (Summer) : 289–93. [Cocktail Party]. "Eliot has emerged as a very distinguished dramatist whose work displays the typical excellences and suffers the typical limitation of a theater of ideas."

1390. Morris, Robert L. "Eliot's 'Game of Chess,' and Conrad's 'The Return.' " *MLN,* 65 (June) : 422–23. [Waste Land]. Thinks the passage owes more to Conrad than to Shakespeare's Cleopatra. Morris's parallel is not convincing.

1391. Murphy, Richard. "The Cocktail Party," *Spectator* 184, no. 6357 (April 28) : 569. Objects to reading the play as if it were prose. (See no. 1340.)

*1392. Murry, J. Middleton. "Mr. Eliot's Cocktail Party." *FR* 168, no. 1008, n.s., (December) : 391–98. [Cocktail Party; Family Reunion]. A lucid comparison and contrast between the two plays, showing the superiority of *The Cocktail Party*. Reprinted in *Unprofessional Essays,* 1956.

1393. Nathan, George Jean. "The Theatre: Clinical Notes." *AM* 70 (May) : 557–58. [Cocktail Party]. Dislikes the idea of the play, and asserts that Eliot is ignorant of the laws of dramatic composition.

1394. O'Connell, Thomas G. V. "T. S. Eliot's 'The Cocktail Party.' " *America* 82 (March 25) : 724–25. A discriminating and sensitive review from the Roman Catholic point of view.

1395. Pappe, H. O. "Some Notes on Mr. Eliot's Culture." *Land-fall* 4 (September) : 230–43. [Notes towards the Definition of Culture]. An attack on Eliot from the liberal-democratic point of view.

1396. Peel, Robert. "A Poetic Exploration of Modern Man's Spiritual Loneliness." *CSM Magazine Section* (March 25), p. 7. [Cocktail Party]. On the various levels of meaning and enjoyment offered by the play.

1397. Peschmann, Hermann. " 'The Cocktail Party': Some Links between the Poems and Plays of T. S. Eliot." *Wind* 7 (Autumn) : 53–58. "What *The Cocktail Party* does is to tighten the threads that bind all Eliot's work into a demonstrable unity, and at the same time to lend special emphasis to a dramatization of the doctrines of *Four Quartets.*" The article is too short for a satisfactory development of his thesis.

*1398. Peter, John. "Sin and Soda." *Scrutiny* 17 (Spring) : 61–66. [Family Reunion; Cocktail Party]. Dwells on the difficulty of effecting a synthesis between the everyday mundane world and the world of belief. He prefers *The Cocktail Party* to *The Family Reunion.*

1399. Phelan, Kappo. "The Stage: The Cocktail Party." *Cweal* 51 (February 3) : 463. She was mystified and bored by the play. (See nos. 1631 and 1662.)

1400. Pick, John. "A Note on the Cocktail Party." *Renascence* 3 (Autumn) : 30–32. Both *Murder in the Cathedral* and *The Cocktail Party* "deal with the making of a saint, and Thomas Becket and Celia Coplestone are set against a contrasting background." The point is neatly made.

1401. Pocock, D. F. "Symposium on Mr. Eliot's 'Notes,' III," *Scrutiny* 17 (Autumn) : 273–76. [Notes towards the Definition of Culture]. Says Eliot's book is sterile, contradictory, and in bad taste. (See no. 1208 and *Scrutiny* 17 (Spring) for pts. 1 and 2.)

*1402. Popkin, Henry. "Theatre Letter." *KR* 12 (Spring) : 337–39. [Cocktail Party]. Eliot is more at ease in the mundane story of the Chamberlaynes than he is in the religious part of the play. An informative review.

*1403. Pound, Ezra. *The Letters of Ezra Pound, 1907–1941,* edited by D. D. Paige. New York: Harcourt, Brace & Co., 1950. Contains letters to Eliot; especially important for the history of "Prufrock," *The Waste Land* and early minor poems. Also contains biographical information. (Two letters of Pound to Eliot and one from Eliot appear also in *Nine* 4 (Summer) : 176–79, with a summarizing paragraph by D. D. Paige.)

1404. Robbins, Rossell Hope. "T. S. Eliot Myth." *ScSo* 14, no. 1 (Winter, 1949–1950) : 1–28. Attacks Eliot as a poet and thinker because he lacks faith in man; a prejudiced and misinformed essay.

1405. Roby, Robert Curtis. "T. S. Eliot and the Elizabethan and Jacobean Dramatists." *Summaries of Doctoral Dissertations* 17, pp. 42–46. Chicago and Evanston: Northwestern University, 1950. Eliot's attitude toward the Elizabethan and Jacobean dramatists is admiration for their language and versification, but disapproval of their unbridled individualism and lack of order and restraint.

1406. "Sagittarius." "Nightingale among the Sweenies." *NSN* 40 (July 29) : 118. [Cocktail Party]. A comic poem on the success of the play.

1407. Seldes, Gilbert. "Life on the Tinsel Standard." *SatR* 33 (October 28) : 10. One paragraph in an article on the decline of culture. He rejects Eliot's views because "he has turned his back on a reasonably possible future."

1408. Sherek, Henry. "On Giving a Cocktail Party." *TAr* 34 (April) : 24–26. Interesting personal reminiscences of Eliot by the producer of *The Cocktail Party*.

1409. Sickels, Eleanor M. "Eliot's The Waste Land I, 24–30, and Ash Wednesday, IV-VI." *Expl* 4, no. 1 (October) : item 4. On the rock symbolism of the two poems. (See no. 1494.)

1410. Smith, Arthur J. M. "Contemporary Literature: Thomas Stearns Eliot (1888–   ) : Gerontion." *An Introduction to Literature and the Fine Arts*, pp. 353–56. East Lansing: Michigan State College Press, 1950. In the light of "Ash Wednesday" and the *Four Quartets* this appears as "a confessional poem," indicating the need for the healing waters of God's grace.

1411. Smith, Chard Powers. "The Cocktail Party." *SatR* 33 (February 25) : 23. This is the first work of Eliot's that he has understood—in answer to J. M. Brown (no. 1328).

*1412. Smith, Grover C. *The Poems of T. S. Eliot, 1909–1928: a Study in Symbols and Sources.* 301 pp. and bibliography. Ph.D. diss., Columbia University, 1950. Ann Arbor: University Microfilms, no. 585000). Letters from Eliot to the author give valuable information on sources. Smith has also assembled a mass of information which is greatly expanded by excursions into mythology and conjecture. Published as *T. S. Eliot's Poetry and Plays: a Study in Sources and Meaning*, Chicago: University of Chicago Press, 1956. 338 pp.

1413. ———. "Charles-Louis Philippe and T. S. Eliot." *AL* 22 (November) : 254–59. [The third "Prelude"; Rhapsody on a Windy Night]. Two of the novels of Philippe were the chief inspiration for these poems.

1414. ———. "Tourneur and *Little Gidding:* Corbière and *East Coker*." *MLN* 65 (June) : 418–21. He says that the "familiar compound ghost" derives not only from Dante, but also from a speech of Borachio in the *Atheist's Tragedy;* and that "In my beginning was my end," derives partially from *Les Amours Jaunes* of Corbière.

1415. Smith, Ray. "Eliot's The Waste Land, I, 74–75." *Expl* 9, no. 1 (October) : item 8. An explanation of the symbolism of the dog. (See also no. 624.)

1416. Speaight, Robert. "Sartre and Eliot." *Drama* 17 (Summer) : 15–17. Sartre has abandoned, Eliot has recovered, "belief in classical man, with the power of reason and the freedom of choice."

*1417. Spender, Stephen. "After the Cocktail Party." *NYTBR* (March 19) , pp. 7, 20. Excellent criticism of the dramatic, poetic, and religious aspects of the play.

*1418. ———. "New Literature. The Cocktail Party." (1950) , pp. 41–42. [This has been seen only as a clipping, and its place of origin and exact date have not been found]. Considers the meaning of the play on several levels; clear, simple. Thinks Eliot dismisses human love too readily.

1419. Stephenson, George R. "The Power of Divinity." Review of *The Descent of the Dove,* by Charles Williams. *NYTBR* (October 1) , p. 32. Mentions Williams's great influence on Eliot and C. S. Lewis.

1420. Stuart, Duane R. "Modernistic Critics and Translators." *PULC* 11 (Summer) : 177–98. Concerning the insufficient classical knowledge on the part of Eliot and other poets, and their borrowings from the classics.

1421. Thompson, David W. "Twentieth Century Poetry in English: Contemporary Recordings of The Poets Reading Their Own Poems, selected and arranged by the Consultants in Poetry in English at the Library of Congress."

AQ 2 (Spring) : 92–93. High praise for Eliot's reading of his poems.

1422. Thurber, James. *"What* Cocktail Party?" *NY* 26 (April 1) : 26–29. Thurber spoofs people who find all sorts of psychoanalytic and impossible meanings in the play.

1423. Trilling, Lionel. "Wordsworth and the Iron Time." *KR* 12 (Summer) : 493–94. [Cocktail Party]. He uses Eliot to explain what he means by Wordsworth's "Judaic quietude." Reprinting in *The Opposing Self,* New York: Viking, 1955, pp. 145–47.

*1424. Unger, Leonard. *Donne's Poetry and Modern Criticism,* pp. 6–9. Chicago: Henry Regnery Company, 1950. An excellent critical summary of Eliot's essay on Donne, and of Eliot's influence on George Williamson's *The Donne Tradition.*

1425. Vassilieff, Elizabeth. "Piers to Cocktails." *Meanjin* 9 (Spring) : 193–203. [Cocktail Party]. A comparison of the play with *Piers Plowman,* both in versification and the fourfold levels of meaning in each work. A poorly organized but stimulating essay.

1426. Vincent, C. J. "A Modern Pilgrim's Progress." *QQ* 57 (Autumn) : 346–52. [Cocktail Party]. Eliot has progressed through an Inferno, and a Purgatorio, and has arrived at glimpses of a Paradiso.

*1427. Waggoner, Hyatt Howe. "T. S. Eliot: at the Still Point." *The Heel of Elohim: Science and Values in Modern American Poetry,* pp. 61–104; *passim.* Norman: University of Oklahoma Press, 1950. [Dry Salvages]. In a penetrating study, Waggoner discusses the philosophic influences which have led to Eliot's attitude toward science and his combination of respect for real, and condemnation of false, science; and analyzes "The Dry Salvages" for its attitude toward science and Christian thought.

*1428. Weitz, Morris. *The Philosophy of the Arts,* pp. 93–107; *passim.* Cambridge: Harvard University Press, 1950. [Prufrock]. A sensitive and intelligent analysis of "Prufrock" as a work of art.

1429. White, Jon Manchip. "What a Party!" *Poetry L,* no. 19 (August), pp. 24–27. [Cocktail Party]. The characters are dull, the plot is anemic, and the verse opaque.

*1430. Williams, William Carlos. "It's about 'Your Life and Mine, Darling.'" *New York Post* (March 12), M18.

[Cocktail Party]. A brief but excellent article, chiefly concerned with the verse.

1431. Williamson, George. Review of *T. S. Eliot: a Symposium,* edited by R. March and Tambimuttu, and of Kristian Smidt, *Poetry and Belief in the Work of T. S. Eliot, AL* 22 (November) : 363–65. In the *Symposium* "one may discover the basis of Eliot's international reputation and the extent to which it reflects his English reputation." Although Mr. Smidt's book has weaknesses, it "makes a valuable examination of the relations between philosophy and poetry in Eliot's work."

1432. ———. "The Structure of *The Waste Land." MP* 47 (February) : 191–206. An exploration of the materials involved in the genesis of the poem, and a critical examination of its structure. Specialized, scholarly.

*1433. Wimsatt, W. K., Jr. "Arts and Letters: Eliot's Comedy." *SR* 58 (Autumn) : 666–78. [Cocktail Party]. "Eliot's play is perhaps the best morality play in English since *Everyman,* and the only comical-morality." A scholarly study.

1434. Wool, Sandra. "Weston Revisited." *Accent* 10 (Autumn) : 207–12. *The Cocktail Party* interpreted in terms of Weston's *From Ritual to Romance* and in terms of Eliot's earlier use of Weston in *The Waste Land.*

1435. Worsley, T. C. "The Second Cocktail Party." *NSN* 39 (May 13) : 543. A criticism of the acting by the members of the second London company.

1436. Wyatt, Euphemia V. Review of *The Cocktail Party. CathW* 170 (March) : 466–67.

1437. Wynn, Dudley. "The Integrity of T. S. Eliot." *UDPSH,* no. 1—"Writers of Our Years," edited by A. M. I. Fiskin, pp. 59–78. Denver: University of Denver Press, 1950. Drawing his material chiefly from other writers, Wynn traces the development of Eliot's religious ideas in the poems and plays.

1951

1438. Anon. Notice of *Poetry and Drama. NY* 27 (April 28) : 106. Complimentary.

1439. ———. "The Habit." *Time* 57 (January 1) : 45. Concerning a letter written by Eliot to the London *Times* on the television habit.

1440. ———. "Pioneering Poetic Drama." *TLS,* no. 2594 (Oc-

tober 19), p. 661. [Poetry and Drama.] A sober summary of the book.

*1441. Blackmur, R. P. "Unappeasable and Peregrine: Behavior
and the Four Quartets." *Thought* 26 (Spring) : 50–76.
A difficult but rich essay on the interaction of experience and expression in the *Four Quartets*.

1442. ———. "In the Hope of Straightening Things Out," *KR*
13 (Spring) : 303–14. Eliot's personality gives unity to
his criticism.

1443. Bogan, Louise. *Achievement in American Poetry, 1900–
1950*, pp. 66–75, 86, 98–99, 107–9. Chicago: Henry
Regnery, 1951. A competent, though rapid, survey of
Eliot's poetry and criticism as part of the history of
American poetry since 1917.

*1444. Bradbury, John M. "Four Quartets: the Structural Sym-
bolism." *SR* 59 (Spring) : 254–70. Drawing upon Dante
and Heraclitus, "Eliot has made use, and extraordinary
use, of a symbolic system quite as coherent as that of
Yeats." An excellent article.

*1445. Brett, R. L. "Ambiguity and Mr. Eliot." *English* 8 (Autumn) : 284–87. [Waste Land; Four Quartets]. Eliot's
later poems are better than the earlier ones because in
them his images are not left to make their appeal only
to the unconscious mind but also to the conscious mind.

1446. Brown, John Mason. "When Words Sing." *SatR* 34 (April
28) : 24–26. [Poetry and Drama]. Disagrees with Eliot's
opinion that the audience should be so accustomed to
verse in drama that they will cease to be conscious of it.

*1447. Child, Ruth C. "The Early Critical Work of T. S. Eliot:
an Assessment." *CE* 12 (February) : 269–75. A reasoned
and intelligent analysis of the influence of Eliot on the
"New Criticism," both good and bad. He has encouraged interest in "tone" and in "wit," he has set up a
new standard of judgment for poetry, which has elevated
the metaphysical poets and disparaged the Romanticists,
and he has made current such terms as "objective correlative" and "impersonality."

1448. Clancy, Joseph P. Review of *Poetry and Drama. Thought*
26 (Winter, 1951–52), 103–5. "The discussion is admirably lucid, frequently witty, and refreshingly candid
in its admission of mistakes."

1449. Clutton-Brock, Alan. "Letters to the Editor: T. S. Eliot
and Conan Doyle." *TLS*, no. 2555 (January 19), p. 37.
Makes the point that Grover Smith (see no. 1181) had

made, that four lines in *Murder in the Cathedral* are derived from A. Conan Doyle's *The Musgrave Ritual*.

1450. Coffman, Stanley K. *Imagism: a chapter for the history of modern poetry,* pp. 42–43, 216–21. Norman: University of Oklahoma Press, 1951. On Eliot's connections with the imagist movement, both critical and poetic.

1451. Day-Lewis, Cecil. *The Poet's Task,* pp. 18–20. Oxford: Clarendon Press, 1951. Suggests that Eliot is more tolerant of many kinds of poetry than are some of his followers, but notes his moral disapproval of Hardy.

1452. Dunkel, Wilbur Dwight. "An Exchange of Notes on T. S. Eliot: a Rejoinder." *Theol* 7 (January) : 507–8. In no. 1341 Dunkel criticized *The Cocktail Party,* drawing a reply from Eliot and from Smith (no. 1481). This is good-tempered, intelligent controversial writing.

1453. Dwyer, Daniel N. "Eliot's The Love Song of J. Alfred Prufrock." *Expl* 9, no. 5 (March) : item 38. Objects to the identification of Lazarus with the beggar, as proposed by Fish (no. 1346).

1454. Fergusson, Francis. "Backstage with Mr. Eliot." *NYTBR* (June 10) , p. 14. [Poetry and Drama]. A brief summary and favorable comment.

1455. Fitzell, Lincoln. "The Sword and the Dragon." *SAQ* 100 (April) : 226–27. [Gerontion]. Two paragraphs saying that the poem is both satirical and tragic.

1456. Friar, Kinon, and Brinnin, J. M. *Modern Poetry American and British,* pp. 459–98. New York: Appleton-Century-Crofts, 1951. [Burnt Norton; Ash Wednesday; Waste Land; Gerontion]. A very detailed explanation of the background and allusions of *The Waste Land* and less detailed explanations of the other two poems.

*1457. Gegenheimer, Albert Frank. Reviews of *T. S. Eliot: a Symposium,* edited by R. March and Tambimuttu; Drew: *T. S. Eliot: the Design of His Poetry;* Gardner: *The Art of T. S. Eliot;* in *ArQ* 7 (Summer) : 186–92. An extensive and sound criticism of these studies.

1458. Glicksberg, Charles I. "Thomas Stearns Eliot." *American Literary Criticism: 1900–1950,* edited by C. I. Glicksberg, pp. 129–33. New York: Hendricks House, 1951. A textbook introduction to the criticism, stressing the evolution of Eliot's doctrine.

1459. Hall, Donald Andrew. "The Lady with a Past." *HAB* 53 (February 24) : 427–28. On the development of style in

Eliot's early poems reprinted in the *Harvard Advocate Fifty-Year Book.*

1460. Henn, T. R. "Two Kinds of Obscurity: Blake's *The Sick Rose:* and a Passage from T. S. Eliot's *The Waste Land.*" *The Apple and the Spectroscope,* pp. 42–46. London: Methuen & Co., 1951. [Waste Land]. Examination of a long extract from "The Fire Sermon" to show how Eliot uses words and phrases from previous poems to extend his own meaning.

1461. Isaacs, J. "T. S. Eliot and Poetic Drama." *An Assessment of Twentieth-Century Literature,* pp. 134–60. London: Secker and Warburg, 1951. [Sweeney Agonistes; The Rock; Family Reunion; Cocktail Party]. A radio address on Eliot's use of myth and allegory—a criticism of the four plays, of which he thinks *The Family Reunion* the most successful. He is interested in Eliot's dramatic theory, and says: "the creative writing of today has been largely dominated or directed by the critical writing of Mr. Eliot."

1462. Kenner, Hugh. *The Poetry of Ezra Pound.* London: Faber and Faber, 1951. Throws light on Eliot's poetry by comparing it with Pound's. Throughout Kenner relies on Eliot's criticism, and makes scattered allusions to the technique and meaning of his poetry. Kenner weakens his analysis by overemphasis.

*1463. Knox, George A. "Quest for the Word in Eliot's 'Four Quartets.'" *ELH* 18 (December): 310–21. An explanation of the central religious idea of the poem by way of a subtle analysis of the passage on the poetic struggles with language.

1464. Leavis, F. R. "Mr. Eliot and Lawrence." *Scrutiny* 18 (June): 66–73. Leavis accuses Eliot of snobbery toward Lawrence in his preface to Tiverton's *D. H. Lawrence and Human Existence.*

1465. ———, and Wagner, Robert D. "Correspondence: Lawrence and Eliot." Scrutiny 18 (Autumn): 136–43. [Cocktail Party]. A letter from Wagner attacks Leavis (no. 1464). Leavis replies in a vigorous controversial essay, denouncing the worldliness of *The Cocktail Party.*

1466. Lynch, William (Father). "Confusion in Our Theatre." *Thought* 26 (Autumn): 351. [Cocktail Party]. This play shows that Eliot has pushed "into the morass out of which no deeper tragedy comes. . . ." He calls the play a new Waste Land.

1467. Melchiori, Giorgio. "Echoes in 'The Waste Land.' " *ES* 32, no. 1 (February) : 1–11. The author traces the use of materials below the conscious level which went into the building of the "Game of Chess" section of *The Waste Land*. He finds they came from Keats's "Lamia," Joyce's "Ulysses," the "Ancient Mariner," *Cymbeline,* and "The Eve of Saint Agnes," of which *Cymbeline* is the most important.

1468. Meyer, Christine. "Some Unnoted Religious Allusions in T. S. Eliot's 'The Hippopotamus.' " *MLN* 66 (April) : 241–45. A routine investigation pointing out parallels in the Unitarian and Methodist hymnals to lines in Eliot's poem.

*1469. Miles, Josephine. *The Primary Language of Poetry in the 1940's,* pp. 408–17, 484–90. Pt. 3 of *The Continuity of Poetic Language.* University of California Publications in English, vol. 19. Berkeley: University of California Press, 1951. Presents both interesting detailed analyses of Eliot's vocabulary and broadly based generalizations on his use of language.

1470. Munz, Peter. "Devil's Dialectic, or The Cocktail Party." *HJ* 49 (April) : 256–63. [Cocktail Party; Family Reunion; Murder in the Cathedral]. Because Eliot tempers the doctrine of absolute Christian love with worldly wisdom, he has rejected Christ in favor of the devil, and is unable to understand true saintliness.

*1471. Murry, J. Middleton. "A Note on the 'Family Reunion.' " *EIC* 1 (January) : 67–73. Finds a moral confusion in this play, "as though there were an element irreducibly pagan at the heart of a Christian mystery."

*1472. Pinto, Vivian de Sola. "T. S. Eliot." *The Crisis in English Poetry 1880–1940,* pp. 158–86. London: Hutchinson's University Library, 1951. A mature and temperate survey of the whole of Eliot's poetry aside from the plays; especially good for *The Waste Land.*

1473. Redman, Ben Ray. "New Editions." *SatR* 34 (February 17) : 27. [Selected Essays]. Summary.

1474. Reed, Henry. "Towards 'The Cocktail Party.' " *Listener* 45 (May 10 and May 17) : 763–64, 803–4. Praises the verse because in it "lyric has given way to drama, and the verse has for the first time achieved the state of luminous transparency in which the characters can be clearly seen . . . and in which the action can thus be seen also."

1475. Robbins, Rossell Hope. *The T. S. Eliot Myth*, 226 pp. New York: Henry Schuman, 1951. The longest and most bitter attack on Eliot that has yet appeared; Robbins judges all of Eliot's poems from a leftist political point of view.

1476. Rothbard, Lorraine. "Eliot." *Diameter* 1 (March): 31–38. [Cocktail Party].

1477. Scott, Nathan A., Jr. "T. S. Eliot's 'The Cocktail Party': of Redemption and Vocation." *RL* 20 (Spring): 274–85. A long summary of the play followed by a confused restatement of the theological problems which it raises. Revised, enlarged, and reprinted in *Man in the Modern Theater*, 1965, pp. 13–39.

1478. Sergeant, Howard. *Tradition in the Making of Modern Poetry*, vol. 1. London: Britannicus Liber Limited, 1951. Includes Eliot's definition of tradition, a short account of his early life, and scattered references to his relations with Pound.

1479. Sitwell, Edith. *The American Genius*, pp. xvii–xix. London: John Lehmann, 1951. [Sweeney Agonistes; Sweeney among the Nightingales]. An impressionistic analysis of the musical effects of lines in these two poems.

1480. Smith, James Harry and Parks, Edd Winfield. "Thomas Stearns Eliot." *The Great Critics*, pp. 710–13. New York: W. W. Norton, 1951. A clear though brief statement of Eliot's major critical beliefs and of his relations to other critics.

1481. Smith, R. Gregor. "An Exchange of Notes on T. S. Eliot: a Critique." *Theol* 7 (January): 503–6. [Cocktail Party]. Protests against Dunkel's statement (no. 1341) that there is nothing "at all that cannot be found apart from the church" in this play. Smith makes the obvious points.

1482. Spender, Stephen. "Meeting T. S. Eliot." *EngSW* 33 (February): 13–15. On the myth that has grown up around Eliot, the man. "He retains his mystery." Slight but pleasant.

*1483. ———. "On 'The Cocktail Party.'" *The Year's Work in Literature, 1950*, edited by John Lehmann, pp. 17–23. Published for the British Council by Longmans, Green & Co., London, 1951. A highly competent early explanation of the play which contemporary critics found difficult, combined with perceptive criticism, especially of the verse.

1484. ———. *World within World*. New York: Harcourt, Brace, 1951. Scattered personal recollections showing a young poet's admiration for an older one more disciplined and traditional than himself.

1485. Stein, Sol. Review of *Poetry and Drama*. *ArQ* 7 (Summer) : 179–80. He disagrees with Eliot's view that his drama is constantly improving.

1486. Stepanchev, Stephen. "The Origin of J. Alfred Prufrock." *MLN* 66 (June) : 400–401. "The name . . . was probably suggested by the Prufrock-Littau Company . . . in St. Louis."

1487. Symes, Gordon. "T. S. Eliot and Old Age." *FR* 169, no. 1011, n.s. (March) : 186–93. [Prufrock; Gerontion; Ash Wednesday; the Ariel poems; Four Quartets]. "Starting from a natural fear and revulsion, the poet has moved by tentative steps toward an evaluation of old age, an elucidation of its special grace and an appreciation of its special function in the progress of the soul."

1488. Theall, Donald F. "Traditional Satire in Eliot's 'Coriolan.'" *Accent* 11 (Autumn) : 194–206. [Triumphal March, Difficulties of a Statesman]. The poems are a satirical treatment of man's government in the tradition of More, Swift, Rabelais, and Joyce. Considerable attention is given to sources.

1489. Thomas, R. Hinton. "Culture and T. S. Eliot." *MQ* (London) 6 (Spring) : 147–62. [Notes towards the Definition of Culture]. An analysis of Eliot's political and social thought from the point of view of the extreme left. Reasonable in tone but not in idea.

1490. Thompson, Francis J. "Bases of Ascent: The Harvard Advocate Anthology." *HR* 4 (Summer) : 60–61. [Humouresque (after J. Laforgue)]. This early poem illustrates Eliot's persistent belief that the poet must "turn the unpoetical into poetry." (Quotation from Eliot.)

*1491. Tinsley, E. J. "Aldous Huxley and T. S. Eliot: A Study in Two Types of Mysticism." *LS* 6 (October) : 119–30. Huxley's mysticism is "vedantic," Oriental; Eliot's is Christian. Scholarly.

1492. Tschumi, Raymond. "Thought in T. S. Eliot's Poetry." *Thought in Twentieth-Century English Poetry*, pp. 119–56. London: Routledge and Kegan Paul, Ltd., 1951. [Prufrock; Waste Land; Ash Wednesday; Burnt Norton]. This chapter attempts to summarize Eliot's ideas on religion and tradition, and to provide detailed analyses of some of the poems. Disorganized and lacking in perception.

1493. Wagner, Robert D. "Correspondence: Lawrence and Eliot." *Scrutiny* 18 (Autumn) : 136–43. A letter attacking Leavis for accusing Eliot of snobbery toward Lawrence.

1494. Weathers, Willie T. "Eliot's Waste Land, I, 24–30." *Expl* 9, no. 4 (February) : item 31. Suggests persuasively that the "red rock" is a fertility symbol as explained in Weston's *From Ritual to Romance*. (See no. 1409.)

1495. Whicher, George F. "Analysts of Decay." *The Literature of the American People,* edited by A. H. Quinn, pp. 873–78. New York: Appleton-Century Crofts, 1951. A brief summary of the themes and techniques of the poems to 1930.

1496. ———. "Loopholes of Retreat." *The Literature of the American People,* edited by A. H. Quinn, pp. 896–99. New York: Appleton-Century Crofts, 1951. [Four Quartets]. Poetry and drama from 1930 to 1950. Good brief analysis of the *Four Quartets*. "No poem of our time has greater depth and resonance."

*1497. Williams, Raymond. "Criticism into Drama, 1888–1950." *EIC* 1 (April) : 131–38. [Sweeney Agonistes; Murder in the Cathedral; Family Reunion; Cocktail Party]. Because of its unity of feeling, *Murder in the Cathedral* is Eliot's most successful play; form in *The Family Reunion* fails, whereas *The Cocktail Party* triumphantly succeeds. Reprinted in *Drama from Ibsen to Eliot,* London: Chatto and Windus, 1952, pp. 273–77.

1498. Williamson, Audrey. "Poetry in the Theater; Eliot and Fry." *Chrysalis* 4, nos. 5–6 (1951) : 3–19. [Murder in the Cathedral; Family Reunion; Cocktail Party]. Considers the place of poetry in the theater, the stage history of Eliot's three plays, summarizes the plots. The reviewer prefers *The Family Reunion* to the other two because it has "continuous tension" and better poetry. Reprinted in *Theatre of Two Decades,* London: Rockliff, 1951, pp. 134, 144, and *passim*.

1499. Yoklavich, John M. "Eliot's *Cocktail Party* and Plato's *Symposium*." *N&Q* 196, no. 25 (December 8) : 541–42. Points out a "slender Platonic parallel" between the two works, centering on Harcourt-Reilly as a kind of Socrates.

1952

1500. Aiken, Conrad. *Ushant, an Essay.* New York: Duell, Sloan & Pearce, 1952. Personal reminiscences of Eliot.

1501. Ames, Russell. "Decadence in the Art of T. S. Eliot." *ScSo* 16 (March) : 193–221. [Prufrock]. Criticism from the socialist point of view, which finds that Eliot has broken up artistic form and produced poor art that has abandoned reason.

1502. Anon. "Books and T. S. Eliot." *SatR* 35 (March 8) : 23. Letters from Frank S. MacShane, Christopher E. Fullman, and Diana S. Purrington defending Eliot against the attack by Van Wyck Brooks (no. 1508) and the editorial by H. Smith (no. 1539) on the same date.

1503. ———. "Eliot Complete." *Time* 60 (December 22) : 68–70. [Complete Poems and Plays]. The poems "contain the comment of one highly civilized brain and a poetic talent as deep, constricted and penetrating as an oil well, on the human condition in today's world."

1504. Bain, Richard. *The Unholy Trade,* pp. 130–46 and *passim.* London: Gollancz, 1952. [Sweeney Agonistes, The Rock, Murder in the Cathedral, Family Reunion, Cocktail Party]. ". . . his plays are lonely, austere artifacts, inimitable, but he has shown the way for the next generation; he has redeemed the poetic drama." Chiefly skillful summaries.

1505. Bateson, F. W. "The Critical Forum. 'Dissociation of Sensibility.' " *EIC* 2 (April) : 213–14. A rebuttal of Eric Thompson's article in this issue. ". . . the fact must be faced that, however much we dress it up, the Dissociation of Sensibility cannot be made respectable."

1506. Blackmur, R. P. "Lord Tennyson's Scissors, 1912–1950." *KR* 14: 1–20. Praise of Yeats, Pound, and Eliot for having learned to fuse music with meaning.

1507. Brooks, Harold F. " 'The Family Reunion' and 'Colombe's Birthday.' " *TLS,* no. 2654 (December 12) , p. 819. Suggests that the influence of Browning's play on Eliot's, though imprecise and general, is observable.

1508. Brooks, Van Wyck. "Faith vs. Doubt in Literature." *The Confident Years.* New York: E. P. Dutton & Co., 1952. Also in *SatR* 35 (February 2) : 11–12 ff. In believing in the doctrine of original sin, Eliot has abandoned, or even reversed, the best American tradition.

1509. Colum, Mary. "St. Louis over Bloomsbury." *SatR* 35 (December 27): 17–18. [Complete Poems and Plays]. A review expressing the commonplaces of Eliot criticism, that the early poetry is the best, that the poems and plays are limited in their emotional range, and that he deserved the Nobel Prize.

1510. Coulon, H. J. "T. S. Eliot and Anglo-Catholicism." *SatR* 35 (April 5): 23. A letter saying that Eliot's social and political views have nothing to do with Anglo-Catholicism.

1511. Czamanake, Palmer, and Hertz, Karl. "The Beginning of T. S. Eliot's Theory of Culture." *Cresset* 15: 9–21. Traces the idea of *Notes towards the Definition of Culture* through Eliot's earlier writings.

1512. Durrell, Lawrence. "T. S. Eliot." *Key to Modern British Poetry*, pp. 143–63. London: Peter Nevill, Ltd., 1952. [Waste Land, Four Quartets]. First given as a lecture, this is an agreeable but somewhat diffuse explanation of the two poems.

1513. Freedman, Morris. "Jazz Rhythms and T. S. Eliot." *SAQ* 51 (July): 419–35. [Sweeney Agonistes, Old Possum's Book of Practical Cats]. A provocative analysis of Eliot's technique in using jazz rhythms in relation to his meaning. ". . . in succumbing to the attraction of jazz—and, by extension, to the modern world—Eliot deals that world of vulgarity and jazz a blow with its own weapon in *Sweeney Agonistes*."

1514. Friar, Kinon. "Politics and Some Poets." *NR* 127 (July 7): 17–18. Rejects Eliot's political ideas from the standpoint of one to whom "a natural faith" alone is valid.

1515. Frohock, W. M. "The Morals of Mr. Eliot." *SWR* 37 (Spring): viii, x, xi, 163–66. [Review of R. H. Robbins's *The T. S. Eliot Myth*]. Points out the weakness of this book, that Robbins's condemnation of Eliot rests on his dislike of Eliot as sometimes anti-Semitic and always a social reactionary.

*1516. Gallup, Donald. *T. S. Eliot: a Bibliography, Including Contributions to Periodicals and Foreign Translations*, 177 pp. London: Faber and Faber, 1952. A model bibliography, the authoritative work on Eliot's own writing. Revised in 1969.

1517. Howes, A. B. "T. S. Eliot's 'A Cooking Egg.'" *HumY* 1 (March): 1–5. The speaker is a man who cannot find a meaningful existence in modern society.

1518. Kee, Howard C. "The Bible and the Work of Eliot and Sitwell." *FrI* 109 (November 8): 641–42. [Cocktail Party]. Eliot's use of the Bible is unsatisfactory to the author because Eliot does not fully appreciate man's moral responsibility; he is a Calvinist.

1519. Kelly, Robert. *The Premises of Disorganization: A Study of Literary Form in Ezra Pound, T. S. Eliot, James Joyce, and Dorothy Richardson*, pp. 226–28. Stanford University Abstracts of Dissertations, 1952. [Waste Land]. Assuming that the "objective correlative" is anti-rational and that it dominates the structure of the poem, he concludes that the poem lacks rational organization.

1520. Leavis, R. R. *The Common Pursuit.* New York: George W. Stewart, 1952. Reprints of nos. 434, 1067, and 1258.

1521. Levý, Jiří. "Synthesis of Antitheses in the Poetry of T. S. Eliot." *EIC* 2 (October): 434–43. "The synthesis of antitheses by undermining the belief in the reliability of human concepts focuses the attention *beyond* the things and actions of objective reality, and endows metaphysical conclusions with the appearance of greater comparative reality." The study is based on Eliot's diction.

1522. Lonkon, R. "T. S. Eliot's Recent Work." *ConR* 182 (July): 34–37. [Notes towards the Definition of Culture; Cocktail Party]. Praises these as the fruits of Eliot's mature wisdom.

*1523. Marshall, William H. "The Text of T. S. Eliot's 'Gerontion.'" *SB* 4 (1951–52): 213–17. A meticulous collation of the seven published texts of the poem, with Eliot's final approval of an "eclectic" text compiled by University of Virginia scholars.

*1524. Maxwell, D. E. S. *Poetry of T. S. Eliot*, 223 pp. London: Routledge and Kegan Paul, 1952. Richard Ludwig says: "a major contribution." Maxwell "ranged beyond the poetry into history, French symbolism, poetic drama, and humanist philosophy." He is particularly good on the critical background (what Eliot opposed in the Georgians and what he substituted), the new classicism, and the orthodoxy of humanist philosophy, "yet he never fails to integrate these matters with the elucidation of the poetry."

*1525. McCarthy, Harold E. "T. S. Eliot and Buddhism." *PhilEW* 2 (April): 31–55. [Four Quartets]. A mature, well-balanced analysis of Eliot's relation to Buddhism as shown in the poem. "Although Eliot's general problem is universal, it could still appear . . . that his particular formulation of the problem is strikingly similar to that of Buddhism."

1526. Mellers, Wilfrid. "Recent Trends in British Music." *MusQ* 38 (1952): 185–201. On Eliot's lecture on Milton at the British Academy.

1527. Musgrove, Sydney. *T. S. Eliot and Walt Whitman,* 89 pp. Wellington: University of New Zealand Press, 1952. "The purpose of this essay is to examine what there is in Eliot that can be ascribed to an abiding memory of Whitman." A chapter entitled "Eliot and Tennyson" is reprinted in Hugh Kenner's *Eliot,* pp. 73–85.

1528. Paul, David. "Euripides and Mr. Eliot." *TC* 152 (August): 174–80. [Cocktail Party]. The didacticism of the play, particularly in the figure of the psychiatrist, precludes the sympathy essential to drama. The adaptation of figures from *Alcestis* is unsuccessful.

1529. Payne, Robert. *The Great God Pan,* p. 75. New York: Hermitage House, 1952. On the possible identification of Sweeney as "Sweeny Todd, of penny-dreadful fame."

1530. Peter, John. "A New Interpretation of *The Waste Land.*" *EIC* 2 (July): 242–66. Offers as the central theme of the poem the love of the protagonist for a man, now drowned, his horrified reactions to his love, and his turning to religion.

1531. Popkin, Henry. "Poets as Performers: revival of poetry-reading." *TAr* 36 (February): 74. Eliot is modest, objective, impersonal in reading his poetry. "There is a striking parallel between the manner of Eliot's platform appearance and the matter of his poems."

*1532. Pritchett, V. S. "An American Puritan in England." *NYTBR* 7 (November 30), pp. 1, 36. [Complete Poems and Plays]. A discriminating analysis. Eliot is a Puritan in his longing for a lost past, in his separation of the mind, body, and senses, and in his insistence that poetry comes of suffering.

*1533. Ranson, John Crowe. "The Poems of T. S. Eliot: a Perspective." *NR* 127 (December 8): 16–17. [Four Quartets; Waste Land; Ash Wednesday]. A broad and sensitive survey of Eliot's poetic career, with special reference to his religious evolution. "The Quartets . . . may well come to be for us the poem of the century."

1534. Redman, Ben Ray. "Critical Appraisal." *SatR* 35 (February 2) : 19. [Review of *The T. S. Eliot Myth* by R. H. Robbins]. An attack on Eliot in the course of praising Robbins's book.

1535. Richman, Robert. "The Quiet Conflict: the Plays of T. S. Eliot." *NR* 127 (December 8) : 17–18. [Cocktail Party; Murder in the Cathedral; Ramily Reunion]. Defends Eliot for writing metaphysical plays, in which meditation is more important than action.

*1536. Scott, Nathan. "T. S. Eliot: a Contemporary Synthesis." *Rehearsals of Discomposure,* pp. 178–245. New York: King's Crown Press, 1952. [Waste Land; Family Reunion; East Coker]. In the course of a sensitive and informed discussion of Eliot's relevance to contemporary problems, Scott presents an excellent analysis of *The Waste Land* and briefer analyses of *The Family Reunion* and *East Coker.*

1537. Shulenberger, Arvid. "Mr. Eliot's Sunday Morning Service." *Expl* 10, no. 4 (February) : item 29. Interprets the poem as a dramatic opposition between the Church's present low state and its past splendor.

*1538. Smith, Grover. "Mr. Eliot's New 'Murder.'" *NMQ* 22 (Autumn) : 331–39. [The film of *Murder in the Cathedral*]. A luminous essay on the central meaning of the play, comparing the stage and motion picture versions.

1539. Smith, Harrison. "Strange Paradox." *SatR* 35 (February 9) : 20. Praises Van Wyck Brooks for condemning Pound and Eliot because they have abandoned America and American optimism.

1540. Thompson, Eric. "The Critical Forum, 'Dissociation of Sensibility.'" *EIC* 2 (April) : 207–13. In pointing out indebtedness to F. H. Bradley's philosophy, Thompson clarifies Eliot's use of the term. He denies Bateson's assertion that Remy de Gourmont is the chief influence on Eliot.

1541. Thorlby, Anthony. "The Poetry of the Four Quartets." *CamJ* 5 (February) : 280–99. A difficult but suggestive essay on the inhibiting effect of Eliot's critical analysis of life on his poetry, an inhibition which is common in our age.

1542. Vassilieff, Elizabeth. "The Quiddity of *Four Quartets.*" *Direction* (Melbourne), no. 1 (May), pp. 34–45. In spite of an error in fact and a questionable interpretation, this is a sound and readable study of the poem.

1543. Weisstein, Ulrich. *"The Cocktail Party:* An Attempt at Interpretation on Mythological Grounds." *WR* 16 (Spring) : 232–41. Beginning with likenesses between the play and *Alcestis,* the author plunges deeper and deeper into unsupported interpretations. Julia, he holds, is both one of the Fates and God, while Harcourt-Reilly is the Devil.

1544. Weitz, Morris. "T. S. Eliot: Time as a Mode of Salvation." *SR* 60 (Winter) : 48–64. [Prufrock; Four Quartets]. "To apprehend the immanence of God in the temporal is not to deny the reality of the temporal or to proclaim its illusory character; but to comprehend its mode of reality for the first time as a creation of God, with its own characteristic of individuality." He reads "Prufrock" as a Christian poem.

*1545. Williams, Raymond. "T. S. Eliot," *Drama from Ibsen to Eliot,* pp. 223–46. London: Chatto and Wildus, 1952. [Sweeney Agonistes; Murder in the Cathedral; Family Reunion; Cocktail Party; Rock]. Highly competent criticism. Williams thinks that *Murder in the Cathedral* is "the best example in the years I have been considering of the discovery of an adequate form for serious drama." Reprints and expands no. 1497.

1546. Wimsatt, W. K., Jr. "Prufrock and Maud: From Plot to Symbol." *YFS,* no. 9 (1952) , pp. 84–92. Overtones of "Maud" echo in "Prufrock"; but a comparison of the two poems reveals the development of the use of symbolism from Tennyson's era to Eliot's.

1547. Wood, Frank. "Rilke and Eliot: Tradition and Poetry." *GR* 27 (December) : 246–59. A tentative analysis of affinities between the two poets. While their idea of tradition differs, both are concerned with preserving tradition in the modern world. Both admire Baudelaire, and have similar themes.

1548. Worsley, T. C. "The Second Cocktail Party." *The Fugitive Art; Dramatic Commentaries 1947–51,* pp. 144–46. London: John Lehmann, 1952. [Cocktail Party]. Chiefly on the production in London with a new cast.

1953

1549. Abel, Darrel. "R.L.S. and 'Prufrock.' " *N&Q* 198: 37–38. The poem contains resemblances to Stevenson's "Crabbed Age and Youth."

1550. Allen, Gay Wilson. "The Poet and the Personality." *NYTBR* 7 (November 29), p. 24. [Musgrove's *T. S. Eliot and Walt Whitman*]. Calls it a "subtle and illuminating study of the unconscious influence of Whitman on Eliot's imagery."

1551. Anon. *On the Four Quartets of T. S. Eliot, with a Foreword by Roy Campbell,* 64 pp. London: V. Stuart, 1953. [In the 1965 American edition the author is identified as Constance De Masirevich]. An almost hysterically enthusiastic interpretation of the poem.

1552. ———. "Source Hunting." *TLS* (February 20). [Musgrove's *T. S. Eliot and Walt Whitman*]. A brief, laudatory review.

1553. ———. "Poet and Critic." *TLS* (March 27). [Selected Prose]. Eliot's earlier criticism is more valuable than his later because he was imaginatively closer to his subject.

1554. ———. "The Waste Land Revisited." *TLS,* no. 2691 (August 28), pp. viii, ix. "The mood and imagery of the poem have had an oblique rather than direct influence. It exhibits a belief which is 'radical and reactionary, as opposed to a liberal and progressive, attitude toward the disorders of modern society.' " From *AL*.

1555. ———. "Three-Stringed Lyre." *TLS* (November 27). Skillful summary of "The Three Voices of Poetry," given as a lecture.

1556. ———. "The Eliot Family and St. Louis." *WUS,* n.s., Language and Literature, no. 23, 1953. An appendix to "American Literature and the American Language," an address delivered by Eliot at Washington University on June 9, 1953. All the descendents of Eliot's grandfather, William Greenleaf Eliot, were strongly motivated toward public service.

1557. Atkinson, Brooks. "Triumph at Old Vic. Eliot's 'Murder in the Cathedral' Gains Fresh Values in Its New Production." *NYT* 2 (April 26), p. 1. Enthusiastic praise of the play as "magnificent theatre" and of this production.

1558. Auden, W. H. "T. S. Eliot So Far." *Griffin* 2: 1–3. A sympathetic and discriminating essay on Eliot's career as poet and playwright.

1559. Bateson, F. W. " 'A Cooking Egg': Three Postscripts." *EIC* 3 (October): 476–77. Summarizes interpretations of Pipit as 1) a child spirit control of an elderly medium (essay by Mrs. Adeline Glasheen) ; 2) the screen is one behind which the speaker kissed the child Pipit (suggestion by Grover Smith) ; 3) explanation of some of the key phrases of the poem (by Constance I. Smith).

1560. ———. "The Function of Criticism at the Present Time." *EIC* 3 (January) : 1–27. [A Cooking Egg]. Suggests a reading of "A Cooking Egg" which became the center of animated discussion.

1561. ———. "The Critical Forum. 'A Cooking Egg.'" *EIC* 3 (July) : 353–57. Reaffirms his earlier position, no. 1560, that Pipit is a "Bloomsbury demivierge."

1562. Beare, Robert L. "T. S. Eliot and Goethe." *GR* 28 (December) : 243–53. A tentative but thoughtful explanation of Eliot's reasons for denying Goethe a central position among the great poets.

1563. Beaver, Joseph. "T. S. Eliot's Four Quartets." *Expl* 9, no. 5 (March) : item 37. Proposes a purely scientific explanation for the lines in "East Coker," "Out at sea the dawn wind/ Wrinkles and slides" and a more rewarding scientific explanation of "unimaginable zero summer" from "Little Gidding, I." *Zero* is absolute zero $(-273\,^{\circ}\text{C})$ and is unimaginable because it is theoretical. At this temperature stillness is achieved.

1564. Bland, D. S. "Mr. Eliot on the Underground." *MLN* 68 (January) : 27–28. [Four Quartets]. The "Inner Circle" of the London Tube "can be conceived as a symbol of almost Dantesque power" and is basic to *Four Quartets.*

1565. Blisset, William. "Pater and Eliot." *UTQ* 22: 261–68. "Eliot's denigration of Pater may be a natural reaction from an early enthusiasm; cites resemblances in expression, imagery, taste, and preoccupation." From *AL.*

1566. Bodelsen, C. A. "Two Difficult 'Poems by T. S. Eliot.'" *ES* 34 (February) : 17–22. [Burnt Norton]. The children are those that might have been born, and symbolize what the protagonist missed in life. The second group of lines (1–15 of sec. 2) are tentatively interpreted as describing "one, partial and imperfect, kind of detachment from time and the material world."

1567. Brown, Spencer. Review of George Williamson's *Reader's Guide to T. S. Eliot. Poetry* 82 (August) :287–91. Although "this is surely The Book on Eliot," Williamson's "tremendous labor of love" is weakened by its preoccupation with the intellectual structure behind the poems and is insufficiently aware of Eliot's deficiencies.

1568. Carroll, Joseph. "T. S. Eliot Arrives in the Theatre, not with a Bang but a Whimper." *TAr* 37 (February) : 12–13, 94–95. [Cocktail Party; Family Reunion; Murder in the Cathedral]. *The Cocktail Party* is a very boring play, *The Family Reunion* is a little better; in *Murder in the Cathedral* he came closer to success than in the others.

1569. Carter, Paul J., Jr. "Who Understands 'The Cocktail Party?' " *ColQ* 2 (Autumn) : 193–205. A summary of some contradictory opinions concerning the play, concluding that "Eliot's admonition is cheerless, austere, and ambiguous."

1570. Crawford, Ian. "More Mirth Than Mysticism." *TAr* 37 (November) : 81–82. [Confidential Clerk]. The reviewer is not sure of the intellectual meaning of the play, but "no play from his pen so well bears being seen."

1571. Cunningham, Gilbert F. "The Critical Forum. 'A Cooking Egg.' " *EIC* 3 (July) : 347–50. Pipit is the speaker's fiancée; they are, in their thirties, embarking on a marriage of convenience.

1572. Dobrée, Bonamy. Review of *Selected Prose*, edited by John Hayward, p. 582. *NSN* 45 (May 16). Eliot is "all of a piece" and you do not need to agree with him to find him stimulating.

1573. Donald, Henry. "Edinburgh Festival." *Spectator* 191 (September 4) : 238. [Confidential Clerk]. "This is a maddening, broken-backed play."

1574. Drew, Elizabeth. "The Critical Forum, 'A Cooking Egg.' " *EIC* 3 (July) : 353. Miss Drew is indebted to I. A. Richards for her earlier interpretation of Pipit. She reasons that Pipit was a childhood playmate, now a spinster of thirty.

1575. Edman, Irwin. "The Spoken Word: England and New England." *SatR* 36 (April 25) : 71. [Waste Land; Sweeney among the Nightingales; Ash Wednesday]. Notes the "bland semi-international English," the dryness, the cadence, and the clerical intonation of Eliot's voice, but admits its "magic and . . . power."

1576. ———. "Words and Drama; Recording of Murder in the Cathedral." *SatR* 36 (November 28) : 88. "It is hard to say which is the greater miracle, the performance or the recording of it."

1577. Engle, Paul. "Why Modern Poetry." *CE* 15 (October): 7-11. [Prufrock]. The "ragged claws" lines are used as an illustration of the compressed suggestiveness of modern poetry. A clear, sensible introduction for the beginner.

1578. Fell, Kenneth. "From Myth to Martyrdom: Towards a View of Milton's *Samson Agonistes.*" *ES* 34 (August): 145-55. [Murder in the Cathedral]. Treats Eliot's play as the final stage in the development of Samson's story from its original mythical form through a story of revenge in Milton to the "maturer reading of God's intention in Eliot."

1579. Findlater, Richard. "The Camouflaged Drama." *TC* 154 (October): 311-16. [Confidential Clerk.] "Though Eliot's new play . . . promises to be a great box office success, it is a failure because it lacks emotional unity." From *AL*.

1580. Fowler, D. C. *"The Waste Land:* Mr. Eliot's 'Fragments.' " *CE* 14 (January): 234-35. Suggests that the bundle of quotations at the end of the poem is a charm to break the spell of the waste land.

*1581. Goheen, Robert F. " 'Burbank with a Baedeker,' the Third Stanza: Thematic Intention through Classical Allusion." *SR* 61 (Winter): 109-19. A fine exploration of the classical sources of the stanza, broadening into insights into "the deep-set and fecund life of the mind in which Eliot shares to an important degree."

1582. Greenberg, Clement. "The Plight of Our Culture: Industrialism and Class Mobility." *Commentary* 15 (June): 558-66. [Notes towards the Definition of Culture]. "The main trouble with [his position] is less that it is reactionary than that it is irrelevant."

1583. ———. "The Plight of Our Culture: Work and Leisure under Industrialism," pt. 2. *Commentary* 16 (July): 54-62. He now leaves Eliot and proposes his own solution.

1584. Gwynn, Frederick L. "Eliot's 'Sweeney among the Nightingales' and *The Song of Solomon.*" *MLN* 68 (January): 25-27. Notes verbal and conceptual echoes from the Bible.

1585. ———. "Faulkner's Prufrock—and Other Observations." *JEGP* 52 (January): 63-70. Faulkner's *Mosquitoes* has

many verbal echoes of Eliot's early poems, not well assimilated into the novel.

1586. Hassan, Ihab H. "French Symbolism and Modern British
Poetry: with Yeats, Eliot and Edith Sitwell as Indices."
DA 13: 232–33. (Pennsylvania). No conclusions are
given here, but only a discussion of Mr. Hassan's method.

*1587. Heilman, Robert B. *"Alcestis* and *The Cocktail Party." CL*
5 (Spring) : 105–16. Eliot uncovers the "symbolic possibilities" of the literal story by interpretation and by
subtle changes in situation and character.

1588. Hewes, Henry. "A Bang and a Whimper." *SatR* 36 (September 12) : 44–46. [Confidential Clerk]. The play is
a comedy but "in addition there are moments of sad
profundity scattered" throughout.

1589. ———. "T. S. Eliot—Confidential Playwright." *SatR* 36
(August 29) : 26–28. [Cocktail Party; Confidential
Clerk]. In an interview, Eliot commented on his method
of playwriting, his intentions in these plays, his metrics,
and his sources.

1590. Karlin, Ken. "Critical Notes." *ChiR* 7: 52–54. ". . . Eliot
believes it impossible . . . to experience love in normal
human intercourse," because people inevitably misun-
derstand each other.

1591. Kirk, Russell. "Two Plays of Resignation." *Month* 10 (October) : 223–25. [Confidential Clerk]. The play "will be
remembered more for its occasional lines of melancholy
beauty and its penetration into the recesses of Self than
as a neat and close-knit play. . . ." Finds echoes of Ibsen,
Wilde, and Shaw.

1592. Leavis, F. R. "The State of Criticism: Representations to
Fr. Martin-Jarrett-Kerr." *EIC* 3 (April) : 219. In an
article replying to Jarrett-Kerr's criticism of him, Leavis
says that Eliot is now "a safe academic classic" and opposes the doctrinal approach to Eliot's poetry.

*1593. Lehmann, John. "T. S. Eliot Talks about Himself and the
Drive to Create." *NYT* 7 (November 29) , pp. 5, 44.
Eliot gives Lehmann valuable information on outside
events that led to his writing the Ariel poems, *Ash
Wednesday, The Rock, Murder in the Cathedral,* and
Four Quartets; also spoke on his dislike of repeating the
same techniques.

1594. Mairet, Philip. "The Confidential Clerk." *NR* 129 (September 21) : 17–18. This comedy of manners has so

much plot that it comes near to melodrama. Mairet supposes that Colby is Sir Claude's son.

1595. Melchiori, Giorgio. "Eliot and the Theatre." *EM,* no. 4 (1953), pp. 187–233. "Eliot's plays, . . . are all based on the same situation and deal with the same characters. The development is in the direction of a more and more open statement of his aims." But the situation, the sense of sin, never becomes dramatically vital.

1596. ———. "The Moment as a Time-Unit in Fiction." *EIC* 3 (October) : 434–36. A clear summary of the meaning of Eliot's "Moment in the rose garden," depending on Unger, no. 1191 and Martz, no. 1073.

1597. Moorman, Charles. "Order and Mr. Eliot." *SAQ* 52 (January) : 73–87. "The sacramental point of view which finds its method in the constant reconciling of disparate elements can be said to underlie all of Eliot's work and is the foundation upon which he has constructed his poetry, his critical theory, and his conception of the nature of culture in a Christian society." From *AL.*

1598. Morgan, F. Bruce. "The Cocktail Party." *Crossroads* 3 (July-September) : 79–81. A much-simplified account of the Christian doctrine of the play.

1599. Morris, David. *The Poetry of Gerard Manley Hopkins and T. S. Eliot in the Light of the Donne Tradition. A Comparative Study,* 143 pp. Bern: Arnaud Druck, 1953. Eliot resembles Donne in intelligence, complexity of thought, unity of thought and feeling, his use of wit and the intellectual conceit. Both poets move from worldly to spiritual preoccupations; both experiment with verse forms.

1600. Morrissette, Bruce A. "T. S. Eliot and Guillaume Apollinaire." *CL* 5 (Summer) : 262–68. "Eliot develops with great skill some of Apollinaire's 'insights, tonalities, devices, and themes.'" From *AL.*

1601. Peacock, Ronald. "Public and Private Problems in Modern Drama." *BJRL* 36 (1953–54) : 38–55. Reprinted in the *Tulane Drama Review* 3 (March, 1959) : 69–72. [Family Reunion; Cocktail Party]. Compares Ibsen, Georg Kaiser, Giraudoux, and Eliot to show their portrayal of the relationship between the social world and an individual's world. Eliot's method is to use "ritualistic realism."

1602. Peter, John. "Murder in the Cathedral." *SR* 61 (Summer) : 362–83. ". . . the play is lucid and integral in a way in which the later plays are not." Reprinted in Kenner's *Eliot*, pp. 155–72.

1603. Ramsay, Warren. "Irony and Legend." *Jules Laforgue and the Ironic Inheritance*, pp. 192–94, 197–204. New York: Oxford University Press, 1953. Brief but authoritative on Eliot's debt to Laforgue, which Ramsay manages to keep in proper perspective.

1604. Read, Herbert. *The True Voice of Feeling, Studies in English Romantic Poetry*, pp. 139–50. London: Faber and Faber, 1953. [Family Reunion; Cocktail Party]. As part of an inquiry into the meaning of "organic form" Read examines Eliot's distinction between "verse" and poetry, and questions whether poetry can be successful in drama.

1605. Reed, Henry. "If and Perhaps and But." *Listener* 49 (June 18): 1017–18. [Selected Prose]. On Eliot's prose style; a thoughtful essay.

1606. Robbins, Rossell Hope. "A Possible Analogue for *The Cocktail Party*." *ES* 34: 165–67. Charles Williams's novel, *Descent into Hell*, is suggested.

1607. Robinson, D. E. "Economics and the Possibility of Civilization: Four Judgments." *QJE* 67 (February): 50–75. [Notes towards the Definition of Culture]. The book is summarized as one of four eminent essays on civilization which tend to refute Keynes's assertion that economists are trustees of the "possibility of civilization."

1608. Ross, Malcolm Mackenzie. "Conclusion: the Firmament Arrested." *Poetry and Dogma*, pp. 249–51; *passim*. New Brunswick: Rutgers University Press, 1954. [Ash Wednesday; Four Quartets]. Whereas "Ash Wednesday" is a fine failure as a Christian poem because it depends on an understanding of liturgy which most readers do not possess, this difficulty is overcome in the great achievement of the *Quartets*.

1609. Sastri, P. S. "T. S. Eliot and the Contemporary World." *ModR* 83 (March): 233–36. A rapid survey of all of Eliot's poems, centering on their religious and philosophical "message."

1610. Schwalb, Harry M. "Eliot's A Game of Chess." *Expl* 11, no. 6 (April). [Waste Land]. Finds a parallel between scenes in Shakespeare's *Antony and Cleopatra* I.i and I.ii and the boudoir-pub scenes of the "Game of Chess."

1611. Schwartz, Edward. "Eliot's *Cocktail Party* and the New

Humanism." *PQ* 32 (January): 58–68. "Humanism, for Eliot, may be only ancillary to Christianity, but it nevertheless is a powerful influence . . . in his writing."

1612. Simon, Irene. "Echoes in *The Waste Land.*" *ES* 34 (April): 64–72. A tentative suggestion that the "Game of Chess" section of this poem may owe something to "The Rape of the Lock."

1613. Simons, Jack W. "Eliot and His Critics." *Cweal* 57: 515–16. [Waste Land]. Since some Americans expect ideology in poetry, readers who found in this poem their own disillusionment came to look on Eliot as a false seer when he did not lead them to a utopia.

1614. Spender, Stephen. "Rilke and the Angels, Eliot and the Shrines." *SR* 61 (Autumn): 557–81. [Four Quartets]. A contrast between the attitudes toward life of the two poets.

*1615. Stein, Arnold. *Answerable Style*, pp. 132–34. Minneapolis: University of Minnesota Press, 1953. Examines Eliot's assertion that Milton does violence to language, and in a fine comparison between a passage from Milton and sec. 6 of "Ash Wednesday" illuminates both poetic styles.

*1616. Stein, Walter. "After the Cocktails." *EIC* 3 (January): 85–104. [Cocktail Party]. A careful and provocative discussion of the play as a failure because its author has lost faith in the Christian solution and has substituted for it Manicheanism.

1617. Stinton, T. C. W., and Browning, I. R. "The Critical Forum. 'A Cooking Egg.'" *EIC* 3 (July): 350–53. Pipit is the nurse, and the poem is "the poignant contrast between the way the world looked to the boy, and the way it looks to the man."

1618. Tillyard, E. M. W. "The Critical Forum. 'A Cooking Egg.'" *EIC* 3 (July): 345–47. [Also "Sweeney Agonistes"]. Pipit is a homely girl whom the speaker had played with as a child. Concerning Sweeney, Eliot told Tillyard that he was a professional boxer who kept a bar.

1619. Trewin, John Courtney. "Mr. Eliot." *Dramatists of Today*, pp. 102–10. London, New York: Staples Press, 1953. [Murder in the Cathedral; Family Reunion; Cocktail Party]. Finds the plays dull as theatre.

1620. Weightman, J. G. "Edinburgh, Elsinore and Chelsea." *TC* 154 (October): 302–10. [Confidential Clerk]. Admires the form but doubts the quality of the content of this play; finds Act III lacking in taste.

1621. West, Ray B., Jr. "Personal History and the *Four Quartets*." *NMQ* 23: 269–82. Eliot's poem has been seen as primarily religious, but it contains much personal history.

*1622. Williamson, George. *A Reader's Guide to T. S. Eliot: a Poem by Poem Analysis*, 248 pp. New York: The Noonday Press, 1953. "No attempt has been made to give full readings or analyses of the poem; nor to recover all the borrowings or erudition of the poet; only to offer some guidance to the evident but not obvious pattern of the poems, at most to chart their course." One of the most complete studies of the poems.

1623. Worsley, T. C. "The Confidential Clerk." *NSN* 46 (September 5) : 256. Criticizes the play on grounds of the confused impression it makes, even though it can rivet the attention of the audience.

1954

1624. Adams, Robert M. "Donne and Eliot: Metaphysicals," *KR* 16 (Spring) : 278–91. "Eliot, like Donne, heroically turned the stream of English verse into dramatic channels and thereby liberated the energy which arises from contrasts and disorder." From *AL*.

1625. Aldington, Richard. *Ezra Pound and T. S. Eliot. A Lecture*, 20 pp. Reading: Peacock Press, 1954. The book was written "about fifteen years ago" as part of a series of lectures given at an eastern American University. Attacks Eliot for pessimism, triviality, and for borrowing without acknowledgment.

1626. Anon. "T. S. Eliot on Life and Its Paradoxes." *NYTM* 6 (February 21) , p. 16. [Confidential Clerk]. The play represents "the high poetic powers of a master of language."

1627. ———. "First Night: The Confidential Clerk." *Newsweek* 43 (February 22) : 94. "His failure lies in trying to play showman at the expense of the detached genius who wrote 'Murder in the Cathedral' and 'Sweeney Agonistes.' "

1628. ———. "The Confidential Clerk." *TAr* 38 (April) : 22–25. Four pages of photographs of the New York stage production, summary, and quotations from the play.

1629. ———. "The Confidential Clerk." *Time* 63 (February 22): 80, 83. "However accomplished and distinctive in places, *The Confidential Clerk* suggests a clever prestidigitator rather than the greatest poet alive."

1630. Arrowsmith, William. "The Comedy of T. S. Eliot." *English Stage Comedy*, edited by W. K. Wimsatt, Jr., pp. 148–72. New York: Columbia University Press, *English Institute Essays*, 1954. Argues that "where Euripides, in dealing with supernatural events in a naturalistic manner, did justice to both planes, Eliot's comedies fail because they do not adequately realize the natural relations through which they seek to convey supernatural relations."

*1631. ———. "Menander and Milk Wood." *HudR* 7 (Summer): 291–96. [Confidential Clerk]. By insisting on renunciation and nothing else, Eliot has impoverished his play, which is further weakened by stark, deprived language.

1632. Atkinson, Brooks. "T. S. Eliot's 'Clerk.'" *NYT* 2 (February 21), p. 1. The play "represents a consistent retreat from poetry over a period of nineteen years" and the result is a commonplace drama.

1633. Baldridge, Marie. "Some Psychological Patterns in the Poetry of T. S. Eliot." *Psychoanalysis* 3 (Fall): 19–47. She is concerned with the pattern of desire, guilt, renunciation, punishment, and salvation, chiefly in the poems between 1910 and 1930. She cannot accept his religion.

1634. Bateson, F. W., and Richards, I. A. "'A Cooking Egg': Final Scramble." *EIC*, 4 (January): 106–8. "What, . . . on my reading, is the structural core of "A Cooking Egg'? To put it crudely, I suggest that the poem's meaning is built around the social [class] implications of the various phrases and images."

1635. Beach, Joseph W. "Conrad Aiken and T. S. Eliot: Echoes and Overtones." *PMLA* 69: 753–62. Beach presents detailed evidence that Eliot's "Prufrock" influenced Aiken's "The Jig of Forslin," and that possibly Aiken gave Eliot hints for the Tarot cards and the voices out of empty cisterns in *The Waste Land*.

1636. Becker, William. "Broadway: Classics and Imports." *HudR* 7 (Summer): 269–71. [Confidential Clerk]. The plot is improbable, the Christianity ambiguous, but the language was good to hear.

1637. Bellow, Saul. "Pleasure and Pains of Playgoing." *PR* 21

(May) : 313–15. [Confidential Clerk]. Calls the play a version of *The Importance of Being Ernest*. Bellow cannot see "salvation in being . . . three parts iced over."

1638. Bentley, Eric. "Old Possum at Play." *NR* 130 (February 22) : 22. [Confidential Clerk]. As dramaturgy, the play marks an advance over Eliot's previous ones in that it has a plot, but it fails because it is not supported by comic rhythm. It is difficult to appraise the play.

1639. ———. "Theatre," *NR* 131 (August 9) : 22. [Murder in the Cathedral; Family Reunion; Cocktail Party; Confidential Clerk]. Eliot's modern plays suffer from his belief that relationships between human beings are neither possible nor desirable, but in spite of this, they are full of "incidental felicities." His best play is *Murder in the Cathedral*.

1640. Berland, Alwyn. "Some Techniques of Fiction in Poetry." *EIC* 4 (October) : 380–85. [Prufrock]. A complex analysis of point of view and scene in the poem.

1641. Blau, Herbert. "W. B. Yeats and T. S. Eliot: Poetic Drama and Modern Poetry." *DA* 14: 523–24. (Stanford). Both Yeats and Eliot represent "tardy Romanticism"; both are extreme representatives of "dissociation of sensibility."

1642. Bodelsen, Merete, and Bodelsen, C. A. "T. S. Eliot's Jewelled Unicorns." *ES* 35 (June) : 125–26. [Ash Wednesday]. Proposes that the line "While jewelled unicorns draw by the gilded hearse" was suggested by a picture, perhaps by Botticelli, in the Turin Pinakothek.

1643. Bodelsen, C. A. Review of George Williamson's *A Reader's Guide to T. S. Eliot. ES* 35 (April) : 88–91. "Taking it by and large, this is a commentary which will be useful to students."

1644. Breit, Harvey. "An Unconfidential Close-up of T. S. Eliot." *NYTM* (February 7) , pp. 16, 24–25. Dwells on the paradoxes of Eliot's personality and the consistency of his work.

1645. Broadbent, J. B. "The Critical Forum. Sixteenth-Century Poetry and the Common Reader." *EIC* 4 (October) : 425–26. [East Coker]. Finds examples of sixteenth-century rhetorical figures. "Eliot's poetry is strong because it has a rhetorical backbone."

1646. Brombert, Victor. "T. S. Eliot and the Romantic Heresy."

YFS 13: 3–16. A defense of Romanticism against Eliot's attack.

1647. Brooke, Nicholas. *"The Confidential Clerk:* A Theatrical Review." *DUJ* 46 (March) : 66–70. The play makes for an entertaining evening of theatre, but "a depressing one afterward" because of its mixture of genres and dullness of the character of Colby.

1648. Brown, John Mason. "Not with a Bang." *SatR* 37 (February 27) : 26–28. [Confidential Clerk]. ". . . Mr. Eliot never seems to have made up his mind what kind of play he was writing, and . . . in both its serious and farcical moods so much of it is a waste land in which only the most avid meaning-hunters among his devotees will find the pleasure we all hoped for."

1649. Brown, Spencer. "T. S. Eliot's Latest Poetic Drama." *Commentary* 17 (April) : 367–72. [Confidential Clerk]. Says this play proves that Eliot is a second-rate playwright.

1650. Butz, Hazel E. "The Relation of T. S. Eliot to the Christian Tradition." *DA* 14: 1213–14. (Indiana). An attempt at a complete analysis of Eliot's religious development. His relation to the Christian tradition is "thoroughgoing and Catholic."

1651. Caldwell, James R. "States of Mind, States of Consciousness." *EIC* 4 (April) : 171–74. [Whispers of Immortality]. An analysis of the organization of the poem illustrates Caldwell's belief that "ordered states of consciousness can be attained without emotional or logical structure."

1652. Clurman, Harold. "Theater." *Nation* 178 (February 27) : 184–87. [Confidential Clerk]. "In this play about fathers who do not know their sons and sons who do not know their fathers, the surface is all urbanity and deferential smiles, the core is a resigned but basic misanthropy."

1653. Colby, Robert A. "The Three Worlds of the Cocktail Party; the Wit of T. S. Eliot." *UTQ* 24 (October) : 56–69. The worlds are the Community of Christians, represented by Celia; the Christian State, by Sir Henry, Alex, and Julia; the Christian Community, by Edward and Lavinia.

1654. Cook, Harold E. "A Search for the Ideal: an Interpretation of T. S. Eliot's 'Marina.'" *BuR* 5, no. 1 (December) : 33–41. A sensitive interpretation by a musician, emphasizing the sound and rhythm as they combine to clarify the meaning.

*1655. Dobrée, Bonamy. "The Confidential Clerk." *SR* 62 (January): 117–31. A thoughtful and penetrating essay on the structure of the play, characterization, verse form, levels of meaning, and final meaning. Dobrée concludes: "He is trying to do, at the same time, two extremely difficult things: the first, to gain acceptance for a morality to which in 1953 most people will be refractory; the second, to create a new kind of play, new in the form used as vehicle for an idea, new in the way the impact on the audience is effected."

1656. Drew, Arnold P. "Hints and Guesses in *Four Quartets*." *UKCR* 20 (Spring): 171–75. "These hints and guesses, these fragments, transitory flashes by which the poet sees the vague outline . . . of the truth are to be found both in the imagery and in the argument of *Four Quartets*." From *AL*.

1657. Evans, David W. "The Domesticity of T. S. Eliot." *UTQ* 23 (July): 380–85. "Eliot is at home with homeliness . . . begins of necessity with the realities." Superficial.

1658. ———. "T. S. Eliot, Charles Williams, and the Sense of the Occult." *Accent* 14 (Spring): 148–55. Points out that Eliot shared Williams's interest in the occult, and suggests that he knew the Tarot playing cards better than, in the notes to *The Waste Land*, he says he does.

1659. Fergusson, Francis. "On the Edge of Broadway." *SR* 67 (Summer): 475–78. [Confidential Clerk]. "Eliot was apparently trying to control the medium of parlor comedy, the theatrical language acceptable to the carriage trade, for the purpose of the poetry, but in the struggle poetry lost." He considers the play pleasant but insignificant.

1660. Fitzgerald, Robert. "Generations of Leaves: The Poet in the Classical Tradition." *Perspectives USA*, no. 8, pp. 68–85. A provocative but sometimes obscure essay on the nature of classicism. The "rose leaves" of *Burnt Norton* and some of their antecedents are considered.

1661. Gardner, Helen. Review of *The Confidential Clerk*. *NSN* 47 (March 20): 373. "The rather weary blend of the comedy of manners with a kind of divine comedy [in *The Family Reunion* and *The Cocktail Party*] has given way to another kind of comedy, something nearer to the comedy of humours." She finds in this play more homogeneity than in the two earlier comedies.

1662. Gassner, John. "The Poet as Anti-Modernist." *The Theatre in Our Time*, pp. 267–81. New York: Crown Publishers, 1954. [Cocktail Party]. Although he is respectful of Eliot's dramatic achievements, Gassner concludes that too much insistence on "a dichotomy between worldlings and the elect tends to depersonalize both," and produce desiccated drama.

1663. Gibbs, Wolcott. "The Importance of Being Eliot." *NY* 30 (February 20): 62, 64–65. [Confidential Clerk]. The ideas are expressed well, but "they are not conspicuously novel and they are often seriously diminished by the farcical framework on which they are hung."

1664. Gwynn, Frederick L. "Sweeney among the Epigraphs." *MLN* 69: 572–74. Light on "Sweeney among the Nightingales" from the epigraph from *The Reign of King Edward the Third* (1590?) which the poet dropped in the 1920 *Poems*.

1665. Hartley, Anthony. "The Drama and Mr. Eliot." *Spectator* 192 (March 26): 364–65. [Confidential Clerk]. Praises this, and hopes that Eliot will go further in writing a more frankly poetic drama.

1666. Hayes, Richard. Review of *The Confidential Clerk*. *Cweal* 59 (March 19): 599–600. Sees the play as a "possible masterpiece."

1667. Hivnor, Mary. "Theatre Letter." *KR* 16: 463–65. [Confidential Clerk]. ". . . feeling comes out as a design, in reminiscence, as life abstracted."

1668. Hockwald, Ilse E. "Eliot's *Cocktail Party* and Goethe's *Wahlverwandtschaften*. *GR* 29: 254–59. Theorizes that Eliot used *Die Wahlverwandtschaften* in addition to *Alcestis* as a conscious source of his play.

1669. Hynes, Sam. "Religion in the West End." *Cweal* 59 (February 12): 475–76. [Confidential Clerk]. Compares this unfavorably to Graham Greene's *The Living Room*. In the play comedy and religiosity are at odds—they blend imperfectly."

1670. Jones, A. E. "Poet as Victim." *CE* 16 (December): 167–71. New Criticism can be carried too far in its insistence that "the critic should possess the right of eminent domain over the poet's property." Eliot is quoted as abetting this trend.

*1671. Kenner, Hugh. "Possum by Gaslight." *Poetry* 85 (October) : 47–54. [Cocktail Party; Confidential Clerk]. Discussion of these plays with reference to themes developed from Eliot's earlier plays and poetry. A Victorian "period wash" over the tone of *The Confidential Clerk* is perhaps "protective coloration" to conceal defects. Reprinted and revised in *T. S. Eliot, the Invisible Poet,* 1959.

1672. Lambert, J. W. "The Verse Drama." *Theatre Programme,* edited by J. C. Trewin, pp. 63–66. London: Frederick Muller Ltd., 1954. The plays have steadily become less dramatic as the poetry has more nearly approached prose.

1673. Lawlor, John. "The Formal Achievement of *The Cocktail Party.*" *VQR* 30 (Summer) : 431–51. "The decorum of this play is in its unique blending of satirical comedy and the high comedy of 'Romance,' a formal achievement issuing in the consulting-room scene." From *AL*.

1674. Lehmann, John. "The Other T. S. Eliot." *Listener* 51 (January 28) : 178–79; 182. Report of an interview with Eliot in which he talked of his work as editor of *The Criterion* and about the history of his own writing.

1675. Liddell, Robert. "Lawrence and Dr. Leavis: The Case of *St. Mawr.*" *EIC* 4 (July) : 321–23. One of Liddell's objects is to show "that Mr. Eliot's so much criticized notion of the uncouth, untutored Lawrence is not quite without foundation."

1676. Lynch, Father William. "Theology and the Imagination." *Thought* (Spring) , pp. 82, 84. [Cocktail Party]. The play is not satisfactory from a theological point of view because, like most modern tragedy, it is guilty of unintentional Manicheanism.

1677. Matthews, T. S. "T. S. Eliot Turns to Comedy." *Life* 36 (February 1) : 56–58 ff. [Confidential Clerk]. The essential facts of Eliot's life are mingled with a summary of the play. Matthews says cautiously that it will be compared with Ibsen or Shaw.

1678. Melchiori, Giorgio. "The Lotus and the Rose. D. H. Lawrence and Eliot's *Four Quartets.*" *EM,* no. 5 (1954) , pp. 203–16. Reprinted in no. 2144. "The lotus, thanks to the significance it had acquired in the pages of Proust and Lawrence, set the mood in which the basic theme of the *Four Quartets* (the moment of Incarnation) could be expressed. Having performed this essential function, the lotus disappeared. . . ." The rose, symbol of the mystical interpretation of timelessness, replaced it.

1679. ———. *"The Waste Land* and *Ulysses." ES* 35 (April): 56–68. "Eliot's *Waste Land* derives from Joyce's *Ulysses* to a degree in general method, imagery, symbolism, and vocabulary." From *AL.*

1680. Moakley, Gertrude. "The Waite-Smith 'Tarot.' A footnote to *The Waste Land." BNYPL* 58 (October): 471–75. Produces evidence to show that it is not the traditional Tarot pack of cards which is used in *The Waste Land,* but modern cards designed by Pamela Smith and Arthur Waite.

1681. Morris, George L. K. "Marie, Marie, Hold on Tight." *PR* 21 (March-April): 231–33. Reprinted in Kenner's *T. S. Eliot, the Invisible Poet.* An account of Morris's chance discovery of a hitherto unknown source of a line in *The Waste Land*—Countess Marie Larisch's *My Past.*

1682. Muir, Kenneth. "Kipling and Eliot." *N&Q,* n.s.1, no. 9 (September): 400–401. The influence of "Wee Willie Winkie" is all-pervasive in "The Journey of the Magi."

1683. Musgrove, Sydney. "James Picot's Use of T. S. Eliot." *Meanjin* 13 (Autumn): 88–95. Detailed analysis of Eliot's influence on *For It Was Early Summer* by the Australian poet.

1684. Noon, William T. "Four Quartets: Contemplatio ad Amorem." *Renascence* 7 (Autumn): 3–10, 29. A comparison of the four points of Ignatius Loyola's *Contemplatio ad Amorem* with the fourfold theme of *Four Quartets* illuminates the poem.

1685. Nott, Kathleen. "Mr. Eliot's Liberal Worms." *The Emperor's Clothes.* Bloomington, Indiana University Press, 1954. Mrs. Nott repeats the usual criticisms of those who do not like Eliot's religion.

1686. Orsini, Gian N. G. "T. S. Eliot and the Doctrine of Dramatic Conventions." *TWA* 43: 189–200. Criticism of Eliot's "conception of convention as a productive factor" and of Miss Bradbrook's similar idea in *Themes and Conventions in Elizabethan Tragedy.* There is no "magic power" in a dramatic convention; a more fruitful approach to literary criticism is "the study of the artistic personality of individual writers."

1687. Richards, I. A. " 'A Cooking Egg': Final Scramble." *EIC* 4 (January): 103–5. Richards thinks that in the controversy about the meaning of the poem the critics are on the wrong track because they are looking for a story, "whereas the movement of the line" will give the right clue.

1688. Saunders, J. W. "Poetry in the Managerial Age." *EIC* 4 July) : 243–81. In a useful article on poets and their readers, references throughout to Eliot's readers, his business career, and his remarks on the business of poetry.

1869. Schwartz, Delmore. "T. S. Eliot's Voice and His Voices." *Poetry* 85 (December 1954) : 170–76; (January) : 232–42. Analysis of Eliot's style and idiom as a poet. His method is called "sibylline (or subliminal) listening." Schwartz considers it an important new method, originated by Pound, which gives energy, mobility, and freedom to use a variety of older methods at will, but it has its dangers. (See no. 1734.)

1690. Seif, Morton. "The Impact of T. S. Eliot on Auden and Spender." *SAQ* 53 (January) : 61–69. "The specific debts of these two poets, widely divergent in aims and achievements, to Eliot demonstrates his wide-ranging influence on the generation of poets that followed him." From *AL*.

1691. Smith, Grover. "The Fortuneteller in Eliot's *Waste Land*." *AL* 25 (January) : 490–92. Sources for the character of Madame Sosostris.

1692. Spelvin, George. "Confidentially, 'Clerk' Had 'em Confused." *TAr* 38 (May) : 77. "A spirited twitting of the reviewers of . . . *The Confidential Clerk*." From *AL*.

1693. Stevenson, David L. "An Objective Correlative for T. S. Eliot's Hamlet." *JAAC* 13: 69–79. The "objective correlatives" for Hamlet's emotional state are his awareness of the indifference of Gertrude and Claudius to their own moral taint, and Hamlet's "naked and unnameable rivalry and hostility" toward Claudius.

1694. Tate, Allen. "Thomas Stearns Eliot." *Sixty American Poets 1896–1944*, pp. 24–39, 153–54. Washington: Library of Congress, 1954. A bibliography of Eliot's writing and a selection of books about him.

1695. Virtue, John. "Eliot's The Love Song of J. Alfred Prufrock, 121." *Expl* 13, no. 2 (November) : item 10. To wear the bottoms of his trousers rolled is Prufrock's "trying to conceal his lack of virility by aping the appearance of the swaggering young males around him."

*1696. Wagner, Robert D. "The Meaning of Eliot's Rose Garden." *PMLA* 69 (March) : 23–33. [Four Quartets]. The moment in the rose garden is marked by unselfconsciousness, a childhood experience when we were at one with reality. That moment, as remembered, is not for Eliot merely the product of the imagination, but stands as a reality beyond imagination. A subtle and thoughtful essay.

1697. Webster, H. T., and Starr, H. W. "Macavity: An Attempt to Unravel His Mystery." *BSJ* 4 (October) : 205–10. [Old Possum's Book of Practical Cats]. Written in a mock-serious style, the authors find the original of Macavity in Conan Doyle's "Moriarity" in *The Final Problem*.

1698. Weedon, William S. "Mr. Eliot's Voices." *VQR* 20 (Autumn) : 610–13. [Three Voices of Poetry; Confidential Clerk]. "It has been the hypothesis of this review that 'The Three Voices of Poetry' and 'The Confidential Clerk' are . . . concerned with . . . much the same subject. Of the two, the latter is by far the more interesting and articulate expression of the problem."

*1699. Wheelwright, Philip. "Pilgrim in the Wasteland." *The Burning Fountain. A Study in the Language of Symbolism,* pp. 330–64. Bloomington: Indiana University Press, 1954. [Waste Land; Four Quartets]. An ingenious and sensitive exploration of several poetic themes, presented tentatively and gracefully.

1700. Wilkinson, Burke. "A Most Serious Comedy by Eliot." *NYT* 2 (February 7) , pp. 1, 3. [Confidential Clerk]. An interview with Martin Browne, director of the play. Browne says that Eliot means that man must adjust, almost resign himself to his lot, and that he comes close to God in the discovery of that lot. Eggerson is the only "*developed* Christian in the play."

1701. Williams, Raymond. *Drama in Performance,* pp. 109–16. Chester Springs, Pa.: Dufour editions, 1954. The clash between verse and naturalistic acting and settings makes Eliot's plays impossible to perform satisfactorily.

1702. ———. "Editorial Commentary." *EIC* 4 (1954) : 341–44. Takes Eliot to task for a paragraph in *The London Magazine* in which he criticizes two existing types of magazines.

1703. Wills, John Howard. "Eliot's The Journey of the Magi." *Expl* 12, no. 5 (March) : item 32. Interprets the narrator as an egoist rather than a holy man. Mr. Wills quotes Eliot's analysis of Othello's last speech, showing it as an effort to think well of himself, and says that the Magus is doing the same thing.

1955

1704. Anon. "Author against Critics." *TLS*, no. 2775 (May 6), p. 237. A competent report of Eliot's address to the Authors' Club, entitled "Author and Critic."

*1705. Arrowsmith, William. "Transfiguration in Eliot and Euripides." *SR* 63 (Summer): 421–42. Included in *English Institute Essays* (1954), pp. 148–72, under the title, "The Comedy of T. S. Eliot." [Confidential Clerk]. A sensitive and clear explanation of the Christian meaning of Eliot's plays in relation to their dramatic structure, and in contrast to those of Euripides. Eliot's failure is his inability to "accept the reality of illusion in this world." Reprinted in *Arion* 4 (1965): 21–35.

1706. Bateson, F. W. "Editorial Commentary." *EIC* 5 (October): 427–34. [Author and Critic]. A defense of his interpretation of Wordsworth's *Lucy* poems against a criticism by Eliot. Also a defense of criticism in general against Eliot's statement that the meaning of a poem is "communicated first emotionally (by the rhythms and the imagery)."

1707. Branford, W. R. G. "Myth and Theme in the Plays of T. S. Eliot." *Theoria* (University of Natal) 7 (1955): 101–9. [Murder in the Cathedral; Family Reunion; Cocktail Party; Confidential Clerk]. Suggests tentatively that in *The Cocktail Party* and *The Confidential Clerk* Eliot has used myth less obviously than he did in *Murder* and *The Family Reunion*.

1708. Breit, Harvey. "Tea." *NYTBR* 7 (June 26), p. 8. An interview with Eliot touching on his novel reading, pugilism, Ralph Hodgson, the poet, ocean liners, and tea.

1709. Funato, Hideo. "T. S. Eliot's Idea of Time." *RR*, no. 16 (1955), pp. 19–51. Drawing on other critics and on most of Eliot's work, the essay is an earnest attempt to understand the relations of past, present, and future, and of time and eternity. The author admits that he is handicapped by his lack of knowledge of Christianity, but his essay is sound as far as it goes.

*1710. Fussell, B. H. "Structural Methods in Four Quartets."

ELH 22 (September) : 212–41. A useful restudy of opposites and their reconciliation in this poem.

1711. Fussell, Paul, Jr. "The Gestic Symbolism of T. S. Eliot." *ELH* 22 (September) : 194–211. In using gestures as symbols, Eliot "has presented the poetic emblem that is the most precise equivalent of his central concern with reunion and integration." A pleasant and suggestive analysis.

1712. Glicksberg, Charles I. "The Journey That Must Be Taken: Spiritual Quest in T. S. Eliot's Plays." *SWR* 40 (Summer) : 203–10. [Murder in the Cathedral; Family Reunion; Cocktail Party; Confidential Clerk]. An oversimplified explanation of the moral and religious meaning of the plays.

1713. ———. "The Spirit of Irony in Eliot's Plays." *PrS* 29 (Fall) : 222–37. [Murder in the Cathedral; Family Reunion; Cocktail Party; Confidential Clerk]. "Though he is fundamentally serious . . . he is too complex and various a personality not to be aware of and give expression to the comic aspects of life." A thoughtful essay.

1714. Graves, Robert. "These Be Your Gods, O Israel." *EIC* 5 (April) : 140–45. Appeared also in *New Republic,* February 27, 1956. A slangy attack on Eliot as a man and as a poet. His style, F. W. Bateson says, is one of "cheerful dogmatic impudence."

1715. Gross, Harvey Seymour. *The Contrived Corridor: A Study of Modern Poetry and the Meaning of History.* Ann Arbor: University Microfilms, 1955. [Gerontion; Four Quartets]. Eliot's view of history has developed, and he has transcended "the impossible glorification of the past."

1716. Gywnn, Frederick L. "Correction to 'Sweeney among the Epigraphs.'" *MLN* 70 (November) : 490–91. [Supplements the note in *MLN* 69 (1954) : 572–74, no. 1664]. Corrects the erroneous impression that he found the source of the second epigraph.

1717. Hamalian, Leo. "The Voice of This Calling: a Study of the Plays of T. S. Eliot." *DA* 15 (May–August) : 1398–99. (Columbia). "This study combines historical criticism with textual analysis."

1718. Harding, Joan N. "T. S. Eliot, O.M." *ConR* 187, no. 1072 (April) : 239–43. [Murder in the Cathedral; Family Reunion; Cocktail Party]. In a brief discussion the author attempts to show that Eliot's humanistic ideals of 1930 are still operative, though supplemented by Christianity.

1719. Hoffman, Frederick J. *The Twenties: American Writing in the Post-War Decade,* pp. 291–303. New York: The Viking Press, 1955. [Waste Land]. A matter-of-fact, clear paraphrase of the poem.

1720. Holbrook, David. "Mr. Eliot's Chinese Wall." *EIC* 5 (October) : 418–26. Eliot has erected a wall between his two selves, one of "terrifying honesty" and the other, a didactic and snobbish preacher.

*1721. Holyrod, Stuart. "The Poet, the Saint, and the Modern World." *Poetry R* 46 (July–September, 1955) : 149–53; pt. 2, *Poetry R* 46 (October–December) : 223–27. [Four Quartets]. A comparison of Eliot and Rilke. The "saint" of the title is Eliot himself; his peculiar achievement is religious rather than poetical. Brief, but authoritative.

*1722. Jayne, Sears. "Mr. Eliot's Agon." *PQ* 34 (October) : 395–414 [Sweeney Agonistes]. A detailed and subtle explanation of the religious meaning of the play.

1723. Kunitz, Stanley J., and Colby, Vineta. "Eliot, Thomas Stearns." *Twentieth Century Authors, First Supplement,* pp. 303–4. New York: H. W. Wilson Company, 1955. Brings up to date the account first published in 1942. See no. 2494.

1724. Margolis, Joseph. "The Love Song of J. Alfred Prufrock." In *Interpretations. Essays on Twelve English Poems,* edited by John Wain, pp. 179–93. London: Routledge and K. Paul, 1955. A pretentious and ill-considered explanation.

1725. Martin, Percival William. *Experiment in Depth; a Study of the Work of Jung, Eliot, and Toynbee.* New York: Pantheon, 1955. Interprets Eliot's poems and his personal journey to God as an example of the use of the "mythical method" which Jung and Toynbee also used.

*1726. Martz, Louis L. "The Saint as Tragic Hero: *Saint Joan* and *Murder in the Cathedral.*" *Tragic Themes in Western Literature,* edited by Cleanth Brooks, pp. 150–78. New Haven: Yale University Press, 1955. A well-balanced comparison of the two plays, concluding that both are tragedies, though not Aristotelian.

1727. Merchant, W. M. "The Verse-Drama of Eliot and Fry." *NS* 3: 97–106. Thinks that poetry is more suitable than prose for our day.

1728. Nelson, Armour H. "The Critics and *The Waste Land,* 1922–1949." *ES* 36: 1–15. Bibliographical essay.

1729. Nicholas, Constance. "The Murders of Doyle and Eliot." *MLN* 70 (April): 269–71. Ten lines of *Murder in the Cathedral* are taken from *The Musgrave Ritual.*

1730. Palette, Drew B. "Eliot, Fry, and Broadway." *ArQ* 11 (Winter): 342–47. [Confidential Clerk]. Questions whether Eliot is afraid to use poetry or is afraid of his new public.

1731. Raleigh, John H. "Revolt and Revaluation in Criticism, 1900–1930." *The Development of American Criticism,* edited by Floyd Stovall, pp. 159–98. Chapel Hill: University of North Carolina Press, 1955. Generalization on Eliot's and Pound's influence on American criticism in the 1920s. "Against America and the present, they asserted Europe and the past."

1732. Richards, Robert Fulton. *Concise Dictionary of American Literature,* pp. 43, 44, 45, 46, 48, 73–75, 177, 178, 179, 180. New York: Philosophical Library, 1955. A short article summarizing Eliot's life and work under "T. S. Eliot," and references to his work elsewhere; flippant.

1733. Schanzer, Ernest. "Mr. Eliot's Sunday Morning Service." *EIC* 5 (April): 153–58. A careful examination of the meaning of the poem, concluding with a judgment of its artistic merit.

1734. Schwartz, Delmore. "T. S. Eliot's Voice and His Voices." *Poetry* 85 (January): 232–42. [Conclusion of no. 1689]. Tries to define what he calls "sibylline (or subliminal listening)" as a characteristic of Eliot's poetry; has difficulty in making the meaning clear.

1735. Shanahan, C. M. "Irony in Laforgue, Corbière, and Eliot." *MP* 53 (November): 117–28. "Irony . . . as found in Laforgue and Corbière, in its various uses helped Eliot to express personal emotions while retaining as great a reserve as that of Leconte de Lisle."

1736. Siegel, Eli. "T. S. Eliot and W. C. Williams: a Distinction." *UKCR* 22 (October): 41–43. Eliot is a craftsman, but lacks the true poetic feeling of Williams.

1737. Sochatoff, A. Fred. "The Use of Verse in the Drama of T. S. Eliot." *Lectures on Some Modern Poets,* pp. 59–75. Carnegie Series in English, no. 2, 1955. Repeats well-known observations on Eliot's verse form in *Sweeney Agonistes, The Rock, Murder in the Cathedral, The*

Family Reunion, The Cocktail Party, and *The Confidential Clerk.*

1738. Stanford, Donald L. "Two Notes on T. S. Eliot." *TCL* 1 (October): 133–34. [Hollow Men; Burbank with a Baedeker]. 1) Finds the origin of the lines "Here we go round the prickly pear" in primitive fertility rites. 2) The first four lines of "Burbank . . ." are verbally like the first four lines of Tennyson's "The Sisters."

1739. Turner, W. Arthur. "The Not So Coy Mistress of J. Alfred Prufrock." *SAQ* 54 (October): 516–22. Reads the poem as "a companion piece to *Portrait of a Lady* and as a poem in the direct tradition of *To His Coy Mistress.*"

1740. Van Vechten, Carl. "C–a–t spells Rawsthorne." *SatR* 38 (November 26): 48, 69. [Old Possum's Book of Practical Cats]. A complimentary comment on six of these poems set to music by Alan Rawsthorne and recited by Robert Donat.

1741. Vickery, John Britton. "T. S. Eliot and *The Golden Bough:* the Archetype of the Dying God." University of Wisconsin: Summaries of Doctoral Dissertations 16 (1955): 560–61. The central myth in Eliot's poetry is that of the dying and reviving god, and is probably derived from *The Golden Bough.*

1742. Watson-Williams, Helen. "The Blackened Wall; Notes on Blake's *London* and Eliot's *The Waste Land.*" *English* 10 (Summer): 81–84. The essay seeks to show fundamental similarities between the two poets, but it rests on a misunderstanding of Eliot's position.

1743. Weigand, Elsie. "Rilke and Eliot: the Articulation of the Mystic Experience." *GR* 30 (October): 198–210. A discussion centering on the *Eighth Duino Elegy* and *Burnt Norton.*

1956

1744. Anon. "Lecturer in the Arena." *Newsweek* 47 (May 14): 72. An account of Eliot's lecture in Minneapolis, "The Frontiers of Criticism."

1745. Baker, John Ross. "Eliot's *The Waste Land, 77–93.*" *Expl* 14: item 27. Suggests that the "seven-branched candelabra" parallels the candlestick which Jehovah commanded Moses to fashion for the temple.

1746. Blackmur, R. P. "Irregular Metaphysics." *Anni Mirabilis 1921–1925,* pp. 26–32. Washington: Library of Congress,

1956. [Waste Land]. Reprinted in Kenner, *T. S. Eliot*. An abstruse essay on analogy as an organizing principle of structure.

1747. Boulton, J. T. "The Use of Original Sources for the Development of a Theme: Eliot and *Murder in the Cathedral*." *English* 11 (Spring) : 2–8. "Eliot visualized his theme—the conflict of the religious and secular values and attitudes—with precision, in terms of human nature at a given point in time and . . . his use of original sources . . . released imaginative energy for other important tasks."

1748. Davie, Donald. "T. S. Eliot: the End of an Era." *TC* 159 (April) : 350–62. [Dry Salvages]. Reprinted in Kenner's *T. S. Eliot*. *The Dry Salvages* is unaccountably bad unless it is seen as intentional parody, the voice of the speaker being that of a Whitmanesque American.

1749. Evans, David W. "Case Book of T. S. Eliot." *MLN* 71 (November) : 501. A note saying that "crime fiction in general has had an influence on Eliot's work."

*1750. Fergusson, Francis. "Three Allegorists: Brecht, Wilder, and Eliot." *SR* 64 (Autumn) : 544–73. [Confidential Clerk]. The play "is an allegory about Providence. All the characters wish for things in youth which (by God's Providence) they get later in life; the moral is that we had better take care *what* we wish for, lest we get just that, we had better 'make perfect our will.' " The play fails as theatre because the distance between Eliot's real meaning and what the comedy seems to say is too great.

1751. Freedman, Morris. "Meaning of T. S. Eliot's Jew." *SAQ* 55 (April) : 198–206. Eliot's unfriendly portraits of Jews in his early poems reveal that "for many years, he was incapable of sympathy, not alone with Jews, but with humanity at large."

1752. Hardenbrook, Don. "T. S. Eliot and the *Great Grimpen Mere* by Gaston Huret III." *BSJ* 6, n.s.: 88–93. A pretended translation from the French, discussing the relation of the *grimpen* in *East Coker* to the mere in Conan Doyle's *The Hound of the Baskervilles*.

*1753. Harding, D. W. "Progression of Theme in Eliot's Modern Plays." *KR* 18 (Summer) : 337–60. [Family Reunion; Cocktail Party; Confidential Clerk]. The theme of all three plays is that of separation. "In *The Confidential Clerk* the assertion that the hero must accept some form

of martyred loneliness has become less convincing, and
less convinced, than it ever was in the earlier work."

1754. Henn, T. R. "Mr. Eliot's Compromise." *The Harvest of
Tragedy*, pp. 217–32. London: Methuen & Co., Ltd.,
1956. [Murder in the Cathedral; Family Reunion; Cocktail Party]. Considers that *Murder in the Cathedral* contains theologically questionable doctrine, and that the
other two plays are confused both in idea and technique.

*1755. Keeley, Edmund. "T. S. Eliot and the Poetry of George
Seferis." *CL* 8 (September) : 214–26. ". . . Eliot, along
with the French symbolists and surrealists, helped Seferis
to find in his own tradition the least exhausted sources,
and . . . he opened to the Greek poet several significant
possibilities for the further development of his art."

1756. Kerr, Walter. *How Not to Write a Play*, pp. 230–31. London: Max Reinhardt, 1956. ". . . Eliot is mentally a
lyric poet, not a dramatic one."

1757. Krieger, Murray. "T. S. Eliot." *The New Apologists for
Poetry*, pp. 46–56. Minneapolis: University of Minnesota Press, 1956. Examines the concepts of the "unified
sensibility" and the "objective correlative" and finds
contradictions in them.

1758. Laurentia, Sister M. "Structural Balance and Symbolism
in T. S. Eliot's 'Portrait of a Lady.'" *AL* 27: 409–17.
Overinsists on the structural similarities between the
epigraph and the poem, and on the musical motifs
associated with the man and with the woman.

1759. Deleted.

1760. Lumley, Frederick. "T. S. Eliot as Dramatist." *Trends in
Twentieth-Century Drama: A Survey since Ibsen and
Shaw*, pp. 80–90. London: Barrie and Rockliff, 1956.
A survey of Eliot's drama. ". . . in diluting his poetry,
Eliot has removed the power which, above all others,
he possesses."

1761. Lyman, Dean B., Jr. "Aiken and Eliot." *MLN* 71 (May) :
342–43. Offers addenda to Beach, no. 1635, pointing out
similarities between Eliot and Aiken.

1762. Melchiori, Grigorio. *The Tightrope Walkers*, "Echoes in
'The Waste Land,'" pp. 53–88; "The Lotus and the
Rose," pp. 89–103; "Eliot and the Theatre," pp. 109–
49. London: Routledge and Paul, 1956. Repeats commonplaces of Eliot criticism.

1763. Murry, J. Middleton. "The Plays of T. S. Eliot." *Unpro-*

fessional Essays, pp. 151–90. London: J. Cape, 1956. [Family Reunion; Cocktail Party; Confidential Clerk]. A pleasantly written essay analyzing Eliot's rejection of love between men and women, and relating that rejection to passages in some of the poems.

1764. Musurillo, Herbert. "A Note on *The Waste Land* (Part IV)." *CP* 51 (July) : 174–75. Suggests a meaning for *Phlebas* from the *Palatine Anthology.*

1765. Powers, Lyall H. "Eliot's 'The Love Song of J. Alfred Prufrock.'" *Expl* 14: item 39. Disagrees with Virtue, no. 1695, and George Williamson, no. 1622, on the meaning of "trousers rolled." Prufrock is not emulating swaggering young men.

*1766. Smith, Grover, Jr. *T. S. Eliot's Poetry and Plays: a Study in Sources and Meaning,* 338 pp. Chicago: University of Chicago Press, 1956. The most complete study of sources.

1767. Steinmann, Martin, Jr. "Coleridge, T. S. Eliot, and Organicism." *MLN* 71 (May) : 339–40. Points out Eliot's indebtedness in "Ben Jonson" to Coleridge's theory of organicism.

*1768. Unger, Leonard. "Laforgue, Conrad, and Eliot." *The Man in the Name,* pp. 190–242. Minneapolis: University of Minnesota Press, 1956. Reprinted with slight changes in *T. S. Eliot: Moments and Patterns,* University of Minnesota Press, 1966. Excellent; a model of what studies of influences should be.

*1769. Wellek, René. "Criticism of T. S. Eliot." *SR* 64 (Summer) : 398–443. A critical analysis of Eliot's critical principles, their self-contradictions and their relation to his role as critic, covering all the important topics. Eliot's taste is called "medieval-baroque-symbolist." His later criticism, committed to supra-literary standards, has "weakened the impact of his own achievement as a literary critic." But his early work is "very great indeed."

*1770. Williams, Raymond. "Second Thoughts: I—T. S. Eliot on Culture." *EIC* 6 (July) : 302–18. [Idea of a Christian Society; Notes towards the Definition of Culture]. A thoughtful examination, sympathetic yet critical.

1771. Williamson, Audrey. "Eliot, Whiting and Fry." *Contemporary Theatre, 1953–56,* pp. 22–26; 98–100. London: Rockliff, 1956. [Family Reunion; Confidential Clerk]. Chiefly on the acting and staging of the two plays. Photographs of *The Confidential Clerk.*

1772. Young, Philip. "Scott Fitzgerald's Waste Land." *KM* 24: 73–77. Tentatively suggests that there was "unconscious influence" from *The Waste Land* on *The Great Gatsby*.

1957

1773. Anon. "Poet's Shoptalk." *Time* 70 (September 16: 125–26. [On Poetry and Poets]. A notice of the book.

1774. ———. "Who Myra Buttle Is." *Newsweek* 50 (November 4) : 116. Myra Buttle is identified as Victor Purcell, a lecturer at Cambridge.

*1775. Alvarez, A. "Eliot and Yeats: Orthodoxy and Tradition." *TC* 162 (August–September): 149–63, 224–34. Reprinted in *The Shaping Spirit: Studies in Modern English and American Poets*, pp. 11–47. London: Chatto and Windus, 1958. The New York edition is called *Stewards of Excellence*. In the course of contrasting the orthodoxy of Eliot and the traditionalism of Yeats, Alvarez isolates Eliot's leading qualities as a poet, and considers influences on him and his influence on others. A rich essay.

1776. Anthony, Mother Mary [Weining]. *Diction, Syntax, and Rhetoric in T. S. Eliot's Four Quartets, with a Concordance. DA* (Fordham). [I have seen this in mimeographed form only. Presumably it is in *DA,* but I have not found it.] A line-by-line examination of the poem.

*1777. Beare, Robert L. "Notes on the Text of T. S. Eliot: Variants from Russell Square." *SB* 9: 21–49. [The Poems and Plays]. A carefully detailed record of variants in the plays and poems throws light on the author's method of composition. There is "a sizeable collection of variants."

1778. Beringause, A. F. "Journey through The Waste Land." *SAQ* 56 (January): 79–90. An essay claiming that Eliot's poem is built upon Fitzgerald's translation of *The Rubaiyat* and James Thomson's *The City of Dreadful Night*. No convincing evidence is presented.

1779. Blum, Margaret. "The Fool in the Love Song of J. Alfred Prufrock." *MLN* 72 (June) : 424–26. She suggests that Eliot had Yorick in mind.

*1780. Bollier, Ernest Philip. "Mr. Eliot's 'Tradition and the Individual Talent' Reconsidered." *UCSLL:* no. 6 (January), pp. 103–18. A careful examination based on everything that Eliot has written, with resulting new insight and clarity on the vexed question of Eliot's development as a critic. Bollier says that Eliot "has never abandoned his belief in the esthetic integrity of the poem."

1781. Brown, Robert M., and Yokelson, Joseph B. "Eliot's 'Gerontion,' 56–61." *Expl* 15: item 31. The authors think that this passage is directed to God, not, as Unger suggests, to a lady.

1782. Browne, E. Martin. Introduction to *Four Modern Verse Plays*, pp. 8–10. Harmondsworth, Middlesex: Penguin Books: 1957. [Family Reunion]. After a brief but excellent summary of Eliot's previous plays, Browne presents the essentials for appreciating this one.

1783. Buttle, Myra [pseud. of Victor William Williams Saunders Purcell]. *The Sweeniad*, 66 pp. New York: Sagamore Press, 1957. The most elaborate of the parodies of Eliot's poems, partly in prose, partly in verse. Ineffective primarily because it is an indiscriminate attack on the entire style and content of Eliot's work.

1784. Cargill. Oscar. "Mr. Eliot Regrets. . . ." *Nation* 184 (February 23) : 170–72. Examines Eliot's prejudice against the Irish, Jews, and Cockneys, and his confession of remorse in *Little Gidding*.

1785. Colby, Robert A. "Orpheus in the Counting House: The Confidential Clerk." *PMLA* 72 (September) : 791–802. Calls our attention to Eliot's interest in one of the "most perplexing paradoxes confronting twentieth century man," his loneliness in crowds and his insecurity amid prosperity as presented in *The Confidential Clerk*.

1786. Enright, D. J. "On Not Teaching *The Cocktail Party:* A Professorial Dialogue." *The Apothecary's Shop, Essays on Literature*, pp. 206–11. London: Secker and Warburg, 1957. Pros and cons on the merits of the play.

1787. Fowlie, Wallace. "Jorge Guillén, Marianne Moore, T. S. Eliot: Some Recollections." *Poetry* 90 (May) : 107–9. Not only recollections of Eliot at Harvard in the 1930s, but also good remarks on "Prufrock."

1788. Gregory, Horace. "The Authority of T. S. Eliot." *Cweal* 67 (November 8) : 148–50. [On Poetry and Poets]. A pleasant, complimentary review.

1789. Gross, Seymour L. "Laurence Sterne and Eliot's 'Prufrock'; an Object Lesson in Explication." *CE* 19 (November) : 72–73. After Gross had correlated the "Fool" with a sentence in a letter by Sterne, Eliot said that he had never seen the letter.

1790. Hardy, John Edward. "An Antic Disposition." *SR* 65 (Winter): 50–60. [Cocktail Party]. Eliot does not intend for Harcourt-Reilly to be a Christ-figure, but he has pretensions to divinity.

1791. Hart, Jeffery P. "T. S. Eliot: His Use of Wycherley and Pope." *N&Q* 4, n.s.: 389–90. Points out echoes between lines in Wycherley's *Plain Dealer* and Eliot's "Portrait of a Lady," Pope's *Dunciad,* Book III, and "Gerontion."

1792. Holyrod, Stuart. "T. S. Eliot and the 'Intellectual Soul.'" *Emergence from Chaos,* pp. 191–217. Boston: Houghton Mifflin; London: Gollancz, 1957. Traces Eliot's spiritual biography; uncritically admiring.

*1793. Howarth, Herbert. "Eliot, Beethoven, and J. W. N. Sullivan." *CL* 9: 322–32. Eliot chose Beethoven's *Opus 132* as his model for *Four Quartets* and had been impressed by Sullivan's book on Beethoven. (See Harvey Gross, no. 1921.)

1794. Joseph, Brother F. S. C. "The Concept of 'Poetic Sensibility' in the Criticism of T. S. Eliot." *Fresco* 8: 40–47. A restatement of points made by Eric Thompson and F. O. Matthiessen.

*1795. Kenner, Hugh. "Prufrock of St. Louis." *PrS* 31 (Spring): 24–30. [Prufrock]. A difficult but perceptive essay on the expert verbalism of the poem, which Kenner admires. Reprinted in his *T. S. Eliot, the Invisible Poet.*

*1796. Kermode, Frank. "Dissociation of Sensibility." *KR* 19 (Spring): 169–94. A wide-ranging and penetrating study of the meaning of the phrase.

*1797. ———. *Romantic Image.* London: Routledge and Paul, 1957. Sees Eliot as a critic and poet in the Romantic-Symbolist tradition. Judicious criticism.

1798. Marsh, T. N. "The Turning World, Eliot and the Detective Story." *EM* 8: 143–45. Notes a resemblance between the associated figures of the "dance" and "still center" in Eliot and their use in Dorothy Sayer's *Gaudy Night.*

1799. Martin, Philip Montague. *Mastery and Mercy, A Study of Two Religious Poems, The Wreck of the Deutschland by G. M. Hopkins, and Ash Wednesday by T. S. Eliot,* pp. 84–148. London and New York: Oxford University Press, 1957. The author, a churchman, emphasizes that these poems were written from within the church; he presents a simple reading for Christians, but is not without feeling for poetic beauty.

*1800. Mary Eleanor, Mother. "Eliot's Magi." *Renascence* 1 (Autumn) : 26–31. [Journey of the Magi]. The poem may be read on a literal, a symbolic, or universal level. Most attention is given to the second level.

1801. McElderry, B. R., Jr. "Eliot's Shakespeherian Rag." *AQ* 9 (Spring) : 185–86. Identifies l. 128 of *The Waste Land* as coming from a song hit of 1912 called "That Shakesperian Rag."

1802. ———. "Santayana and Eliot's 'Objective Correlative,'" *BUSE* 3 (Autumn) : 179–81. On Santayana's possible influence.

1803. Mizener, Arthur. "To Meet Mr. Eliot." *SR* 55 (Winter) : 34–49. An easy-going, appreciative introduction to Eliot's poetic career. Reprinted in Kenner's *T. S. Eliot, a Collection of Critical Essays,* 1962.

1804. Pound, Ezra. "Mr. Eliot and Mr. Pound." *TLS* (July 26), p. 457. Pound writes to correct the legend that he taught Eliot to write poetry.

1805. Pratt, William C., Jr. "Revolution without Betrayal: James, Pound, Eliot and the European Tradition." *DA* 17 (September–December) : 2600. (Vanderbilt). This thesis studies the ideal society envisaged by each of three writers.

1806. Rahv, Philip. "T. S. Eliot, the Poet as Playwright." *Image and Idea: Twenty Essays on Literary Themes,* pp. 196–202. London: Weidenfeld and Nicholson, 1957. [Poetry and Drama; Cocktail Party]. Prefers his theory to his practice in *The Cocktail Party.*

1807. Rodman, Selden. "The Moral Value of Verse." *SatR* 40 (November 9) : 14. [On Poetry and Poets]. The reviewer commends Eliot for his "new emphasis on content."

1808. Sen, Mihar-Kumar. "A Psychological Interpretation of The Waste Land." *LitC* 3: 29–44. This analysis is an interesting combination of Freudian thought with Indian morality and Christian doctrine.

1809. Shuman, R. Baird. "Buddhistic Overtones in Eliot's *The Cocktail Party.*" *MLN* 72 (June, 1957), 426–27. Says that Celia works out her salvation by implicitly subscribing "to the four noble truths of Buddhism."

1810. Spector, Robert Donald. "Eliot, Pound, and the Decline of the Conservative Tradition." *HIN* 3 (January) : 2–5. [Prufrock]. Based on the theory that Prufrock is identical with the author of the poem, Spector concludes that Eliot rejects society because it has rejected him.

1811. Vickery, John Britton. "T. S. Eliot's Poetry: The Quest and the Way, Part I." *Renascence* 10 (Autumn) : 3–10, 31; pt. 2 (Winter, 1958) : 59–67. An over-schematic but ingenious study of the evolution of Eliot's poetry as falling into three stages: the quest for a hero, the quest of the hero, and the tracing out of the Way.

1812. Walcutt, Charles Child. "Eliot's 'The Love Song. . . .' " *CE* 19 (October) : 71–72. Argues that Prufrock is "primarily thinking about proposing to the lady at the tea party."

1813. Wrenn, C. L. "T. S. Eliot and the Language of Poetry." *Thought* 32 (Summer) : 239–54. [Poems; Murder in the Cathedral; Family Reunion; Cocktail Party; Confidential Clerk]. ". . . a distinction is to be drawn between the Eliot of the *Four Quartets* where his aims in poetic language seem good and have been splendidly achieved, and the Eliot who has steadily withdrawn the diction of his plays from poetry . . . until *The Confidential Clerk* with its so often merely ordinary flatness."

1958

1814. Anon. Criticism of *The Elder Statesman*. *Time* 72 (September 8) : 43 f. Quotes from favorable British criticisms.

1815. ———. "Old Possum at Seventy." *Time* 72 (September 29) : 98. Eliot credits his new-found love of life to his second marriage.

1816. Ap Ivor, Dennis. "Setting 'The Hollow Men' to Music." Braybrooke, *T. S. Eliot: A Symposium for His Seventieth Birthday*, pp. 89–91. New York: Farrar, Straus and Cudahy, 1958. Ap Ivor's score combines the rhythms of jazz and liturgical chant.

1817. Arden, Eugene. "The Echo of Hell in 'Prufrock.' " *N&Q* 5, n.s.: 363–64. Although Prufrock echoes Dante in the *Inferno,* Canto II, in saying "I am not Prince Hamlet," he is no more a lost soul than Dante was.

1818. Bacon, Helen H. "The Sibyl in the Bottle." *VQR* 34 (Spring) : 262–76. [Waste Land]. On the influence of Petronius's *Satyricon* on the poem.

1819. Barber, C. L. "The Power of Development . . . in a Different World." Final chapter of the 3rd ed. of F. O. Matthiessen's *The Achievement of T. S. Eliot,* pp. 198–243. New York: Oxford University Press, 1958. Treats 1) the criticism, 2) *The Confidential Clerk,* 3) *The Cocktail Party.* Judicious, but lacks the freshness and drive of the earlier chapters.

1820. Barnes, Djuna. "Fall-out Over Heaven." Braybrooke, *T. S. Eliot: A Symposium for His Seventieth Birthday,* p. 27. New York: Farrar, Straus and Cudahy, 1958. Ten-line lyric based on Eliot's "I'll show you fear in a handful of dust."

1821. Barry, Michael. "Televising *The Cocktail Party.*" Braybrooke, *T. S. Eliot: A Symposium for His Seventieth Birthday,* pp. 85–88. New York: Farrar, Straus and Cudahy, 1958. A sketch of changes made in transforming the stage play into the medium of T.V.

1822. Beharriell, Frederick J. "Freud and Literature." *QQ* 65 (Spring) : 118–25. Contains a few references to Eliot.

1823. Betjeman, John, "T. S. Eliot the Londoner." Braybrooke, *T. S. Eliot: A Symposium for His Seventieth Birthday,* pp. 193–95. New York: Farrar, Straus and Cudahy, 1958. ". . . London percolates most of his poems."

*1824. Bodelsen, C. A. *T. S. Eliot's Four Quartets: a Commentary,* 128 pp. Copenhagen: Rosenkilde and Bagger, 1958. Says too modestly that his explanation of the meaning of the poem is intended for the ordinary reader; the book is admirably lucid and deserves to be read.

*1825. Bollier, Ernest Philip. "T. S. Eliot and John Milton: a Problem in Criticism." *TSE* 8: 165–92. Holds that no radical change occurred in Eliot's attitude toward Milton, and what did occur can be seen as his interest shifted from a concern with the practicing poet to the relation of the poet to the common reader. A broadly based essay.

1826. Braybrooke, Neville. "T. S. Eliot." *ConR,* no. 1113 (September) , pp. 123–26. A wandering personal reminiscence of Eliot's influence since the 1930s.

1827. ———, ed. "A Garland from the Young," *T. S. Eliot: A Symposium for His Seventieth Birthday,* pp. 102–18. New York: Farrar, Straus and Cudahy, 1958. Impressions of Eliot's work by school children.

1828. ———, ed. *T. S. Eliot: A Symposium for His Seventieth Birthday,* 221 pp. New York: Farrar, Straus and Cudahy,

1958. Comments on Eliot and his work from many points of view. Each item is entered separately in this bibliography under the name of the author.

1829. Brien, Alan. "The Invisible Dramatist." *Spectator* (September 5), pp. 305-6. [Elder Statesman]. This is a "zombie play designed for the living dead."

1830. Browne, E. Martin. "From *The Rock* to *The Confidential Clerk*." Braybrooke, *T. S. Eliot: A Symposium for His Seventieth Birthday*, pp. 57-69. New York: Farrar, Straus and Cudahy, 1958. Practical view of production problems, with respect for the spirit of the plays, by the first producer of all of Eliot's plays.

1831. Cameron, J. M. "T. S. Eliot as a Political Writer." Braybrooke, *T. S. Eliot: A Symposium for His Seventieth Birthday*, pp. 138-51. New York: Farrar, Straus and Cudahy, 1958. The author, a Roman Catholic, raises questions about the logic of Eliot's basing his "Christian society" on Anglicanism.

1832. Causley, Charles. "Down by the Riverside." Braybrooke, *T. S. Eliot: A Symposium for His Seventieth Birthday*, p. 28. New York: Farrar, Straus and Cudahy, 1958. A poem for Eliot.

1833. Cauthen, I. B., Jr. "Another Webster Allusion in *The Waste Land*." *MLN* 73: 498-99, pt. 2, pp. 117-26, echoes *The White Devil*, V. vi, pp. 223-27.

1834. Colum, Padraic. "A Commemorative Book: 'T. S. Eliot: Symposium.'" *SatR* 41 (September 13): 31. A reminiscence of the state of literature when Eliot appeared.

1835. Cronin, Vincent. "T. S. Eliot as a Translator." Braybrooke, *T. S. Eliot: A Symposium for His Seventieth Birthday*, pp. 129-37. New York: Farrar, Straus and Cudahy, 1958. His translations of Laforgue and Saint-John Perse had a decisive impact on his own poetry.

1836. Culbert, Taylor. "Eliot's 'Gerontion.'" *Expl* 17: item 20. Suggests that *gutter* means "a fire which burns fitfully."

1837. Dinwiddy, Hugh. "Reading T. S. Eliot with Schoolboys." Braybrooke, *T. S. Eliot: A Symposium for His Seventieth Birthday*, pp. 92-97. New York: Farrar, Straus and Cudahy, 1958. These poems help boys to mature.

1838. English, Isobel. "Rose of Memory." Braybrooke, *T. S. Eliot: A Symposium for His Seventieth Birthday*, pp. 185-86. New York: Farrar, Straus and Cudahy, 1958. What Eliot meant to the author.

1839. Espey, John J. "The Epigraph to T. S. Eliot's 'Burbank with a Baedeker: Bleistein with a Cigar.'" AL 29 (January) : 483–84. Suggests that part of the epigraph came from Ford Maddox Ford.

1840. Evans, David W. "The Penny World of T. S. Eliot." *Renascence* 10 (Spring): 121–28. [A Cooking Egg]. A serio-comic review of critical opinion on this poem, and an interpretation by Evans.

1841. Fraser, G. S. "W. B. Yeats and T. S. Eliot." Braybrooke, *T. S. Eliot: A Symposium for His Seventieth Birthday,* pp. 196–216. New York: Farrar, Straus and Cudahy, 1958. The two poets are contrasted in many phases of their attitudes toward life.

*1842. Gardner, Helen. "The 'Aged Eagle' Spreads His Wings. A 70th Birthday Talk with T. S. Eliot." *Sun Times* (September 21) , p. 8. Eliot talks freely with Miss Gardner about his poems and plays, correcting some misconceptions. Valuable.

1843. Graves, Robert. "Sweeney among the Nightingales." *TQ* 1 (Spring) : 83–102. A gay, impudent essay which dismisses most modern poets, including Eliot, because they do not worship the White Goddess, Aphrodite.

*1844. Gross, Harvey Seymour. "Gerontion and the Meaning of History." *PMLA* 73 (June) : 299–304. One of the fullest and most probing studies of the poem.

1845. Hamilton, Elizabeth. "Teaching 'The Four Quartets' to Schoolgirls." Braybrooke, *T. S. Eliot: A Symposium for His Seventieth Birthday,* pp. 98–101. New York: Farrar, Straus and Cudahy, 1958. Good students are responsive to the poem.

1846. Hewes, Henry. "Eliot on Eliot. 'I Feel Younger than I did at 60.'" *SatR* 41 (September 13) : 32. Eliot is quoted on a variety of topics.

1847. ———. "T. S. Eliot at Seventy." *SatR* 41 (September 13) : 30–32. [Elder Statesman]. A summary of the plot and brief comment.

1848. Hoellering, George. "Filming *Murder in the Cathedral.*" Braybrooke, *T. S. Eliot: A Symposium for His Seventieth Birthday,* pp. 81–84. New York: Farrar, Straus and Cudahy, 1958. An account of Eliot's intimate involvement in the making of the film.

1849. Jacobs, Arthur. "*Murder in the Cathedral* as an Opera."

Listener 59 (March 20) : 504–5. Praise for the operatic version by Pizzetti given in Milan.

1850. Jarrett-Kerr, Martin. "Not Much about Gods." Braybrooke, *T. S. Eliot: A Symposium for His Seventieth Birthday,* pp. 176–80. New York: Farrar, Straus and Cudahy, 1958. The "most profoundly religious elements in his poetry" lie in moments of nostalgia for lost innocence.

1851. Jennings, Paul. "O City City." Braybrooke, *T. S. Eliot: A Symposium for His Seventieth Birthday,* pp. 45–48. New York: Farrar, Straus and Cudahy, 1958. Fancies touched off by Eliot's early career as a banker.

1852. Kermode, Frank. "T. S. Eliot on Poetry." *ILA* (London) 1: 131–34. [On Poetry and Poets]. Eliot reaffirms in these essays the organic roots of his criticism. Most of the essay is on Eliot's high praise of Virgil.

1853. Knight, W. F. Jackson. "T. S. Eliot as a Classical Scholar." Braybrooke, *T. S. Eliot: A Symposium for His Seventieth Birthday,* pp. 119–28. New York: Farrar, Straus and Cudahy, 1958. His classical knowledge permeates his work.

1854. Leavis, F. R. "T. S. Eliot's Stature as Critic, a Revaluation." *Commentary* 26 (November) : 399–410. While professing admiration for Eliot's poetic gifts and some of his early criticism, Leavis attacks him for his "radical conventionality of judgment."

1855. Leggatt, Alison. "A Postscript from Mrs. Chamberlayne and Mrs. Guzzard." Braybrooke, *T. S. Eliot: A Symposium for His Seventieth Birthday,* pp. 79–80. New York, Farrar, Straus and Cudahy, 1958. Says that playing these two roles was the highlight of her theatrical career.

1856. Lelièvre, F. J. "Parody in Juvenal and T. S. Eliot." *CP* 53 (January) : 22–26. A judicious examination of similarities between the two poets.

1857. Levy, William Turner. "The Idea of the Church in T. S. Eliot." *ChS* 41 (December) : 587–600. A clear exposition based on Eliot's essays, a sermon, and a poem.

1858. Livesay, Dorothy. "London Notes." *CF* 38 (November) : 171–72. [Elder Statesman]. Says it is dull.

1859. Macaulay, Rose. "The First Impact of *The Waste Land.*" Braybrooke, *T. S. Eliot: A Symposium for His Seventieth Birthday,* pp. 29–33. New York: Farrar, Straus and Cudahy, 1958. She sensed both strangeness and recognition.

1860. Mairet, Philip. "Memories of T. S. Eliot." Braybrooke, *T. S. Eliot: A Symposium for His Seventieth Birthday*, pp. 36–44. New York: Farrar, Straus and Cudahy, 1958. An appreciation of Eliot's encouragement of new writers and magazines.

1861. Manning, Hugo. "Onorate l'Altissimo Poeta." Braybrooke, *T. S. Eliot: A Symposium for His Seventieth Birthday*, pp. 181–84. New York: Farrar, Straus and Cudahy, 1958. Says he comes close to uniting the insights of Lucretius, Dante, and Goethe.

1862. Maxwell, D. E. S. "The Cultivation of Christmas Trees." Braybrooke, *T. S. Eliot: A Symposium for His Seventieth Birthday*, pp. 190–92. New York: Farrar, Straus and Cudahy, 1958. An appreciation of the spiritual qualities of the poem.

1863. Miller, James E., Jr. "Whitman and Eliot: the Poetry of Mysticism." *SWR* 43 (Spring): 113–23. [Four Quartets]. Much is made of similarities in diction and images in *Song of Myself* and Eliot's poem.

1864. Moorman, Charles. "Myth and Organic Unity in *The Waste Land*." *SAQ* 57 (Spring): 194–203. The unifying factor in the poem is the use of the major symbol, the sterility theme of the Fisher King-Waste Land myth.

1865. Mudrick, Marvin. "The Two Voices of Mr. Eliot." *HudR* 10 (Winter, 1957–1958): 599–605. As poet critic, Eliot is great; as Dean of English Letters, he is diffuse and slippery.

1866. Mueller, W. R. " 'Murder in the Cathedral': an Imitation of Christ." *RL* 27 (Summer): 414–26. Argues unconvincingly that Thomas's murder is completely predestined, and that the murderers are "loyal servants of God."

1867. Murdoch, Iris. "T. S. Eliot as a Moralist." Braybrooke, *T. S. Eliot: A Symposium for His Seventieth Birthday*, pp. 152–60. New York: Farrar, Straus and Cudahy, 1958. Objects to Eliot's rejection of liberalism in favor of dogma and authority.

1868. Nathan, Norman. "Eliot's Incorrect Note on 'C. i. f. London' " *N&Q* 5, n.s.: 262. [Waste Land]. Says that the abbreviation means "cost, insurance, freight."

1869. Newton, Frances J. "Venice, Pope, T. S. Eliot and D. H. Lawrence," *N&Q* 5, n.s.: 119–20. Pope and Lawrence, like Eliot, use Venice as a symbol of squalor.

1870. Nicholson, Harold. " 'My Words Echo.' " Braybrooke,

T. S. Eliot: A Symposium for His Seventieth Birthday, pp. 34–35. New York: Farrar, Straus and Cudahy, 1958. Gratitude to Eliot both for the liberating influence of his style and for his acceptable message of hope.

1871. Parkinson, Thomas. "Intimate and Impersonal: An Aspect of Modern Poetics." *JAAC* 16 (March): 373–83. An intelligent examination of the modern theory of impersonality in art as a reaction to the Romantic theory of personality. He concludes that Eliot does not go so far in advocating impersonality as some critics do. He allows for "the Reek of Humanity."

*1872. Preston, Raymond. "T. S. Eliot as a Contemplative Poet." Braybrooke, *T. S. Eliot: A Symposium for His Seventieth Birthday,* pp. 161–69. New York: Farrar, Straus and Cudahy, 1958. On despair as a stage in religion and in poetry, and on spiritual progress from the *Waste Land* to the *Quartets.*

1873. Rambo, Dorothy Ellen. "An Analysis of *Four Quartets* by T. S. Eliot with Particular Respect to Its Prosody." *DA* 19: 1476. (Northwestern). Provides material to aid in oral reading of the poem, but also considers other aspects.

1874. Read, Herbert. "Poetry in My Time." *TQ* 1 (February): 87–100. Considers Eliot's place in the poetic revolution of Pound and Yeats.

1875. Rosenberg, John. "Anatomist and Poet." Braybrooke, *T. S. Eliot: A Symposium for His Seventieth Birthday,* pp. 187–89. New York: Farrar, Straus and Cudahy, 1958. A nonbeliever finds more help in Eliot's portrayal of doubt than in his overtly religious affirmations.

1876. Rosenthal, M. L. "Satire and Criticism." *Nation* 186 (March 8): 211. [On Poetry and Poets]. Calls *The Sweeniad* by Victor Purcell bad poetry; praises Eliot's book, though with some reservations.

1877. Salmon, Christopher and Paul, Leslie. "Two Views of Mr. Eliot's New Play." *Listener* 60 (September): 340–41. [Elder Statesman]. Salmon says that the play never comes to life; Paul is noncommittal.

1878. Sewell, Elizabeth. "Lewis Carroll and T. S. Eliot as Nonsense Poets." Braybrooke, *T. S. Eliot: A Symposium for His Seventieth Birthday,* pp. 49–56. New York: Farrar, Straus and Cudahy, 1958. Ingenious and possibly serious discussion of Eliot's poems as examples of the art form of Nonsense.

1879. Skinner, A. E. "New Acquisitions: Rare Book Collections, II, T. S. Eliot." *LCUT* 6: 46–50. An incomplete account of their Eliot holdings.

1880. Smith, Stevie. "History or Poetic Drama?" Braybrooke, *T. S. Eliot: A Symposium for His Seventieth Birthday*, pp. 170–75. New York: Farrar, Straus and Cudahy, 1958. [Murder in the Cathedral]. An emotional attack on Eliot for his turning to religion.

1881. Speaight, Robert. "Interpreting Becket and Other Parts." Braybrooke, *T. S. Eliot: A Symposium for His Seventieth Birthday*, pp. 70–78. New York: Farrar, Straus and Cudahy, 1958. The actor who played the part of Becket over one thousand times prefers the poetry to the plays.

1882. ———. "T. S. Eliot, O.M.: a Birthday Tribute." *Listener* 60 (September 25) : 455–57. Says that Eliot's "achievement has been due to the courage, and also the modesty, with which he has recalled literature to order."

1883. Stanford, Derek. "Mr. Eliot's New Play." *ConR*, no. 194, pp. 199–201. [Elder Statesman]. In this play "Eros and Agape are brought into balance, and this equilibrium is a lovely thing." (Amplified in "T. S. Eliot's New Play," *QQ* 65, [Winter, 1959]: 682–89.)

1884. Steadman, John M. "Eliot and Husserl: The Origin of the Objective Correlative." *N&Q* 5, n.s.: 261–62. Husserl used the term in 1900.

*1885. Strothmann, Friedrich W. and Ryan, Lawrence V. "Hope for T. S. Eliot's 'Empty Men.'" *PMLA* 73 (September) : 426–32. [Hollow Men]. The authors argue that the poem offers hope to "empty" men who are not the same as "hollow" men.

*1886. Vickery, John Britton. "Gerontion: The Nature of Death and Immortality." *ArQ* 14 (Summer) : 101–15. A clear, sensitive explication of the poem.

1887. Virginia, Sister Marie. "Some Symbols of Death and Destiny in *Four Quartets*." *Renascence* 10 (Summer) : 187–91. [Dry Salvages; Little Gidding]. An intensive analysis of the symbols of water, fire, the desert, and the city-block-cluster in these two poems.

1888. Wain, John. "A Walk in the Sacred Wood." *LonM* 5 (January) : 45–53. [On Poetry and Poets]. Eliot's book is used chiefly as a springboard for Wain's reflections on other subjects.

1889. Watkins, Vernon. "Ode." Braybrooke, *T. S. Eliot: A Sym-*

posium for His Seventieth Birthday, pp. 24–26. New York: Farrar, Straus and Cudahy, 1958. A birthday tribute.

1890. Weightman, J. G. "After Edinburgh." *TC* 164 (October): 342–44. [Elder Statesman]. Praises the first two acts, but thinks that the third is a failure.

1891. Whitfield, J. H. "Pirandello and T. S. Eliot: An Essay in Counterpoint." *EM* 9: 329–57. It is paradoxical that it is Pirandello who offers hope for life, and Eliot who offers despair.

1892. Williamson, Mervyn Wilton. "A Survey of T. S. Eliot's Literary Criticism, 1917–1956." *DA* 18 (May-June): 2131. (Texas). Eliot's criticism is less a consistent aesthetic theory than it is "the 'workshop' criticism of a practicing poet."

1893. Wilson, Edmund. "Books: 'Miss Buttle' and 'Mr. Eliot.'" *NY* 34 (May 24): 119–50. Affirms his long-standing conviction that Eliot's poetry has an "emotional vibration" which one cannot forget, but he dislikes Eliot's concern with religion and his political views.

1894. Worsley, T. C. "Mr. Eliot at Colonus." *NSN* 56 (August 30): 245–46. [Elder Statesman]. A mildly favorable review.

1959

1895. Allen, Walter. "Kosmos, of Manhattan the Son." *NSN* 58 (September 12): 327–28. Briefly points out two general resemblances between *Leaves of Grass* and *The Waste Land.*

1896. Austin, Allen C. "T. S. Eliot as a Literary Critic." *DA* 19 (March-June): 3301–2. (N.Y.). Eliot's value as a critic is highly overestimated.

1897. ———. "T. S. Eliot's Objective Correlative." *UKCR* 26: 133–40. Argues that the term refers to the "necessity of a motive for the character's emotion."

1898. Balakian, Nona. "Affirmation and Love in Eliot." *NewL* 42 (May 11): 20–21. [Elder Statesman]. She approves of the philosophy of the play, but not of the plot or characterization.

1899. Baumgaertel, Gerhard. "The Concept of the Pattern in the Carpet: Conclusions from T. S. Eliot." *RLV* (Bruxelles) 25: 300–306. An inconclusive essay on Eliot and Henry James.

1900. Benziger, James. "The Romantic Tradition: Wordsworth and T. S. Eliot." *BuR* 8 (December) : 277–86. Resemblances between the thought and technique of the two poets.

*1901. Bergsten, Steffan. "Illusive Allusions: Some Reflections on the Critical Approach to the Poetry of T. S. Eliot." *OL* 14: 9–18. [Burbank . . . ; Four Quartets]. A sound study on the use and abuse of identifying allusions and quotations in Eliot's poetry.

1902. Bloom, Harold. "Lawrence, Blackmur, Eliot, and the Tortoise." *A D. H. Lawrence Miscellany,* pp. 360–69. Carbondale: Southern Illinois University Press, 1959. Passing allusions to Eliot, whom Blackmur defends, and whom Bloom dislikes.

*1903. Bollier, Ernest Philip. "T. S. Eliot and John Donne: A Problem in Criticism." *TSE* 9: 103–18. A good study, based on all that Eliot has written about Donne.

1904. ———. "T. S. Eliot and the Idea of Literary Tradition." *DA* 20: 1023. (Columbia). Eliot's idea is "a directive to consider the whole of literature as a constantly growing body of data in which a constantly modified order of value may be discovered."

1905. Braybrooke, Neville. "Eliot's Search for a Lost Eden." *CathW* 190 (December) : 151–56. Eliot's attitude toward children and *vice versa.*

1906. Buckley, Vincent. "T. S. Eliot: Impersonal Order"; "T. S. Eliot: The Question of Orthodoxy." *Poetry and Morality: Studies on the Criticism of Matthew Arnold, T. S. Eliot and F. R. Leavis,* pp. 87–157. London: Chatto and Windus, 1959. A serious and prolix study, adding to rather than resolving confusion.

1907. Burne, Glenn S. "T. S. Eliot and Remy de Gourmont." *BuR* 8 (February) : 113–26. Gourmont's influence on Eliot was important up to 1927.

1908. Cleophas, Sister Mary. *"Ash Wednesday:* The Purgative Modern Mode." *CL* 11 (Fall) : 329–39. A subtle and sometimes over-ingenious correlation of the poem and Cantos IX through XXVIII of the *Purgatorio.*

1909. Cross, Gustav. "A Note on *The Waste Land." N&Q* 6, n.s.: 286–87. Suggests that the "red rock" is the Church, or Christ, as well as suggesting other meanings pointed out earlier by other critics.

1910. Cruttwell, Patrick. "One Reader's Beginning." *OL* 14:

1–8. When Cruttwell first read Eliot in 1939, it was the rhythms that appealed to him.

1911. Dahlberg, Edward, and Read, Herbert. "Robert Graves and T. S. Eliot." *TC* 166: 54–62. [Waste Land]. Dahlberg attacks Eliot, whom Read defends, saying, "Eliot was the prophetic poet of our time."

1912. Daniels, Edgar F. "Eliot's Gerontion." *Expl* 17: item 58. On a possible allusion to Marvel's "a green thought in a green shade."

1913. Dobrée, Bonamy. "The London Stage." *SR* 67 (Winter): 109–15. [Elder Statesman]. On the basis of the fact that this play has a clearer meaning than the others, this is his best.

1914. Donoghue, Denis. "Eliot in Fair Colonus. 'The Elder Statesman.'" *Studies* 48 (Spring): 49–58. A perceptive review, comparing the play with earlier ones. He finds it more human and that it "shows a greater trust in the possibility of verbal communication." The most serious defect is the lack of a satisfactory climax.

*1915. ———. *The Third Voice* pp. 76–179. Princeton: Princeton University Press, 1959. [Murder in the Cathedral; Family Reunion; Cocktail Party; Confidential Clerk; Elder Statesman]. Using sophisticated methods of literary criticism with intelligence and sensitivity, Donoghue examines the major plays and concludes that *The Confidential Clerk* and *The Elder Statesman* are the best. There is also an excellent chapter on Eliot's verse.

*1916. Duncan, Joseph Ellis. "Eliot and the Twentieth Century Revival." *The Revival of Metaphysical Poetry,* pp. 143–64; *passim.* Minneapolis: University of Minnesota Press, 1959. A careful, well-informed study of the relation between Eliot's criticism and poetry to that of the metaphysical poets of the seventeenth century.

1917. Gerard, Sister Mary. "Eliot of the Circle and John of the Cross." *Thought* 34 (Spring): 107–27. [Four Quartets]. At the center of the poem "stands an impersonal, Platonic God, rather than the personal Incarnate God of the Cross."

1918. Gerstenberger, Donna L. "Formal Experiments in Modern Verse Drama." *DA* 19 (January): 1757–58. (Oklahoma). Eliot, like the other poets studied, is aware of the influence of poetic language on total artistic expression.

1919. Giannone, Richard J. "Eliot's 'Portrait of a Lady' and Pound's 'Portrait d'une Femme.' " *TCL* 5 (October): 131–34. Relates Eliot's and Pound's theories of the dramatic monologue to these poems.

1920. Grigson, Geoffrey. "Leavis against Eliot." *Encounter* 12: 68–69. A sharp rejoinder to Leavis, no. 1854.

*1921. Gross, Harvey Seymour. "Music and the Analogue of Feeling, Notes on Eliot and Beethoven." *CentR* (Michigan State) 3 (Summer): 269–88. A sensitive and rich exploration of the likenesses between *Four Quartets* and the quartets of Beethoven. See no. *2175.

*1922. Hall, Donald Andrew "The Art of Poetry I: T. S. Eliot, an interview." *ParR*, no. 21 (Spring-Summer), pp. 47–70. An important record of a long interview with Eliot, in which he frankly answered intelligent questions. Reprinted in *Writers at Work. Paris Review Interviews, Second Series,* 1963.

1923. Headings, Philip Ray. "The Tiresias Tradition in World Literature." *DA* 19: 2337–38. (Indiana). The figure of Tiresias has been widely used, but without any concord of interpretation.

1924. Homann, Elizabeth R. "Eliot's 'Sweeney among the Nightingales,' 8." *Expl* 17 (February): item 34. Proposes an entirely new and religious meaning for "horn'd gate."

1925. Hovey, Richard P. "Psychiatrist and Saint in Eliot's *The Cocktail Party.*" *LitPsy* 9 (Summer and Fall): 51–55. The inadequate understanding of depth psychology in this play impairs Eliot's Christianity in that he undervalues the role of human love.

*1926. Howarth, Herbert. "Eliot: the Expatriate as Fugitive." *GaR* 13 (Spring): 5–17. A pleasant and suggestive essay on the causes and results of Eliot's leaving America for Europe.

*1927. ————. "T. S. Eliot's *Criterion:* The Editor and His Contributors." *CL* 11 (Spring): 97–110. The periodical was a catalyst for Eliot's own poems and plays. A richly rewarding essay.

1928. Jarrett-Kerr, Martin. "The Poetic Drama of T. S. Eliot." *ESA* (Johannesburg) 2 (March): 16–33. A general review of all the plays except *The Elder Statesman.*

1929. Kahn, Sholom J. "Eliot's 'Polyphilprogenitive.' Another Whitman Link?" *WWR* 5 (June): 52–54. [Mr. Eliot's Sunday Morning Service]. Kahn's attempt to relate the word to Whitman is repudiated in a letter from Eliot to Mr. Kahn.

*1930. Kenner, Hugh. *The Invisible Poet: T. S. Eliot,* 346 pp. New York: McDowell, McDowell, Obolensky, 1959. Brilliant, subtle criticism, which assumes that its readers know Eliot's work thoroughly. Less attention is given to the plays than to the nondramatic poems and criticism. The book is full of fresh expression and insights.

1931. ———. "For Other Voices." *Poetry* 95 (October) : 36–40. [Elder Statesman]. Kenner paradoxically intimates that this is a good play because it is written for a theatre that does not exist.

1932. Kermode, Frank. "What Became of Sweeney?" *Spectator* 202 (April 10) : 513 [Elder Statesman]. It is the mass audience that Eliot considered so carefully that has sabotaged his theatre.

1933. Kline, Peter. "The Spiritual Center in Eliot's Plays." *KR* 21 (Summer) : 457–72. Analyzes the plays, especially *Murder in the Cathedral,* in terms of their Christian significance, and finds them effective dramatically.

1934. Kornbluth, Martin L. "A Twentieth-Century *Everyman.*" *CE* 21: 26–29. A detailed comparison of *Murder in the Cathedral* and *Everyman.*

1935. Levy, Jiří. "Rhythmical Ambivalence in the Poetry of T. S. Eliot." *Anglia* 77, no. 1: 54–64. A technical analysis of the effect of the frequent run-on line in Eliot's poetry.

1936. Licht, Merete. "What Is the Meaning of Happening?" *OL* 14: 19–32. By uniting seemingly incompatible elements, Eliot has "infused into his plays a doubleness which contributes to restoring drama to . . . reality after years of . . . naturalistic drama."

1937. Loesch, Katherine. "A Dangerous Criminal Still at Large." *N&Q* 6, n.s. (January) : 8–9. Proof that Eliot's Macavity is derived from Conan Doyle's Professor Moriarity in *The Memoirs of Sherlock Holmes.* No. 1697 anticipates this.

1938. MacGregor-Hastie, Roy. "*Waste Land* in Russell Square." *Trace,* no. 32 (June-July) , pp. 1–5. Report of an interview with Eliot.

1939. Major, John A. " 'Gerontion' and *As You Like It.*" *MLN* 74 (January) : 28–31. Finds analogies between Touchstone, Jacques, and "Gerontion."

1940. Marsh, Florence. "The Ocean-Desert: *The Ancient Mariner* and *The Waste Land.*" *EIC* 9 (April) : 126–33. The article is focused on Coleridge, but the comparison illuminates both poems.

1441. Marshall, William H. "Eliot's *The Waste Land,* 182." *Expl* 17 (March) : item 42. A comment on the use of *Leman.*

1942. ———. "A Note on 'Prufrock.' " *N&Q* 6, n.s. (May) : 188–89. Counters Arden, no. 1817, saying that "Prufrock is not Dante, nor was meant to be." Marshall's point is well taken.

1943. Møller, Kai Friis. Review of C. A. Bodelsen's *T. S. Eliot's Four Quartets. A Commentary. OL* 14.

1944. Preston, Priscilla. "A Note on T. S. Eliot and Sherlock Holmes." *MLR* 54 (July) : 397–99. Suggestions concerning Eliot's indebtedness to Conan Doyle.

1945. Raleigh, John H. "The New Criticism as an Historical Phenomenon." *CL* 11 (Winter) : 21–28. Complex forces which formed the New Criticism had two main streams: Coleridge-Eliot, and Bentham-Richards." It managed "to equip the basically unscientific attitude of Coleridge with the scientific precision of Bentham."

1946. Rickman, H. P. "Poetry and the Ephemeral: Rilke's and Eliot's Conceptions of the Poet's Task." *GL&L* 12 (April) : 174–85. [Four Quartets]. A questionable assertion of similarity of language in the two poets.

1947. Schaar, Claes. "Palimpsest Technique in 'Little Gidding': The Second Movement and the Inferno, XV." *OL* 14 (1959) : 33–37. What Eliot does is "to superimpose the description of one world upon that of another, and these two worlds are fundamentally different," thus making it an indirect valuation of the world of the Divine Comedy.

1948. Senior, John. "The Detail of the Pattern, Eliot." *The Way Down and Out: the Occult in Symbolist Literature,* pp. 170–98. Ithaca: Cornell University Press, 1959. Presents evidence that Eliot is an occultist: his central ideas derive from an occult point of view; his central method, the epiphany, is designed to achieve an occult response; he uses an occult method in *The Waste Land* and *Four Quartets,* and he quotes from obscure occult sources.

1949. Shuman, R. Baird. "Eliot's The Cocktail Party." *Expl* 17 (April) : item 46. Harcourt-Reilly represents a needed primitive element in Christianity.

1950. Simons, Jack W. "Beliefs and Poetry of T. S. Eliot." *Cweal* 71 (October 30) : 160–61. Catholics should accept Eliot's work for what it can give—poetry, not doctrine.

*1951. Smidt, Kristian. "Point of View in T. S. Eliot's Poetry." *OL* 14: 38–53. [Prufrock; La Figlia che Piange; Waste Land]. As Eliot's philosophical certainty increased "the point of view in his poetry became increasingly stable."

1952. Stanford, Deker. "T. S. Eliot's New Play." *QQ* 65 (Winter) : 682–89. [Elder Statesman]. Summary of the plot, noncommittal criticism.

1953. Strandberg, Victor. "Eliot's 'Whispers of Immortality.' " *Expl* 17 (May) : item 53. The poem means that "the flesh of Griskin must clothe . . . the skeleton of metaphysics."

1954. Terrell, Carroll Franklin. "The Bone on the Beach, The Meaning of T. S. Eliot's Symbols." *DA* 19 (March–June) : 3310. (N.Y.). Although Eliot is not a mystic, he uses mystical symbols coming from the great forces of the universe—fire, earth, water, and air.

1955. "Thespis," "Theatre Notes." *English* 12 (Spring) : 139–40. [Elder Statesman]. Summary and brief criticism.

1956. Vergmann, Finn. " 'Ash Wednesday': A Poem of Earthly and Heavenly Love." *OL* 14: 54–61. An attempt is made to treat recurring symbols from the early poems and *Ash Wednesday* to throw light on larger aspects of the poetry.

1957. Voaden, Herman Arthur, ed. *Murder in the Cathedral.* Faber and Faber, 1959. I have not been able to see a copy of this edition.

1958. Waterman, Arthur E. "Eliot's 'The Love Song of J. Alfred Prufrock,' 15–22." *Expl* 17: item 67. The fog of these lines suggests not isolation, but beauty.

1959. Watson, Ernest Bradlee, and Pressey, Benfield, eds. Introduction and notes to *Murder in the Cathedral, Contemporary Drama: Fifteen Plays,* pp. 354–55. New York: Charles Scribner's Sons, 1959. Conventional criticism.

1960. Weisstein, Ulrich. "Form as Content in the Drama of T. S. Eliot." *WR* 23 (Spring) : 239–46. [Murder in the Cathedral]. Analyzes the temptation scene in an attempt to discover the relation between rhythm and language, and meaning.

*1961. Williamson, Mervyn W. "T. S. Eliot's 'Gerontion'; a Study in Thematic Repetition and Development." *TxSE* 36:

110–26. The author weaves swiftly back and forth among all of Eliot's major poems in order to show that the theme of spiritual decay looks forward to later work. A perceptive study.

1960

1962. Adams, J. Donald. *Copey of Harvard,* pp. 158–64. Boston: Houghton, Mifflin Co., 1960. Describes Eliot's composition on Kipling and Copeland's treatment of it.

1963. Anthony, Mother Mary [Weining]. "Verbal Pattern in 'Burnt Norton, I.' " *Criticism* 2 (Winter) : 81–89. A close grammatical textual analysis of the first 48 lines.

1964. Arden, Eugene. "The 'Other' Lazarus in 'Prufrock.' " *N&Q* 7, n.s.: 33, 40. Suggests that the Lazarus of Luke 16:19–31 and not of John 11:1–46 is the man Eliot had in mind.

1965. Austin, Allen. "T. S. Eliot's Quandary." *UKCR* 27: 143–48. A useful collection of quotations illustrating Eliot's changing opinions on the problem of belief in literary judgment.

1966. Barnhill, Viron Leonard. "Poetic Context in the Collected Poems (1909–1935) of T. S. Eliot: A Linguistic Investigation of Poetic Context." *DA* 21 (November–February, 1960–61) : 2284. (Mich.). The poems are studied on "three levels constituting the linguistic layer . . . the phonological, the lexical, and the syntactical."

*1967. Bergsten, Steffan. *Time and Eternity: A Study of the Structure and Symbolism of T. S. Eliot's Four Quartets,* 258 pp. Studia Litterarum Upsaliensia, 1. Stockholm: Bonniers, 1960. A fine study of the poem, covering a rich variety of points, but admirably unified.

1968. Bland, D. S. "T. S. Eliot's Case-Book." *MLN* 75 (January) : 23–26. Suggests Ivy Compton-Burnett's *Men and Wives* as a source for *The Family Reunion.*

1969. Bolgan, Anne C. *Mr. Eliot's Philosophical Writings, or "What the Thunder Said."* Ottawa: National Library of Canada, *Canadian Theses, 1960–61.* I have not seen this doctoral dissertation.

1970. Bollier, Ernest Philip. "T. S. Eliot and *The Sacred Wood.*" *ColQ* 8 (Spring) : 308–17. Asserts the permanent and beneficial importance of this book, which taught the value of literary explication.

1971. Brett, R. L. "T. S. Eliot's *Four Quartets.*" *Reason and*

Imagination: a Study of Form and Meaning in Four Poems, pp. 108–35. London, New York: Oxford University Press, 1960. [Waste Land; Ash Wednesday; Family Reunion; Four Quartets]. Retraces familiar ground in showing Eliot's poetic evolution.

1972. Christian, Henry. "Thematic Development in T. S. Eliot's 'Hysteria.'" *TCL* 6 (April): 76–80. An explication of the poem with special attention to sound in relation to theme.

1973. Church, Margaret. "Eliot's 'Journey of the Magi.'" *Expl* 18: item 55. Suggests that the white horse may come from Rilke's Sonnet XX in pt. I of *Sonette am Orpheus.*

1974. Clowder, Felix. "The Bestiary of T. S. Eliot." *PrS* 34 (Spring): 30–37. [Old Possum's Book of Practical Cats]. Suggests, half seriously, that some of the poems have theological meanings.

1975. Craig, David. "The Defeatism of *The Waste Land.*" *CritQ* 2: 241–52. Reprinted in R. F. Knoll's *Storm over the Waste Land,* 1964, pp. 122–35. Asserts that Eliot glorifies the Renaissance at the expense of the present.

1976. Cronin, Anthony. "A Question of Modernity." 10 (October): 283–92. What Pound, Yeats, Joyce, and Eliot did was to achieve "a return of psychological precision and a gain in honesty, complexity, wholeness."

1977. Donoghue, Denis. "Eliot in the Sibyl's Leaves." *SR* 68 (Winter): 138–43. In this review of Kenner's book on Eliot he takes issue with some of Kenner's conclusions, but says: "*The Invisible Poet* is a formidable book; it offers a challenge. Only a fool or a megalomaniac will ignore its existence."

1978. Dye, F. "Eliot's 'Gerontion.'" *Expl* 18: item 39. This interpretation of the poem depends on the meaning of "Christ the Tiger."

1979. Gerstenberger, Donna. "The Saint and the Circle: The Dramatic Potential of an Image." *Criticism* 2 (Fall): 336–41. [Murder in the Cathedral]. The play presents, on all levels, an emblem of the turning wheel of the world and the still center of the saint.

*1980. Gillis, Everett A., Ryan, Laurence V., and Strothman, Friedrich W. "Hope for Eliot's Hollow Men?" *PMLA* 75 (December): 635–38. Gillis answers no. 1885 by arguing that the poem has a sonata-like structure, and that *hollow* and *empty* are synonyms, and he is answered by

Ryan and Strothman. The series of articles is useful.

1981. Gleckner, Robert F. "Eliot's 'The Hollow Men' and Shakespeare's *Julius Caesar.*" *MLN* 75: 26–28. The positive actions of the characters in Shakespeare intensify the nullity of Eliot's hollow men.

1982. Grigsby, Gordon Kay. "The Modern Long Poem: Studies in Thematic Form." *DA* 21 (July–October): 622–23. (Wis.). [Waste Land; Four Quartets]. *The Waste Land* is less coherent and more limited in scope than has been generally supposed; *Four Quartets* is structurally the most successful of the five poems studied.

1983. Hamalian, Leo. "Wishwood Revisited." *Renascence* 12 (Summer): 167–73. [Family Reunion]. ". . . the Eumenides are pivots in the pattern of the play . . . and not merely adjuncts to the action."

1984. Hanzo, Thomas. "Eliot and Kierkegaard: 'The Meaning of Happening' in *The Cocktail Party.*" *MD* 3 (May): 52–59. [Cocktail Party; Family Reunion]. If the spiritual meaning of "happening" is an awareness of despair, then Eliot has not successfully realized his intention in any of his plays.

*1985. Hough, Graham Goulden. *Image and Experience, Studies in a Literary Revolution.* London: Duckworth, 1960. [Waste Land; Prufrock]. Guardedly critical of the literary revolution headed by Eliot, Pound, Joyce, and Wyndham Lewis because, being deprived of connections with the outside world, it has had no lasting influence.

1986. Howarth, Herbert. "Eliot and Hofmannsthal." *SAQ* 59 (Autumn): 500–509. Reprinted in *Notes on Some Figures behind T. S. Eliot.* Howarth shows how Eliot's interest in Hofmannsthal began in 1911 and influenced his drama.

1987. Jackson, James L. "Eliot's 'The Love Song of J. Alfred Prufrock.'" *Expl* 18: item 48. The word *overwhelming* is part of the sea imagery as well as descriptive of the *question.*

*1988. Jones, David Edwards. *The Plays of T. S. Eliot,* 242 pp. Toronto: University of Toronto Press, 1960. An excellent study, sympathetic in tone, using earlier criticism.

1989. Kaplan, Robert B., and Wall, Richard J. "Eliot's 'Journey of the Magi.'" *Expl* 19 (November): item 8. The horse symbolizes the death of paganism.

1990. Korg, Jacob. "Modern Art Technique in *The Waste Land*." *JAAC* 18 (June) : 456–63. A provocative essay, claiming a resemblance between the techniques of this poem and the techniques of modern artists.

1991. Krause, Sydney. "Hollow Men and False Horses." *TSLL* 2 (Autumn) : 368–77. A fairly good explication, but over-emphasizes a passage in *Julius Caesar* in which the phrase *hollow men* occurs.

1992. Lucy, Seán. *T. S. Eliot and the Idea of Tradition*, 222 pp. New York: Barnes and Noble, 1960. This study, concentrating on Eliot's criticism, is not completely in control of the material.

1993. Lund, Mary Graham. "The Androgynous Moment: Woolf and Eliot." *Renascence* 12 (Winter) : 74–78. Both of these writers, "particularly in *The Cocktail Party* and *The Waves* are concerned not only with the individuation process but with the *return* of the individual to the society of men."

1994. Monteiro, George. "Eliot's 'Gerontion' 65–75." *Expl* 18: item 30. *The Education of Henry Adams* has influenced these lines.

1995. Moorman, Charles. "T. S. Eliot." *Arthurian Triptych; Mythic Material in Charles Williams, C. S. Lewis, and T. S. Eliot*, 163 pp. Berkeley: University of California Press, 1960. [Waste Land]. Argues that the poem achieves unity through the use of the Fisher-king-waste land parallel, and that it is therefore a religious poem.

1996. Nagano, Yoshio. "The Stream of Consciousness in *The Waste Land* by T. S. Eliot. Its Linguistic and Technical Problem." *SELit,* no. 10 (March) . The absence of conjunctions and subordinate clauses is necessitated by the author's intention of reproducing consciousness.

1997. Oden, Thomas C. "The Christology of T. S. Eliot: A Study of the *Kerygma* in 'Burnt Norton.' " *Encounter* 21: 93–101. A tendentious reading of the poem as consisting of these parts: I. The Garden of Gethsemene, II. The Crucifixion, III. The Descent to Hell, IV. The Tomb and the Resurrection, V. The Creation of the Church.

1998. Peake, Charles. "Sweeney Erect and the Emersonian Hero." *Neophilogus* (Groningen) 44: 54–61. Sweeney is Emerson's hero carried to the logical extreme.

1999. Ramamrutham, J. V. "T. S. Eliot and Indian Readers." *LitHY* (Bangalore) 1: 46–54. Written for the Indian reader in an attempt to help him overcome the major obstacles to understanding Eliot's poetry.

2000. Rumble, Thomas. "Some Grail Motifs in Eliot's 'Prufrock.' " *LSUAL*, no. 8, pp. 95–103. A parallel, pushed rather far, of likenesses between this poem and an early version of the Grail quest, by Von dem Turlîn.

2001. Shapiro, Karl. "T. S. Eliot: The Death of Literary Judgment." *SatR* 43 (February 27) : 34–36. Reprinted in *In Defense of Ignorance,* New York, 1960. An intemperate attack on Eliot's religion in the guise of criticism of his poetry.

2002. Simister, O. E. "The Four Quartets and Other Observations." *AWR* (Pembroke Dock) 10: 39–45. An easy, chatty essay, with abundant quotation.

2003. Sinha, Krishna Nandaw. "Imagery and Diction in Eliot's Later Poetry." *IJES* (Calcutta) 1: 79–90. Relies on other critics for sound commonplaces.

*2004. Smith, Grover, Jr. "Getting Used to T. S. Eliot." *EJ* 49 (January) : 1–9, 15. An Eliot scholar presents an introduction to the poetry, rich in compressed meaning.

2005. ———. "The Ghosts in T. S. Eliot's 'The Elder Statesman.' " *N&Q* 7, n.s.: 233–35. An interesting essay on ghosts in several of Eliot's works, and antecedents for those in this play.

2006. Spratt, P. "Eliot and Freud." *LitHY* (Bangalore) , no. 1, pp. 55–68. The ultimate in a mechanical application of popular Freudian theories to the entire body of Eliot's work.

2007. Vickery, John. "A Comment on Two Phrases in The Waste Land." *LitPsy* 10 (Winter) : 3–4. Suggests Freud's *Totem and Taboo* as the source.

2008. Walmsley, D. M. "Unrecorded Article by T. S. Eliot." *BoC* 9 (Summer) : 198–99. Notes an article entitled "Modern Tendencies in Poetry." *Shama'a* 1 (April 1920) : 9–18.

2009. Wasser, Henry. "A Note on Eliot and Santayana." *BUSE* 4 (Summer) : 125–26. [The end of "The Hollow Men"]. A possible source for this is the comment on the world of Dante in *Three Philosophical Poets.*

2010. Whitfield, J. H. "T. S. Eliot's *Four Quartets* and Their Italian Version." *EM* 11: 211–21. A review of the translation and an attack on the pessimism of the poem.

2011. Wright, George Thaddeus. "Eliot: the Transformation of a Personality." *The Poet in the Poem; the Personae of Eliot, Yeats, and Pound,* pp. 60–87. Berkeley, University of California Press, 1960. Eliot's personae are ritual performers who speak in conversational tones.

1961

2012. Allen, Walter. "The Time and Place of T. S. Eliot." *NYTBR* (April 9), pp. 1, 40–41. The reviewer sees the reaction against Eliot, especially his criticism, as a sign of "current English provincialism."

2013. Anon. "An Individual Talent." *TLS* (March 10), p. 152. A review of Seán Lucy, *T. S. Eliot and the Idea of Tradition;* David E. Jones, *The Plays of T. S. Eliot;* and George T. Wright, *The Poet in the Poem.* Praises Lucy and Jones. There is independent criticism in this review.

2014. Boardman, Gwenn R. "T. S. Eliot and the Mystery of Fanny Marlow." *MFS* 7 (Summer) : 99–105. On various works by "F.M." in the *Criterion,* suggestive of Eliot.

*2015. Clubb, Merrel D., Jr. "The Heraclitean Element in Eliot's 'Four Quartets.'" *PQ* 60 (January) : 19–33. A temperate and rich essay on Eliot's use of Heraclitus's dialectic of paradox.

2016. Fleming, Rudd. "The Elder Statesman and Eliot's 'Programme for the Metier of Poetry.'" *WSCL* 2: 54–64. Pushes a little too hard the parallels between this play and *Oedipus at Colonus.* Also suggests likenesses to *Samson Agonistes.*

2017. Gerstenberger, Donna. *"The Waste Land* in *A Farewell to Arms." MLN* 76 (January) : 24–25. Suggests that Hemingway was influenced by Eliot's poem.

2018. Gibson, William M. "Sonnets in T. S. Eliot's *The Waste Land." AL* 32 (January) : 465–66. By his use of a double sonnet in lines 236–65, Eliot "heightens a major theme of the entire work."

2019. Gillis, Everett A. "The Spiritual Status of T. S. Eliot's Hollow Men." *TSLL* 2 (Winter) : 464–75. The same point was made in no. *1980.

2020. Hasegawa, Mitsuaki. "Human Salvation: an Appreciation of The Cocktail Party." *Eigo to Kyoiku or English and Education,* pp. 65–72. 1961. Eliot shows the levels of spirituality of the characters in the play, which leads to the conclusion that humanity has its full meaning for him only when divinity is related to humanity. Consequently his sympathy with humanity has the form of prayer.

2021. Harvey, Versa R. "T. S. Eliot's 'The Love Song of J. Alfred Prufrock.'" *IEY*, no. 6, pp. 29–31. A mechanical interpretation of the poem, line by line.

2022. Hoskot, S. S. *T. S. Eliot, His Mind and Personality*, 297 pp. Bombay: University of Bombay, 1961. This doctoral dissertation suffers from a misunderstanding of America and England, and from a lack of clear thinking.

2023. Howarth, Herbert. "T. S. Eliot and the "Little Preacher.'" *AQ* 13 (Summer) : 179–87. On likenesses between Eliot and his abolitionist grandfather, William Greenleaf Eliot. Reprinted in Howarth's *Notes on Some Figures behind T. S. Eliot.*

*2024. ———. "Eliot and Milton: The American Aspect." *UTQ* 30 (January) : 150–62. "Milton was what the Jungians would call Eliot's 'shadow figure': a . . . secret self from whom he must avert his gaze, or, if he gazed, burst out in protest at the self revealed." A stimulating essay.

2025. Hyman, Stanley Edgar. "Poetry and Criticism: T. S. Eliot." *ASch* 30 (Winter) : 43–55. [Sweeney among the Nightingales; Tradition and the Individual Talent]. A sophisticated essay on the relation between the poem and the essay.

2026. Kaplan, Robert B. and Wall, Richard J. "Eliot's 'Gerontion.'" *Expl* 19: item 36. The authors suggest that Dedalus's vision of hell in *The Portrait of the Artist as a Young Man* is close to the old man's reverie in this poem.

2027. Knieger, Bernard. "The Dramatic Achievement of T. S. Eliot." *MD* 3 (February) : 387–92. [The plays]. The plays are studied for dramatic conflict and use of language. Praises *Murder in the Cathedral* for its poetry and the heroic character of Thomas.

2028. Major, Minor Wallace. "A St. Louisan's View of Prufrock." *CEA* 23 (September) : 5. Reads this poem as a "satire on St. Louis society."

2029. Marion, Sister Thomas. "Eliot's Criticism of Metaphysical Poetry." *Greyfriar* 4: 17–23. Accuses Eliot of unintelligibility in his use of the phrase "unified sensibility." This essay magnifies the difficulty of the phrase.

2030. Moynihan, William T. "The God of the Waste Land Quest." *Renascence* 30 (Summer) : 171–79. An extreme example of archetypal criticism, concentrating on the epical and spiritual levels of man's search for eternal life.

2031. Porter, Katherine Anne. "On First Meeting T. S. Eliot." *Shenandoah* 12 (Spring) : 25–26. She was favorably impressed by Eliot's courtesy and self-possession at a raucous cocktail party.

2032. Stelzmann, Rainulf A. "The Theology of T. S. Eliot's Dramas." *XUS* 1 (April) : 7–17. A slight essay.

2033. Stickey, William J. "Eliot's 'The Love Song of J. Alfred Prufrock.' " *Expl* 20: item 10. There is a resemblance between "Prufrock" and *The Divine Comedy,* but the experience of Prufrock contrasts with that of Dante.

2034. Sugiyama, Yoko. *"The Waste Land* and Contemporary Japanese Poetry." *CL* 13 (Summer) : 254–62. A group of poets, the *Arechi,* "has contributed to Japanese poetry new rhythms, realistic images, a haunting melancholy, a deep though pessimistic faith in humanity—all through the stimulus of Eliot's *Waste Land."*

*2035. Unger, Leonard. *T. S. Eliot,* 48 pp. Pamphlets on American Writers, no. 8. Minneapolis: University of Minnesota, 1961. Reprinted as "T. S. Eliot's Magic Lantern." *Moments and Patterns,* pp. 7–40. Minneapolis: University of Minnesota, 1966. A mature and luminous criticism covering all of Eliot's work by a critic who knows and understands him thoroughly.

2036. White, Robert. "Eliot's 'The Love Song of J. Alfred Prufrock,' Epigraph." *Expl* 20: item 19. Not only the epigraph, but the entire poem, supports the likeness between Prufrock and Guido da Montefeltro.

2037. Winter, Jack. " 'Prufrockism' in *The Cocktail Party."* *MLQ* 22 (June) : 135–48. A wide-ranging study of Eliot's theology.

2038. Wooton, Carl. "The Mass: 'Ash Wednesday's' Objective Correlative." *ArQ* 17 (Spring) : 31–42. An explication of the parallels in the Mass for Ash Wednesday and the poem.

1962

2039. Anon. "T. S. Eliot. An Interview." *GrR* (Westminster School) 24, no. 3. Eliot answers questions on a variety of subjects, including "Prufrock."

2040. ———. "The Waste Land Forty Years On." *TLS,* no. 3161

(September 28) , p. 760. [The Preludes; Waste Land].
A rapid survey of differing opinions of *The Waste Land,*
and a conclusion that its magic "still works."

2041. Austin, Allen C. "T. S. Eliot's Theory of Dissociation."
CE 23 (January) : 309–12. A careful analysis of the
meaning of the phrase "dissociation of sensibility."

2042. Barth, J. Robert. "T. S. Eliot's Image of Man: a Thematic
Study of His Drama." *Renascence* 14 (Spring) : 126–
38, 165. The theme of the dramas is "the problem of
isolation from reality, leading to the . . . action of
striving for union with reality—oneself, the world, other
men, God." Competent.

2043. Boardman, Gwenn R. "Ash Wednesday: Eliot's Lenten
Mass Sequence." *Renascence* 15 (Fall) : 28–36. The
structure of the poem is found in the Roman Catholic
mass. The author insists on finding a strict correspondence between the parts of the mass and the parts of
the poem.

2044. Bullaro, John Joseph. "The Dantean Image of Ezra
Pound, T. S. Eliot, and Hart Crane." *DA* 22 (April–
June) : 4012. (Wisconsin). Eliot believed that in the
selection and ordering of his images he was following
Dante.

2045. Carew, Rivers. "Georges Rouault and T. S. Eliot: a Note."
HJ 60 (April) : 230–35. A quick summary of *Four
Quartets;* any parallel with the painter is insufficiently
developed.

2046. Carey, Sister M. Cecelia. "Baudelaire's Influence in *The
Waste Land.*" *Renascence* 14: 185–92, 198. Influence
may be seen in the borrowing of lines from *Les Fleurs
du Mal,* choice of subject, and a concern with the problem of good and evil.

2047. Cornwell, Ethel F. "Eliot's Concept of the 'Still Point.'"
*The 'Still Point'; Theme and Variations in the Writings
of T. S. Eliot, Coleridge, Yeats, Henry James, Virginia
Woolf, and D. H. Lawrence,* pp. 17–63. New Brunswick:
Rutgers University Press, 1962. An earnest attempt to
clarify the concepts embodied in the phrase.

2048. Falck, Colin. "Hurry Up Please! It's Time." *Review* 1
(November) : 59–64. [Notes towards the Definition of
Culture; After Strange Gods]. Rejects Eliot's concept
of the impersonality of the poet while arguing for a
dynamic humanism to counter the destructive forces of
the present time.

2049. Freed, Louis. *T. S. Eliot, Aesthetics and History,* 235 pp. LaSalle, Ill.: Open Court, 1962. Most of the book is concerned with Aristotle, Kant, and F. H. Bradley as background for understanding Eliot's views on criticism, metaphysics, and religion.

2050. Gaskell, Ronald. "The Family Reunion." *EIC* 12 (July): 292–301. A sophisticated essay saying that the choice of naturalism as a mode of development for this play results in failure, because it is at odds with Eliot's lack of interest in the natural world.

2051. Hathorn, Richard Y. *Tragedy, Myth, and Mystery,* pp. 195–216. Bloomington: Indiana University Press, 1962. [Murder in the Cathedral]. Becket goes beyond the stoic virtues to the Christian ones.

2052. Hidden, Norman. "Studying T. S. Eliot in the Sixth Form." *English* 14 (Summer): 53–56. Seventeen-year-old students found the study of Eliot rewarding.

2053. Holland, Norman N. "Realism and the Psychological Critic; or, How Many Complexes had Lady Macbeth." *LitPsy* 10 (Winter): 5–8. Points out that Eliot did not intend Harcourt-Reilly to be a real psychiatrist.

2054. Inserillo, Charles R. "Wish and Desire: Two Poles of the Imagination in the Drama of Arthur Miller and T. S. Eliot." *XUS* 1:247–58. [Family Reunion; Cocktail Party; Confidential Clerk]. *Wish* (desiring an impossibility) is represented by Loman; *desire* (wanting a realistic potentiality) is represented by Harry, Celia, and Colby. Eliot is a classicist, Miller a romanticist.

2055. Jenkins, William D. "The Sherlockian Eliot." *BSJ* 12: 81–84, 128. Concerns the debt of Eliot to Holmes's stories.

2056. Kameyama, Masaka. "An Essay on T. S. Eliot—His Idea of Tradition." *CEKWJC,* no. 6 (December), pp. 72–88. A clear restatement of Eliot's ideas, and a conclusion on Eliot's relevance for modern Japan.

2057. Kenner, Hugh. "Art in a Closed Field." *VQR* 38: 597–613. [Waste Land]. An analogy between the literature of the past one hundred years and the modern mathematical concept of the closed field.

2058. ———. *T. S. Eliot; a Collection of Critical Essays.* Englewood Cliffs: Prentice-Hall, 1962. "Introduction," Hugh Kenner; "To Meet Mr. Eliot," Arthur Mizener; "Early London Environment," Wyndham Lewis; "Bradley,"

Hugh Kenner; "Irregular Metphysics," R. P. Blackmur; "Lewis Carroll and T. S. Eliot as Nonsense Poets," Elizabeth Sewell; "Eliot and Tennyson," Sydney Musgrove; "Marie, Marie, Hold on Tight," George L. K. Morris; "The Waste Land," F. R. Leavis; "T. S. Eliot, 1925–1935," D. W. Harding; "T. S. Eliot's Later Poetry," F. R. Leavis; " 'Little Gidding,' " D. W. Harding; "On Ash Wednesday," Allen Tate; "In the Hope of Straightening Things Out," R. P. Blackmur; "Mr. Eliot's Solid Merit," Ezra Pound; "The Style of the Master," William Empson; "Murder in the Cathedral," John Peter; "The Cocktail Party," Denis Donoghue; "For Other Voices," Hugh Kenner; "T. S. Eliot: the End of an Era," Donald Davie. Each of these essays is entered separately in this bibliography.

2059. Kligerman, Jack. "An Interpretation of T. S. Eliot's 'East Coker.' " *ArQ* 18 (Summer) : 101–12. A good reading of the poem, concentrating on details.

2060. Knust, Herbert. "The Artist, the King, and 'The Waste Land': Richard Wagner, Ludwig II, and T. S. Eliot." *DA* 22 (January–March) : 2398. (Penn State). A study of possible sources of the poem.

*2061. Mason, William Heppell. *Murder in the Cathedral*, 73 pp. Oxford: B. Blackwell, 1962. An introduction, accomplishing admirably its purpose, to give necessary background and to indicate the main areas of critical interest.

2062. Mathewson, George. "The Search for Coherence: T. S. Eliot and the Christian Tradition in English Poetry." *DA* 23 (July–September) : 225–26 (Princeton). [Murder in the Cathedral]. Concentrates on *Murder* and on Eliot's attitude toward Shelley.

2063. McConnell, Daniel J. *"The Heart of Darkness* in T. S. Eliot's 'The Hollow Men.' " *TSLL* 4 (Summer) : 141–53. The "heart of darkness" in both Conrad and Eliot is the international cities of Europe whose corruption has doomed humanity.

2064. Ong, Walter J. " 'Burnt Norton' in St. Louis." *AL* 33 (January) : 522–26. Suggests that Eliot's memories of girls at a school next door to him influenced the first section of the poem.

2065. Palmer, Richard E. "Existentialism in T. S. Eliot's *The Family Reunion*." *MD* 5 (September) : 174–86. Overemphasizes the existentialist aspect of the play.

*2066. Perkins, David. "Rose Garden to Midwinter Spring: Achieved Faith in the *Four Quartets*." *MLQ* 23 (March) : 41–45. A rich and suggestive essay.

2067. Rees, T. R. "T. S. Eliot, Remy de Gourmont, and Dissociation of Sensibility," edited by W. F. Neir, pp. 186–98. *Studies in Comparative Literature*, No. 7, Baton Rouge, La., 1962. A close scrutiny of the meaning of "dissociation of sensibility," defending Eliot's and de Gourmont's use of the term.

*2068. Rillie, John A. M. "Melodramatic Device in T. S. Eliot." *RES* 13 (August) : 267–81. Melodrama is the "technical correlation of [Eliot's] distinctive sensibility, a form adaptable to an almost Manichean view of the world, and a judgment of that world." A penetrating study.

2069. Robson, W. W. "Eliot's Later Criticism." *Review* 1 (November) : 52–58. [On Poetry and Poets]. While centering on *On Poetry and Poets,* Robson runs through much of Eliot's critical writings sometimes responding favorably and sometimes unfavorably. His perceptions are neither original nor completely developed.

2070. Shapiro, Karl. "The Three Hockey Games of T. S. Eliot." *AR* 22 (Fall) : 284–86. Chiefly an attack on the New Criticism, and peripherally on Eliot.

2071. Sinha, Khrishna Nandan. "The Intimate and the Unidentifiable: Feeling in T. S. Eliot's *Four Quartets*." *LitC* 5: 128–40. A derivative and rambling paraphrase of the poem.

2072. Smith, Carol Hertzig. "From *Sweeney Agonistes* to *The Elder Statesman*: a Study of the Dramatic Theory and Practice of T. S. Eliot." *DA* 23 (July–September) : 635–36. (Mich.). A study of Eliot's themes and dramatic methods.

2073. Smith, Gerald. "Eliot's 'The Love Song of J. Alfred Prufrock.'" *Expl* 21: item 17. The "pair of ragged claws" is a beautifully chosen symbol for Prufrock's sexual desire.

2074. Wasserstrom, William. "T. S. Eliot and *The Dial*." *SR* 70: 81–92. Contains information on *The Dial* award to *The Waste Land.*

2075. Weatherhead, A. Kingsley. "*Four Quartets*: Setting Love in Order." *WSCL* 3 (Spring–Summer) : 32–49. Tries to show that "the most significant strand in the evolution of the Quartets . . . is the metamorphosis of love and the discovery of a proper context for it." Much of the evidence is tenuous.

2076. Winston, George P. "Washington Allston and the Objective Correlative." *BuR* 11 (December) : 95–108. Suggests that he borrowed the term from Allston's *Lectures on Art,* 1850.

2077. Woodward, Daniel H. "John Quinn and T. S. Eliot's First Book of Criticism." *PBSA* 56: 259–65. Quinn was the instigator of Eliot's first book of criticism, *Ezra Pound: His Metric and Poetry.*

1963

*2078. Adams, John F. "The Fourth Temptation in *Murder in the Cathedral.*" *MD* 5 (February) : 381–88. The peculiarly modern questions raised for Thomas by the Fourth Tempter concerning motives for martyrdom involve the reader also. A subtle and fine analysis.

2079. Barnes, W. J. "T. S. Eliot's 'Marina'; Image and Symbol." *UKCR* 29 (Summer) : 297–305. A prolix interpretation of the poem primarily on the literal level.

*2080. Bollier, Ernest Philip. "From Scepticism to Poetry; A Note on Conrad Aiken and T. S. Eliot." *TSE* 13: 95–104. An authoritative account of Eliot's attitude toward reality and toward poetry.

*2081. ———. "T. S. Eliot and F. H. Bradley: A Question of Influence." *TSE* 12: 87–111. "Like Dante's Vergil, I suggest Bradley led Eliot not only into the Inferno, but through Purgatory to within sight of Paradise itself." An excellent study.

2082. Brooks, Cleanth. "T. S. Eliot: Discourse to the Gentiles." *The Hidden God: Studies in Hemingway, Faulkner, Yeats, Eliot, and Warren,* pp. 68–97. New Haven: Yale University Press, 1963. A clear explanation of why Eliot uses analogy and indirection in writing of Christianity.

2083. Bullough, Geoffrey. "Christopher Fry and the 'Revolt' against Eliot." *Experimental Drama,* edited by W. A. Armstrong, pp. 56–78. London: G. Bell and Sons, Ltd., 1963. There are only passing references to Eliot here.

2084. Carnell, Corbin. "Creation's Lonely Flesh: T. S. Eliot and Christopher Fry on the Life of the Senses." *MD* 6 (September) : 141–49. Eliot is less "orthodox and less successful in his handling of Christian belief" than Fry is, because Eliot does not delight in God's created world.

2085. Chaturvedi, B. N. *T. S. Eliot,* 93 pp. Allahabad: Kitab Mahal, 1963. Intended primarily for Indian readers.

2086. Costello, Harry Todd. *Josiah Royce's Seminar, 1913–14.* Edited by Grover Smith. New Brunswick: Rutgers University Press, 1963. Class notes include some of Eliot's notes and questions. This volume contains fresh information on Eliot's early interests.

2087. Davie, Donald. "Mr. Eliot." *NSN* 66 (October 11) : 496–97. [Collected Poems, 1909–1962]. Eliot has made poetry into music, which means "making the only events in the poem to be the happening of its constituent words as one by one they rise and explode on our consciousness."

2088. Dunn, Ian S. "Eliot's 'The Love Song of J. Alfred Prufrock.'" *Expl* 22: item 1. Suggests an etymology for *Prufrock.*

2089. Fortin, René E. "Eliot's *The Waste Land,* 207–214." *Expl* 21: item 32. Explores the connection between *currants* and *currents.*

*2090. Frye, Northrop. *T. S. Eliot* (Writers and Critics) , 106 pp. Edinburgh and London: Oliver and Boyd, 1963. A fine study, clear enough for the beginning student, and full enough for the expert. Frye considers all of Eliot's work.

2091. George, Arapura Ghevarghese. *T. S. Eliot: His Mind and Art, Literary Perspectives,* 256 pp. Bombay and New York: Asia Publishing House, 1963. This book claims too much for existentialism in Eliot's work.

2092. Greenheet, Morris. "Sources of Obscurity in Modern Poetry; The Examples of Eliot, Stevens, and Tate." *CentR* 7 (Spring) : 171–90. Though some of Eliot's poetry is not obscure, *The Waste Land* is, and Eliot's example has been the cause of obscurity in Stevens and Tate.

2093. Griffith, Clark "Eliot's 'Gerontion.'" *Expl* 21: item 46. Considers the meaning of the "boy" who reads aloud and the "jew" landlord.

2094. Hasegawa, Mitsuaki. "Poet's Communication of Meaning: An Approach to T. S. Eliot." *HSLL* 9: 66–74. Published by the English Literary Association of Hiroshima University. Eliot "is . . . struggling to communicate what is meaningful to his community of human beings, where it is essential to be conscious of moral[ity] upon the foundation of tradition and orthodoxy." [Summary by the author]. The style of the essay is difficult.

2095. Hathaway, Richard D. *"The Waste Land's* Benediction." *AN&Q* 2 (December) : 53–54. Relies on the onomatopoeia of the thrice-repeated *Shanti* which he says suggests falling rain, to conclude that the poem ends on a note of hope.

2096. Kermode, Frank. "Reading Eliot Today." *Nation* 197 (October 26) : 263–64. [Collected Poems, 1909–1962]. "Eliot is matched only by Pound and Yeats . . . in the intensity of his effort . . . to give a whole mind to poetry."

2097. Kuna, F. M. "T. S. Eliot's Dissociation of Sensibility and the Critics of Metaphysical Poetry." *EIC* 13: 241–52. A closely argued essay which seeks to prove that "all the well-known statements in [the review of Grierson's *Metaphysical Poets*] can be applied only to modern poetry," and do not apply to seventeenth-century metaphysical poetry.

2098. Lee, Joe Ho. "Alexander Pope in Eliot's 'East Coker.' " *N& Q* 10, n.s.: 381. Similarities between sec. IV of Eliot's poem and *The Essay on Man,* sec. II, ll. 143–46.

2099. Locke, Frederick W. "Dante and T. S. Eliot's Prufrock." *MLN* 78 (June) : 51–59. A leisurely and well-mannered examination of the epigraph, leading to the conclusion that the "I" of the poem is the reader.

2100. Maxwell, J. C. "Flaubert in *The Waste Land." ES* 44: 279. Line 80 recalls a description of a cupid in the hotel where Emma Bovary and Leon met.

2101. Narayana, K. S. "T. S. Eliot and the Bhagavad Gita." *AQ* 15 (Winter) : 573–58. [To the Indians Who Died in Africa]. On the close resemblances between certain stanzas in Eliot's poem and the Indian epic.

2102. Nelson, C. E. "Saint-John Perse and T. S. Eliot." *WHR* 17 (Spring) : 163–71. Because of differences in attitude toward mankind and life, Eliot has not done justice to Perse in his translation of *Anabase.*

2103. Nemerov, Howard. "Twenty-five Years with Mr. Eliot." *NewL* 46 (December 9) : 28–29. After a spirited, irreverent, and personal beginning, the author thanks Eliot for his services to poetry and criticism.

2104. Nims, John Frederick. "Greatness in Moderation." *SatR* 46 (October 19) : 25–27. [Collected Poems, 1909–1962].

Although a great poet, Eliot suffers because his poetry lacks exhilaration. It shows man as shrunken rather than as "larger, more alive than we thought."

2105. Rehak, Louise R. "On the Use of Martyrs: Tennyson and Eliot on Thomas Becket." *UTQ* 33: 43–60. A balanced assessment of the virtues and defects of both plays.

2106. Rickey, Mary Ellen. " 'Christabel' and *Murder in the Cathedral.*" *N&Q* 10, n.s.: 151. Points out similarities between sec. I of the poem and a section near the end of Act I of the play.

2107. Scrimgeour, C. A. "*The Family Reunion.*" *EIC* 13 (January) : 104–6. [Reply to Ronald Gaskell, July 1962]. This essay criticizes no. 2050 by asserting that in the character of Amy, Eliot maintains dramatic tension between the natural and supernatural worlds.

2108. Sinha, Krishna Nandan. *On Four Quartets of T. S. Eliot,* 127 pp. Ifracombe: A. H. Stockwell, 1963. The author leans heavily on other commentators, not all of whom he comprehends.

*2109. Smith, Carol H. *T. S. Eliot's Dramatic Theory and Practice, from Sweeney Agonistes to The Elder Statesman,* 249 pp. Princeton: Princeton University Press, 1963. One of the best studies of Eliot. "Eliot found in drama, because of its ritual origins and its capacity to present a completely ordered dramatic world, the perfect vehicle for the expression of his religious insight."

2110. Spanos, William V. "*Murder in the Cathedral*: the *Figura* as Mimetic Principle." *DramS* 3 (October) : 206–23. By means of the figural aesthetic, Eliot "transcends the univocal realism of naturalistic drama without resorting to the strategy that altogether by-passes or dissolves concrete reality."

2111. Speaight, Robert. "The Plays of T. S. Eliot." *Month* 30 (October) : 209–13. A review of Carol Smith's *T. S. Eliot's Dramatic Theory and Practice,* praising it for its clarity. He doubts that Eliot "has the theatre in his bones."

2112. Thompson, Eric. *T. S. Eliot: The Metaphysical Perspective,* 186 pp. Crosscurrents: Modern Critiques. Carbondale: Southern Illinois University Press, 1963. The author relates Eliot's doctoral thesis on F. H. Bradley to his criticism and to "Burnt Norton." The persistent reader can profit by this book.

*2113. Williams, Raymond. "Tragic Resignation and Sacrifice."
CritQ 5 (Spring) : 5–19. [Murder in the Cathedral;
Cocktail Party]. By means of a clear and subtle analysis
of the meaning of *sacrifice* the theme of the two plays
is clarified.

1964

2114. Andreach, Robert J. "The Spiritual Life in Hopkins,
Joyce, Eliot, and Hart Crane." *DA* 25: 467. (New York
University) [Ariel poems, Four Quartets, the plays].
Chiefly a contrast between Eliot and Hopkins. "Where
Hopkins emphasizes the progression of the spiritual life
and the possibility of a higher spiritual state, Eliot em-
phasizes the discovery of the spiritual life and the pos-
sibility of a transformed earthly life."

2115. ———. *Studies in Structure: The Stages in the Spiritual
Life of Five Modern Authors,* pp. 72–101. New York:
Fordham University Press, 1964. Contrasts and compares Eliot with Hopkins and Joyce; technical and over-
literal.

2116. Anon. "People." *Time* 84 (October 2) : 72. On Eliot's receiving the Medal of Freedom from United States Am-
bassador Bruce. Photograph.

2117. Bates, Ronald. "A Topic in *The Waste Land:* Traditional
Rhetoric and Eliot's Individual Talent." *WSCL* 5 (Summer) : 85–104. Traces earlier uses of the rhetorical figure of architectural description and shows how Eliot
uses it.

2118. Bellis, William Ward. "Thomas Becket: An Emerging
Myth." *DA* 25: 2976–77. (Ind.) . Considers Becket as a
mythic figure in Eliot's, Anouilh's, and Fry's plays. Eliot
"shows Thomas as a saint and, through him, the in-
scrutable mystery which sanctity poses for the world."

*2119. DeLaura, David J. "The Place of the Classics in T. S.
Eliot's Christian Humanism." *Hereditas: Some Essays
in the Modern Experience of the Classical,* edited by
Frederic Will, pp. 153–97. Austin: University of Texas
Press, 1964. A well-informed and wide-ranging essay on
Eliot's humanism, religion, view of civilization, and
primarily his view of the classics. DeLaura shows that in
spite of a failure on Eliot's part to be "the ideal ex-
ponent of Christian humanism for our time," he has

struggled valiantly to reconcile Christianity and classical paganism.

2120. Dickerson, Mary Jane. *"As I Lay Dying* and *The Waste Land:* Some Relationships." *MissQ* 17 (Summer) : 129–35. Both authors use vegetation myths.

2121. Dorris, George E. "Two Allusions in the Poetry of T. S. Eliot." *ELN* 2 (September): 54–57. [Sweeney Agonistes; Waste Land]. An allusion in *Sweeney* to a scene in James's *The Ambassadors,* and one in *The Waste Land* (ll. 266–306) to Puccini's *Madam Butterfly.*

2122. Edmonds, Dorothy. "T. S. Eliot: Toward the 'Still Point.' " *BSTCF* 5: 49–54. The prize-winning essay in the *Atlantic's* contest for young writers. It is a clear and refreshing survey of Eliot's poetry, from "Sweeney among the Nightingales" to *Four Quartets.*

2123. French, A. L. "Criticism and *The Waste Land." SoRA* 1, no. 2 (1964) : 69–81. Rejects Eliot's notes, and with them Leavis's influential interpretation of the poem. An interesting point of view.

*2124. Gardner, Helen Louise. "Shakespeare in the Age of Eliot." *TLS,* no. 3243 (April 23) , p. 335. A masterly essay on Eliot's influence on Shakespeare criticism between 1916 and 1964.

2125. Geier, Norbert Joseph. "The Problem of Aesthetic Judgment and Moral Judgment of Literary Value in the Critical Theories of Irving Babbitt, Paul Elmer More, Yvor Winters, and T. S. Eliot." *DA* 24: 4188. (Wisconsin). Of the four critics, Eliot suggests the best pragmatic approach to the problem, though he gives no demonstrable solution.

2126. Gibbs, A. M., Magarey, Kevin, and French, A. L. "Critical Exchange: Mr. French's Mr. Eliot." *SoRA* 1: 82–88. [Waste Land]. (See no. 2123.) A lively and reasoned argument against no. 2123. French replies (pp. 85–88) with a vigorous rejoinder.

2127. Gillis, Everett A. "Religion in a Sweeney World." *ArQ* 20 (Spring) : 55–63. [Sweeney among the Nightingales]. A highly subjective interpretation, reading the poem as concerned with the "impotency of sacrificial death."

*2128. Headings, Philip R. *T. S. Eliot,* 191 pp. New York: Twayne, 1964. An illuminating study of the poems and dramas with emphasis on the influence of Dante. The author knows the major critics of Eliot and uses them intelligently.

2129. Holder, Alan. "T. S. Eliot on Henry James." *PMLA* 79 (September) : 490–97. A careful analysis of Eliot's admiration for James the novelist, and his failure to appreciate him as critic.

*2130. Howarth, Herbert. *Notes on Some Figures behind T. S. Eliot,* 396 pp. Boston: Houghton Mifflin, 1964. A study of Eliot's family, teachers, and friends, providing an intellectual background for his work.

2131. Howell, John Michael. "The Waste Land Tradition in the American Novel." *DA* 24: 3337. (Tulane). The influence of *The Waste Land* on Fitzgerald, Hemingway, Faulkner, and Salinger.

*2132. Jones, Genesius. *Approach to the Purpose: A Study of the Poetry of T. S. Eliot,* 351 pp. New York: Barnes and Noble, 1964. In this fine study, Father Jones approaches the poetry from: I. The Perspective of Religion, II. of History, III. of Language, IV. of Art, V. of Science, VI. of Myth. Within each chapter the poems are studied chronologically. He has assimilated the best of Eliot scholarship and brings illumination to the subject.

2133. Joselyn, Sister M. "Twelfth Night Quartet: Four Magi Poems." *Renascence* 16 (Winter) : 92–94. A brief comparison of Yeats's "The Magi," John Peale Bishop's "Twelfth Night," Edgar Bowers's "The Wise Men," and Eliot's "The Journey of the Magi."

2134. Kaul, R. K. "Rhyme and Blank Verse in Drama. A Note on Eliot." *English* 15 (Summer) : 96–99. An inconclusive essay, comparing Eliot's and Samuel Johnson's views.

2135. Kennedy, Richard S. *Working Out Salvation with Diligence: the Plays of T. S. Eliot,* 11 pp. Wichita: University Studies 59, University of Wichita, 1964. The mysticism of *The Cocktail Party, The Family Reunion, The Confidential Clerk,* and *The Elder Statesman* work against their dramatic success. *Murder in the Cathedral,* which is not mystical, is his greatest achievement.

2136. Kenner, Hugh. "The Seven-Year Shaman." *NaR* 16 (February 11) : 113–14. For seven years between 1916 and 1923, Eliot was a "shaman-poet, shaking with a civilization fever, and confronting its demons with an incantation."

2137. Knoll, Robert E. *Storm over the Waste Land,* 163 pp. Chicago: Scott, Foresman, 1964. Introduction, ten reprinted essays and chapters from books, a list of questions for students, and a brief bibliography. Each of the essays is entered separately in this bibliography.

2138. Koppenhaver, Allen John. "T. S. Eliot's *Murder in the Cathedral.*" DA 25 (October-December) : 2983. (Duke). Traces as completely as possible the religious, literary, and musical elements that flowed together to create the play.

2139. Lees, F. N. "T. S. Eliot and Nietzsche." *N&Q* 11, n.s.: 386–87. Notes two similarities between the work of the two men.

2140. Lightfoot, Marjorie Jean. "T. S. Eliot's *The Cocktail Party:* An Experiment in Prosodic Description." *DA* 25: 6630. (Northwestern). A technical study concluding, "Character, mood, situation and style are given poetic dimension through immediately and recollected patterns, while conversational 4-stress accentual verse establishes a norm for versification."

2141. ———. *"Purgatory* and *The Family Reunion.* In Pursuit of Prosodic Description." *MD* 7: 256–66. Thinks there are four stresses per line in the play, as there are in Yeats's *Purgatory.*

2142. Lorch, Thomas M. "The Relationship between *Ulysses* and *The Waste Land.*" *TSLL* 6 (Summer) : 123–33. Concludes on the basis of verbal parallels between the two works that Eliot was influenced on the unconscious level by Joyce's work.

2143. Marks, Emerson R. "T. S. Eliot and the Ghost of S. T. C." *SR* 72 (Spring) : 262–80. [Idea of a Christian Society; Notes towards the Definition of Culture]. The originality of this essay lies in pointing out the strong similarities between Eliot's and Coleridge's ideas on society and politics.

2144. Maxwell, J. C. " 'The Dry Salvages'; A Possible Echo of Graham Greene." *N&Q* 11, n.s.: 387. Similarity of wording with Greene's *The Man Within* (1929).

2145. ———. "Eliot and Husserl." *N&Q* 11, n.s.: 74. Suggests that the source of Eliot's phrase "objective correlative" may be Santayana's *Interpretations of Poetry and Religion.*

2146. Mayer, John Theodore, Jr. "The Dramatic Mode of T. S. Eliot's Early Poetry." *DA,* 25 (July-September) : 1918.

(Fordham). "This study explicates all Eliot's major early works by approaching each as an interior utterance that unfolds a psychic action."

*2147. McGill, Arthur C. *The Celebration of Flesh: Poetry in Christian Life*, pp. 38–91. New York: Association Press, 1964. [Waste Land]. Concentrating on language, the author sensitively explores the meaning of the poem for Christians. By "flesh" he means immediate concrete experience.

2148. Melchiori, Giorgio. "Eliot and Apollinaire." *N&Q* 11, n.s.: 385–86. A suggestive note on the possibility that Apollinaire's *Les Mamelles de Tirésias* suggested *Sweeney Agonistes*.

2149. Merritt, James D. "Eliot's *The Waste Land*, 74–75." *Expl* 23 (December): item 31. Interprets the "Dog" of these lines as "God" spelled backwards.

2150. Mowat, John. "Samuel Johnson and the Critical Heritage of T. S. Eliot." *SGG* 6: 231–47. Emphasizes the interest of both critics in the tensions between the general and the particular in criticism and their interest in the relation between the real and the ideal.

2151. Musacchio, George L. "A Note on the Fire-Rose Synthesis of T. S. Eliot's *Four Quartets*." *ES* 45 (June): 238. "Eliot's fusion of the fire and the rose . . . has a greater similarity to Tennyson's union of the two [in *Maud*] than it has to Dante's separate symbols."

2152. Ramsay, Warren. "The *Oresteia* since Hofmansthal: Images and Emphases." *RLC* 38 (July-September): 359–75. [Family Reunion]. Chiefly summary, concluding that "the play seems to have grown away from the legend."

2153. Randall, Dale B. J. "The 'Seer' and 'Seen.' Themes in *Gatsby* and Some of Their Parallels in Eliot and Wright." *TCL* 10 (July): 51–63. [Waste Land]. An attempt that promises more than it achieves.

2154. Rao, K. S. Narayana. "Addendum on Eliot and the Bhagavad-Gita." *AQ* 16 (Spring): 102–3. (See no. 2101.) Verbal changes in the revision of "To the Indians Who Died in Africa" detract from its original emphasis on Indian thought.

2155. Reckford, Kenneth J. "Heracles and Mr. Eliot." *CL* 16 (Winter): 1–18. [Cocktail Party]. The drinking and singing, and eccentric behavior of Harcourt-Reilly-Heracles derive from the Alcestis myth, but are pointed in a specifically Christian way. An interesting point of view.

2156. Rogers, Daniel John. "Dramatic Use of the Liturgy in the Plays of T. S. Eliot: a Secular Evolution." *DA* 24 (April-June) : 4198. (Wisconsin). "Eliot evolved a liturgy proper to the stage that was not the same as, but akin to, a religious liturgy."

2157. Rubin, Larry. "T. S. Eliot: a Revaluation." *ModA* 8, no. 2 (Spring) : 221-23. [Collected Poems, 1909-1962]. Most of these poems fail because of "intellectual pretentiousness"; *Prufrock* is an exception.

*2158. Seferis, George. "Letter to a Foreign Friend." *Poetry* 105 (October) : 50-59. An expansion of "T. S. Eliot in Greece," in March and Tambimuttu (1948), no. 1174. Distinguished criticism by a poet on Eliot's poetry as it seems to a Greek.

2159. Shaw, Sam. "T. S. Eliot's Theory of Tradition." *DA* 25: 1924-25. (New York). Offers a "close analysis of the inconsistencies of Eliot's criticism."

*2160. Stead, C. K. " 'Classical Authority' and 'The Dark Embryo': a Dichotomy in T. S. Eliot's Criticism." *AUMLA*, no. 22, pp. 200-207. Eliot's work is in the Romantic tradition, and his self-announced classicism is an attempt to solve the romantic dilemma of Beauty on the one hand and Truth on the other.

*2161. ———. *The New Poetic: Yeats to Eliot*, 125-87, *passim*. London: Penguin Books, 1964. A stimulating and original point of view, placing Eliot in the line of romantic poets, arguing that his best poems, especially *The Waste Land*, come from levels deeper than the conscious mind. Well-balanced criticism.

2162. Talley, Jerry B. "Religious Themes in the Dramatic Works of George Bernard Shaw, T. S. Eliot, and Paul Claudel." *DA* 25 (October-December) : 3750. (Denver). Surveys the themes of purgation, confusion, and adaptation to Christian function.

2163. Toms, Newby. "Eliot's *The Cocktail Party*: Salvation and the Common Routine." *ChS* 47 (Summer) : 125-38. A turgid examination of the morality and religion of the play.

2164. Warren, Austin. "Continuity in T. S. Eliot's Criticism." *EWR* (Kyoto) 1 (Spring) : 1-12. The essay, now first published, was probably written in 1940. It emphasizes the influence of Irving Babbitt on Eliot.

2165. Watkins, Floyd C. "T. S. Eliot's Painter of the Umbrian School." *AL* 36 (March) : 72–75. [Mr. Eliot's Sunday Morning Service]. Identifies the painting as Piero della Francesca's "The Baptism of Christ."

*2166. Watson, C. B. "T. S. Eliot and the Interpretation of Shakespearean Tragedy in Our Time." *EA* 17: 502–21. Eliot's accusation that Shakespeare had an inferior moral philosophy has led to excesses of allegorical interpretation in an effort to redeem him. A scholarly essay.

2167. West, William Channing. "Concepts of Reality in the Poetic Drama of W. B. Yeats, W. H. Auden, and T. S. Eliot." *DA* 25: 6120–21. (Stanford). In Eliot's plays his prime subject has been "the definition of the experience of religious illumination and the relation of this experience to quotidian life."

2168. Wilbur, Robert Henry Hunter. "George Santayana and Three Modern Philosophical Poets: T. S. Eliot, Conrad Aiken, and Wallace Stevens." *DA* 26: 2228. (Columbia). Santayana believed that poetry and religion were essentially the same. Eliot rejects this belief; he also denies Santayana's insistence on "rational" poetry.

2169. Wolheim, Richard. "Eliot, Bradley, and Immediate Experience." *NSN* 67 (March 13) : 401–2. [Knowledge and Experience in the Philosophy of F. H. Bradley]. A review of Eliot's doctoral dissertation.

*2170. Woodward, Daniel H. "Notes on the Publishing History of *The Waste Land.*" *PBSA* 58: 252–69. An account, based partly on letters from Eliot to Mr. Woodward.

2171. Yerbury, Grace D. "Of a City Beside a River: Whitman, Eliot, Thomas, Miller." *WWR* 10 (June): 67–73. [Waste Land]. Not much is gained by the conjunction of the four authors treated here.

1965

2172. Aiken, Conrad. "T. S. Eliot." *Life* 58 (January 15) : 92–93. Aiken knew Eliot for fifty-seven years, but this article deals only with superficialities.

2173. Anon. "Last Trip to East Coker." *ChC* 82 (January 20) : 68. Grudging praise of the poet together with regrets for his anti-Semitism and snobbishness.

2174. ———. "On the Death of T. S. Eliot; Poems." *Cweal* 81 (January 29) : 576. Four poems: "T.S.E. 1888–1965," Joseph P. Clancy; "For the Giver of Gods," Harold

Isbell: "Impromptu Blues for Mr. Eliot," William Mc-
Laughlin; "The Death," Kenneth J. Reckford.

2175. ———. "Eliot and an Age of Fiction." *NSN* 59 (January
8): 47. "That Eliot, who was neither a novelist nor a
critic of fiction, should have had such authority in what
seems the age of the novel makes his achievement at once
more vulnerable and more impressive."

2176. ———. "Notes and Comments." *NY* 40 (January 16): 25.
Brief but discriminating praise of Eliot's qualities as a
man and as a poet.

2177. ———. "T. S. Eliot 1888–1965." *Newsweek* 65 (January
18): 70–71. In a series of clichés, Eliot is considered as
a "mug" and a man.

2178. ———. "Obituary Note." *PW* 187 (January 11): 69–70.
Biography.

*2179. ———. "T. S. Eliot." *Time* 85 (January 15): 86–87. A
packed, readable account of Eliot's life and work, well
illustrated by quotations from his poetry.

2180. ———. "A Great Man Gone." *TLS* (January 7), p. 9. A
weary and conventional assessment of Eliot as critic,
dramatist, social and religious writer, and poet.

2181. ———. "Critic Criticized." *TLS* (December 16), p. 1177.
[To Criticize the Critic and Other Writings]. Calls the
style inconsistent and most of the essays perfunctory.

2182. Avery, Helen P. *"The Family Reunion* Reconsidered."
ETJ 17 (March): 10–18. In 1965 the play is more
relevant than it was when it was first written (1938)
because it "reflects the prevailing tenor of disillusionment and restless search for values," using many of the
techniques of the Theatre of the Absurd.

*2183. Blanshard, Brand. "Eliot in Memory." *YR* 54 (Summer):
635–40. Praises Eliot's wide learning, his poetry, and his
goodness as a person. His weakness was that he could not
make Christianity attractive or intelligible.

2184. Bowers, John L. *T. S. Eliot's Murder in the Cathedral,*
mimeographed, 18 pp. Capetown: University of Cape
Town, Department of English, 1965. A mimeographed
lecture, presented as an introduction to the play which
was performed at the university. It emphasizes the character of Becket.

2185. Browne, E. Martin. "T. S. Eliot as Dramatist." *Drama* 76
(Spring): 41–43. ". . . as time goes on men will come . . .
to value Eliot the dramatist as the one who, avoiding

the self-pity and self-excuse which vitiate so much of today's 'realism,' gives the most penetrating account of the rootless twentieth century soul." Well-balanced criticism.

*2186. Carne-Ross, D. S. "T. S. Eliot: Tropheid." *Arion* 4 (Spring) : 5–20. An essay on the "place of classical literature in Eliot's critical work." In a fine essay on the meaning of the classics to modern man, the author analyzes Eliot's high regard for the classics and his subordination of them to Christianity.

2187. Carruth, Hayden. "Upon Which to Rejoice." *Poetry* 106 (June) : 239–41. [Collected Poems 1909–1962; Knowledge and Experience in the Philosophy of F. H. Bradley]. Eliot had philosophical gifts, but in 1915 the way of philosophy was closed. As a poet, his great virtue is in his technical departures, not only in his advances. His weakness is his coldness.

2188. Chatterji, Nimai. "A Letter from Mr. Eliot." *NSN* (March 5) , p. 361. Reprints a short letter from Eliot written in 1935 on what he meant by the objective correlative.

2189. Chaturvedi, B. N. "The Indian Background of Eliot's Poetry." *English* 15: 220–23. Influence of Indian religious literature on *The Waste Land* and *Four Quartets*.

2190. Ciardi, John. "Thomas Stearns Eliot." *SatR* 48 (January 23) : 34–36. [Prufrock; Spleen; Waste Land; Hollow Men; Ash Wednesday]. Ciardi unifies his brief discussion of the poems by tracing Eliot's growing religious convictions.

2191. Dallas, Elizabeth. "Canon Cancrizans and the *Four Quartets*." *CL* 17 (Summer) : 193–208. Miss Dallas asserts that the Heraclitean theme of opposites meeting at a still midpoint which forms the basis of the formal structure of the *Quartets* is exactly paralleled by the structure of Machaut's rondeau, "Ma fin est mon commencement." The parallel is not entirely convincing.

2192. Day, Robert A. "The 'City Man' in *The Waste Land;* The Geography of Reminiscence." *PMLA* 80 (June) : 285–91. A stimulating essay on the contrasting figures of the "City Man" and the sailor and on the two churches, St. Mary Woolnoth and St. Magnus Martyr. One of the sources of the poem is Eliot's personal experiences as a Londoner.

2193. DeLaura, David J. "Pater and Eliot: the Origin of the

Objective Correlative." *MLQ* 26 (Summer) : 426–31. A tenuous connection is suggested between Pater's approval of creative criticism, Eliot's condemnation of that kind of criticism, and the doctrine of the objective correlative.

*2194. Donoghue, Denis. "T. S. Eliot's *Quartets:* a New Reading." *Studies* 54 (Spring) : 41–62. A sensitive reading of the poem with emphasis on the doctrinal content, but much awareness of the poem as poetry. Special attention is given to "The Dry Salvages" which he thinks is inferior to the three other parts because Eliot uses too many voices. Donoghue wishes that Eliot had "an even warmer sense of human value in all its limitation."

2195. Driver, Tom F. "T. S. Eliot: 1888–1965." *ChrC* 25 (February 8) : 2–3. Though Eliot thought that in his drama he was writing about people like ourselves, the rapport between him and the modern world has been broken. For this reason, the poetry will outlast the drama.

*2196. Durrell, Lawrence. "The Other T. S. Eliot." *Atlantic* 215 (May) : 60–64. Durrell knew Eliot as a publisher for many years, and presents a sympathetic and penetrating character sketch, emphasizing his friendliness and humor. Two letters from Eliot criticizing an article and a play are printed here.

2197. Ellmann, Richard. "Yeats and Eliot." *Encounter* 25 (July) : 53–55. Yeats was always critical of Eliot's poetry and of his religion, but after first disapproving of Yeats's private religion, Eliot was to say at Yeats's death that he was the greatest of contemporary poets. The compound ghost in "Little Gidding" is primarily Yeats. Reprinted in *Tri-Quarterly,* 1965, pp. 77–80.

2198. Elmen, Paul. "Magical Journey of T. S. Eliot." *ChC* 82 (May 19) : 649–50. [Journey of the Magi]. Uses the poem to construct a questionable history of Eliot's conversion and its results.

2199. Ferry, David. "The Direction of American Poetry." *American Poetry,* edited by Irvin Ehrenpreis, pp. 135–53. Vol. 7 of Stratford-Upon-Avon Series. London: Edward Arnold, 1965. [Rhapsody on a Windy Night. Prufrock]. A good brief analysis of the new colloquial language used by Eliot, William Carlos Williams, and e. e. cummings. Most of the essay concerns Williams.

2200. Foster, Steven. "Relativity and *The Waste Land:* a Postulate." *TSLL* 7: 77–95. A reading of the entire poem to show that it is based on the beliefs that subjective experience is the only value and that absolutes have no validity. The thesis is pushed to extremes.

2201. Gerstenberger, Donna. "Steinbeck's American Waste Land." *MFS* 11 (Spring) : 59–65. Asserts that *The Winter of Our Discontent* owes much to *The Waste Land* in general pattern as well as an ironic frame of meaning. The point is not well sustained.

*2202. Greene, David Mason. *The Waste Land, a Critical Commentary,* 84 pp. New York: American R.D.M. Corporation, 1965. A useful volume containing a section-by-section analysis, a discussion of the Grail myth, identification of the symbols, allusions, and proper names, an essay on Eliot's approach to poetry, and a short bibliography. The text of the poem is not included.

2203. Gross, John. "Eliot: From Ritual to Realism." *Encounter* 24 (March) : 48–50. Eliot's true importance in the theatre lies in his essays, in *Murder,* and in his nondramatic poetry. He is at his best in writing ritualistic drama, and less good when he abandons it for realism.

2204. Gupta, N. Das. "T. S. Eliot." *Plato to Eliot: a Literary Criticism,* pp. 185–98. London: Probsthain, 1965. Survey of Eliot's critical principles, repeating commonplaces.

2205. Guttmann, Allen. "From Brownson to Eliot: The Conservative Theory of Church and State." *AQ* 17 (Fall) : 483–500. The last five pages of the essay are a rapid review of Eliot's ideas on church and state; Mr. Guttmann points out that Eliot is almost alone in championing the union of church and state.

2206. Hacikyan, A. "Art of T. S. Eliot's Imagery." *RUS* 5: 155–60. A diffuse essay based on part of an M.A. thesis, repeating well-known generalizations without examples.

2207. Halper, Nathan. "Joyce and Eliot: a Tale of Shem and Shaun." *Nation* 200 (May 31) : 590–95. A punning, half-serious essay in which Halper suggests that Joyce regarded Eliot as the stand-pat Shem.

*2208. Harvey, C. J. D. "T. S. Eliot: Poet and Critic." *Standpunkte* (Capetown) 18: 5–10. [Morning at the Window; Burbank with a Baedeker]. Prefers Eliot's early poetry to his later, praises his early criticism, and gives an excellent explication of the two poems.

2209. Hewes, Henry. "Journey to Simplicity." *SatR* 48 (January 23) : 53–54. A few paragraphs on Eliot's ideas on death, and one each on his plays.

2210. Hewitt, Elizabeth K. "Structure and Meaning in T. S. Eliot's 'Ash Wednesday.'" *Anglia* 83: 426–50. The paper proposes to describe the meter and rhythm in the poem and to relate description to the meaning. The first section is highly technical.

2211. Holder, Alan. "Three Voyagers in Search of Europe: a Study of Henry James, Ezra Pound, and T. S. Eliot." *DA* 26: 1646–47. (Columbia). Eliot's attitude toward America and Europe is compared and contrasted with that of the other two authors.

2212. Hyman, Stanley Edgar. "T. S. Eliot: 1888–1965." *NewL* 48 (February 1): 21–22. An appreciative review of his work, especially of the *Four Quartets*.

2213. Janoff, Ronald W. "Eliot and Horace—Aspects of the Intrinsic Classicist." *Cithara* 5 (November): 31–44. [Waste Land]. The two poets are "particularly similar in the nature of their poetic gifts, their method and their diction." This judgment is supported by a comparison of "The Burial of the Dead" and "Ode to Pyrrha." Janoff finally prefers Horace.

2214. Jones, P. Mansell. "Laforgue's 'Vers Libre' and the Form of 'The Waste Land.'" *The Assault on French Literature and Other Essays,* pp. 141–44. Manchester, England: Manchester University Press, 1965. Suggests that both Pound and Eliot learned "disruption and alternation of theme, tone and tempo" from Laforgue.

2215. Kameyama, Masako. "An Essay on T. S. Eliot: On the Function of Poetry." *CEKWJC,* no. 9 (December, 1965), pp. 117–31. [The Social Function of Poetry]. A skillful summary and interpretation of the essay, and reflections on its meaning for Japanese.

2216. Kenner, Hugh. "T. S. Eliot. R I P." *NaR* 17 (January 26) : 63–64. A eulogy of the man and his work, emphasizing his many roles.

2217. Kermode, Frank. "Eliot's Dream." *NSN* 69 (February 19) : 280–81. [Waste Land]. Eliot is more like Milton in his attitude toward life than he would have admitted. *"The Waste Land* is . . . an imperial epic; but such comforts as it can offer are not compatible with any illusions, past, present, or future."

2218. Kilgallin, Anthony R. "Eliot, Joyce, and Lowry." *CanAB*

41 (Winter) : 3–4, 6. Asserts that Malcolm Lowry's *Under the Volcano* owes its mythic method and some of its phrases to *The Waste Land* as well as to Joyce.

2219. Kingham, G. L. "T S [*sic*] Eliot," *WT* 14 (January) : 78. A brief factual account of Eliot's work, adding, "as a man, he was universally liked."

2220. Knust, Herbert. "Eliot's *The Waste Land,* 74." *Expl* 23 (May) : item 74. Proposes that the dog in this line is related to the Greek *kynikos,* and is cynical in the correct sense of the word, i.e., a eulogistic one.

2221. ———. "What's the Matter with One-Eyed Riley?" *CL* 17 (Fall) : 289–98. [Cocktail Party]. The author believes that "the northern myth of Wotan and Brunhild is relevant for the circumstances of Reilly and Celia . . . as well as for the constellation of the one-eyed merchant and of Belladonna . . . in the fortune telling scene of *The Waste Land.*" The parallels are worked out ingeniously.

2222. Levi, Peter, S.J. "The Death of Poets." *Month* 33 (February) : 114–19. Unrestrained adulation.

2223. Levy, William Turner. "A Memoir of T. S. Eliot." *NYTBR* (January 31) , pp. 34–35. In this unusual glimpse of Eliot, written by an Anglican cleryman, a priestlike Eliot emerges.

2224. Linton, Calvin D. "T. S. Eliot: Prophet with Honor." *ChrT* (March 26) , pp. 10–12. [Prufrock; Waste Land; Ash Wednesday; Four Quartets]. An appreciative essay for the general reader, interpreting all the poems as Christian.

2225. Marks, Emerson R. "Thomas Stearns Eliot (1888–1965) ." *Criticism* 7 (Spring) : 115. Praises his criticism and leaves the poetry to the judgment of posterity.

2226. Matthews, T. S. "Interview with Eliot." *Mademoiselle* 61 (May) : 68. Report of an interview in 1958 covering aspects of his life, work, and opinions; repeats well-known information.

2227. McCord, Howard. "The Wryneck in 'The Waste Land.' " *CJ* 60 (March) : 270–71. Suggests that "jug, jug" in lines 103 and 204 refers to the cry of the wryneck (woodpecker) , associated with physical lust.

2228. McLuhan, Herbert Marshall. "T. S. Eliot." *CanF* 44: 243–44. An appreciation, concentrating on Eliot's influence at home and abroad.

2229. Morison, Samuel Eliot. "The Dry Salvages and the Thacker Shipwreck." *AN* 25 (October) : 233–47. The historian, Eliot's cousin, provides useful information about the Dry Salvages and why they inspired Eliot.

2230. Nimkar, B. A. "T. S. Eliot: The Interpreter of the Intellectual Crisis." *ModR* 117: 148–50. This essay, purporting to show that Eliot's pessimism has been exaggerated, is confused and self-contradictory.

*2231. Nitchie, George W. "Eliot's Borrowing: A Note." *MR* 6 (Winter–Spring) : 403–6. An intelligent defense of the notes in *The Waste Land,* broadening into a discussion of the way Eliot's mind absorbed its reading.

2232. Oden, Thomas C. "A Meditation for Ash Wednesday." *CrC* 15 (Winter) : 1–8. A paraphrase of "Ash Wednesday" as a liturgical poem following the Anglo-Catholic service for that day: I. Act of Confession; II. Act of Absolution; III. Preparation for Holy Communion; IV. Holy Communion; V. Gloria in Excelsis; VI. Benediction.

2233. Panter-Downs, M. "Letter from London; Homage to Eliot at Globe Theatre." *NY* 41 (June 26) : 84 ff. An account of music by Stravinsky, readings of his poems, and a production of *Sweeney Agonistes* (a memorial service).

*2234. Paul, Leslie. "A Conversation with T. S. Eliot." *KR* 27 (Winter) : 11–21. An interview in 1958 ranging over politics, the poet in society, religion, Eliot's prosody, and the fate of the manuscript of *The Waste Land.* A revealing interview. Reprinted in *Quadrant,* March 1965, pp. 50–55.

2235. ———. "Elusive Genius of T. S. Eliot." *Reporter* 32 (April 22) : 33–35. Friendly memories of Eliot, and a remark that the sibilance of his poetry is its keynote; "Something of the dryness of the times . . . is symbolized in that insistent whispering sound."

2236. Petersen, Sven. "Mr. Eliot in 'The Sacred Wood.'" *Greyfriar* 8: 33–43. Examines Eliot's theory of impersonality as a necessity for the critic, and concludes that the theory is incoherent because it neglects the necessity of grasping the universal principle behind shifting impressions.

2237. Porter, Katherine Anne. "From the Notebooks of Katherine Anne Porter—Yeats, Joyce, Eliot, Pound." *SoR* 1: 570–73. An excellent description of Eliot reading in Sylvia Beach's bookshop; one paragraph.

2238. Puhvel, Martin. "Reminiscent Bells in 'The Waste Land.'" *ELN* 2 (June) : 286–87. Suggests that the bells parallel in idea as well as phrasing lines 193–98 in Browning's "Childe Roland to the Dark Tower Came."

2239. Rago, Henry. "T. S. Eliot: a Memoir and a Tribute." *Poetry* 105 (March) : 392–95. Reminiscences of Eliot's conversation, and a tribute which Rago gave when he introduced Eliot at a lecture in 1959 on his having given our age its "complete expression."

*2240. Rayan, Krishna. "*Rasa* and the Objective Correlative." *BJA* 5 (July) : 246–60. A distinguished study clarifying the meaning of Eliot's term by showing its similarity to Sanskrit critical theory, and illustrating it by numerous examples, some from *The Waste Land.*

2241. Rexine, John E. "Classical and Christian Foundations of T. S. Eliot's *Cocktail Party.*" *BA* 39 (Winter) : 21–26. "The acknowledged model for the play is Euripides' *Alcestis,* but 'the similarities to *Alcestis* are closely interwoven with Christian symbolism, other Greek myths, and similarities to . . . *The Waste Land.*'" [From *TCL*].

2242. Ricks, Christopher. "Errors of Tone." *NSN* (November 26), pp. 832–34. [To Criticize the Critic and Other Writings]. Accuses Eliot of having become disillusioned about literary criticism and of having written essays which are both distinguished and unimportant.

2243. Robson, W. W. "T. S. Eliot as a Critic of Dr. Johnson." *NewR,* p. 42. A report of a lecture which began by praising Eliot as a critic of "London" and "The Vanity of Human Wishes."

2244. Roy, Emil. "The Becket Plays: Eliot, Fry, and Anouilh." *MD* 8: 268–76. In attempting to cover too much ground, the article covers no one point adequately.

2245. Russell, Francis. "Some Non-encounters with Mr. Eliot." *Horizon* 7 (Autumn) : 36–41. Reminiscences of seeing, but never talking to, Eliot, from 1932 onwards. There are speculations about his private life, and an appreciation of *The Four Quartets.*

2246. Sena. "Henrik Ibsen and the Latest Eliot." *LitC* 6: 19–25. [Elder Statesman]. "*The Elder Statesman* and *The Pillars of Society* . . . display a correspondence of *outer* and *inner structure,* of the framework of plot and its directing theme and psychology." The correspondences are accidental.

2247. Seymour-Smith, Martin. "Out into the Open." *Spectator* 215 (November 12) : 624. [To Criticize the Critic and Other Writings]. An indication of the contents of the volume.

2248. ———. "The Revolutionaries." *Spectator* (March 12) , p. 331. The author politely questions Eliot's sincerity as a Christian and his excellence as a poet while admitting his great influence on the poetic revolution.

2249. Smidt, Kristian. "T. S. Eliot and W. B. Yeats." *RLV* 31: 555–67. A careful study of the personal relations between the two poets, Yeats's influence on Eliot's poetry and criticism, and Eliot's possible influence on Yeats.

2250. Smith, Janet Adam. "T. S. Eliot and 'The Listener.'" *Listener* 73 (January 21) : 105. Reprints a critical report from Eliot on the contemporary poetry being published in the *Listener*.

*2251. Spanos, William V. "T. S. Eliot's *The Family Reunion*: The Strategy of Sacramental Transfiguration." *DramS* 4: 3–27. [Murder in the Cathedral; Family Reunion]. Considers that Eliot's world is one in which, because of the Incarnation, man may integrate two spheres, that of time and of timelessness. This is done more successfully in *The Family Reunion* than in *Murder in the Cathedral*. Considers also the use of Greek myths, style, and Eliot's theology.

*2252. Spender, Stephen. "Remembering Eliot." *Encounter* 24 (April) : 3–14. A rich essay combining anecdotes of Eliot's behavior and conversation, the meaning of his early poems to their readers, and perceptive comments on Eliot's personal and literary career. A well-balanced article.

2253. ———. "The Influence of Yeats on Later English Poets." *Tri-Quarterly*, no. 4, pp. 82–89. Chiefly on Yeats, but offers brief contrasts with Eliot on diction and religion. Spender considers Yeats the greater poet.

2254. Stanford, Derek. "Concealment and Revelation in T. S. Eliot." *SWR* 50 (Summer) : 243–51. Eliot was helped in writing his poetry of communication rather than poetry of expression by the examples of Pound and Dante, and by his discovery of the objective correlative.

2255. Stravinsky, Igor. "Memories of T. S. Eliot." *Esquire* 64 (August) : 92–93. Interesting personal memories, based on three meetings, one in 1956 and two later.

2256. Sweeney, Francis. "In Memoriam: T. S. Eliot." *America* 112 (January 23): 120–21. Routine praise, with emphasis on Eliot's love of order.

*2257. Unger, Leonard. "A Tribute, T. S. Eliot: The Intimate Voice." *SoR* 1: 731–34. ". . . in Eliot's poetry we find the intimate voice of the modern sensibility."

2258. ————. "T. S. Eliot, 1888–1965. Viva il poeta!" *MR* (Spring–Winter), pp. 408–10. Reminiscences of brief meetings with Eliot, and of the impact first made by his poetry; remarks on why Eliot's later poetry, as well as his earlier, is "contemporary."

*2259. Wain, John. "T. S. Eliot." *Encounter* 24 (March): 51–53. [The Music of Poetry]. A brief but balanced study of Eliot's diction. ". . . up to about 1930 his work was iconoclastic in relation to the English poetic tradition; . . . thereafter . . . he turned inwards . . . and began to refine and at the same time, deepen his harmonies."

2260. ————. "On T. S. Eliot." *LanM* 59: 371–75. Before "Ash Wednesday" Eliot was an innovator in language; afterward, he saw that it was necessary to deepen and refine it.

2261. Watson, George. "The Triumph of T. S. Eliot." *CritQ* 7 (Winter): 328–37. Eliot's success "was total and instantaneous within the terms it had set itself; the capture of young intellectuals of creative energy in England and the United States in the 1920's."

2262. Weatherhead, A. Kingsley. "Baudelaire in Eliot's *Ash Wednesday,* IV." *ELN* 2 (June): 288–89. The cadences in Baudelaire's "Bohemiens en Voyage" are strikingly similar to those in Eliot's passage on the Lady of *Ash Wednesday* IV, and probably "is one of those instances where Eliot's verse has grown up out of a cadence running through his mind."

2263. Whittemore, Reed. "T. S. Eliot: 1888–1965." *NR* 152 (January 16): 28. Describes himself as a "reluctant long time admirer," after saying that Eliot has been dead for a decade now.

2264. Williams, Philip Eugene. "The Biblical View of History: Hawthorne, Mark Twain, Faulkner, and Eliot." *DA* 25 (January–March): 4159 (Penn.). "More affirmative— and more American—than Eliot's other poetry, *Four Quartets* reflects a view of human experience founded on that of the Gospel of John with its stress on transforming grace."

*2265. Williamson, George. "T. S. Eliot: 1888–1965." *ModA* 9 (Fall) : 399–407. A fine survey of all of Eliot's work by a leading scholar.

2266. Wilson, Richard. "The Continuity of T. S. Eliot." *KanoS,* no. 1, pp. 24–32. A mélange of quotations intended to illustrate the unity of the poems.

2267. Wright, Keith. "Rhetorical Repetition in T. S. Eliot's Early Verse." *REL* 6 (April) : 93–100. A factual account of Eliot's use of rhetorical figures such as *anaphora* and *anadiplosis,* with some attention to their effects.

APPENDIX

1920

2268. Anon. Review of *Poems, Baltimore Evening Sun* (May 15). [Clipping so dated, but incorrectly, in the Eliot Collection at Harvard]. A brief notice that the poems will fill you with a vague uneasiness."

2269. ———. *Brooklyn Eagle* (April 23). Quotes with approval Robert Lynd's denunciation of Eliot's criticism of *Hamlet*.

2270. ———. "New Light on Old Literature." *Edinburgh Evening News* (November 18). [So dated in the Eliot Collection, but the review was not found under this date]. [Sacred Wood]. A brief paragraph praising the essays.

2271. ———. Notice of *The Sacred Wood. Glasgow Herald* (August 11). [So dated in the Eliot Collection, but the review was not found on that date.] Calls the essays "scholarly, delicate, and stimulating."

2272. ———. Review of *The Sacred Wood. Liverpool Post* (November 24). Eliot "has the power of reaching bed rock in a sentence."

2273. ———. *Morning Post* (London) (May 28). [I have seen this item as a clipping in the Eliot Collection, but have been unable to check it.] Reference to Eliot as a "so-called poet," and a quotation from "Prufrock."

2274. ———. "Some Recent Verse." *Oakland Tribune* (California) (April 4), p. 7. [Poems]. "He startles, he shocks, and he is very, very clever."

2275. ———. Review of *Poems*. A Philadelphia newspaper (April 4). [The clipping is in the Eliot Collection, but I have been unable to identify it. The following papers have been checked: *Press, Inquirer, Record, Public Ledger,* and *North American.*] "Mr. Eliot has a brisk brain, a feeling for character (of a wild sort), and a cleverness in metaphor."

2276. ———. "Poems by T. S. Eliot." *Sun and New York Herald* (April 11), sec. 3, p. 9. The reviewer says "it is not wise to ignore men like Eliot, who are actually opening new fields and modes in verse." Brief.

2277. ———. Note on "A Brief Treatise on the Criticism of Poetry." *Sunday Chronicle* (London) (May 28). [So dated in the Eliot Collection, but incorrectly, since May 28, 1920, fell on Friday.] Favorable.

2278. W.S.B. [William Stanley Braithwaite]. "A Scorner of the Ordinary Substance of Human Nature." *Boston Evening Transcript* (April 14), pt. 2, p. 6. [Poems]. Reading these "poems (?) is like being in a closed room full of foul air."

2279. S.T.C. [Samuel T. Clover]. Review of *Poems, 1919. Richmond Evening Journal* (Virginia) (April 17), p. 7. He says that "to those who have cut their literary wisdom teeth the volume is a veritable treasure trove."

2280. R.C.R. "Making a Playgoer." *Birmingham Post* (November 13), p. 10. [Sacred Wood]. A friendly disagreement with Eliot's theories on poetic drama.

2281. Sampson, George. Review of *The Sacred Wood. Daily News* (London) (December 16), p. 7. Dislikes Eliot's lack of clarity in prose.

2282. H.T. "The Bookshelf." *Star* (London) (November 23), p. 3. [Sacred Wood]. Prefers Robert Lynd's criticism to Eliot's.

2283. W.S.T. "An Irritable Intelligence." *Boston Herald* (April 14). [Ara vos Prec]. "There is no intellectual synthesis in Mr. Eliot's work; it is an unusually sensitive register of sense impressions."

1921

2284. Anon. "Three Essayists." *Church Times* (London) (January 14), p. 28. [Euripides and Professor Murray]. A notice praising Eliot's criticism of Gilbert Murray.

2285. ———. "Books of the Day." *Morning Post* (London) (January 14), p. 3. [Sacred Wood]. One paragraph. "It is good to see such kindly severity."

2286. ———. Notice of *The Sacred Wood. Scotsman* (January 17), p. 2. Complimentary.

2287. Preston, Keith. "Respecting the Handy Man." *Chicago Daily News* (February 9), p. 12. [Sacred Wood]. Quotation from the essay on Blake.

2288. Wells, Charles. "Written in a Library." *Bristol Times and Mirror* (June 4), p. 15. [Poetry in Prose]. A reference to Eliot's essay in the April *Chapbook* defining a prose poem.

1922

2289. Anon. "The New Books." *New York Evening Post Literary Review* (February 18), p. 435. [Sacred Wood]. A brief note, expressing surprise at the contrast between this volume and Eliot's poems.

2290. ———. " 'Hamlet' as Fine Art." *New York Evening Post Literary Review* (September 9), p. 5. [Review of Clutton-Brock's *Shakespeare's 'Hamlet'*]. In his first essay "Mr. Clutton-Brock assails, with skill and an array of facts, the themes of J. M. Robertson and T. S. Eliot."

2291. ———. Advertisement for *The Waste Land. New York Evening Post Literary Review* (October 28), p. 159. "Those who have read it are unanimous in believing that it is a work of profound significance." This is an advertisement by *The Dial.*

2292. ———. "The Sporting Spirit." *New York Evening Post Literary Review* (November 11), p 1. [Waste Land]. The poem "may be nonsense as a whole, but is certainly a sporting attempt to turn accident into substance."

2293. ———. "The Muse of the Uneasy." *Times* (London) (November 5), p. 8. [Review of *Modern American Poets*]. A disparaging reference to "The Love Song of J. Alfred Prufrock."

2294. ———. "Medallions. III. Mr. T. S. Eliot. The Exact Critic." *Times* (London) (June 13), p. 14. [Sacred Wood]. Eliot's criticism, interesting and important as it is, does not attract English readers because he prefers intellect to instinct.

2295. Butcher, Fanny. "Award by *The Dial*." *Chicago Tribune* (December 3), pt. 7, p. 23. [Waste Land]. A garbled story on Eliot's receiving the *Dial* award for *The Waste Land.*

2296. Dodd, Lee Wilson. "The New Curiosity Shop, Panjandremonium." *New York Evening Post Literary Review* (November), p. 243. [Waste Land]. [This was seen as a clipping in the Eliot Collection, but has not been found in the issues for November 1922.] On the unintelligibility of the poem.

2297. "Pendennis." "Shakespeare under the Microscope—Was
Hamlet Mad?" *Pall Mall Gazette,* no. 17772 (May 18),
p. 7. [Hamlet and His Problems]. Says he has no
desire to make the acquaintance of "a Mr. Eliot," whom
Clutton-Brock has reproved.

2298. Rascoe, Burton. Review of *The Waste Land* in *New York
Tribune* (October 26). [So dated in the Eliot Collection, but not found in the paper for this date.] It is a
"thing of bitterness and beauty." Rhapsodic praise.

2299. ———. *New York Tribune* (December 3), sec. 6, p. 18.
On Eliot's receiving the *Dial* award; says he is in bad
health and financial straits.

2300. ———. "A Bookman's Day Book." *New York Tribune,*
review of *The Waste Land* (November 5), sec. 5, p. 8.
"It is perhaps the finest poem of this generation."

1923

2301. Anon. "The Dial's Prize." *Boston Herald* (January 27),
p. 6. [Waste Land]. The writer is distressed at the award.

2302. ———. *Boston Herald* (February). [The clipping is so
dated in the Eliot Collection, but a search of the paper
for February does not reveal the article.] [Waste Land].
A dramatic monologue by a flighty woman excited by
The Waste Land.

2303. ———. *Brooklyn Eagle* (March). [The clipping is so
dated in the Eliot Collection, but a search of the paper
for March does not reveal the story.] [Waste Land].
A slangy comment on the poem as a hoax.

2304. ———. *CSM* (March 23), p. 18. [Waste Land]. An editorial suggesting that Eliot wrote *The Waste Land* as
a hoax.

2305. ———. " 'Spoofing' the Philistines." *NYT* (March 4), sec.
2, p. 4. [Waste Land]. A confused editorial questions
whether or not Edith Sitwell and T. S. Eliot are "spoofing" the public.

2306. ———. "Interview with Ezra Pound on Bel Esprit Fund."
NYT (June 17), sec. 3, p. 18. (See Pound, *Letters,* 172–
76.) On collecting funds for Eliot to go to Lausanne
for his health.

2307. ———. Review of *The Waste Land. Oregonian* (Portland)
(February 11), sec. 5, p. 3. "In treatment he is somewhat similar to Rupert Brooke."

2308. Butcher, Fanny. "Help, Help." *Chicago Tribune* (February 4), pt. 7, p. 23. [Waste Land]. She does not understand the poem, nor does she want to. (Article reprinted in the *New York Daily News,* February 1923.)

2309. Dawson, N. P. "Theodoro, the Sage." *New York Globe and Commercial Advertiser* (April 12), p. 17. [Waste Land]. The poem is the result of a toothache.

2310. ———. "Books in Particular." *New York Globe and Commercial Advertiser* (April 17), p. 14. A letter from Eliot denies that he told Ben Hecht that *The Waste Land* is a hoax.

2311. Drury, John. "World's Greatest Poem." *Chicago Daily News* (February 14), p. 15. [Waste Land]. This is the "greatest poem so far written in contemporary literature."

2312. Duffus, Robert L. "Genius and the Guffaws of the Crowd." *New York Globe and Commercial Advertiser.* (February 28), p. 16. [Waste Land]. Protests against Drury's assertion (no. 2311) that the guffaws of the crowd prove the greatness of the poem.

2313. Hart, Henry G. "New Plays and Poems." *Philadelphia Record* (April 1), sec. T, p. 6. [Waste Land]. Part of an omnibus review. "To us 'The Waste Land'—in toto —is a fly speck," but not a hoax.

2314. Heller, Otto. "T. S. Eliot Awarded $2,000 Prize for 'The Waste Land.' " *St. Louis Post Dispatch* (February 24), p. 10. An earnest but confused attempt to understand the poem. "He has got into bad company for the time being, as young poets will."

2315. Hoffenstein, Samuel. "The Moist Land—a Parody of Eliot's Poem." *New York Tribune* (January 28), magazine, p. 24. [Waste Land]. A long, elaborate parody. Reprinted in *Year In, You're Out.* New York: H. Liveright, 1930.

2316. Lewis, Tracy H. "Painless Parker Poetry." *New York Morning Telegraph* (March). [The clipping is so dated in the Eliot Collection, but a search of the paper for March does not reveal the article.] Suggests that it is the musings of a woman in the dentist's chair.

2317. Moody, W. S. "Poetry, Transformed and Deformed." *New York Herald* (March 11), p. 5. [Waste Land]. He protests against the award of the *Dial* prize to Eliot.

2318. Morley, Christopher [pseud., "E. Tenebris Lux"]. "South

Ferry." *New York Evening Post* (January 8), p. 8. [Waste Land]. A parody of the poem, including the notes.

2319. Pettus, Clyde. "The Dial Prize Winner." *Atlanta Constitution* (January). [The clipping is so dated in the Eliot Collection, but a search of the paper for January does not reveal the article.] [Waste Land]. "The Waste Land, after the first curiosity of the seekers of the bizarre in literature has been satisfied, will make its appeal only to those who delight in the solving of literary puzzles." Draws on Edmund Wilson for a summary.

2320. C.P. [Charles Powell]. Review of *The Waste Land. Manchester Guardian* (October 31), p. 7. To all but anthropologists and *literati,* the poem is waste paper.

2321. Rascoe, Burton. "In Defense of T. S. Eliot." *New York Tribune* (January 7), sec. 6, p. 22. [Waste Land]. The reporter lunched with G. Seldes and Edmund Wilson, who made merry over critics who do not understand Eliot. Article reprinted in the *Fort Wayne Journal Gazette,* also in *A Bookman's Day Book,* New York: Horace Liveright, 1929, pp. 60–64.

2322. ———. "A Bookman's Day Book." *New York Tribune* (January 14), sec. 6, p. 23. [Waste Land]. A paragraph explaining four lines in *The Waste Land.* Reprinted in *A Bookman's Day Book,* New York: Horace Liveright, 1929, pp. 71–72.

2323. ———. "A Bookman's Day Book." *New York Tribune* (January 21), sec. 6, p. 27. [Waste Land]. He defends himself and Edmund Wilson against the charge of being uncritically enthusiastic. (See no. 110.) Reprinted in *A Bookman's Day Book,* New York: Horace Liveright, 1929, pp. 80–81.

2324. ———. "Personal Letters Which All May Read." *New York Tribune* (January 28), sec. 6, pp. 21, 26. [Waste Land]. Consists of 1) an anonymous letter stating that Eliot told the writer *The Waste Land* was a hoax; 2) a reply by Rascoe defending Eliot; 3) and 4) an exchange of letters between Untermeyer and Rascoe. (See nos. 2322 and 110.)

2325. ———. *New York Tribune* (April 1), sec. 6, p. 27. [Sacred Wood; Waste Land]. Four lines dismissing the essays in *The Sacred Wood* as tedious and pedantic, and a note on the assertion that *The Waste Land* is a hoax.

2326. ———. "A Bookman's Day Book." *New York Tribune* (April 22), sec. 6, p. 22. Quotes John Gould Fletcher on Eliot's future plans for work and as saying, "Eliot has the finest intellect of any man I know:" Rascoe also reports that Eliot has denied saying that *The Waste Land* was a hoax, in letters to the *Chicago Daily News* and the *New York Globe*. Reprinted in *A Bookman's Day Book*, New York: Horace Liveright, 1929, pp. 291–93.

2327. Shanks, Edward. "Books and Authors—New Poets." *Daily News* (London) (October 8), p. 9. [Waste Land]. Likes certain passages, but the sense of the whole poem escapes him. "Mr. Eliot is a man of great intelligence and some poetic sensibility, but in him these qualities do not unite."

2328. Stallings, Laurence. "Enter Robert Lynd with Flare of Critical Brass." *New Work World* (March 25), sec. E, p. 9. [Sacred Wood; Waste Land]. Praises Lynd for his attack on Eliot's essay on *Hamlet*. Also attacks *The Waste Land*.

2329. Van de Water, F. "Books and so Forth." *New York Tribune* (January 28), p. 19. [Waste Land]. Wonders whether the poem is a hoax, but concludes, "We're almost tempted to fall on our knees and call T. S. Eliot great."

2330. Weaver, John V. A. "Personally Conducted." *Brooklyn Eagle* (April). [So dated in the Eliot Collection, but the item has not been found in April issues.] [Waste Land]. Calls it "humbug."

2331. Wood, Clement. "If There Were a Pillory for Poets. The Waste Land." *New York Herald* (April 15), pp. 3, 6. "It is a vast hoax, conscious or unconscious; . . . it is erudite gibberish."

1924

2332. J.M.H. "Poetry: Old and New." *Freeman* (Dublin) (February 9), p. 9. [Waste Land]. Praises the poem in the usual terms.

2333. N.T. [Netta Thompson]. "Modern American Poetry." *Aberdeen Press* (May 26), p. 3. "An undoubted vogue he has, but it is with the 'intellectuals.' the Sitwells, and other British insurgents who juggle with acrobatic satire."

1925

2334. Haywood, A. Richard, "Mr. Aldington's New Book." *Northern Whig* (February 14), p. 10. Says that in *A Fool in the Forest* Aldington has copied Eliot's technique in *The Waste Land*.

2335. Paul, Elliot H. "From a Litterateur's Notebook." European edition of the *New York Herald* (December), p. 5. [I have seen this only as a clipping in the Eliot Collection.] [Poem, 1909–1925]. Chiefly quotation; calls Eliot a lawyer. Reprinted in *Chicago Tribune,* April 3, 1926.

2336. Porter, Alan. "Dryden and Poetry." *Spectator* 135, no. 5070 (August 29): 337–38. [Homage to John Dryden]. Attacks Eliot by asking, "What is man to decide what poetry is?" Nothing on Eliot's essay.

2337. "Z". "Opacities." *Liverpool Post* (December 8). [I have not been able to verify this item, which I have seen only as a clipping]. [Poems, 1909–1925]. Admires the combination of "philosophical and lyrical intuition," but finds the poems difficult.

1926

2338. C.P. [Charles Powell]. Review of Poems, 1909–1925. *Manchester Guardian* (February 9), p. 9. Dislikes all the poetry except two verses of "Sweeney among the Nightingales."

1927

2339. F. P. A[dams]. "Jack and Jill, or the Waste Paper." *New York World* (November 16). [Clipping so dated in the Eliot Collection, but item has not been found in the issue for this date.] [Waste Land]. Parody.

2340. Anon. "The Ariel Poems." *Aberdeen Press* (September 20), p. 2. [Journey of the Magi]. "Is Mr. Eliot part of the drift back to the Church and Christianity that seems to be seizing on the younger poets of Britain and France?"

2341. ———. "The Sad Young Cynics." *New York Sun* (February 19), p. 11. [Poems, 1909–1925]. Accuses Eliot of "languid pessimism."

2342. ———. "T. S. Eliot, Former St. Louis Poet, Now a British

Subject." *St. Louis Globe-Democrat* (November 26).
Biographical.

1928

2343. ———. "Poetry of the Future." *Daily Express* (London)
(March 14), p. 9. [Prufrock; Sweeney among the Night-
ingales]. Commonplace article defending modernist
poetry against a charge of obscurity and lack of rhyme.

2344. ———. "Ariel Poems and Others." *Observer* (December
23), p. 5. Notice of the Ariel booklets, especially "A
Song for Simeon."

2345. ———. "T. S. Eliot." *Times* (Bombay) (December). [For
Lancelot Andrewes]. [I have not been able to see files
of this paper in order to get the exact date.] His new
religious bias makes him unfair to his opponents.

2346. Fry, Varian. "A Bibliography of the Writings of Thomas
Stearns Eliot." *HH* 1 (March): 214–18; (June): 320–
24. Superseded by Gallup, no. 1516.

1929

2347. Britten, Clarence. "T. S. Eliot Dazes 'Waste Landers' in
Plea for Religion." *New York Post Magazine Section*
(April 6), p. 10. [For Lancelot Andrewes]. Enthusiastic
praise. He often disagrees with Eliot, but is "not so rash
as to undertake rebuttal until more of his case is in."

1930

2348. Anon. "Among These Rocks." *TLS,* no. 1478 (May 29),
p. 452. [Ash Wednesday]. Briefly summarizes the poem,
which the reviewer does not understand.

2349. Leavis, F. R. *Mass Civilization and Minority Culture.*
Cambridge, England: Minority Press, 1930. Barely mentions Eliot, *The Waste Land,* and *The Criterion.*

1931

2350. Anon. Review of "Ariel Poems." *TLS,* no. 1556 (November 26), p. 944 [Triumphal March]. A few lines of comment.

2351. ———. "Harvard Invites T. S. Eliot to be Lecturer on
Poetry." *NYHT* (December 16), p. 21. Announcement

of Eliot's appointment to the Charles Eliot Norton professorship of poetry for 1932–33.

2352. Schwartz, Jacob. *1100 Obscure Points; the Bibliographies of 25 English and 21 American Authors*, pp. 51–52. London: The Ulysses Bookshop, 1931. Bibliographical description of eleven of Eliot's books.

1932

2353. Agate, James. "Profundity." *Daily Express* (London) (September 15), p. 8. [Selected Essays]. Eliot has every good quality except a sense of fun, and he is therefore unreadable.

2354. Anon. "Mr. Eliot as Critic." *CSM* (October 1), p. 6. [Selected Essays]. High praise for the essays except for their "formalistic" religion.

2355. ———. "T. S. Eliot." *Church Times* (London) (September 16), p. 307. [Selected Essays]. Admires Eliot, but is worried by his admiration for D. H. Lawrence and James Joyce.

2356. ———. "T. S. Eliot." *Scotsman* (October 24), p. 2. Review of Hugh Ross Williamson's *The Poetry of T. S. Eliot*. "He has done his work well, and those who know little of Eliot's verse . . . will find the path smoothed for them by Mr. Williamson."

2357. ———. "The Modernist." *Southport Guardian* (England) (October 8). [Selected Essays 1917–1932]. A good critic, "rarefied in his knowledge, austere in his style, a modernist yet never an iconoclast."

2358. Dahlberg, Edward. "Poetic Garland for John Donne." *New York Evening Post* (March 26), sec. 1, p. 7. [Donne in Our Time]. Summarizes and praises the essay.

2359. Grattan, C. Hartley. "T. S. Eliot's Influence on the British Puzzles Critics; A Typical Product of T. S. Eliot's Mind." *New York World-Telegram* (November 8), p. 15. [John Dryden, the Poet, the Dramatist, the Critic]. Patronizing, slight.

2360. Gregory, Horace. "T. S. Eliot Survives His 'Lost' Youth." *New York Evening Post* (September 15), p. 11. [Selected Essays 1917–1932]. A critical summary of the volume, and remarks on Eliot's growth toward maturity.

2361. Grigson, Geoffrey. "The Modern Arnold." *Yorkshire Post* (October 19), p. 6. [Selected Essays 1917–1932]. A good, sympathetic analysis of the reasons for Eliot's un-popularity with certain critics.

2362. R.A.L. "Clever Essays." *Bristol Evening Post* (October 29). [Selected Essays 1917–1932]. Commonplace praise.

2363. Lynd, Robert. "Mr. Drinkwater's Early Struggles." *News Chronicle* (London) (October 7), p. 4. [Selected Essays 1917–1932]. Eliot has "a peculiar gift for misunderstanding and for giving his misunderstandings an appearance of authoritativeness."

2364. ———. "The Reputation of T. S. Eliot." *John O'London's Weekly* (October 22), p. 113. [Selected Essays 1917–1932]. Same point of view as the preceding.

2365. Nicholls, Norah. "A Bibliography of T. S. Eliot." *Bookman* (English) 82 (September): 309. Superseded by Gallup, no. 1516. Appeared also in *The American Book Collector: a Monthly Magazine for Book Lovers* 3 (February): 105–6.

2366. C.P. [Charles Powell]. "Mr. Eliot's Poetry." Review of H. R. Williamson's *The Poetry of T. S. Eliot,* in *Manchester Guardian Weekly* (November 11), p. 395. Protests that Eliot is unintelligible, in spite of Williamson's good book.

2367. Priestley, J. B. "Pompous Criticism." *Evening Standard* (London) (September 22), p. 7. [Selected Essays 1917–1932]. Eliot is narrow.

2368. Schriftgiesser, Karl. "Some Inquiries about T. S. Eliot." *Boston Evening Transcript* (September 24), book section, p. 1. Long article on Eliot's coming to Harvard as Norton Professor of Literature.

2369. Wood, Frederick T. "Mr. T. S. Eliot." *Sheffield Daily Telegraph* (September 22). [Selected Essays 1917–1932]. Objects to stylistic peculiarities, but "the book remains a valuable collection of critical documents."

1933

2370. Anon. "Poetry and Criticism: Mr. T. S. Eliot's New Volume." *Cambridge Daily News* (England) (November 22), p. 3. [The Use of Poetry and the Use of Criticism]. Brief, favorable.

2371. ———. "The Course of English Poetry." *Glasgow Herald* (December 28). [The Use of Poetry and the Use of Criticism]. A clear exposition of the book, with a number of fresh critical judgments.

2372. ———. "New Essays in Criticism—About It and About." *Irish Independent* (Dublin) (December 12) , p. 4. [The Use of Poetry and the Use of Criticism]. Says that these lectures leave the reader where they found him.

2373. ———. "The Poet as Critic, T. S. Eliot's American Lectures." *Morning Post* (London) (November 28) . [The Use of Poetry and the Use of Criticism]. Cautious disapproval of the inconclusiveness of the volume.

2374. ———. *New York Globe* (February) . [So dated in the Eliot Collection, but the story has not been found in the *Globe* for February]. Burton Rascoe is reported to have said, "not wholly convincingly, however," that he and some friends decided to "hoax the public" by praising *The Waste Land*. The news account questions his statement.

2375. ———. "T. S. Eliot Analyzes Poet in Lecture to 400 Here." *NYHT* (April 21) , p. 13. An account of Eliot's lecture on April 20 at the New School for Social Research on "Meaning in Poetry."

2376. ———. "Eliot Recites His Poems at Social Research Hall." *NYHT* (April 28) , p. 11. An account of a lecture and reading of his poems at the New School for Social Research on April 27.

2377. ———. "Vassar Players Mix Classics with Moderns." *NYHT* (May 7) , sec. 1, p. 22. [Sweeney Agonistes]. Account of a performance of "Sweeney Agonistes" at Vassar.

2378. ———. "T. S. Eliot Hails End of 'College Spirit.'" *NYT* (April 22) , p. 16. In an interview, Eliot expresses himself on the subject of athleticism, book clubs, and radio broadcasting.

2379. ———. "20,000 Throng Campus at Columbia's 179th Commencement." *NYT* (June 7) , p. 26c. Citation of Eliot for the honorary degree of doctor of letters.

2380. ———. "Poetry and Criticism." *Northern Echo* (Darlington, England) (November 22) , p. 8. [The Use of Poetry and the Use of Criticism]. Praises the clarity of the volume.

2381. ———. "Distinguished St. Louis Poet, T. S. Eliot Reads Detective Thrillers." *St. Louis Globe-Democrat* (January 16) . Interview, account of his family and early life, announcement of his lecture, "The Study of Shakespeare Criticism."

2382. Becker, May Lamberton. "The Reader's Guide." *SatR* 9 (May 13) : 598. A short list of books and articles dealing with Eliot.

2383. Fausset, Hugh I'Anson. "T. S. Eliot's Harvard Lectures on Poetry." *Yorkshire Post* (November 22), p. 6. [The Use of Poetry and the Use of Criticism]. Summary.

2384. G.R.B.R. "T. S. Eliot Discourses on the Use and Function of Poetry." *Boston Evening Transcript* (December 9), book section, p. 1. [The Use of Poetry and the Use of Criticism].

2385. B.S. "Mr. Eliot's Criticism." *Manchester Guardian* (November 16), p. 5. [The Use of Poetry and the Use of Criticism]. Chiefly summary: objects to Eliot's "tone of pomposity."

2386. Lynd, Robert. "The Explorations of Mr. Eliot." *News Chronicle* (London) (December 8), p. 4. [The Use of Poetry and the Use of Criticism].

1934

2387. Anon. Review of *The Rock*. *Cambridge Daily News* (England) (June 13), p. 3. Based on a reading of the play; praises the choruses.

2388. ———. "A Poet Discourses on Poetry." *Catholic Times* (London) (January 5). [The Use of Poetry and the Use of Criticism].

2389. ———. "Among the New Books. The Antidote to Literary Paganism." *Catholic Times* (London) (March 2). [After Strange Gods]. Valuable only as expressing a Roman Catholic approval of the book.

2390. ———. "The Cult of Subjectivity." *Church Times* (London) (March 9), p. 291. [After Strange Gods]. Chiefly sympathetic summary. "Mr. Eliot has done yeoman service to the cause of Christian sanity."

2391. ———. " 'The Rock' at Sadler's Wells: a Provocative Passion Play." *Church Times* (London) (June 1), p. 677. Finds the chorus the most interesting feature of the play.

2392. ———. "Mr. T. S. Eliot's Triumph." *Church Times* (London) (June 8), p. 710. [The Rock].

2393. ———. "Our Mr. Eliot." *Church Times* (London) (October 5), p. 355. [Elizabethan Essays]. The Anglican Church is proud of Eliot, though it finds him bewildering.

2394. ———. "T. S. Eliot's Pageant Play." *Evening News* (Glasgow) (June 23), supplement, p. 2. [The Rock]. "It forms an important link with the past of 'The Waste Land' and the work that is sure to come." Superficial.

2395. ———. "Modern Morality Play." *Glasgow Herald* (June 14). [The Rock]. Routine newspaper criticism, favorable.

2396. ———. "Literary Notes." *Inverness Courier* (March 13), p. 3. [After Strange Gods]. Notes on the attitudes of several reviewers toward the book.

2397. ———. "Mr. T. S. Eliot's Literary Faith." *Inverness Courier* (March 20), p. 3. [After Strange Gods]. A defense of Eliot's religious position against John Beevers (no. 401).

2398. ———. "Tradition and Orthodoxy." *Irish Times* (March 3), p. 4. [After Strange Gods]. A summary.

2399. ———. "Mr. Eliot's Pageant Play." *Irish Times* (June 23), p. 5. [The Rock]. A routine review. Likes the choruses best.

2400. ———. Notice of *After Strange Gods. LQHR* 159 (July), p. 419. A descriptive notice.

2401. ———. *Manchester Guardian* (June 13), p. 7. [The Rock]. Summary.

2402. ———. "A Notable Pageant." *Morning Post* (London) (May 29), p. 14. [The Rock]. The reviewer rather likes the pageant, but "what leaves one most in doubt . . . is the insistent and not entirely justified pessimism of his outlook."

2403. ———. Review of *After Strange Gods. NewL* (New York) (March 23), p. 5. One paragraph. "The large assumptions behind [this book] take one's breath away.

2404. ———. "The Function of Criticism." *Oxford Times* (March 30), p. 10. [The Use of Poetry and the Use of Criticism]. Good ordinary criticism. Brief.

2405. ———. Review of *After Strange Gods. Scotsman* (March 12), p. 2. Says "It is to be commended."

2406. ———. "Is It Poetry?" *Sheffield Daily Telegraph* (December 4, 5). Correspondence regarding the critique of *The Waste Land* by Geoffrey Bullough (No. 543).

2407. ———. "What Use Is the Critic?" *Sun* (Sydney) (June 3), p. 10. [The Use of Poetry and the Use of Criticism]. Fairly good newspaper review.

2408. ———. "Church Pageant at Sadler's Wells." *Times* (London) (May 29), p. 12. [The Rock]. Says he has "created a new thing in the theatre, and made smoother the path towards a contemporary drama."

2409. ———. "Mr. Eliot's Pageant." *Yorkshire Post* (August 8), p. 6. [The Rock]. No reasons for disliking the pageant are given, but an anti-religious bias is implied.

2410. Bullough, Geoffrey. "Is It Poetry?" *Sheffield Daily Telegraph* (December 5). [I have seen this item only as a clipping.] [Waste Land]. A letter to the editor explaining the soda-water lines.

2411. T.D. "It Takes a Poet to Know a Poet." *Daily Herald* (London) (February 27). [After Strange Gods]. A good brief summary.

2412. ———. "East End Vicar as Stage Star." *Daily Express* (London) (May 29), p. 9. [The Rock]. Thought the pageant was too long.

2413. B.I.E. "Mr. Eliot's Criticism." *Glasgow Herald* (March 1). [After Strange Gods]. A protest, from a liberal and patriotic critic, against Eliot's point of view.

2414. "Enterkin" [William Power]. "T. S. Eliot and Heresy." *Evening News* (Glasgow) (March 24), supplement, p. 4. [After Strange Gods].

2415. P.J.F. "Some Recent Works of Critics and Poets." *Methodist Times and Leader* (March 22), p. 9. [The Use of Poetry and the Use of Criticism]. A favorable opinion of the book.

2416. Fausset, Hugh I'Anson. "Mr. Eliot as Moralist." *Yorkshire Post* (March 14), p. 6. [After Strange Gods]. Eliot's orthodoxy is negative "because it is the expression of distrust rather than of faith, and because it would at best curb the ego from without instead of really transforming it from within."

2417. Grigson, Geoffrey. "Tradition in Life and Letters." *Morning Post* (London) (March 2). [After Strange Gods]. Intelligent, sympathetic summary.

2418. R. H. "A Missionary Poet: Mr. T. S. Eliot's Parable of The Rock." *Morning Post* (London) (June 12). Finds the clarity of this play surprising after the obscurity of *The Waste Land*.

2419. W.H.H. "Pageant Play at Sadler's Wells." *Evening Standard* (London) (May 29). [The Rock]. Likes the choruses, but not the Cockney humor or the "deadly effect of the clerical voice."

2420. Hayward, John. "London Letter." *New York Sun* (May 19), p. 30. [The Rock]. Announcement of forthcoming production at Sadler's Wells Theatre.

2421. "Mr. Dangle." "Unusual Pageant Play." *Oxford Times* (July 6), pp. 68–69. [The Rock]. Lukewarm praise.

2422. R.C.R. "Plays and Players, a Book of Words." *Birmingham Post* (June 9), p. 8. [The Rock]. The reviewer says "there is no question that in *The Rock* Mr. Eliot . . . has given to the stage the possibilities of a new idiom."

2423. Sewell, J. E. "Satire in Church Pageant Play." *London Telegraph* (May 29). [The Rock]. "It is all tremendously alive."

2424. Strong Robert. Review of *After Strange Gods. Methodist Times and Leader* (May 10), p. 13. Favorable criticism from the professional religious point of view.

1935

2425. Anon. "T. S. Eliot's Selected Essays." *Catholic Times* (London) (October 21). Objects to his too great admiration for tradition and for classicism, caused by his being an Anglo-Catholic and an American.

2426. ———. *Harvard College Class of 1910 Twenty-fifth Anniversary Report* (Cambridge, Mass., 1935), pp. 219–21. A bibliography of Eliot's writings, superseded by no. 1516.

2427. ———. "Book Notes." *NYHT* (July 2), p. 15. [Murder in the Cathedral]. One paragraph saying that *Murder in the Cathedral* was given in Canterbury, and that it will be published by Harcourt Brace on August 8.

2428. ———. Review of *Murder in the Cathedral. Times* (November 2), p. 10. "This is the one great play by a contemporary dramatist now to be seen in England."

2429. Hayward, John. "London Letter." *New York Sun* (June 15), p. 21. [Murder in the Cathedral]. A carefully written news story on the forthcoming production at Canterbury.

2430. Lucas, E. V. "The Guilty Knights." *Sunday Observer* (London) (July 27). [Murder in the Cathedral]. Lucas has discovered that three of the four actual murderers of Becket died within three years of the assassination.

2431. Muir, Edwin. "Literature at the Start of 1935." *Yorkshire Post* (January 15), p. 6. [The Use of Poetry and the Use of Criticism; After Strange Gods]. One short paragraph of favorable comment.

2432. Nicoll, Allardyce. "Eliot Play Opens in London Theatre." *NYT* (November 2), p. 12. [Murder in the Cathedral]. Report of the opening of Ashley Dukes's production at the Mercury Theatre, London. Quotes part of the London *Times* review.

2433. Roberts, R. Ellis. "T. S. Eliot's Drama of Faith." *Church Times* (London) (June 14), p. 729. [Murder in the Cathedral]. Written from the Anglican point of view. The critic is interested in the religious aspect of the play.

2434. H.S. "T. S. Eliot's Confidence in the Superiority of the Past Colors His Latest Work." *Dallas News* (September 22). [Murder in the Cathedral]. The subject matter of the play seems remote and "arty" to the reviewer.

2435. Tilghman, Tench. "Realm of Poesy." *Baltimore Evening Sun* (November 9), p. 6. [Murder in the Cathedral]. "It is a beautiful and important production."

2436. Wall, Bernard. "Murder in the Cathedral." *Catholic Herald* (London) (June 29), p. 15. Reproaches Eliot for not being Roman Catholic. "The simple contrast of this play being acted in the Canterbury chapter house serves to emphasize how far Canterbury has departed from Becket."

1936

2437. Anderson, John. "Federal Project Actors Present Drama of Thomas à Becket." *New York Evening Journal* (March 23), p. 16. The play is dull.

2438. Anon. "U.S. Culture Satisfies T. S. Eliot, Back from 'Exile' in Great Britain." *Boston Evening Transcript* (September 30), p. 22. A report of an interview on a wide range of political, literary, and religious subjects.

2439. ———. "Federal Theater Presents a Play." *Brooklyn Eagle* (March 21), p. 15. [Murder in the Cathedral]. The play can leave the spectator bored, for it is wordy.

2440. ———. "Willed to Virginia. David Schwab's T. S. Eliot Collection Goes to University." *NYT* (March 15), sec. 2, p. 11. The bequest consists of 380 items, by and about Eliot.

2441. Atkinson, Brooks. "The Play. Meditation of a Martyr in T. S. Eliot's 'Murder in the Cathedral.'" *NYT* (March 21), p. 13. "Sometimes he writes more like a scholastic than a bard," but "the general impression he leaves is superb." A review of the WPA Theatre Project production.

2442. Barnes, Howard. "'Murder in the Cathedral.' T. S. Eliot's Poetic Melodrama Opens at the Manhattan." *NYHT* (March 21), p. 12. "If the author has neglected frequently the shrewd sleight-of-hand of the theatre for the sheer music of words, he has still achieved a fervent and moving drama with moments of majestic beauty."

2443. ———. "Play Bill." *NYHT* (March 29), sec. 5, p. 1. [Murder in the Cathedral]. Ordinary, favorable criticism of the New York production.

2444. Boie, Mildred. "Book Reviews." *NorAR* 242 (Autumn): 189–92. [Collected Poems 1909–1925; Matthiessen's *The Achievement of T. S. Eliot*].

2445. Brown, John Mason. "The High Excitements of 'Murder in the Cathedral.'" *New York Evening Post* (March 30), p. 18. Reprinted in *Two on the Aisle,* New York: W. W. Norton and Co., 1938, pp. 124–26. Finds the play undramatic until the last act, which is "magnificent."

2446. J.C. "WPA Stages T. S. Eliot's Poetic Drama." *New York Daily News* (March 21), p. 27. [Murder in the Cathedral]. It is "dramatically placid."

2447. Carroll, Joseph. "The Dry Crackle of 'The Waste Land' Haunts His Measures." *Chicago Daily News* (June 3), p. 19. [Collected Poems 1909–1935]. Eliot is less vigorous in acceptance than he was in protest.

2448. "Cyrano." *Town Topics* (New York) 10. Comment on *Murder in the Cathedral* (April 17), p. 17. A long paragraph of favorable comment.

2449. Gabriel, Gilbert W. "Murder in the Cathedral." *New York American* (March 21), p. 11. This play is better, because simpler in content and form than Tennyson's play on the same subject. Praises the nobility of cadence and fervency of idea.

2450. Garland, Robert. "WPA Presents Drama of Thomas à Becket." *New York World-Telegram* (March 21), p. 6C. [Murder in the Cathedral]. Says the "Federal Theater's latest undertaking is a dignified, pictorial and talky—oh how talky! theater-piece with overtones of melodrama, undertones of psychology and devastating tones of high-falutin-hocus-pocus."

2451. Gilmore, William. "The Poetry of Eliot. An Oasis in the Waste Land." *Brooklyn Daily Eagle* (May 24), pp. 10, 11C. [Collected Poems 1909–1935]. Gilmore thinks *The Waste Land* is a failure because of its subject matter, and likes Eliot's later poetry.

2452. Hall, Theodore. "The Voice of General Despair." *Washington Post* (December 20), sec. B, p. 7. A confused review saying that Eliot is not really a poet, but a moralist.

2453. Holmes, John. "T. S. Eliot." *Boston Evening Transcript Book Review Section* (June 6), p. 6. [Collected Poems 1909–1935].

2454. Lockridge, Richard. "The Stage in Review: Poetic Martyrdom." *New York Sun* (March 21), p. 9. [Murder in the Cathedral]. The verse is too epigrammatic for the theatre, but the play is "unquestionably a poetic drama of vitality." Also comments on the production.

2455. Marx, Carolyn. "Book Marks for Today." *New York World-Telegram* (March 14), sec. 3, p. 3. Notices of the opening of *Murder* at the Manhattan Theatre on March 20, 1936.

2456. ———. "Book Marks for Today." *New York World-Telegram* (March 21), sec. 3, p. 3. The opening of *Murder in the Cathedral* has created a new interest in the book.

2457. Maynard, Theodore. "The Book of the Day. An Influence on the Wane; the Work of a Poet of Disillusionment." *New York Sun* (June 10), p. 29. [Collected Poems 1909–1935].

2458. Waldorf, Wilella. " 'Murder in the Cathedral' Given by Federal Actors." *New York Evening Post* (March 21), p. 8. After the "merry interlude" of the speeches of the four knights, Eliot "reverted to his earlier and more tedious mood while the women of Canterbury moaned rhythmically over the corpse of their saint until the curtain fell."

2459. Watts, Richard, Jr. "Bringing the Middle Ages to Broadway." *NYHT* (March 29), sec. 5, pp. 1, 5. [Murder in the Cathedral]. Compares this play and Shaw's *St. Joan.* Eliot "lacks the flaming eloquence and heroic spirit of the tragedy written by the unpoetic Irishman." "The Beckets of this world will always seem too inhuman for the normal taste."

1937

2460. Anon. "Murder in the Cathedral." *Boston Herald* (March 20), p. 7. An account of the first of five performances given by the Poets' Theatre of Harvard in the Fogg Art Museum.

2461. ———. "Edinburgh, Graduation." *Scotsman* (July 3), p. 18. Prints the citation of Eliot for the degree of Litt.D. from the University of Edinburgh.

2462. Frank, Joseph. "The Cloisters of T. S. Eliot." *WSCR* 1 (March): 3, 18–19. [Essays Ancient and Modern]. A youthful critic deplores Eliot's lack of knowledge of the present day.

2463. Gallup, Donald C. *A Catalogue of English and American First Editions of Writings by T. S. Eliot: Exhibited in the Yale University Library 22 February to 20 March, 1937,* 42 pp. New Haven: Yale University Library, 1937. An early version of Gallup's bibliography, no. 1516.

1938

2464. Anon. "Eliot Tragedy at the Shubert Monday Week." *Boston Evening Transcript* (January 22), pt. 4, p. 7. [Murder in the Cathedral]. Announcement of the production on January 31, 1938.

2465. ———. "Religion and Poetry: an Interview with Mr. T. S. Eliot." *Church Times* (London) (April 22), p. 467. Eliot talks about his religious history, his experiments with verse drama, and obscurity in poetry.

2466. ———. "Rejected Painter Lashes the Academy." *Evening News* (London) (April 21). Wyndham Lewis expresses his annoyance at the rejection by the Royal Academy of his portrait of Eliot.

2467. ———. "New Cambridge Doctors." *Times* (London) (June 10), p. 8. Account of Eliot's receiving the degree of Doctor of Letters.

2468. Atkinson, Brooks. "T. S. Eliot's Murder . . . Performed by the English Company." *NYT* (February 17), p. 16. Anticipates the same criticism as in the May 1, 1938, article (no. 658).

2469. Hall, Mordaunt. " 'Murder in the Cathedral' is Presented at the Shubert," *Boston Evening Transcript* (February 1), p. 6. Bright, cheerful journalese.

2470. Lawson, Arthur. "The Soul of a Poet." *Star* (London) (February 24), p. 2. Interview in which Eliot expresses his difficulty in getting good material for *The Criterion* from dictator countries, and comments on his use of poetry for the stage.

2471. Mantle, Burns. "Murder . . . English Version, Shown in Ritz Theatre." *New York Daily News* (February 17), p. 41. [Murder in the Cathedral]. Good comparison of the staging of this version with that of the Federal Theatre project. The latter was "an effective shadow."

2472. Rogers, Robert E. "Shubert's Play Novel 'Mystery.'" *Boston Evening American* (February 1), p. 9. [Murder in the Cathedral]. He thinks the play is interesting, but does not understand it.

2473. Sherrill, Henry Knox. "Bishop Sherill Writes Review of 'Murder in the Cathedral.' Finds Becket a Symbol of Today." *Boston Evening Transcript* (February 2), p. 1. Clear explanation of the meaning of the play.

2474. Sloper, L. A. "With and Without Scenery." *CSM* (February 1), p. 8. [Murder in the Cathedral]. Repeats familiar material; the news story is about the Boston production of the play.

2475. Watts, Richard, Jr. "Martyr of Canterbury." *NYHT* (February 18), p. 14. [Murder in the Cathedral]. Finds the play obscure in meaning. The passion for martyrdom "is an emotion not easy to appreciate in the theatre."

2476. Webster, Clifford J. "The Chorus: T. S. Eliot." *McMUQ* (Ontario, Canada) 48, no. 1 (November): 40–49. [Murder in the Cathedral]. An undergraduate paper.

1939

2477. Anon. "T. S. Eliot's New Play." *Manchester Guardian* (March 22), p. 13. [Family Reunion].

2478. ———. "Wasteland of Words." *News Chronicle* (London) (March 22), p. 8. [Family Reunion].

2479. ———. "Entertainments: Westminster Theatre." *Times* (London) (March 22), p. 12. [Family Reunion]. The verse is good, but the plot is badly managed.

2480. ———. "Leeds Confers Five Honorary Degrees." *Yorkshire Post* (July 4), p. 5. Photograph and account of Eliot's receiving an honorary doctorate from Leeds University.

2481. Darlington, W. A. "T. S. Eliot's New Verse Play." *Morning Post* (London) (March 22). [Family Reunion]. This play is not so good as *Murder in the Cathedral* because tension falls in Act III.

2482. Gallup, Donald C. "T. S. Eliot Imitates Greeks." *Dallas Morning News* (April 2), sec. 2, p. 9. [Family Reunion]. Summary, with little comment. " 'The Family Reunion' is of importance as an attempt to revitalize the influence of Greek poetry upon contemporary English literature."

2483. Holmes, John. "Eliot on Roistering Cats." *Boston Evening Transcript* (November 15), p. 15. [Old Possum's Book of Practical Cats]. ". . . it should have been prevented."

2484. R.E.R. "Mr. Eliot's New Play." *Church Times* (London) (March 24), p. 305. [Family Reunion]. Summary and favorable criticism.

2485. Thompson, Ralph. "Books of the Times." *NYT* (March 30), p. 21. [Family Reunion]. *"The Family Reunion* suggests that he is still more of a poet than a dramaturge, but on the brink of becoming more of a metaphysician than either."

1940

2486. Anon. "Sandburg Denounces T. S. Eliot as Royalist and 'Close to Fascist.' " *NYHT* (October 24), p. 18. Sandburg says, "I'm off him, to use a truck-driver's phrase, and we've got to consider the truck drivers in the present hour, rather than the intellectual."

2487. ———. "Maugham Cites U.S. and British Cultural Bond." *NYHT* (October 24), p. 17. In a speech Maugham said, "If we have a great poet in England today," it is Eliot.

2488. ———. "For 'Christian Society.' T. S. Eliot Outlines a Religious System." *Springfield Republican* (Massachusetts) (January 7), p. 7e. [Idea of a Christian Society]. The reviewer is reluctant to accept Eliot's idea of an authoritarian church.

2489. Imberman, A. A. "Mr. T. S. Eliot Will Save You. If You'll Wear Your Sunday Clothes All Week." *Des Moines Register* (February 4), society sec., p. 7. [Idea of a Christian Society].

2490. Thompson, Ralph. "Books of the Times." *NYT* (January

8), p. 13. [Idea of a Christian Society]. Makes fun of the book.

2491. Waller, John. "An Old Man and a Young Maiden." *Poetry R,* 31 (December) : 431–35. [East Coker].

1941

2492. Darlington, W. A. "Canterbury Play in a Shelter." *Daily Telegraph and Morning Post* (March 25), p. 3. [Murder in the Cathedral]. The working-class audience gave the play its earnest attention.

2493. Harper, Allanah. "A Magazine and Some People in Paris." *PR* 9 (July-August) : 311–12. Says *Échanges,* No. 1 (December, 1929), contains Eliot's *A Brief Introduction to the Method of Paul Valéry.*

2494. Kunitz, Stanley J., and Haycraft, Howard. *Twentieth Century Authors,* pp. 420–22. New York: H. W. Wilson and Co., 1942. Biography, list of works, short bibliography of critical works on Eliot. Factually correct.

2495. Oxenford, Mabel. *Murder in the Cathedral,* English Pamphlet Series no. 2. Buenos Aires: Argentine Association of English Culture, 1942.

2496. Rezzano (de Martini), Maria Clotilde. *The Family Reunion,* English Pamphlet Series no. 2, pp. 13–25. Buenos Aires: Argentine Association of English Culture, 1942. Summary with an attempt at interpretation.

1943

2497. Anon. "Eliot on Kipling." *NYHTB* (September 26), p. 25. [A Choice of Kipling's Verse]. Brief summary of Eliot's introduction.

2498. ———. "Ambassadors for Books." *TLS,* no. 2160 (June 26), p. 307. Expresses pleasure that Eliot has been elected president of the English Circle of Books across the Sea.

2499. Emmart, A. D. "Mr. Eliot's Four Quartets." *Baltimore Evening Sun* (May 8), p. 4.

2500. Maynard, Theodore. Review of *Four Quartets. CathW* 157 (August) : 553–54.

2501. Rillo, Lila C. *Aldous Huxley and T. S. Eliot,* English Pamphlet Series no. 3, pp. 5–14. Buenos Aires: Argentine Association of English Culture, 1943. Superficial comparisons between passages in Huxley's novels and in Eliot's poems; much quotation with but little analysis.

2502. Strachan, Pearl. "The World of Poetry." *CSM, Weekly Magazine Section* (May 29), p. 11. [Four Quartets].

2503. Varley, Lee. "T. S. Eliot's 'Four Quartets.'" *Springfield Republican* (Massachusetts) (May 23), p. 7e. [Four Quartets]. Complimentary.

1944

2504. Anon. "Notes on Current Books: Poetry." *VQR* 20 (Winter): xi–xii. [A Choice of Kipling's Verse].

2505. Scott, Edmund. "There Is Humor in Mr. T. S. Eliot." *CSM* (January 11), p. 6. An easy-going brief defense of Eliot, considering not only humor, but also the music of his poetry, and other topics. Chiefly quotation.

1945

2506. Anon. On *Murder in the Cathedral. Life* 19, no. 14 (October 1): 123–27. A short article and nine photographs of the play as presented at Hobart College.

2507. ———. "Radical Only in a Great Sense." *SenS* 46 (April 9): 16. A simplified one-column summary of Eliot's life and work.

1947

2508. Anon. "You Must Meet Mr. Eliot." *SenS* 50 (February 10): 19. Popularization for high-school students.

2509. ———. "T. S. Eliot's Lecture Illustrates Development of Striking Trends," *Wellesley College News* (May 8), pp. 5, 6. An account of Eliot's reading his poems and the report of an interview.

2510. ———. "Eliot Will Read Poem Selections in Sprague Hall." *Yale News* (May 26), p. 1.

2511. Battenhouse, Henry M. "T. S. Eliot." *Poets of Christian Thought*, pp. 153–72. (New York: Ronald Press, 1947). Uses Eliot to illustrate his own point of view.

2512. L. F. "T. S. Eliot's 'Family Reunion' in Cherry Lane." *NYT* (November 29), p. 9. "It is completely lacking in any dramatic structure or conflict."

1948

2513. Anon. "Honors List Cites Laboring Britons." *NYT* (January 1), p. 4. Eliot is to receive the Order of Merit.

2514. ———. "T. S. Eliot Receives 1948 Nobel Award." *NYT* (November 5), p. 1. News story and photograph.

2515. ———. "T. S. Eliot Receives British Order of Merit." *PW* 153 (January 31): 632.

2516. ———. "Books of the Day. Culture and Religion." *Scotsman* (December 16). [Notes towards the Definition of Culture]. A full and fair summary.

2517. ———. "The New Year Honours. O.M. for Mr. T. S. Eliot." *Times* (London) (January 1), p. 6. Announcement that he is to receive the Order of Merit.

2518. ———. "The Meaning of Culture. Mr. Eliot on Educationists." *Times* (London) *Educational Supplement* (December 4), p. 678. [Notes towards the Definition of Culture].

2519. ———. "New Year Honours List." *Times Weekly Edition* (London) (January 7), p. 9. Photograph and notice that Eliot has received the Order of Merit.

2520. Bayley, John. "T. S. Eliot, Poet and Portent." Review of *T. S. Eliot: a Symposium, NaR* 131 (November): 481–82.

2521. Childe, W. R. "Mr. T. S. Eliot Looks at Society." *Yorkshire Post and Leeds Mercury* (November 19), p. 2. [Notes towards the Definition of Culture]. The reviewer laments that Eliot has forsaken poetry for sociology.

2522. Dash, Thomas R. "The Family Reunion." *Women's Wear Daily* (New York) (December 1). "On its philosophical plane it is challenging, even if it is not always too clear what the author intends to convey."

2523. Glicksberg, Charles I. Review of Unger's *T. S. Eliot: a Selected Critique, ArQ* 4 (Winter): 374–76.

2524. Lister, R. P. "Mr. Bluefrock Considers It All." *Atlantic* 182 (September): 52. [Prufrock]. Doggerel parody.

2525. Minney, R. J. "T. S. Eliot's views on 'Culture' as a Way of Life." *Church of England Newspaper* (November 5), p. 8. [Notes towards the Definition of Culture]. "Whether you agree with him or not, you will find his arguments interesting."

2526. Walker, Kenneth. "What is Culture?" *Sun Times* (London) (November 14), p. 3. [Notes towards the Definition of Culture].

1949

2527. Anon. "The Cocktail Party: Poet uses worldly scene for a Christian comedy." *Life* 27 (September 26) : 18, 20, 23. Summary of the play by means of judiciously chosen quotations; photographs of scenes.

2528. ———. "Ties with Canada Hailed at Yale." *NYT* (June 19) , p. 6. Citation of Mr. Eliot for the degree of Doctor of Letters.

2529. ———. "The Festival, The Cocktail Party: New T. S. Eliot Play." *Scotsman* (August 23) , p. 6. Wit sparkles throughout the comedy, but it is put there to balance the serious philosophic purpose.

2530. ———. "The Edinburgh Festival, 'The Cocktail Party.'" *Times* (London) (August 24) , p. 8. It is a "story highly ingenious in its construction, witty in its repartee, and impregnated with Christian feeling."

2531. Calta, Louis. "New T. S. Eliot Play to Bow in January." *NYT* (October 15) , p. 11. [Cocktail Party].

2532. Darlington, W. A. "Fine Play by T. S. Eliot." *Daily Telegraph and Morning Post* (London) (August 23) , p. 5. [Cocktail Party]. "Unless I am carried away by the excitement of the moment, this play is one of the finest dramatic achievements of our time."

2533. ———. "London Letter. Edinburgh Festival Has Two New Plays." *NYT* (September 11) , p. 2x. [Cocktail Party]. "This play leaves us as poetry should, with the feeling that we have been dealing with immensities."

2534. Dent, Alan. "Accent in Edinburgh." *News-Chronicle* (London) (August 27) , p. 4. [Cocktail Party]. The play is a "finely acted piece of flapdoodle."

2535. R. P. M. G. "Première of T. S. Eliot's Play. 'The Cocktail Party' at Edinburgh." *Daily Telegraph and Morning Post* (London) (August 22) , p. 6. Announcement of the world première of the play on August 22, 1949.

2536. Hayes, Walter. "The Poet with the L. S. D. Touch." *Daily Sketch and Daily Graphic* (London) (August 23) , p. 4. A slangy summary of Eliot's biography, written after the opening of *The Cocktail Party*.

2537. Hobson, Harold. "Opera, Ballets, Orchestras, Eliot's 'The Cocktail Party.'" *CSM* (September 17) , p. 8. Summary of the plot, and praise of the dialogue.

2538. McCord, Bert. "To Produce New Eliot Play." *NYHT* (August 2), p. 10. [Cocktail Party]. Announcement of the forthcoming production in Edinburgh.

2539. Poore, Charles [incorrectly attributed to Orville Prescott]. "Books of the Times." *NYT* (March 3), p. 23. [Notes towards the Definition of Culture]. He dislikes the book, but does not give his reasons.

2540. Robinson, Kenneth J. "Contemporary Arts. The Theatre." *Spectator* 183, no. 6323 (September 2): 294. [Cocktail Party].

2541. Stevenson, J. W. Review of *The Cocktail Party*. [An Edinburgh newspaper, date unknown]. "Fundamentally it is a study of the 'dark night of the soul' in which faith is born, the despair which is the creative moment of hope." Expresses the idea clearly.

2542. Trewin, John Courtney. "Symbols and Saints." *Illustrated London News* 125 (September 10): 388 [Cocktail Party]. A brief review saying "it does not fire the spirit."

2543. Wilson, Cecil. "Festival Play Was Eliot's Little Joke." *Daily Mail* (London) (August 23), p. 3. [Cocktail Party]. The joke is that the play is called a comedy.

2544. Zolotow, Sam. "Miller Importing Cast for Comedy." *NYT* (November 30), p. 35: [Cocktail Party]. The Sherek players from London will appear in New York in the play.

1950

2545. Anon. "New English Favorite in T. S. Eliot's Cocktail Party." *Brooklyn Eagle* (January 22), p. 27. Chiefly about the actor, Alec Guiness.

2546. ———. *Chicago Sunday Tribune* (October 15), pt. 4, p. 14. [Introduction to Adventures of Huckleberry Finn].

2547. ———. "T. S. Eliot, Delighted but a Little Baffled." *CSM* (August 19), p. 18. An interview with Eliot on his working habits; how to read a poem; the role of the church in the conflict between East and West.

2548. ———. "T. S. Eliot's Murder in the Cathedral Presented in a Number of Italian Churches to Large Audiences." *Church Times* (London) (October 20), p. 772.

2549. ———. "A Play by a Poet." *Cue* (January 14), p. 12. [Cocktail Party]. On the London success of the play, and a brief summary. Pictures.

2550. ———. "T. S. Eliot's Play Tops a Full Week." *Cue* (January 28) , p. 18. [Cocktail Party].

2551. ———. "Eliot Says Play Is to Entertain." *NYHT* (May 14) , sec. 5, p. 2. [Cocktail Party]. Eliot says he will begin a new play. Information on his working habits.

2552. ———. "T. S. Eliot Arrives in New York on the DeGrasse. Going to Chicago to Give Four Lectures on 'The Aims of Education.' " *NYHT* (October 4) , p. 19.

2553. ———. "T. S. Eliot Sees the Cocktail Party in New York." *NYHT* (December 6) . [The clipping is so dated in the Eliot Collection, but the news story has not been found in this issue.]

2554. ———. "Eliot Play Raises Issue." *NYT* (January 6) , p. 24. The *London Times* dramatic critic has protested against *The Cocktail Party* opening in New York before it did in London, since Eliot is a British subject.

2555. ———. "Broadway Angels Called Cagey Birds." *NYT* (February 10) , p. 18. Mrs. Howard Cullman was one of two "outside" backers for *The Cocktail Party*.

2556. ———. " 'Cocktail Party' for London?" *NYT* (March 2) , p. 32. Feelings were hurt in London because the play came first to New York; it is to go to London next.

2557. ———. "From the Drama Mailbag." *NYT* (April 2) , sec. 2, p. 2x. [Cocktail Party]. Three letters condemning the play for obscurity and for misinterpreting the psychiatrist.

2558. ———. "Pulitzer Prize Next." *NYT* (April 6) , p. 33. Speculation on whether *The Cocktail Party* will win the prize.

2559. ———. "8 Perry Awards Go to 'South Pacific' . . . T. S. Eliot's 'Cocktail Party' Captures 'Tony.' " *NYT* (April 10) , p. 14. These are prizes given for "notable contributions to the theatre."

2560. ———. Cartoon in Book Review Section by Burr Shafer. *NYT* (April 30) , p. 2. A sailor at a "tattoo parlor," chest bared, says "I have in mind a couple of lines by T. S. Eliot."

2561. ———. "T. S. Eliot's Comedy Unveiled in London." *NYT* (May 4) , p. 33. [Cocktail Party]. Summarizes the generally favorable comments of reviewers in London.

2562. ———. "Radio and Television." *NYT* (May 13) , p. 32. [Family Reunion]. The play is to be broadcast over B.B.C. on June 11, 1950.

2563. ———. "T. S. Eliot Aiding Arts Group." *NYT* (July 1), p. 9. Notice that Eliot has been appointed to the National Arts Foundation Committee of New York.

2564. ———. "Y.M.H.A. Poetry Center under the direction of John Malcolm Brinnin Presents T. S. Eliot in a Reading." *NYT* (October 22).

2565. ———. "$2,800 Awarded T. S. Eliot. He wins *London Sunday Times'* Prize for 'Cocktail Party.'" *NYT* (November 6), p. 33. Gives a short stage history of the play.

2566. ———. "T. S. Eliot's 'The Cocktail Party' has a single performance at the Teatro Agiuleon in Mexico City." *NYT* (November 16), p. 39. The play was given under the auspices of the National Institute of Fine Arts.

2567. ———. "On the Radio. Rebroadcast of T. S. Eliot's Poetry Reading Given in Chicago Nov. 12, 1950." *NYT* (November 18), p. 18.

2568. ———. "The Cocktail Party." *NY* 26 (March 18): 110. A short note saying that it is fortunate that the book has been published while the play is arousing so much comment.

2569. ———. "The Theatre. By Slow Stages to a Sand bar." *NY* 26 (October 7): 51–52. [Cocktail Party]. A flippant comparison of the psychiatrists in *The Cocktail Party* and *Black Chiffon,* concluding more seriously, "I won't continue to bracket Mr. Eliot's eloquent and troubling piece with Miss Storm's overwrought and narrow one."

2570. ———. Notice of *The Adventures of Huckleberry Finn.* *NY* 26 (November 11): 154. [Introduction to *Adventures of Huckleberry Finn*]. A notice, and a few quotations from the introduction.

2571. ———. "T. S. Eliot Flails at Modern Education." *Record* (Stockton, California) (October 30), p. 13. A short account of Eliot's Chicago lectures.

2572. ———. "Stage." *Reynolds News* (London) (May 7). [Cocktail Party]. Says that the play is "lucidly written and beautifully constructed," but does not like the idea of the play.

2573. ———. "Theatre." *Sunday Dispatch* (London) (May 7). [Cocktail Party]. Report of Eliot's curtain speech.

2574. ———. "Portrait Gallery." *Sun Times* (London) (September 3), p. 6. Picture and three paragraphs summarizing his paradoxical career. He is "the only Englishman alive to be honored with both the Order of Merit and the Nobel Prize for Literature."

2575. ———. "The New Plays." *TAr* 34 (April) : 8, 10. [Cocktail Party]. Chiefly summary.

2576. ———. *ThW* (London) 46, no. 305 (June) : 11–18. [Cocktail Party]. Seventeen photographs of the first London production, with a brief summary of the plot.

2577. ———. "American Production of Mr. Eliot's Play." *Times* (London) (January 5) , p. 4. An article by the dramatic critic protesting *The Cocktail Party* opening in New York before it played in London.

2578. ———. "Entertainments. New Theatre. 'The Cocktail Party.' " *Times* (London) (May 4) , p. 2. "Mr. Eliot has picked a form which prose realism has worked to the point of exhaustion, and into it he has breathed new life" by writing in poetry.

2579. ———. "Miller Taking in Some Outside Coin on 'Party.' " *Variety* (January 18) . On financing the American production.

2580. ———. "The Cocktail Party." *Vogue* 115 (April) : 122–23. Two pages, pictures of the cast, summary of the play, and quotations.

2581. Atkinson, Brooks. "At the Theatre." *NYT* (January 23) , p. 17. [Cocktail Party]. The reviewer is "impressed without being enlightened."

2582. Barber, John. "T. S. Eliot's 'Party' Witty, Brutal . . . Valuable." *Daily Express* (London) (May 4) . [Cocktail Party]. Says that "no more valuable play has been seen in 20 years."

2583. Baxter, Beverley. "I'm Not Drinking." *Evening Standard* (London) (May 5) . [Cocktail Party]. He does not like the play.

2584. Benét, William Rose. Review of *The Cocktail Party*. *SatR* 33 (February 11) : 48. A flippant review.

2585. Blackman, M. C. "Middlebrow Enjoys 'Cocktail Party' Too." *NYHT* (March 26) , sec. 5, p. 3. The reviewer is happy to stay on the surface of the play and enjoy it.

2586. ———. "The Cocktail Party." *NY* 26 (March 18) : 110. (January 15) , sec. 2, p. 3. [Murder in the Cathedral; Family Reunion; Cocktail Party]. An easy popular account by a friend of Eliot's of what he is trying to achieve in his plays.

2587. Butcher, Fanny. "The Literary Spotlight." *Chicago Tribune* (October 22), pt. 4, p. 2. An account of Eliot's first lecture on education at the University of Chicago.

2588. Calta, Louis. " 'Cocktail Party' Arrives Tonight." *NYT* (January 21), p. 10. Routine advance publicity.

2589. Cassidy, Claudia. "Broadway Salutes Drama as an Enigmatic Masterpiece." *Chicago Tribune* (May 7). [Cocktail Party]. Finds the play clear in meaning and absorbing as theatre.

2590. Chapman, John. " 'Cocktail Party' a Masterpiece: Cast Gives Superb Performance." *New York Daily News* (January 23), p. 39.

2591. Colby, Ethel. "The Cocktail Party." *New York Journal of Commerce* (January 24), p. 15. Says "the profundities of soul-baring conversation seem too obtrusive to blend with complete comfort."

2592. Coleman, Robert. "Eliot's Fine 'Cocktail Party' Goes Right to the Head." *New York Daily Mirror* (January 23), p. 20. He is enthusiastic about the play and about the "smart audience" which attended.

2593. Crist, Judith. "Theatre in the Living-Room: Current Plays Being Recorded." *NYHT* (February 26), sec. 5, p. 1. [Cocktail Party]. Mr. Rady of Decca's recording department is quoted as saying: "Eliot is quite a vogue. We thought there should be some way of recording it."

2594. Dent, Alan. "Fly in the Ointment." *News-Chronicle* (London) (May 6), p. 4. [Cocktail Party]. The play is undramatic, obscure, and flat.

2595. Drummond, John. "After the Party." *Sunday Chronicle* (London) (May 7). [Cocktail Party]. "I doubt if time will prove this a great play, but it is a good play." Thinks that Eliot's plays lack dramatic form and content.

2596. Field, Rowland. "Cocktail Party." *Newark Evening News* (January 23), p. 12. Enthusiastic.

2597. ———. "Along Broadway; 'The Cocktail Party' is Heady Fare, Affecting Audiences in Various Ways." *Newark Evening News* (July 31), p. 12. On the theatrical history of the play, emphasizing its surprising success.

2598. Funke, Lewis. "News and Gossip of the Rialto: Interview." *NYT* (December 17), sec. 2, p. 3x. [Cocktail Party].

There are different ways to perform the roles, Eliot says. He is working on another verse play.

2599. Gannett, Lewis. "Books and Things." *NYHT* (March 10), p. 17. [Cocktail Party]. "It is better just to enjoy it as one enjoyed Gertrude Stein's *Four Saints in Three Acts* than to attempt to piece the fragments into a coherent pattern."

2600. Garland, Robert. "The Cocktail Party. There's Nothing Like It in Today's Theatre." *New York Journal American* (January 23), p. 8. He thinks it is "Great, but great!!"

2601. Guiness, Alec. "Found in the Drama Mailbag." *NYT* (March 19), drama section, p. 2x. Letter replying to one by Bertram Weis in the March 12, 1950, issue criticizing *The Cocktail Party* as boring. Guiness says that Weis does not understand the play.

2602. Hailey, Foster. "An Interview with T. S. Eliot." *NYT* (April 16), sec. 2, pp. 1, 3. [Cocktail Party]. Eliot gives his views on the characterization and meaning of the play.

2603. Hawkins, William. "T. S. Eliot Analyzes 'The Cocktail Party.'" *New York World-Telegram* (January 23), p. 16. He can see little reason why the American public should go to see this so-called play.

2604. Hobson, Harold. "The Paradoxical Public." *CSM Weekly Magazine Section* (February 25), p. 10. [Cocktail Party]. On the difficulties of getting a London theatre to produce *The Cocktail Party*.

2605. ———. "New Theatre. The Cocktail Party." *Times* (London), p. 2. [I have been unable to check the date of this article further than that it appeared in 1950, and probably in May.] [Cocktail Party]. Is it a great play? "It is . . . near enough to greatness to make the question worth asking."

2606. ———. "The Cocktail Party." *CSM* (May 27), magazine sec., p. 6. Chiefly on the reception of the play, which is succeeding better in London than it did in Edinburgh.

2607. ———. "Too Modest Scotland." *Sun Times* (London) (September 3), p. 2. Mentions *The Cocktail Party* as having been given at the Edinburgh Festival.

2608. Hughes, Elinor. "Eliot's 'The Cocktail Party' Is Fascinating and Controversial." *Boston Herald* (March 19), p. 6c.

2609. Longstreet, Stephen. "Shaggy Grandfathers Sire Strong Breed." *Daily News* (Los Angeles) (May 20), p. 17. [Cocktail Party]. Eliot's prose is "drivel," and his thinking "perverted," but he remains a great poet.

2610. Meyer, Karl. "T. S. Eliot Eats Bacon and Eggs, Chats with Athenaeum Staffers." *Daily Cardinal* (Madison, Wisconsin) (November 15), p. 1. Account of a breakfast with Eliot and remarks on the success of his lecture at the Union Theater on November 13, 1950.

2611. Norton, Eliot. "Most Remarkable Broadway Hit is 'Cocktail Party.'" *Boston Sunday Post* (February 12), p. 31. Summary of the plot.

2612. Ormsbee, Helen. "Irene Worth's Roundabout Trip to a Cocktail Party." *NYHT* (May 7), sec. 5, p. 3. Miss Worth reports her enthusiasm and that of the rest of the cast for the play.

2613. Parsons, Geoffrey. "Solving Some of Eliot's Riddles." *NYHT* (February 12), sec. 5, p. 1. [Cocktail Party]. Interview with Martin Browne, the producer of the play, on its meaning. A welcome light amid the fog of much newspaper criticism.

2614. Pollak, R. An interview with Eliot. *Chicago Daily Sun and Times* (November 12), sec. 2, p. 15. The usual journalistic question, "Why does he write verse plays?"

2615. Pollock, Arthur. "Theatre Time. Eliot's 'The Cocktail Party' Engrossing and Skillful." *Daily Compass* (New York) (January 23), p. 18.

2616. ———. "Theatre Time. 'Cocktail Party' and Green Hills far away." *Sunday Compass* (New York) (January 29), magazine sec., p. 12. The psychiatrist might be suspected of "large scale quackery" and Celia is an escapist, but Eliot is a good playwright.

2617. ———. "Theatre Time. Some Harsh Words about 'Cocktail Party' and $1.80." *Daily Compass* (New York) (March 20), p. 20. A letter from Mr. Goodstein complains about "Benevolent Imperialism" in the play.

2618. Poore, Charles. "Books of the Times." *NYT* (March 16), p. 29. [Cocktail Party].

2619. ———. *NYT* (April 23), sec. 2, p. 3. Protests against allowing Eliot to be compared with Shakespeare. (See no. 2625.)

2620. ———. "From 'Ol' Man River' to T. S. Eliot." *CSM* (No-

vember 11), p. 8. [Cocktail Party]. On the acting of
the play in Mexico City.

2621. Pope, W. Macqueen. "The London Theatre." [News-
paper, unidentified, undated. Seen as a clipping in the
New York Public Library.] [Cocktail Party]. The reviewer compares the play with "The Passing of the
Third Floor Back." He is neutral regarding its value.

2622. Rosten, Norman. *NYT* (May 7), sec. 2, p. 3x. [Cocktail
Party]. A jingle on his bewilderment in answer to a
letter by A. B. Siringo (no. 2625).

2623. Shaeffer, Louis. "Curtain Time: T. S. Eliot's 'The Cocktail Party' Provocative and Superbly Acted." *Brooklyn
Eagle* (January 23), p. 6.

2624. ———. "Margaret Phillips Dominates New Lineup in
'Cocktail Party.' " *Brooklyn Eagle* (June 23), p. 6. The
critic liked the play the first time, and even more the
second.

2625. Siringo, Albert C. "The Drama Mailbag. Eliot and Shakespeare." *NYT* (April 30), sec. 2, p. 4. Answer to a letter
of the week before by C. Poore on *The Cocktail Party*
(no. 2620). Siringo says that Eliot can be legitimately
compared with Shakespeare.

2626. Taubman, Howard. "Records: Cocktail Party." *NYHT*
(June 11). He does not like the mysticism and "pietism"
of the play.

2627. Trewin, John Courtney. " 'The Cocktail Party' Opens in
London." *NYT* (May 7), sec. 2, p. 2x. A useful summary of the mixed reception of the play by critics and
audience.

2628. ———. "Wine and Water." *ILN* 216 (May 20): 792.
[Cocktail Party].

2629. Watts, Richard, Jr. "The Theatre Event of the Season."
New York Post (January 23), p. 32. [Cocktail Party].
Says that it is "absorbing on whatever level it is con-
templated."

2630. Whiting, Charles E. " 'Cocktail' as Hit Baffles Eliot." *Daily
Compass* (May 9). [Cocktail Party]. Report of an interview on the meaning of the play, Eliot's habits of work,
and his plans for the future.

2631. Williams, Stephen. "Why Call It Poetic?" *Evening News*
(London) (May 5). [Cocktail Party]. The play is well
written, but it is not poetic drama.

2632. Zolotow, Maurice: "Psychoanalyzing the Doctor." *NYT*

(February 26), sec. 2, p. 3. [Cocktail Party]. Interview with Alec Guiness on how he thinks the role of Harcourt-Reilly should be acted; Guiness created the role in the original production.

1951

2633. Anon. *Boston Globe* (February 15), pp. 1, 32. The president of the Dell Secretarial School and students testify in court that selections read aloud from Eliot were "shocking and offensive." Eliot replies in the London *Express*.

2634. ———. "Poetry and Design." *Church Times* (London) (January 19), p. 44. [Drew, *T. S. Eliot: the Design of His Poetry*]. "Miss Drew's book is of great interest to those who want to enjoy Dr. Eliot's verse, but find him heavy going." Most of the article is devoted to a defense of studying a poet's technique.

2635. ———. "Studio Exhibition of 'Murder in the Cathedral.' " *Church Times* (London) (January 26), p. 2. "Cutting and editing is now in progress, and the finished production should be ready in April."

2636. ———. "First Irish Production of 'The Cocktail Party.' " *Irish Times* (April 18), p. 3. A flippant review saying that Eliot has done the same thing "very much better" in "The Hollow Men."

2637. ———. "Paris University Honors T. S. Eliot." *NYHT* (December 2), sec. 1, p. 77. He received an honorary doctorate from the University of Paris on December 1, 1951.

2638. ———. "Random Items concerning People and Pictures." *NYT* (January 28), sec. 2, p. 5x. [Murder in the Cathedral]. A paragraph headed "New Medium" states that the film has just been completed.

2639. ———. "Feuilleton." *NYTBR* (February 4), p. 8. A college girl remarked that the trouble with Eliot is that he doesn't use rhymes. Eliot answered, "But I sometimes rhyme in the middle."

2640. ———. "Columbia Doing Eliot Drama." *NYT* (February 14), p. 36. [Murder in the Cathedral]. A presentation by the Columbia University Players is announced for February 24.

2641. ———. "On the Radio: Family Reunion on B.B.C.

Radio." *NYT* (January 13), p. 20. Announcement of broadcast by B.B.C. World Theatre.

2642. ———. " 'Cocktail Party' Tour Set." *NYT* (September 28), p. 26. The tour is to start in San Francisco October 15 and play also in Los Angeles on November 12.

2643. Hoggart, Richard. *Auden, an Introductory Essay.* London: Chatto & Windus, 1951). Casual references to likenesses between Auden and Eliot; brief.

2644. Kennedy, Maurice. "Barley Wine and Some Cocktails." *Sunday Press* (Dublin) (April 22), p. 9. [Cocktail Party]. The play is really a lecture, "delivered by as brilliantly hypnotic a lecturer as any ancient Mariner."

2645. Mordell, Albert. *T. S. Eliot's Deficiencies as a Social Critic,* pp. 2–25. *T. S. Eliot—Special Pleader as Book Reviewer and Literary Critic,* pp. 26–56. No. B–928 (Girard, Kansas: Haldemann-Julius, 1951). These essays show a virulent combination of some factual knowledge, lack of judgment, and hatred.

1952

2646. Crowther, Bosley. "The Screen in Review. Eliot's 'Murder in the Cathedral,' British-Made Film, Shown at Trans-Lux 60th St." *NYT* (March 26), p. 35, col. 2. Says it does not appeal enough to the eye, though it does to the voice.

1953

2647. Anon. *ILN* 223 (September 5): 353. [Confidential Clerk]. Photographs of the Edinburgh Festival production.

2648. ———. "Washington U Honors 10." *NYT* (June 11), p. 31. Eliot receives a doctorate.

2649. ———. "The Confidential Clerk." *NYTM* 6 (September 6): 36–37. Five photographs of the Edinburgh production and a paragraph on the possible meaning of the play.

2650. Calta, Louis. "Sherek May Stage Eliot Play Here." *NYT* (August 29), p. 10. [Confidential Clerk] Sherek will try to get permission from Actors Equity Association to use an all-British cast.

2651. Darlington, W. A. "New Eliot Comedy Cheered by Scots." *NYT* (August 26), p. 22. [Confidential Clerk]. A short, journalistic review of the plot.

2652. Hobson, Harold. "Mr. Eliot in the Saddles." *Sun Times*

(London) (August 30), p. 4. [Confidential Clerk]. Says that Eliot is riding seven horses at once, and has mastered the farcical, poetic, the "well-groomed," emotional, and histrionic ones, while failing to control the dramatic and religious horses.

2653. Marx, Leo. "Mr. Eliot, Mr. Trilling, and Huckleberry Finn." *ASch* 22 (Autumn) : 423–40. A brief section on Eliot's approval of the end of the novel, an approval which Marx attributes to Eliot's too great interest in form.

2654. Panter-Downs, Mollie. "Letter from London." *NY* 29 (May 2) : 87. [Murder in the Cathedral]. Notice of a production at the Old Vic.

2655. ———. "Letter from London." *NY* 29 (October 10) : 110–11. [Confidential Clerk]. A summary of the plot and a note that the play has received "remarkable praise."

1954

2656. Anon. "Drama Mailbag. Reactions to Critic's Review of Play by T. S. Eliot." *NYT* 2 (February 21) : 3. [Confidential Clerk].
   1. Letter from Newell E. Davis—takes issue with the *NYT* reviewer who did not like the play.
   2. Letter from Paul E. Gelfman—the play is stimulating.
   3. Letter from C. C.—the play was not clear.

2657. ———. Letters regarding *The Confidential Clerk. NYT* 2 (February 28) : 3.
   1. Elizabeth Seeger, "Varied Viewpoints from the Drama Mailbag: Ordinary People." Praises the play because it deals with ordinary people.
   2. Charles Reilly, "Concerning an If." Says Eliot is misunderstood in this play.

2658. ———. "Eliot and Hepburn." *NYTM* 6 (March 14) : 6. [Confidential Clerk]. Letters from 1) Dale Guhl, praising Eliot's "mastery of language" and 2) from Mrs. R. J. Beamish, who is "dumbfounded by the lack of poetic quality" in the play.

2659. ———. "T. S. Eliot Wins Goethe Prize." *NYT* (April 3), p. 20. Eliot wins $2,500 and a gold medal in Hamburg.

2660. ———. "T. S. Eliot in London Clinic." *NYT* (April 21), p. 14. "The *London Evening News* said it was understood the playwright was suffering from a heart ailment."

2661. ———. "People Are Talking About . . ." *Vogue* 123 (March 1) : 130–31. [Confidential Clerk]. Picture of the actors and a brief notice.

2662. Atkinson, Brooks. "First Night at the Theatre. Comedy by T. S. Eliot with Ina Claire, Claude Rains and Joan Greenwood." *NYT* (February 12) , p. 22. [Confidential Clerk]. This play "is at least the second step Mr. Eliot has taken to the level of the theatre, and it represents a repudiation of his own genius." Chiefly summary of the plot.

2663. Beaufort, John. " 'The Confidential Clerk' on Broadway." *CSM* (February 20) , p. 10. The reviewer finds the play "mellower" than previous ones, and praises the acting.

2664. Chapman, John. "T. S. Eliot's 'The Confidential Clerk' a Stimulating, Enjoyable Comedy." *Daily News* (New York) (February 12) . "The real value of 'The Confidential Clerk' lies in the surprising realization . . . that one has been led to know a number of interesting people most intimately."

2665. Coleman, Robert. "Eliot's 'Confidential Clerk' is Superlative Theatre." *Daily Mirror* (New York) (February 12) . "Lighthearted on the surface, it has serious undertones." It is the "brightest and easiest to understand of all T. S. Eliot's plays."

2666. Gassner, John. "English Poetic Drama: Eliot and Fry." *Masters of the Drama,* 3rd ed., pp. 729–31. New York: Dover Publications, Inc., 1954. [Murder in the Cathedral; Family Reunion; Cocktail Party].

2667. Hawkins, William. "Comedy, Pathos Mix in 'Confidential Clerk.' " *New York World-Telegram* (February 12) . This play is more lucid and less pretentious than *The Cocktail Party.* It means that "you make your terms with life, or accept the terms it offers."

2668. Kerr, Walter F. "Theater: The Confidential Clerk." *NYHT* (February 12) . The play fails because it is an attempt to combine "soul and slapstick."

2669. ———. "T. S. Eliot Strolls in the Same Garden." *NYHT* 4 (February 21) : 7. [Confidential Clerk]. This play fails to combine serious drama and farce satisfactorily because Eliot "is not by instinct a dramatist."

2670. McClaire, John. "Rewarding Drama; Appreciation of Play Takes Hard Work." *Journal American* (New York) (February 12) . [Confidential Clerk]. The point of the play is that "most of us get our wish in life, but it is rarely granted in the form we desire."

2671. Mosley, Nicholas. "Mr. Eliot's Confidential Clerk; The Importance of Being Amusing." *European* (London), no. 13 (March), pp. 38–44. A superficial review.

2672. Poore, Charles. "Books of the Times." *NYT* (April 8), p. 25. [Three Voices of Poetry]. A brief summary of the contents.

2673. Shawe-Taylor, Desmond. "Youth Has Its Day at Scotland Fete. 'Practical Cats,' a Musical Novelty to T. S. Eliot's Verses, Is Presented at Edinburgh." *NYT* (August 27), p. 11. This work by Alan Rawsthorne "consists of six settings from 'Old Possum's Book of Practical Cats' preceded by a brief overture."

2674. Watts, Richard, Jr. "T. S. Eliot's Confidential Clerk." *New York Post* (February 12). The ideas are less interesting here than they were in *The Cocktail Party*, and the play is wordy.

1955

2675. Anon. "T. S. Eliot Resting in Clinic." *NYT* (January 23), p. 30.

1956

2676. Davidson, Arthur. *The Eliot Enigma, a Critical Examination of The Waste Land*, 48 pp. London: Privately printed, 1956. He is considerably disturbed because Eliot does not write like Longfellow.

2677. Edwards, Oliver. "How to Enjoy." *Times* (London) (November 15), p. 13. [Frontiers of Criticism]. Chiefly appreciative summary of the essay.

1957

2678. Anon. "People Are Talking About . . ." *Vogue* 130 (September 15): 126. A photograph of Eliot.

2679. Davis, Clyde B. "We Are Not Going to the Dogs." *HB* 99 (January): 126. An attack, reprinted from *The Age of Indiscretion*, 1953.

2680. Webster, Margaret. "A Look at the London Season." *TAr* 41 (May): 23–24. [Family Reunion]. A note praising the production.

1958

2681. Anon. "Mr. Eliot's Most Human Play." *Times* (London) (August 26), p. 11. [Elder Statesman]. Praises the play for its "celebration of human love" but finds the characters of the young lovers "exercises in idealization."

2682. Levine, George. "*The Cocktail Party* and *Clara Hopgood*." *Grad* (Minneapolis) 1 (Winter): 4–11. Prefers Mark Rutherford's novel to Eliot's play because the former is more optimistic.

2683. Mathews, R. T. "The Journey of a Magus." *Wingover* 1 (Fall–Winter, 1958–1959): 32–33. I have not been able to find a copy of this publication.

2684. Prichett, V. S. "Our Mr. Eliot Grows Younger." *NYTM* (September 21), pp. 15 f. An interview with Eliot brought out a few interesting pieces of information and opinions.

1959

2685. Anon. On *Family Reunion*. *CathW* 188 (January): 331. A notice of the production at the Phoenix Theatre, concentrating on acting.

2686. ———. "T. S. Eliot Honored. Poet Given Medal by Academy of Arts and Sciences in Boston on October 21." *NYT* (October 22), p. 9.

2687. Braybrooke, Neville. "T. S. Eliot and Children." *DR* 39 (Spring): 43–49. Pleasant and superficial.

1960

2688. Anon. "Random Notes in Washington . . . Kennedy Quotes Eliot to Bolster Arguments." *NYT* (November 7), p. 16. Refers to Eliot's phrase "Their only monument the lost golf balls."

2689. ———. "T. S. Eliot Deplores Modern Verse Study." *NYT* (December 30), pp. 1, 9. Summary of "On Teaching the Appreciation of Poetry." Hillyer's, Williams's, and Auden's comments are quoted.

2690. Calta, Louis. "Students Offer 'The Family Reunion,' at Union Theological Seminary." *NYT* (December 10), p. 26. The play is "pretentious and unresolved."

1961

2691. Joshi, B. N. "Hopkins and T. S. Eliot—A Study in Linguistic Innovation." *OJES* (Hyderabad) , no. 1, pp. 13–16. Asserts that the language of these two poets is "highbrow."

2692. Madhusadan, Reddy V. "The Concept of Time in T. S. Eliot's *The Four Quartets.*" *OJES* (Hyderabad) , no. 1, pp. 31–38. A wandering essay on various concepts of time through the ages from Aristotle to Eliot.

AUTHOR INDEX

Numbers refer to items in the bibliography. Starred items are especially useful.

A., W. J., 49
Abel, Darrel, 1549
Acton, H. B., *1297
Adair, Patricia, *1298
Adams, F. P., 2339
Adams, J. Donald, 1962
Adams, John F., *2078
Adams, Robert M., 1624
Admur, Alice Steiner, 541
Adrian, Brother, 1299
Agate, James, 710, 2353
Aiken, Conrad, 1, 3, 11, *50, 90,
    151, 188, 389, 390, 484, 542,
    654, 1097, 1500, 2172
Aldington, Richard, *51, 52, *72,
    *121, 152, 248, 832, 1025
Ali, Ahmed, 867
Allen, Gay Wilson, 1550
Allen, Walter, 1895, 2012
Alvarez, A., *1775
Ames, Russell, 1501
Anand, Mulk Ray, 868
Anceschi, Luciano, 1098
Anderson, John, 2437
Andreach, Robert J., 2114, 2115
Angioletti, G. B., 1099
Anon., 1551
Anonymous listings
    Aberdeen Press, The, 2340
    Athenaeum, The, 16
    Baltimore Evening Sun, 2268
    Booklist, The, 21
    Bookman, The, 271
    Boston Evening Transcript,
        2438, 2464
    Boston Globe, The, 2633

Boston Herald, The, 2301,
    2302, 2460
Brooklyn Eagle, The, 2269,
    2303, 2439, 2545
Cambridge Daily News, 2370,
    2387
Catholic Times, 2388, 2389,
    2425
Catholic World, 2685
Chicago Sunday Tribune, The,
    2546
Christian Century, 2173
Christian Science Monitor,
    2304, 2354, 2547
Church Times (London), 2284,
    2355, 2389, 2390, 2391, 2392,
    2465, 2548, 2634, 2635
Common Sense, *22
Commonweal, The, 543, 900,
    2174
Contemporary Jewish Record,
    776
Cue, 2549, 2550
Daily Express (London), 2343
Dial, The, 73, 137
Dublin Magazine, The, 249
Edinburgh Evening News, 2270
Evening News (Glasgow), 2394
Evening News, The (London),
    2466
Everyman, 23, 272, 391
Glasgow Herald, The, 273,
    2272, 2371, 2395
Grantite Review, The, 2039
Harvard Alumni Bulletin, 1100
Harvard Class of 1910, 2426

Illustrated London News, 2647

Independent, The, 331

Inverness Courier, The, 2396, 2397

Irish Independent, 2372

Irish Times, The, 2398, 2399, 2636

Isis, 1201

Life, 122, 2506, 2527

Life and Letters, 392

Listener, The, 393, 711, 712

Literary Digest, The, 153

Literary World, The, 4

Little Review, The, 5

Liverpool Post, 2272

Living Age, The, 274

London Quarterly and Holborn Review, The, 2400

Manchester Guardian, The, 394, 713, 2401, 2477

Morning Post, The (London), 2273, 2285, 2373, 2402

Nation, The, 154, 777

Near East, The, 24

New English Weekly, The, 53, 714, 715

New Leader, The, 2403

New Republic, The, 138

New Statesman, The, also called *The New Statesman and Nation*, 6, 53, 123, 171, 901, 980, 2175

New York Post Literary Review, The, 2289, 2290, 2291, 2292

New York Globe, The, 2374

New York Herald-Tribune, The, 2351, 2375, 2376, 2377, 2486, 2487, 2551, 2552, 2553, 2637, 2427

New York Herald-Tribune Weekly Book Review, The, 2497

New York Sun, The, 2341

New York Times, The, 1626, 2205, 2206, 2378, 2379, 2440, 2513, 2514, 2528, 2554, 2555, 2556, 2557, 2558, 2559, 2560, 2561, 2562, 2563, 2564, 2565, 2566, 2567, 2638, 2639, 2640, 2641, 2642, 2648, 2649, 2656, 2657, 2658, 2659, 2660, 2675, 2686, 2688, 2689

New York Times Book Review, The, 25, 74, 1043

New Yorker, The, 655, 1438, 2176, 2568, 2569

News Chronicle (London), 2478

Newsweek, 545, 1300, 1627, 1744, 1774, 2177

Northern Echo, The, 2380

Oakland Tribune, 2274

Observer, The, 26, 2344

Oregonian, The, 2307

Outlook, The, 75

Oxford Times, 2404

Partisan Review, The, 1202

Philadelphia newspaper, a, 2275

Picture Post; Hulton's National Weekly (London), 716

Poetry Review, 485

Publishers' Weekly, 2178, 2514

Punch, 275

Record (Stockton, Cal.), 2571

Religious Book Bulletin, 778

Reynolds News (London), 2572

St. Louis Globe Democrat, The, 2342, 2381

St. Louis Review, 332, 333, 334

Saturday Review, The, 54, 276, 1203, 1502

Schoolmaster, The (London), 335

Scotsman, The, 336, 2286, 2356, 2405, 2460, 2515, 2529

Senior Scholastic, 2507, 2508

Sheffield Daily Telegraph, 2406

Southport Guardian, 2356

Spectator, The, 76

Springfield Republican, The, 2488

Sun, The (Sydney), 2407

Sun and New York Herald, The, 2276

Sunday Chronicle (London), 2277

Sunday Dispatch (London), 2573

Sunday Times (London), 395, 2293, 2574

Tablet, The, 396, 717

Theatre Arts Monthly, also called *Theatre Arts,* 397, 621, 1628, 2575

Theatre World (London), 2576

Theology, 398

Time, 91, 155, 546, 656, 657, 718, 719, 720, 779, 902, 903, 1044, 1101, 1102, 1204, 1205, 1206, 1301, 1302, *1303, 1304, 1305, 1306, 1307, 1308, 1422, 1439, 1503, 1629, 1773, 1814, 1815, *2119, *2179

Time and Tide, 1103

Times, The (Bombay), 2344

Times, The (London), 2293, 2294, 2408, 2428, 2467, 2479, 2517, 2530, 2577, 2578, 2681

Times Educational Supplement (London), 2518

Times Literary Supplement (London), 7, 17, 18, 27, 28, 29, 30, 55, 77, 78, 92, 115, 139, 156, 172, 173, 174, 175, 210, 217, 228, 250, 277, 337, 399, 400, 486, 547, 721, 722, 723, 724, 833, 834, 881, 1005, 1045, 1104, 1309, *1310, 1311, 1440, 1552, 1553, 1554, 1555, 1704, 2013, 2040, 2180, 2181, 2348, 2350, 2498

Times Weekly Edition, The (London), 2519

Vanity Fair, 93, 124

Variety, 2579

Virginia Quarterly Review, The, 2504

Vogue, 1046, 2580, 2661, 2678

Washington University Studies, 1556

Weekly Westminster Gazette, 56

Wellesley College News, 2509

Yale News, 2510

Yorkshire Post, The, 2409, 2480

Anthony, George, 725

Anthony, Mother Mary. *See* Weining

Ap Ivor, Dennis, 1816

Arden, Eugene, 1817, 1964

Arms, George W., 981, 1008, 1312

Arrowsmith, William, *1313, *1314, 1630, *1631, *1705

Arvin, Newton, 548

Atkinson, Brooks, *549, 658, *1315, 1557, 1632, 2441, 2468, 2581, 2612

Auden, W. H., 904, 1106, 1207, 2661

Austin, Allen C., 1896, 1897, 1965, 2041

Avery, Helen P., 2182

B., 278

B., C. E., 550

B., D. W., 189

B., T. F., 726

Bacon, Helen H., 1818

Bailey, Ruth, *727

Bain, Donald, 1316

Bain, Kenneth Bruce, 1597

Bain, Richard, 1504

Baker, Howard, 659

Baker, John Ross, 1745

Balakian, Nona, 1898

Baldridge, Marie, 1633

Bantock, G. H., 1208

Barber, C. L., *780, 1819

Barber, John, 258

Barker, George, 279, 338, 835, 1107

Barnes, Djuna, 1820

Barnes, Howard, 1317, 1318, 2442, 2443

Barnes, T. R., 487

Barnes, W. J., 2079

Barnhill, Viron Leonard, 1966

Barrett, William, *1209, *1319

Barry, Sister Mary Martin, 1108

Barry, Michael, 1821

Barth, J. Robert, 2042

Basler, Roy P., 925, 1009
Bates, Ernest S., 339
Bates, Ronald, 2117
Bateson, F. W., 1320, 1505, 1559, 1560, 1561, 1634, 1706
Battenhouse, Henry M., 2511
Battenhouse, Roy W., 982
Baum, Bernard, 1210
Baumgaertel, Gerhard, 1899
Baxter, Beverley, 2583
Bayley, John, 2520
Beach, Joseph Warren, 551, 1635
Beare, Robert L., 1562, *1776
Beaufort, John, 2663
Beaver, Joseph, 1563
Becker, May Lamberton, 905, 2382
Becker, William, 1636
Beevers, John, 401
Beharriell, Frederick J., 1822
Belgion, Montgomery, *157, 402, 403, 1109
Bell, Bernard Iddings, 552, 781
Bell, Clive, 57, 79, 94, 1110
Bellis, William Ward, 2118
Bellow, Saul, 1637
Benchley, Robert, 553
Benét, William Rose, 95, 211, 340, 404, 405, 906, 1211, 2584
Bennett, Arnold, 341
Bennett, Joan, 342
Bentley, Eric, 1638, 1639
Benziger, James, 1900
Bergsten, Steffan, 1901, *1967
Beringause, A. F., 1778
Berland, Alwyn, 1640
Bernardete, José A., 1212
Berryman, John, 1111, 1112
Betjeman, John, 1113, 1823
Bettany, F. G., 31, 32
Beyer, William Henry, 1321
Bickersteth, G. L., 983
Binsse, Harry A., 782
Birrell, Augustine, 58
Birrell, Francis, 176, 212, 406
Bishop, Virginia Curry, 783
Bixler, J. S., 784
Black, Ivan, 554
Blackman, M. C., 2585

Blackmur, R. P., *177, 213, 343, 407, *488, 622, 660, 785, 950, 1213, *1441, 1442, 1506, 1746, 2058
Blake, Howard, 489
Bland, D. S., 1322, 1564, 1968
Blanshard, Brand, *2183
Blau, Herbert, 1641
Blisset, William, 1010, 1114, *1565
Bloom, Harold, 1902
Blum, Margaret, 1779
Blum, Walter C., 116
Blyth, Ion. See Page, David
Boardman, Gwenn R., 2014, 2043
Bodelsen, C. A., 1566, 1642, 1643, *1824
Bodelsen, Merete, 1642
Bodgener, J. Henry, 984
Bodkin, Maud, 408, 728, 836
Bogan, Louise, 490, 661, 729, 907, 908, 1443
Boie, Mildred, 2444
Bolgan, Anne C., 1969
Bollier, Ernest Philip, *1780, *1825, 1903, 1904, 1970, *2080, *2081
Bose, Amalendu, 1115
Botkin, B. A., 623
Bottrall, Ronald, 1116
Boulton, J. T., 1747
Bovey, John A., 555
Bowers, John L., 2184
Bowra, C. M., 1214
Boyd, Ernest A., 125
Boynton, Grace M., *344
Brace, Marjorie, 1117
Bradbrook, M. C., *869, *870, *909, *1048, *1323
Bradbury, John M., *1444
Bradford, Curtis B., 951, 1215
Braithwaite, William Stanley, 2279
Branford, W. R. G., 1707
Braybrooke, Neville, 1826, 1827, 1828, 1905
Brégy, Katherine, 730
Breit, Harvey, 1118, 1216, 1324, 1644, 1708

Brenner Rica, *837
Brett, R. L., *1445, 1971
Brickell, Herschel, 409
Bridson, D. G., 345, 346, 410
Brien, Alan, 1829
Brightman, Edgar Sheffield, 786
Brinnin, J. M., 1456
Britten, Clarence, 2347
Broadbent, J. B., 1645
Brombert, Victor H., *1217, 1646
Bronowski, J., 178
Brooke, Nicholas, 1647
Brooks, Cleanth, 411, *556, *624,
    625, *662, 731, *1049, 1325,
    *1326, 2082
Brooks, Harold F., 1507
Brooks, Van Wyck, 838, 1508
Brophy, John, 491
Brotman, D. Bosley, 1119
Brown, Alec, 251
Brown, Calvin S., Jr., 663
Brown, E. K., 214, 664
Brown, Harry, 787
Brown, Ivor, 492, 732, 1050, 1327
Brown, John Mason, 1328, 1446,
    1648, 2445
Brown, Leonard S., 347
Brown, Robert M., 1781
Brown, Spencer, 1567, 1649
Brown, Stuart Gerry, 862
Brown, Wallace Cable, 493, 1051,
    1120
Browne, E. Martin, 1052, *1121,
    1782, 1830, 2185, 2350, 2586
Browne, Irene, 910
Buck, Philo M., Jr., *871
Buckley, Vincent, 1906
Bullaro, John Joseph, 2044
Bullett, Gerald, 280
Bullough, Geoffrey, 412, 2083,
    2410
Burdett, Osbert, 413
Burgum, E. B., 788
Burke, Kenneth, 215, 626, 1329
Burne, Glenn S., 1907
Burnet, W. Hodgson, 281
Burnham, Philip, 1330
Bush, Douglas, *627, 985, *1218
Butcher, Fanny, 2295, 2308, 2587

Butler, John F., 628
Buttle, Myra. See Purcell,
    V.W.W.S.
Butts, Mary, 494
Butz, Hazel Emma, 1650

C., A. Y., 158
C., F., 348, 557
C., J., 2446
Cajetan, Brother, 495
Caldwell, James Ralston, 282,
    1651
Calta, Louis, 2531, 2588, 2650,
    2690
Calverton, V. F., 414
Cameron, J. M., 1831
Campbell, Harry M., 952
Campbell, Roy, 179
Canby, Henry Seidel, 216
Cane, Melville, 733
Cantwell, Robert, 283
Carew, Rivers, 2045
Carey, Sister M. Cecelia, 2046
Cargill, Oscar, 839, 1784
Carnell, Corbin, 2084
Carne-Ross, Donald, 1331, *2186
Carroll, Joseph, 1568, 2447
Carruth, Hayden, 1219, 2187
Carter, Barbara B., 558
Carter, Paul J., Jr. 1569
Cassidy, Claudia, 2589
Catlin, George, 415, 1220
Causley, Charles, 1832
Cauthen, I. B., Jr., 1833
Cecchi, Emilio, 1122
Chakravarty, Amiya, *665
Chamberlain, John, 190
Chambers, E. K., 159
Chaning-Pearce, Melville, 911
Chapin, Katherine Garrison, 1053
Chapman, John, 2590, 2664
Charvat, William, 1339
Chase, Richard, 986, 1054
Chatterji, Nimai, 2188
Chaturvedi, B. N., 2085
Chesterton, G. K., 191
Chew, Samuel C., 284, 1123
Child, Ruth C., *1447
Childe, W. R., 2521

Childs, M. W., 217
Christian, Henry, 1972
Church, Margaret, 1973
Church, Ralph W., 666
Church, Richard, 840
Ciardi, John, 2190
Clancy, Joseph P., 1448
Clark, John Abbot, 667, 1221
Clayton, Robert L., 789
Cleophas, Sister Mary, 1055, 1222, 1332, 1908
Clover, Samuel T., 2279
Clowder, Felix, 1974
Clubb, Merrell D., Jr., *2015
Clurman, Harold, 1333, 1652
Clutton-Brock, Alan, 1449
Clutton-Brock, Arthur, 80
Coats, R. H., *1011
Coffman, Stanley K., 1450
Coghill, Nevill, 1124
Cohen, S. Marshall, *1334
Colby, Ethel, 2591
Colby, Reginald, 1223
Colby, Robert A., 1653, 1785
Colby, Vineta, 1723
Coleman, Robert, 2592, 2665
Collier, K. G., 912
Collin, W. E., 252, 253
Collins, Seward, 218, 219
Colton, Arthur, 192
Colum, Mary M., 559, 560, 790, 1509
Colum, Padriac, 33, 1834
Common, Jack, 416
Connolly, Cyril, 561, 734
Connolly, Francis X., 953
Conrad, Sherman, 735
Cook, Harold E., 1654
Cookman, A. V., 1335
Coomaraswamy, Ananda K., 1012
Cormican, L. A., 1336
Cornwell, Ethel F., 2047
Costello, Harry Todd, 2086
Cotten, Lyman A., 954, 1337
Coulon, H. J., 1510
Cowley, Malcolm, 417, 562, 791, 913, 1224, 1225
Coxe, Louis O., 841
Craig, David, 1975

Crawford, Ian, 1570
Crist, Judith, 2593
Cronin, Anthony, 1976
Cronin, Vincent, 1835
Cross, Gustav, 1909
Crowther, Bosley, 2646
Crutwell, Patrick, 1910
Culbert, Taylor, 1836
Cummings, E. E., 34
Cunliffe, J. W., 349
Cunningham, Gilbert F., 1571
Curtius, Ernst Robert, 1125
"Cyrano," 2448
Czamanake, Palmer, 1511

D., A., 1338
D., L. G., 736
D., T., 2411, 2412
Dahlberg, Edward, 1911, 2358
Daiches, David, 792, 1056, 1226, 1339
Dallas, Elizabeth, 2191
Damon, S. Foster, 496
Daniells, J. R., *350
Daniells, Roy, 563
Daniels, Earl, 842
Daniels, Edgar F., 1912
D'Apice, Anthony, *1013
Darlington, W. A., 737, 2481, 2492, 2532, 2533, 2651
Dasgupta, Rabindrakumar, 668
Dash, Thomas, 2522
Davidson, Arthur, 2676
Davie, Donald, 1748, 2058, 2087
Davies, Hugh Sykes, 351
Davies, Leila, 1057, 1058
Davis, Clyde B., 2679
Davis, Robert Gorham, 1227, 1228
Dawson, Christopher, *418, 1229
Dawson, N. P., 96, 2309, 2310
Dent, Alan, 2534, 2594
Day, Robert A., 2192
Day-Lewis, C., *419, 1451
DeLaura, David J., *2119, 2193
Deutsch, Babette, 12, 35, 59, 352, 497, 564, 565, 738, 739, 843, 914
DeVoto, Bernard, 844

Dey, Bishnu, 1126
Dickerson, Mary Jane, 2120
Digby, Kenelm, 60
Diggle, Margaret, *955
Dillon, George, 987
Dinwiddy, Hugh, 1837
Dobrée, Bonamy, *193, 285, 420,
    *1014, *1340, 1572, *1655,
    1913
Dobson, Charles A., 793
Dobson, E. J., 498
Dodd, Lee Wilson, 2296
Dodds, A. E., *566
Donald, Henry, 1573
Donnelly, Ian, 499
Donoghue, Dennis, 1914, *1915,
    1977, 2058, *2194
Dorris, George E., 2121
Douglas, Wallace, 1230
Downey, Harris, 567
Drew, Arnold P., 1656
Drew, Elizabeth, 353, 568, *794,
    *1231, 1574
Driver, Tom F., 2195
Drummond, John, 2595
Drury, John, 2311
Dudgeon, Patrick Orpen, 956
Duffey, Bernard, 1232
Duffus, Robert L., 2312
Dukes, Ashley, 569, 629, *669,
    670, 1127
Duncan, Joseph Ellis, *1916
Duncan-Jones, Elsie E., *1059
Dunkel, Wilbur Dwight, 1341,
    1452
Dunn, Ian S., 2088
Dupee, F. W., 988, 1128
Dur, Philip, *795
Durrell, Lawrence, 1129, 1512,
    *2196
Dutton, Geoffrey, 1342
Dwyer, Daniel N., 1343, 1453
Dye, F., 1978

E., B. I., 2413
E., J., 421
Eastman, Max, 220, 254
Eberhart, Richard, 671

Edman, Irwin, 1233, *1344, 1575,
    1576
Edmonds, Dorothy, 2122
Edwards, F. M., 500
Edwards, Oliver, 2677
Eliot, Henry Ware, Jr., 872
Eliot, T. G., 1359
Elliott, George R., 570
Ellmann, Richard, 2197
Elmen, Paul, 2198
Ely, Catherine B., 81
Emmart, A. D., 2499
Empson, William, *221, 1130,
    2058
Engle, Paul, 1577
English, Isobel, 1838
Enright, D. J., 1786
"Enterkin." See William Power
Eshelman, William R., 1015
Espey, John J., 1839
Evans, B. Ifor, 796, *1131
Evans, David W., 1657, 1658,
    1749, 1840
Every, Brother George, 422, 797,
    989, 1132

F., I., 501
F., L., 2512
F., P. J., 2415
Falck, Colin, 2048
Farber, Marjorie, 915
Fausset, Hugh I'Anson, 2383,
    2416
Fell, Kenneth, 1578
Fergusson, Francis, 160, 194, 423,
    *798, *1060, *1234, *1235,
    1454, 1659, *1750
Fern, Dale E., 1345
Fernandez, Ramon, *161
Ferry, David, 2199
Fiedler, Leslie, 1236
Field, Rowland, 2596, 2597
Fieling, Keith, 571
Findlater, Richard, 1579
Fish, Clifford J., 1346
Fitzell, Lincoln, 1455
Fitzgerald, Robert, 1660
Fleming, Edward Vandemere, 799
Fleming, Peter, 1347

Fleming, Rudd, 2016
Fletcher, John Gould, 630, 916
Flint, R. W., 1133, *1348
Fluchère, Henri, *1134
Ford, Ford Madox, 38
Forster, E. M., 195, 1237, 1349
Fortin, René E., 2089
Foster, Genevieve W., 990, 1016
Foster, Steven, 2200
"Four Winds," 1135
Fowler, D. C., 1580
Fowlie, Wallace, 991, 1136, 1787
Fox, Arthur W., 631
Fox, John J., 1350
Frank, Joseph, 1061, 2462
Frank, Waldo, 286
Frankenberg, Lloyd, *1238, 1351
Fraser, G. S., 1137, 1138, 1841
Freed, Louis, 2049
Freedman, Morris, 1513, 1751
Freeman, John, 126
Freimarck, Vincent, 1352
French, A. L., 2126
Friar, Kinon, 1456, 1514
Friend, Albert C., 287
Frohock, W. M., 1515
Frost, A. C., 196
Fry, Edith, 1139
Fry, Varian, 2346
Frye, Northrop, *2090
Funaroff, S., 672
Funato, Hideo, 1709
Funke, Lewis, 2598
Fussell, B. H., *1710
Fussell, Paul, Jr., 1353, 1711
Fyvel, T. R., 1354

G., H. C., 1355
G., J., 424
G., R. P. H., 2535
Gabriel, Gilbert W., 2449
"Gaffer Peeslake," 354
Gallup, Donald C., 800, *1062,
    *1516, 2463, 2482
Gannett, Lewis, 2580
Gardiner, Harold, 1355
Gardner, Helen Louise, *873,
    *1063, *1239, 1661, *1842,
    *2124

Gardner, W. H., 957
Garland, Robert, 2450, 2600
Garrett, John, 740
Garrison, W. E., 288, 917
Gary, Franklin, 222, 289
Gaskell, Ronald, 2050
Gassner, John W., 572, 1662, 2666
Gaye, Phoebe F., 741
Gegenheimer, Albert Frank,
    *1457
Geier, Norbert Joseph, 2125
"Gens," 874
George, Arapura Ghevarghese,
    2091
George, R. E. Gordon, 290
Gerard, Sister Mary, 1917
Gerstenberger, Donna L., 1918,
    1979, 2017, 2201
Giannone, Richard J., 1919
Gibbs, A. M., 2126
Gibbs, Wolcott, 1356, 1663
Gibson, William M., 2018, 2126
Gidlow, Elsa, 97
Gielgud, Val, 632
Gilbert, Katherine, *992
Gilkes, Martin, 633
Gillis, Everett A., *1980, 2019,
    2127
Gilmore, William, 573, 2451
Glazier, Lyle, 1357
Gleckner, Robert F., 1981
Glicksberg, Charles I., 1140, 1458,
    1712, 1713, 2523
Godolphin, F. R. B., 875
Gohdes, Clarence, 425
Goheen, Robert F., *1581
Goldie, Grace Wyndham, 673
Goldring, Douglas, 36
Goodman, Paul, *918
Gordon, George Stuart, 502
Gorman, H. S., 98
Gorman, William J., *223, 355
Grattan, C. Hartley, 224, 2359
Graves, Robert, 168, 1240, 1714,
    1843
Greenberg, Clement, 958, *1358,
    1582, 1583
Greene, David Mason, *2202
Greenheet, Morris, 2092

Greenleaf, T. E. *See* Eliot, T. G.,
Greenwood, Ormerod, 1360
Gregory, Horace, 255, 426, 574,
 742, *919, 1017, 1788, 2360
Grierson, Herbert J. C., 634, 959
Griffith, Clark, 2093
Grigsby, Gordon Kay, 1982
Grigson, Geoffrey, 1920, 2361,
 2417
Gross, Harvey Seymour, 1715,
 *1844, *1921
Gross, John, *2203
Gross, Seymour L., 1789
Grudin, Louis, 291
Guiness, Alec, 2601
Gupta, N. Das, 2204
Guttmann, Allen, 2205
Gwynn, Frederick L., 1584, 1585,
 1664, 1716

H., C. P., 801
H., I., 1241
H., J. J., 1064
H., J. M., 2332
H., R., 2418
H., W. H., 2419
Hacikyan, A., 2206
Hagstrum, J. H., *1065
Hailey, Foster, 2602
Haldeman-Julius, E., 1242, 1243,
 1244
Hall, Donald Andrew, 1459,
 *1922, 1979
Hall, Mordaunt, 2469
Hall, Theodore, 2452
Hall, Vernon, Jr., 1018
Halper, Nathan, 2207
Hamalian, Leo, 1361, 1717, 1983
Hamburger, Michael, 1141
Hamilton, Elizabeth, 1845
Hamilton, Fyfe, 1245
Hamilton, George Rostrevor,
 *1246, *1362
Hamilton, Iain, 1247
Hannay, A. H., 37
Hanzo, Thomas, 1984
Hardenbrook, Don, 1752
Harding, D. W., *356, *427,

*575, *743, *920, *1753,
 2058
Harding, Joan N., 1718
Harding, M. Esther, 503
Hardy, John Edward, 1790
Hare, John Crosland, 292
Harper, Allanah, 2493
Hart, Henry G., 2313
Hart, Jeffery P., 1791
Hartley, Anthony, 1665
Hartley, Marsden, 13
Harvey, C. J. D., *2208
Harvey, Versa R., 2021
Harvey-Jellie, W., 674
Hasegawa, Mitsuaki, 2020, 2094
Hassan, Ihab H., 1586
Hathaway, Richard D., 2095
Hathorn, Richmond Y., 2051
Haüsermann, H. W., *845, 876,
 *993
Hawkins, Ann, 576
Hawkins, Desmond, 357, 635,
 744, 745, 746, 1142
Hawkins, William, 2603, 2667
Hayakawa, S. Ichiye, 428
Haycraft, Howard, 2494
Hayes, Richard, 1666
Hayes, Walter, 2536
Hayward, John, 577, 994, 1066,
 2420, 2429
Haywood, A. Richard, 2334
Hazlitt, Henry, 293, 294
Headings, Philip Ray, 1923,
 *2128
Heard, Gerald, 225
Heath-Stubbs, John, 1143
Heilman, Robert B., *1587
Heimann, Heidi, 1363
Heller, Otto, 2314
Henderson, Philip, 747
Henn, T. R., 1460, 1754
Heppenstall, Rayner, 429
Hernigman, Bernard, 1144
Hertz, Karl, 1511
Hewes, Henry, 1588, 1589, 1846,
 1847, 2209
Hewitt, Elizabeth K., 2210
Heyl, Bernard C., 226
Heywood, Robert, 1364

Hicks, Granville, 358
Hidden, Norman, 2052
Higgins, Bertram, *256
Higgins, J., 636
Highet, Gilbert, 1248
Higinbotham, R. N., 921
Hillyer, Robert, 359, 1249, 1250, 1365
Hilton, Charles, 257
Hivnor, Mary, 1667
Hobson, Harold, 1366, 1367, 1368, 1369, 2537, 2604, 2605, 2606, 2607, 2633
Hockwald, Ilse E., 1668
Hodgson, R. A., 846
Hodin, J. P., 995
Hoellering, George, 1848
Hoffenstein, Samuel, 2315
Hoffman, Frederick J., 1251, 1719
Hogan, J. P., 877
Hoggart, Richard, 2643
Holbrook, David, 1720
Holden, Raymond, 922
Holder, Alan, 2129, 2211
Holland, Norman N., 2053
Holmes, John, 2453, 2483
Holmes, John Haynes, 578, 802
Holyrod, Stuart, *1721, 1792
Homann, Elizabeth R., 1924
Hood, Arthur, 140
Hook, Sidney, 996
Hope-Wallace, Philip, 1370
Horton, Philip, 637, *748
Hoskot, S. S., 2022
Hough, Graham Goulden, *1985
House, Humphrey, 360
Hovey, Richard P., 1925
Howard, Brian, 227
Howarth, Herbert, *1793, 1926, 1927, 1986, 2023, *2024, *2130
Howarth, R. G., 749
Howell, John Michael, 2131
Howes, A. B., 1517
Hueffer, Ford Madox. See Ford, Ford Madox
Hughes, Elinor, 2608
Hughes, Glenn, 258

Hughes, Josephine, 923
Humphries, Rolfe, 504, 579, 580, 878
Hutchins, Robert Maynard, *1371
Hutchison, Percy, 505
Hyman, Stanley Edgar, 1145, *1252, 2025, 2212
Hynes, Sam, 1669

"Ibee," 581
Iglesias, Antonio, 1372
Imberman, A. A., 2488
Inge, W. Motter, 1373
Inserillo, Charles R., 2054
Irvine, Lyn, 430
Isaacs, Edith J. R., 582
Isaacs, J., 1461
Iyengar, K. R. Srinivasa, *1846

Jack, Peter Monro, 361, 362, 506, 583, 584, 750, 960
Jackson, Elizabeth, 660
Jackson, James L., 1623
Jacobs, Arthur, 1849
James, Bruno S., 997
Jameson, Raymond de Loy, 259
Janoff, Ronald W., 2213
Jarrett-Kerr, Martin, 1850, 1928
Jay, Douglas, 260
Jayne, Sears, *1722
Jenkins, William D., 2055
Jennings, Humphrey, 507
Jennings, Paul, 1851
Jepson, Edgar, 14, 19
John, K., Mrs., 431
Johnson, Maurice, 1253
Jones, A. E., 1670
Jones, David Edwards, 1988
Jones, Genesius, *2132
Jones, Howard Mumford, 585, 803
Jones, P. Mansell, 2214
Joselyn, Sister M., 2133
Joseph, Brother F. S. C., 1794
Joshi, B. N., 2691
Julian, Constance, 1019
Jury, C. R., 295

Kahn, Sholom J., 1929
Kameyama, Masaka, 2056, 2215
Kaplan, Robert B., 1989, 2026
Karlin, Ken, 1590
Kaul, R. K., 2134
Kee, Howard C., 1518
Kelley, Bernard, 751
Keeley, Edmund, *1755
Kelly, Blanche May, 638
Kelly, Robert, 1519
Kemp, Lysander, 1254, 1374
Kenmare, Dallas, 639, 675
Kennedy, Maurice, 2644
Kennedy, Richard S., 2135
Kenner, Hugh, 1255, 1256, 1462,
    *1671, *1795, *1930, 1931,
    2057, 2058, 2138, 2216
Keown, Eric, 1375
Kermode, Frank, *1796, *1797,
    1932, 1947, 2096, 2217
Kerr, Walter F., 1756, 2668, 2669
Kilgallin, Anthony R., 2218
King, Alec, 998
Kingham, G. L., 2219
Kingsmill, Hugh, 363
Kinsman, Robert S., 1376
Kirby, J. P., 981, 1008
Kirk, Russell, 1591
Kirkup, James, 848, 924
Kirschbaum, Leo, 925
Kligerman, Jack, 2059
Kline, Peter, 1933
Knickerbocker, William S., *364
Knieger, Bernard, 2027
Knight, G. Wilson, *365
Knight, Grant C., 296
Knight, W. F. Jackson, 1853
Knights, L. C., 432, 1020
Knoll, Robert E., 2137
Knowlton, Edgar C., 752
Knox, George A., *1463
Knust, Herbert, 2060, 2220, 2221
Koch, Vivienne, 1257, 1377
Koppenhaver, Allen John, 2138
Korg, Jacob, 1990
Kornbluth, Martin L., 1934
Kramer, Hilton, 1378
Krause, Sydney, 1991
Kreymborg, Alfred, 127, 197

Krieger, Murray, 1757
Kronenberger, Louis, 508
Krutch, Joseph Wood, 366, 586,
    587, 1379
Kuna, F. M., 2097
Kunitz, Stanley J., 1635, 2494
Kuntz, Joseph M., 1312

L., N. A. M., 296
L., R. A., 2362
Laboulle, M. J. J., 588
Lal, P., 1380
Lambert, J. W., 1672
Lamson, Roy, 1230
Larrabee, Ankey, 926
Laski, Harold J., *961
Lasky, Melvin, 927
Lattimore, Richmond, 433
Laughlin, James, *509
Laurentia, Sister M., 1758
Lawlor, John, 1673
Lawrence, Seymour, 1381
Lawrence, T. E., 676
Laws, Frederick, 589
Lawson, Arthur, 2470
Lea, Richard, 999
Leavis, F. R., 198, 261, *298, 434,
    590, *879, 928, 929, 1067,
    *1258, 1464, 1465, 1520,
    1854, 2058, 2349, 2660
Lebowitz, Martin, 930
Lee, Joe Ho, 2098
Lees, F. N., 2139
Leggatt, Alison, 1855
Lehmann, John, 804, 1068, *1593,
    1674
Leighton, Lawrence, 228, 677
Lelièvre, F. J., 1856
Leo, Brother, 805, 806
Lerner, Max, 1259
Levi, Peter, 2222
Levine, George, 2682
Levy, William Turner, 1857, 2223
Levý, Jiří, 1521, 1935
Lewis, Arthur O., Jr., 1260
Lewis, Clive Staples, 753
Lewis, Tracy H., 2316
Lewis, Wyndham, 435, 640, 1147,
    2058

Liceaga, Elvira J., 880
Licht, Merete, 1936
Liddell, Robert, 1069, 1675
Lightfoot, Marjorie J., 2140, 2141
Lind, L. Robert, 678
Lindsay, Jack, 180
Linton, Calvin O., 2224
Lister, R. P., 2524
Livesay, Dorothy, 1858
Lobb, Kenneth Martyn, 1382
Locke, Frederick W., 2099
Lockridge, Richard, 2454
Loesch, Katherine, 1937
Loggins, Vernon, 641
Longstreet, Stephen, 2609
Lonkon, R., 1522
Lorch, Thomas M., 2142
Loring, M. L. S., 2430
Lowell, Amy, 82
Lowell, R. T. S., 679
Lucas, E. V., 99, 199, 2430
Lucy, Seán, 1992
Ludowyk, E. F. C., 1148
Lumley, Frederick, 1760
Lund, Mary Graham, 1993
Lyman, Dean B., Jr., 1761
Lynch, Father William, 1466, 1676
Lynd, Robert, 39, 2363, 2364, 2386

M., A., 436, 437, 438
M., H., 511
M., H. J., 83
Macaulay, Rose, 299, 1859
MacCallum, H. Reid, *1070, 1149
MacCarthy, Desmond, 61, 100, 181, 200, 367, 512, 754, 881, 1071
MacGregor-Hastie, Roy, 1938
MacLeish, Archibald, 680, 681, 1383
MacNiece, Louis, 513, 682, 755, *849, 1150
Madge, Charles, 683
Madhusadan, Reddy V., 2692
Magarey, Kevin, 2126
Magny, Claude E., 1151

Mairet, Philip, 514, 591, 1594, 1860
Major, John A., 1939
Major, Minor Wallace, 2028
Mangan, Sherry, 229
Mankowitz, Wolf, 1072
Manning, Hugo, 1861
Mantle, Burns, 2471
March, Richard, 1152, 1153
Margolis, Joseph, 1724
Marks, Emerson R., 2143, 2225
Marion, Sister Thomas, 2029
Marnau, Fred, 1021
Marsh, Florence, 1940
Marsh, T. N., 1798
Marshall, Margaret, 1384
Marshall, William H., *1523, 1941, 1942
Martin, Percival William, 1725
Martin, Philip Montague, 1799
Martinez Diaz (de Vivar), Dora, 882
Martz, Louis L., *1073, *1726
Marx, Carolyn, 2455, 2456
Marx, Leo, 2653
Mary, Mother Eleanor, *1800
Masirevich, Constance de, 1551
Mason, H. A., 515, 1022
Mason, William Heppell, *2061
Masters, Charlie, 850
Mathews, R. T., 2683
Mathewson, George, 2062
Matthews, T. S., 1677, 2226
Matthiessen, F. O., *516, 517, *684, 851, *931, *1074, 1385
Maugham, Somerset, 932
Maxwell, D. E. S., *1524, 1862
Maxwell, Ian R., 1075
Maxwell, J. C., 1386, 2100, 2144, 2145
Mayer, John Theodore, Jr., 2146
Maynard, Theodore, 2457, 2500
McAfee, Helen, 101
McAlmon, Robert, 62, 685
McCarthy, Harold E., *1525
McClaire, John, 2670
McClure, John [?], 102
McConnell, Daniel J., 2063

McCord, Bert, 2538
McCord, Howard, 2227
McElderry, B. R., Jr., 1801, 1802
McGill, Arthur C., *2147
McGreevy, Thomas, 262
McKenzie, Orgill, 230
McLaughlin, John J., *1387
McLuhan, Herbert Marshall, *962, 2228
Meagher, Margaret C., 518
Mégroz, Rodolphe Louis, 368
Melchiori, Giorgio, 1467, 1595, 1596, 1678, 1679, 1762, 2148
Mellers, W. H., 807
Mellers, Wilfrid, 1526
Merchant, W. M., 1727
Meredith, William, 1261
Merritt, James D., 2149
Mesterton, Eric, 933
Meter, W. J., 592
Meyer, Christine, 1262, 1468
Meyer, Karl, 2610
Meyerhoff, Hans, 1154
Miles, George, 1388
Miles, Josephine, *1469
Millar, Moorhouse F. X., 808
Millen, D. J., 1076
Miller, James E., Jr., 1863
Milne, A. A., 519, 520
Mims, Edwin, 1154
Minney, R. J., 2525
Mirsky, D. S., 162, 439
"Mr. Dangle," 2421
Mitchison, Naomi, 300
Mizener, Arthur, 592, 1803, 2058
Moakley, Gertrude, 1680
Møller, Kai Friis, 1943
Moloney, Michael F., 1023, 1024, 1077
Monro, Harold, 103
Monroe, Harriet, 104, 686
Montale, Eugenio, 1156
Monteiro, George, 1994
Montgomerie, William, 852
Moody, W. S., 2317
Moore, Dom Sebastian, *1025, 1078
Moore, Harry Thornton, 440, 809, *1263

Moore, Marianne, 15, 63, 263, *369, 594, 595, 1157
Moore, Merrill, 687
Moore, Nicholas, 1158
Moore, T. Sturge, 182
Moorman, Charles, 1597, 1864, 1995
Mordell, Albert, 2645
More, Paul Elmer, 301
Morgan, F. Bruce, 1598
Morgan, Frederick, 1389
Morgan, Louise, 141
Morgan, Roberta, *688
Morison, Samuel Eliot, 2229
Morley, Christopher, 2318
Morley, F. V., 1159
Morris, David, 1599
Morris, George L. K., 1681, 2058
Morris, Robert L., 1390
Morrissette, Bruce A., 1600
Morrison, Theodore, *689
Morrow, Betty, 642
Morrow, Felix, 231
Mortimer, Raymond, 128
Morton, A. L., *163
Mosley, Nicolas, 2671
Moult, Thomas, 64, 232
Mowat, John, 2150
Moynihan, William T., 2030
Mudrick, Marvin, 1865
Mueller, W. R., 1866
Muir, Edwin, 117, *129, 130, 164, 370, 441, 521, 596, *756, 934, *935, 1000, 1160, 2431
Muir, Kenneth, 1682
Munson, Gorham B., 118, 183, 201, 597, 2318
Munz, Peter, 1470
Murdoch, Iris, 1867
Murdock, James, 522
Murphy, Richard, 1391
Murry, J. Middleton, 40, 65, 66, 84, 106, *142, 165, *184, 202, 264, *1392, *1471, 1763
Musacchio, George L., 2151
Musgrove, Sydney, 1527, 1683, 2058
Musurillo, Herbert, 1764

Nagano, Yoshio, 1996
Narayana, K. S., 2101
Nathan, George Jean, 1393
Nathan, Norman, 1868
Nathan, Paul S., 1264
Naumberg, Carl T., 936
Nelson, Armour H., 1728
Nelson, C. E., 2102
Nemerov, Howard, 2103
Newbolt, Henry, 166
Newton, Frances J., 1869
Nicholas, Constance, 1729
Nicholls, Norah, 2365
Nichols, Robert, 41
Nicholson, Harold, 1870
Nicholson, Norman, 937, 1026, 1161
Nicoll, Allardyce, 442, 1265, 2432
Niebuhr, Reinhold, 810
Nimkar, B. R., 2230
Nimr, Amy, 265
Nims, John Frederick, 2104
Nitchie, George W., *2231
Noon, William T., 1684
Norton, Eliot, 2611
Nott, Kathleen, 1685
Nuhn, Ferner, 883

O'K., D., 757
O'Brien, Bernard, *963
O'Brien, R. D., 964
O'Casey, Sean, 443
O'Connell, Thomas G. V., 1394
O'Connor, William Van, 1079, 1162
Oden, Thomas C., 1997, 2232
O'Donnell, George M., 690
Oldham, J. H., *811, 812, 813
Oliphant, E. H. C., 523
Olivero, Federico, 233
Olson, Elder, 643
O'Malley, Francis J., 814
Ong, Walter J., 2064
Oras, Ants, 301
Ormsbee, Helen, 2612
Orsini, Gian N. G., 1686
Orwell, George, 884, *885, 1163
Osborn, E. B., 67
Osterling, Anders, 1164

Otake, Masaru, 598
Ould, Herman, 691
Oxenford, Mabel, 2495

Page, David, 1047
Palette, Drew B., 1730
Palmer, Herbert Edward, 371, 692
Palmer, Richard E., 2065
Palmer, Winthrop, 1266
Panter-Downes, Mollie, 2234, 2654, 2655
Pappe, H. O., 1395
Parkes, Henry Bamford, 303
Parkinson, Thomas, 1871
Parks, Edd Winfield, 1480
Parsons, Geoffrey, 2613
Parsons, I. M., 304, 305, 524
Partridge, A. C., 644
Passmore, John Arthur, 444
Paul, David, 1001, 1528
Paul, Elliot H., 2335
Paul, Leslie, 1877, *2234, 2235, 2686
Payne, Robert, 1529
Peacock, Ronald, *1027, 1601
Peake, Charles, 1998
Peel, Robert, 445, 446, 1396
Pellegrini, A., *1267
"Pendennis," 2297
Perkins, David, *2066
Peschmann, Hermann, 1002, 1028, 1268, 1269, 1397
Peter, John, 1270, *1398, 1530, 1602, 2058
Petersen, Sven, 2236
Pettus, Clyde, 2319
Phare, Elsie Elizabeth, *372
Phelan, Kappo, 1399
Phillips, Charles W., 693
Phillips, William, 373, 965
Pick, John, 1400
Pinto, Vivian de Sola, *1472
Pocock, D. F., 1401
Pollak, R., 2614
Pollock, Arthur, 2615, 2616, 2617
Pollock, Thomas Clark, 886
Poore, Charles, 2539, 2618, 2619, 2620, 2672
Pope, John C., 1003, 1080

Pope, Myrtle, 1165
Pope, W. Macqueen, 2621
Popkin, Henry, *1402, 1531
Porter, Alan, 2336
Porter, Katherine Anne, 2031, 2237
Porteus, Hugh Gordon, 306, 645, 1081, 1166
Pottle, Frederick A., 525, *758, *853
Pound, Ezra, *8, 9, *374, 447, 448, 449, 450, *451, *452, 815, *1403, 1804, 2058
Powell, Charles, 2320, 2338, 2366
Powell, Dilys, 266, 453, 887
Power, Sister Mary, *694
Power, William, 2414
Powers, Lyall H., 1765
Powys, Llewelyn, 375
Pratt, William C., Jr., 1805
Praz, Mario, 185, *646, 1167
Pressey, Benfield, 1959
Preston, Keith, 2287
Preston, Priscilla, 1944
Preston, Raymond, *1029, *1872
Priestley, J. B., 2367
Prince, Frank, 888
Pritchett, V. S., *1532, 2684
Prokosch, Frederic, 2472
Pryce-Jones, Alan, 307
Puhvel, Martin, 2238
Purcell, Victor William Williams Saunders, 1783
Putt, S. Gorley, 599

Quennell, Peter, 203, 308, 600
Quiller-Couch, Arthur T., 454
Quinn, Kerker, 601

R., C. R., 2280, 2422
R., R. E., 2484
R., G. R. B., 2384
Rago, Henry, *1271, 2230
Rahv, Philip, 309, 602, 1806
Raine, Kathleen, *889, 1168, 1272
Rajan, B., 1082, *1083
Raleigh, John H., 1731, 1945
Ramamrutham, J. V., 1999
Rambo, Dorothy Ellen, 1873

Ramsay, Warren, 1603, 2152
Randall, Dale B. J., 2153
Ransom, John Crowe, 107, *455, 603, 759, 854, *855, 938, *1533
Rao, K. S. Narayana, 2154
Rascoe, Burton, 234, 760, 2298, 2299, 2300, 2321, 2322, 2323, 2324, 2325, 2326
Ratner, Joseph, 816, 817
Rayan, Krishna, *2240
Read, Herbert, 68, 69, 1273, 1604, 1874, 1911, 1933
Reckford, Kenneth J., 2155
Reckitt, Maurice B., *761
Redman, Ben Ray, 1274, 1473, 1534
Reed, Henry, 1030, 1474, 1605
Rees, Garnet, 604
Rees, Goronwy, 1169
Rees, Richard, 526
Rees, T. R., 2067
Reeves, James, 1170
Rehak, Louise R., 2105
Reinsberg, Mark, 1275
Rexine, John E., 2241
Rezzano (de Martini), Maria Clotilde, 1004, 2496
Ribalow, Harold U., 1171
Rice, Philip Blair, 310, 647
Richards, I. A., *143, *144, 166, *235, 527, 966, 1634, 1687
Richards, Robert Fulton, 1732
Richman, Robert, 1535
Rickey, Mary Ellen, 2106
Rickman, H. P., 1946
Ricks, Christopher, 2242
Rickword, Edgell, 42, 131, 376, 377
Riding, Laura, 168
Ridler, Anne, *1084, 1172
Rillie, John A., *2068
Rillo, Lila C., 2501
Robbins, Rossell Hope, 1404, 1475, 1606
Roberts, Michael, 236, 311, 312, 456, 605, 762
Roberts, R. Ellis, 237, 2433
Robinson, D. E., 1607

Robinson, Kenneth J., 2540
Robson, W. W., 2069, 2243
Roby, Robert Curtis, 1405
Rodman, Selden, 1807
Rogers, Daniel John, 2156
Rogers, Robert E., 2472
Rosenberg, John, 1875
Rosenfeld, Paul, 939
Rosenthal, M. L., 1876
Ross, Hugh, 606
Ross, Malcolm MacKenzie, 1608
Rosten, Norman, 2628
Rothbard, Lorraine, 1526
Routh, H. V., 1031, 1085
Rowland, John, 890
Roy, Emil, 2244
Rubin, Levy, 2157
Rumble, Thomas, 2000
Russell, Francis, 2245
Russell, Peter, 1276
Ryan, Lawrence V., *1885, *1886

de S., A., 43
S., B., 2385
S., E., 70
S., H., 2434
Sackville-West, V., 2368
"Sagittarius," 1406
Salmon, Christopher V., 457, 1877
Sampson, Ashley, 458
Sampson, George, 2281
Sansom, Clive, *1086
Sastri, P. S., 1609
Saunders, J. W., 1688
Savage, D. S., *967
Sayers, Michael, 459, 607
Scarfe, Francis, 528, 891, 2505
Schaar, Claes, 1947
Schanzer, Ernest, 1733
Schappes, Morris U., 378
Schenk, W., 1087
Schoeck, R. J., 1173
Schriftgiesser, Karl, 2368
Schwalb, Harry M., 1610
Schwartz, Delmore, *763, 764,
    940, 1005, 1277, 1689, 1734
Schwartz, Edward, 1611
Schwartz, Jacob, 2352
Scott, Edmund, 2505

Scott, Nathan A., Jr., 1477, *1536
Scott-James, R. A., 314
Scrimgeour, C. A., 2107
Seferis, George, 1174, *2158
Seif, Morton, 1690
Seldes, Gilbert, 85, 186, 238, 1407
Sélincourt, Basil de, 379, 460
Sen, Mihar-Kumar, 1808
Sena, 2246
Sengupta, S. K., 461
Senior, John, 1948
Sergeant, Howard, 1478
Severs, Kenneth, 1175
Sewell, Elizabeth, 1878, 2058
Sewell, J. E., 2423
Seymour-Smith, Martin, 2247,
    2248
Shaeffer, Louis, 2623, 2624
Shahani, Ranjee G., 1032, 1278
Shain, Charles Edward, 818
Shanahan, C. M., 1735
Shand, John, *969
Shanks, Edward, 187, 2327
Shapiro, Karl, 1006, 2001, 2070
Shapiro, Leo, 819
Shaw, Sam, 2159
Shawe-Taylor, Desmond, 1279,
    2654
Sherek, Henry, 1408
Sherrill, Henry Knox, 2473
Shewring, Walter, 892
Shillito, Edward, 462, 529
Short, John, 463
Shulenberger, Arvid, 1537
Shuman, R. Baird, 1809, 1949
Shuster, George N., 315
Sickels, Eleanor M., 1176, 1228
Siegel, Eli, 380, 1736
Simister, O. E., 2002
Simon, Brian, 1280
Simon, Irene, 1612
Simons, Jack W., 1613, 1950
Sinclair, May, 10
Sinha, Krishna Nandan, 2003,
    2071, 2108
Siringo, Albert C., 2625
Sisson, C. H., 1177
Sitwell, Edith, *464, 696, 941,
    1178, 1479

Sitwell, Osbert, 316, *1179
Skinner, A. E., 1879
Sloper, L. A., 2474
Smidt, Kristian, *1281, 1951, 2249
Smith, Arthur J. M., 1410
Smith, Bernard, 765
Smith, Carol Hertzig, 2072, *2109
Smith, Chard Powers, 1411
Smith, Francis J., 1033, *1180
Smith, Gerald, 2073
Smith, Grover, 1181, 1282, 1283,
    *1412, 1413, 1414, *1538,
    1691, *1766, *2004, 2005
Smith, H. Jeffrey, 608
Smith, Hallett, 1230
Smith, Harrison, 1539
Smith, J. C., 959
Smith, James Harry, 1480
Smith, Janet Adam, 2250
Smith, Logan Pearsall, 820
Smith, N. A., 530
Smith, R. Gregor, 1088, 1481
Smith, Ray, 1415
Smith, Stevie, 1870
Smyth, Charles, 766
Snell, Reginald, *970
Sochatoff, A. Fred, 1737
Southworth, James G., 821
Spanos, William V., 2110, *2251
Spark, Muriel, 1284
Sparrow, John, 465
Speaight, Robert, 856, 893, 1007,
    1089, 1182, *1285, 1416, 1881,
    1882, 2111
Spector, Robert Donald, 1810
Spelvin, George, 1692
Spencer, Theodore, *381, *697,
    *822
Spender, Stephen, 382, 466, *531,
    767, 823, 857, 858, 942, *1035
    *1036, *1183, *1417, *1418,
    1482, 1483, 1484, 1614, *2252
    2253
Spiller, Robert E., 1184
Spratt, P., 2006
Squire, J. C., 108, 145
Stallings, Laurence, 2328
Stamm, Rudolf, 1286

Stanford, Derek, 1185, 1883, 1952,
    2254
Stanford, Donald L., 1808
Starr, H. W., 1697, 1717
Stauffer, Donald A., 1037, 1287
Stead, C. K., *2160, *2161
Steadman, John M., 1884
Stein, Arnold, *1615
Stein, Gertrude, 145
Stein, Sol, 1485
Stein, Walter, *1616
Steinmann, Martin, Jr., 1767
Stelzman, Rainulf A., 2032
Stepanchev, Stephen, 1486
Stephenson, Ethel, 859, 894, 895,
    971
Stephenson, George R., 1419
Stern, John, 1288
Stevens, Wallace, 698
Stevenson, David L., 1693
Stevenson, J. W., 2541
Stickey, William J., 2033
Stinton, T. C. W., 1617
Stone, Geoffrey, 467, 532, 648
Stonier, George W., 317, 699, 824,
    825
Storman, E. J., *972
Strachan, Pearl, 2502
Strachey, John, 383
Strandberg, Victor, 1953
Stravinsky, Igor, 2255
Stroble, Marion, 44
Strong, L. A. G., 468
Strong, Robert, 384, 2424
Strothman, Friederich W., *1885,
    *1980
Stuart, Duane R., 1420
Stuart-Young, J. M., 147
Sugiyama, Yoko, 2034
Sullivan, A. M., 768
Sunne, Richard, 318, 469
Sweeney, Francis, 2256
Sweeney, James Johnson, *860,
    *943
Sweeney, John L., *794
Swinnerton, Frank A., 470
Symes, Gordon, 1487
Symons, Julian, 769
Sypher, Wylie, 973

T., E. R., 319
T., H., 2282
T., K. S., 471
T., M., 896, 1038
T., W. S., 2283
Talley, Jerry B., 2162
Tambimuttu, 1153, 1186
Tate, Allen, 86, 109, 148, *267, 268, 320, 603, 609, 700, 701, 861, 974, 1694, 2058
Taubman, Howard, 2626
Taupin, René, *321
Taylor, Walter F., 610
"Tellalot, T. S.," 132
Terrell, Carroll Franklin, 1954
Theall, Donald F., 1488
"Thespis," 1955
Thomas, R. Hinton, 1489
Thomas, Wright, 862
Thompson, David W., 1421
Thompson, Eric, 1540, 2112
Thompson, Francis J., 1490
Thompson, Netta, 2333
Thompson, Ralph, 2485, 2490
Thompson, T. H., 472
Thorlby, Anthony, 1541
Thorp, Willard, *1090
Thurber, James, 1422
Tilghman, Tench, 2435
Tillyard, E. M. W., 473, 474, 702, 1618
Tinckom-Fernandez, E. G., 703
Tindall, William York, 1091, 1092
Tinsley, E. J., *1491
Todd, Ruthven, 1187
Tomlin, E. W. F., 533
Toms, Newby, 2163
Toynbee, Philip, 1188
Travers, Pamela, 2471
Traversi, Derek, *1189
Treece, Henry, 1039
Trewin, John Courtney, 1619, 2542, 2627, 2628
Trilling, Lionel, *826, 944, 1423
Troy, William, 475
Trueblood, D. Elton, 649
Tschumi, Raymond, 1492
Turnell, G. Martin, 476, 611, 771
Turner, E. S., 1190

Turner, Luke, 945
Turner, W. Arthur, 1739
Tuve, Rosemond, 1093
Twitchett, E. G., 239

Unger, Leonard, *772, *897, *1191, *1424, *1768, *2035, *2257, 2258
Untermeyer, Louis, 45, 110, 111, 612, *898, 946
Utley, Francis L., *975

Van der Vat, D. G., 704
Van de Water, F., 2329
Van Doorn, Willem, 87, 149
Van Doren, Mark, 46, 71, 119, 204, 322, 385, 534, 613, 773
Van Raalte, George, 535
Van Vechten, Carl, 1740
Vann, Gerald, 827
Varley, Lee, 2503
Vassilieff, Elizabeth, 1425, 1542
Vergmann, Finn, 1956
Vernon, Grenville, 614, 705
Verschoyle, Derek, 477, 774
Vickery, John Britton, 1741, 1811, *1886, 2007
Vincent, C. J., 1426
Vines, Sherard, 169, 205
Vinograd, Sherna S., 1289
Virginia, Sister Marie, 1887
Virtue, John, 1695
Vivas, Eliseo, 976
Voaden, Herman Arthur, 1957
Voight, F. A., 863
Voight, Gilbert P., 615

W., C. H., 478
W., D., 536
W., L. [Leonard Woolf?], 47
Waggoner, Hyatt Howe, *947, *1427
Wagner, Robert D., 1493, *1696
Wain, John, 1888, *2259, 2260
Walcutt, Charles Child, 977, 1192, 1812
Waldorf, Wilella, 2548
Walker, Kenneth, 2526
Wall, Bernard, 1040, 2436

Wall, Richard J., 2009
Waller, John, 2491
Walmsley, D. M., 2008
Walton, Eda Lou, 240, 241, 386, 706
Wanning, Andrews, 864
Ward, Anne, *1290
Warren, Austin, 2164
Warren, C. Henry, 133
Warren, Robert Penn, 625, *662, 707
Wasser, Henry, 2009
Wasserstrom, William, 2074
"Watchman," 775
Waterman, Arthur E., 1958
Waters, Leonard Adrian, 1094
Watkins, Floyd C., 2165
Watkins, Vernon, 1193, 1889
Watson, C. B., *2166
Watson, Ernest Bradlee, 1959
Watson, George, 2261
Watson-Williams, Helen, 1742
Watts, Harold H., 1041
Watts, Richard, Jr., 2459, 2475, 2629, 2674
Waugh, Arthur, 2
Weatherhead, A. Kingsley, 2075, 2262
Weathers, Willie T., 1494
Weaver, John V. A., 2330
Weaver, Raymond M., 48
Weaver, Richard M., 1291
Weber, Brom, 1194
Webster, Clifford J., 2476
Webster, H. T., 1697
Webster, Margaret, 2680
Wecter, Dixon, 479
Wedgwood, C. V., 1195
Weedon, William S., 1698
Weigand, Elsie, 1743
Weightman, J. G., 1620, 1890
Weining, Mother Mary Anthony, 1776, 1963, 1982
Weinstein, Jacob J., 828
Weiss, T., 978, 1042
Weisstein, Ulrich, 1543, 1960
Weitz, Morris, *1428, 1544
Wellek, René, *1769
Wells, Charles, 2288

Wells, H. G., 242
Wells, Henry W., 829, 948
West, Alick, 650
West, Ray B., Jr., 1621
West, Rebecca, 243, 244, 323, 324, 537, 538, 539, 540
West, William Channing, 2167
Wheelwright, Philip, *387, *1095, *1699, *1899
Whicher, George F., 1495, 1496
White, John Manchip, 1429
White, Robert, 2036
Whitfield, J. H., 1891, 2010
Whiting, Charles E., 2630
Whittemore, Reed, 2263
Wilbur, Robert Henry Hunter, 2168
Wilder, Amos N., 830
Wilkinson, Burke, 1700
Williams, Charles, *949
Williams, Charles Walter S., 245
Williams, Orlo, 120
Williams, Philip Eugene, 2264
Williams, Raymond, *1497, 1545, 1701, 1702, *1770, *2113
Williams, Stephen, 2631
Williams, William Carlos, 20, 708, 979, *1430
Williamson, Audrey, 1498, 1771
Williamson, George, *170, *206, 1292, 1293, 1431, 1432, 1622, *2265
Williamson, Hugh Ross, 269, *325, 326, 327, 328, 329, 480
Williamson, Mervyn Wilton, 1892, *1961
Wills, John Howard, 1703
Wilson, Cecil, 2543
Wilson, Edmund, *88, *89, 134, 135, 150, 207, 208, 209, 246, *270, 651, 1096, 1893
Wilson, Francis A. C. C., *1196
Wilson, James Southall, 481
Wilson, Richard, 2266
Wimsatt, W. K., Jr., *1433, 1546
Winkler, R. O. C., 865
Winston, George P., 2076
Winter, Jack, 2037
Winters, Yvor, 652, 866

Wohlstetter, Albert, *688
Wolfe, Humbert, 112
Wolfe, Thomas, 653
Wolff, Charlotte, 616
Wolheim, Richard, 2169
Wood, Clement, 113, 2331
Wood, Frank, 1547
Wood, Frederick T., 2369
Woodward, Daniel H., 2077, *2170
Wool, Sandra, 1434
Woolf, Leonard, *136
Wooton, Carl, 2038
Wormhoudt, Arthur, 1294
Worsley, T. C., 1435, 1548, 1623, 1894
Worthington, Janet, *1295
Wrenn, C. L., 1813
Wright, George Thaddeus, 2011
Wright, Keith, 2267

Wyatt, Euphemia, 617, 1436
Wylie, Elinor, *114
Wyndham, S. J., 1197
Wynn, Dudley, 1437

Yarros, Victor S., 1198, 1199
Yeats, W. B., 618
Yerbury, Grace D., 2171
Yokelson, Joseph B., 1781
Yoklavich, John M., 1499
Young, Charlotte, 1296
Young, Philip, 1772
Young, Stark, 619, 709

"Z," 2337
Zabel, Morton, 247, 330, 388, 482, 483, 620, 831, 1200
Zaturenska, Marya, 1017
Zolotow, Maurice, 2632
Zolotow, Sam, 2544

INDEX TO PERIODICALS

Numbers refer to items in the bibliography. The only newspapers included in this list are the *New York Times Book Review* and the *Times Literary Supplement*. The starred items are especially useful.

Accent, 854, 926, 991, 1034, 1289, 1361, 1434, 1488, 1658

Adam, 1138, 1296

Adelphi, 106, *142, 264, 279, 311, 338, 416, 429, 440, 526, 728, 877, 999, 1028, 1269

Agonia, 956

America, a Catholic Review of the Week, 730, 768, 923, 1024, *1180, 1376, 1394, 2256

American Bookman, 960

American Freeman, 1199, 1242, 1243, 1244

American Literature, *947, 1003, 1080, 1275, *1290, *1295, 1413, 1431, 1691, 1758, 1839, 2018, 2064, 2165

American Mercury, 1365, 1393

American Neptune, 2229

American Notes and Queries, 2095

American Prefaces, 555, 850

American Quarterly, 1421, 1801, 2023, 2101, 2154, 2205

American Review, 532, 570, *625, 648

American Scholar, 606, 739, 988, 1054, 1092, 1228, 2025, 2653

Anglia, 1935, 2210

Anglo-Welsh Review, 2002

Antioch Review, 2070

Arion, *2186

Arizona Quarterly, 1140, *1191, *1457, 1485, 1730, *1886, 2038, 2059, 2127, 2523

Arts Gazette, 31, 32

Asiatic Review, 1032

Athenaeum, 16, 37, 40, 48

Atlantic Monthly, 101, 164, 167, *381, *2196, 2524

Baker Street Journal, 1697, 1752, 2055

Ball State Teachers College Forum, 2122

Bard Review, 1144

Blackfriars, 436, 437, 438, 751, 827, 945, 997

Book Collector, 2008

Booklist, 21

Bookman [American], 48, 183, 218, 219, 244, 271, 290

Bookman [English], 58, 133, 232, 237, 261, 269, 326, 327, 328, 329, 480, 2365

Books Abroad, 2241

Boston University Studies in English, 1802, 2009

Britain Today, 887, *935, *994, 1020, 1272

British Annual of Literature, 1147

British Journal of Aesthetics, *2240

British Weekly, a Journal of Social and Christian Progress, 775

Bucknell Review, 1654, 1900, 1907, 2076

Bulletin of the John Rylands Library, 1601

Bulletin of the New York Public Library, 1601

Calcutta Review, 461, 668
Calendar of Modern Letters, 130, 131
Call Magazine, 113
Cambridge Journal, *1298, 1322, 1541
Cambridge Review, 178, 196, 198, 342, 528
Canadian Author and Bookman, 2218
Canadian Fiction, 2228
Canadian Forum, 214, 563, 1114, 1858
Canisian, *963
Catholic Review, *1013
Catholic World, 495, 518, 558, 617, 638, 1905, 2500, 2616, 2685
C E A Critic, 2028
Centaur, 1021
Centennial Review of Arts and Sciences, *1921, 2092
Chapbook, a Monthly Miscellany, The, 36, 103
Cherwell, 471
Chicago Review, 1041, 1590
Chimera, 875, *1899
Christendom, 649, 784, 982
Christian Century, 288, 462, 529, 917, 2173, 2198
Christian News Letter, *811, 812, 813
Christian Scholar, 1857, 2163
Christianity and Crisis, 2195
Christianity Today, 2224
Chrysalis, 1498
Cithara, 2213
Classical Journal, 2227
Classical Philology, 1764, 1856
Collected Essays, Kyoritsu Women's Junior College, 2056, 2215
College English, 1056, *1447, 1577, 1580, 1670, 1789, 1812, 1934, 2041
Colorado Quarterly, 1569, 1970

Colosseum, a Quarterly Review, 476
Columbia, 806
Commentary, 1582, 1583, 1649, 1854
Commonweal, 315, 388, 467, 543, 614, 667, 693, 705, 782, 900, *1271, 1330, 1350, 1388, 1399, 1613, 1666, 1669, 1788, 1950, 2174
Communist Review, 1280
Common Sense, *22, 810
Comparative Literature, *1587, 1600, *1755, *1793, 1908, *1927, 1945, 2034, 2191, 2155, 2221
Congress Weekly, 1171
Contact, 62
Contemporary Issues, 1197
Contemporary Jewish Record, 776
Contemporary Review, 1522, 1718, 1826, 1883
Cresset, 1511
Criterion, 146, 165, 607
Critical Quarterly, 1975, *2505, 2653
Criticism, 1963, 1979, 2225
Cross Currents, 2232
Crossroads, 1598
Cue, 2549, 2550
Current Literature, 2391

Dalhousie Review, 674, 2687
Dartmouth Quarterly, *1334
Decachord, *163
Dial, 3, 11, 34, 59, 63, 73, *88, 116, 135, 137, 151, 186, 188
Diameter, 1477
Direction, 1542
Dissertation Abstracts, 1586, 1641, 1650, 1717, 1776, 1805, 1873, 1892, 1896, 1904, 1918, 1923, 1954, 1966, 1982, 2044, 2060, 2062, 2072, 2114, 2118, 2125, 2131, 2138, 2140, 2146, 2156, 2159, 2162, 2167, 2168, 2211, 2264
Double Dealer, 102
Downside Review, 1078

Drama, 1416, 2185
Drama Survey, 2110, *2251
Dublin Magazine, 249, 371
Dublin Review, 402, 403, 888, 892, 949, 1007, *1189
Durham University Journal, 1174, 1647

East West Review, 2164
Échanges, 265
Educational Theatre Journal, 2182
Egoist, 9
Eigo to Kyoiku or English and Education, 2020
Empire Review, 181
Encounter, 1920, 1997, 2197, *2203, 2252, *2259
English, 1002, 1362, 1445, 1742, 1747, 1955, 2052, 2134, 2189
English "A" Analyst, 1065
English Journal, 257, 442, *2004
English Language Notes, 2121, 2238, 2262
English Literary History, *1463, *1710, 1711
English Miscellany, 1595, 1678, 1798, 1891, 2010
English Review, 14, 38, 64, 363
English Speaking World, 740, 1482
English Studies, 87, 149, 185, 704, *845, 1286, 1467, 1566, 1578, 1606, 1612, 1642, 1643, 1679, 1728, 2100, 2151
English Studies in Africa, 1928
Esquire, 2255
Essays in Criticism, *1471, *1497, 1505, 1521, 1530, 1540, 1559, 1560, 1561, 1571, 1574, 1592, 1596, 1616, 1617, 1618, 1634, 1640, 1645, 1651, 1675, 1687, 1688, 1702, 1706, 1714, 1720, 1733, 1770, 1940, 2050, 2097, 2107
Ethics, *1297
Études Anglaises, *2166
Études de Lettres, 876
European, 2671
Everyman, 23, 272, 391, 478

Experimental Drama, 2083
Explicator, 925, *962, *975, 977, 981, 1008, 1015, 1018, 1165, 1176, 1192, 1222, 1254, 1260, 1262, 1282, 1337, 1343, 1346, 1352, 1357, 1374, 1376, 1409, 1415, 1453, 1494, 1537, 1563, 1695, 1703, 1745, 1765, 1781, 1836, 1912, 1924, 1941, 1949, 1953, 1958, 1973, 1978, 1987, 1989, 1994, 2026, 2033, 2036, 2073, 2088, 2089, 2093, 2149, 2220

Fantasy, 309
Fireside, 1019
Fortnightly Review, 317, *1392, 1487
Forum, 96, 191, 294, 559, 560, 790
Freeman, 45, *50, 110, 2332
Fresco, 1794
Friend, 463
Friends Intelligencer, 1518
Fugative, 86
Furioso, 1079

Georgia Review, 1926
German Life and Letters, 1946
Germanic Review, 1547, 1562, 1668, 1743
Graduate Student of English, 2682
Granta, 278, 420, 557
Grantite Review, 2039
Greyfriar, 2029, 2236
Griffin, 1558

Harper's Bazaar, 1351
Harper's Magazine, 844
Harvard Advocate, 132, 636, 654, 659, 660, 666, 671, 677, 679, 680, *684, 687, *688, 690, 695, *697, 698, 701, 703, 707, 708
Harvard Alumni Bulletin, 1100, 1459, 1325
Harvard Progressive, *795
Here and Now, *1070
Hibbert Journal, *1011, 1470, 2045

Hiroshima Studies in Language and Literature, 2094
History of Ideas Newsletter, 1810
Hopkins Review, 1490
Horizon, 823, 857, 884, 995, *1035, 2245
Hound and Horn, *177, 194, 228, *267, 407, 423, 2346
House Beautiful, 1782
Hudson Review, *1191, *1231, *1234, *1252, 1255, 1256, 1261, 1273, *1313, *1314, 1389, *1631, 1636, 1865
Humanitas [Brescia], 1020
Humanitas [Manchester], 1087
Humanities [Yokohama], 1517

Illustrated London News, 67, 550, 2542, 2628, 2647
Independent, 331
Indian Journal of English Studies, 2003
Inlander, *223
International Literary Annual, 1852
Iowa English Yearbook, 2021
Isis, 297, 424, 1201

Jewish Frontier, 828
John O'London's Weekly, 1245, 1278, 2364
Journal of Aesthetics and Art Criticism, 1693, 1871, 1990
Journal of Arts and Letters, 1299
Journal of the Australasian Universities Language and Literature Association, 2160
Journal of Bible and Religion, 786
Journal of English and Germanic Philology, 433, 1585

Kano Studies, 2266
Kansas Magazine, 1772
Kenyon Review, *748, *763, 785, 841, 886, 930, *931, 938, 986, *1060, *1209, *1402, 1423, 1442, 1506, 1624, 1667, *1753, *1796, 1933, *2334

Landfall, a New Zealand Quarterly, 1395
Les Langues Modernes, 2260
Library Chronicle of the University of Texas, 1879
Life, 122, 1677, 2172, 2506, 2527
Life and Letters, 195, 199, 203, 266, 392, 742, 852, 868, 941, *993
Life and Letters and the London Mercury and Bookman, 1012
Life of the Spirit, *1491
Listener, The, 285, 313, 351, 393, 418, 512, 673, 711, 712, 767, 1237, 1349, 1474, 1605, 1674, 1877, 1882, 1944, 2250
Literary Criterion, 1808, 2071, 2246
Literary Digest, 153
Literary Digest International Book Review, 98
Literary Half-Yearly, 1999, 2006
Literary Review, 1380
Literary World, 4
Literature and Psychology, 1925, 2007, 2053
Little Review, 5, 10, 13, 19, 20
Living Age, *143, 274
Living Church, 552, 789, 1345
London Aphrodite, 276
London Magazine, 1888
London Mercury, 70, 108, 126, 145, 162, 239, 307, 413, 472, 521, 605, 762
London Quarterly and Holborn Review, 384, 628, 984, 2400
Louisiana State University Studies, Studies in American Literature, 2000
Lutheran Church Quarterly, 615

Mademoiselle, 2226
Massachusetts Review, *2231, 2258
McMaster University Quarterly, 2476
Meanjin, *972, 998, *1036, 1342, 1425, 1683
Measure, *1371

Menorah Journal, 843
Milton Bulletin, 818, *963
Missionary, 805
Mississippi Quarterly, 2120
Modern Age, 2157, *2265
Modern Drama, 1984, 2027, 2065, *2078, 2084, 2141, 2244
Modern Fiction Studies, 2014, 2201
Modern Language Notes, *566, 1173, 1253, 1353, 1390, 1414, 1468, 1486, 1564, 1584, 1664, 1716, 1729, 1749, 1761, 1767, 1779, 1809, 1833, 1939, 1968, 1981, 2017, 2099
Modern Language Quarterly, 2037, *2066, 2193
Modern Language Review, 1944
Modern Monthly, 335, 378, 414
Modern Philology, 1432, 1735
Modern Quarterly, 1489
Modern Review, 1609, 2230
Monologue, 430
Month, 1229, 1386, 1591, 2111, 2222
Musical Quarterly, 1526

Nation [American], 46, 71, 85, 119, *129, 154, 204, 241, 293, 366, 475, 508, 534, 586, 587, 595, 613, 764, 777, 940, 944, 996, 1128, *1191, 1213, 1236, *1358, 1384, 1652, 1784, 1876, 2096, 2207
Nation [English], 39
Nation and Athenaeum, 66, 83, 94, 117, *136, 152, 176, 205, 212
National Review, 983, 2138, 2216, 2520
Near East, 24
Neophilogus, 1998
Die Neuren Sprachen, 1727
New Adelphi, *184, 202, 230
New Age, 49, 68, 69
New-Church Magazine, 890
New Democrat, 1155
New England Quarterly, 359, *689

New English Weekly, 345, 346, 410, 420, 447, 448, 449, 450, *451, *452, 459, *509, 514, 544, 591, 635, 645, 714, 715, 746, *761, 770, 846, 874, 912, *970, 989, 1001, 1057, 1058, 1177, 1744
New Humanist, 493
New Leader, 421, *918, 927, 934, 1354, 1898, 2103, 2212
New Masses, 439, 504, 579, 580, 788
New Mexico Quarterly Review, *1538, 1621
New Oxford Outlook, 360
New Pearson's, 97
New Rambler, 2243
New Republic, 12, 33, 57, 65, 79, 90, 134, 138, 148, 150, 207, 208, 209, 246, 268, 283, 286, 320, 355, 417, 423, 426, 466, 542, 548, 562, 619, 651, 709, 755, 791, 904, 913, 1211, 1225, 1259, 1333, 1514, *1533, 1535, 1594, 1638, 1639, 2263
New Review, 793
New Statesman, 6, 53, 61, 99, 100, 123, *143, 158, 171, 227, 308, 382, 406, 431, 589, 600, 754, 824, 825, 901, 934, 980, 1188, 1279, 1406, 1435, 1572, 1623, 1661, 1894, 1895, 2087, 2169, 2175, 2188, 2217, 2242
New Theatre, 572
New Verse, 507, 683
Newsweek, 545, 760, 1300, 1627, 1744, 1774, 2177
New Yorker, 490, 553, 642, 653, 655, 729, 907, 908, 1096, 1208, 1356, 1422, 1438, 1663, 1893, 2176, 2234, 2425, 2568, 2569, 2570, 2654, 2655
New York Times Book Review, 25, 74, 190, 240, 243, 361, 362, 505, 506, *516, 583, 584, 706, 750, 781, 915, 919, 1043, 1118, 1216, 1233, 1287, 1324, *1417, 1419, 1454, *1532, 1708, 2012, 2223, 2639, 2647

Nine, 1276, 1316

Nineteenth Century, 456, 863, 911, *969

1924, 118

North American Review, 409, 597, 2444

Notes and Queries, 749, 1181, 1283, 1338, 1499, 1549, 1682, 1791, 1817, 1868, 1869, 1884, 1909, 1937, 1942, 1964, 2005, 2098, 2106, 2139, 2144, 2145, 2148

Occidental, 1212

Open Court, 81

Orbis Litterarum, *1901, 1910, 1936, 1943, 1947, *1951, 1956

Osmania Journal of English Studies, 2691, 2692

Outlook, *72, 75, 141

Outposts, 1284

Oxford Magazine, 189

Oxford Outlook, 260

Pacific Weekly, 576

Pagany, 230

Papers of the Bibliographical Society of America, 2077, *2170

Papers of the Manchester Literary Club, 631

Paris Review, *1922

Partisan Review, 602, 731, 745, *826, 950, 958, 965, 966, 973, 1005, 1111, 1112, 1154, 1202, 1227, 1277, *1319, 1637, 1681, 2493

Penguin New Writing, 858, 942, 1052, 1068

Personalist, 608

Perspective (a Quarterly Journal of Literature and the Arts), 1294

Philological Quarterly, 1611, *1722, *2015

Philosophy East and West, *1525

Picture Post: Hulton's National Weekly, 716

PMLA, 990, 1012, 1016, 1635,

*1696, 1785, *1844, *1885, *1980, 2129, 2192

Poetry, *8, 15, 44, 51, 104, 247, 262, 263, 291, *325, 330, 343, *369, 390, 482, 483, 594, 622, 643, 647, 759, 809, 819, 878, 910, 916, *943, 987, 1053, 1219, *1231, *1263, 1293, *1348, 1385, 1567, *1671, 1689, 1734, 1787, 1931, *2158, 2187, 2239

Poetry Journal, 1

Poetry (London), 147, 736, 643

Poetry London, 835, 848, *885, *889, 924, *955, 968, 1081, 1429

Poetry Quarterly, 1257

Poetry Review, 140, 233, 236, 312, 485, *516, 639, 675, 799, 859, 894, 895, 910, 1076, 1185, *1721, 2491

Prairie Schooner, 1713, *1795, 1974

Princeton University Library Chronicle, 1420

Psychoanalysis, 1633

Publications of the University of Pretoria, 644

Publishers' Weekly, 1264, 2178, 2515

Punch, 275, 536, 2495

Purpose, 699, 700, *763, 797

Quadrant, *2334

Quarterly Journal of Economics, 1607

Quarterly Review, 2

Quarterly Review of Literature, 954, 978, 979

Queen's Quarterly, a Canadian Review, 1426, 1822, 1952

Religion in Life, 1477, 1866

Religious Book Bulletin, 778

Renascence, 1332, 1364, *1387, 1400, 1684, *1800, 1811, 1840, 1887, 1983, 1993, 2030, 2042, 2043, 2046, 2133

Reporter, 2235

Review, 2048, 2069
Review of English Literature, 2267
Review of English Studies, *2068
Review of Politics, 814
Revue des Langues Vivantes, 1899, 2249
Revue de Littérature Comparée, 588, 604, 2152
La Revue de l'Université de Sherbrooke, 2206
Rikkyo Review, 1709
Rivista di Letterature Moderne, 1331
Rocky Mountain Review, 952

St. Louis Review, 287, 332, 333, 334
Saturday Evening Post, 238
Saturday Review, 54, 187, 276, 281, 458
Saturday Review of Literature [later Saturday Review], *157, 192, 211, 216, 282, 301, 340, 386, 404, 405, *455, 517, 568, 569, 592, 733, 735, 783, 816, 817, 847, 906, 922, 936, 939, 1117, *1191, 1198, 1203, 1220, 1249, 1250, 1274, 1292, 1328, *1344, 1372, 1407, 1411, 1446, 1473, 1502, 1508, 1509, 1510, 1534, 1539, 1575, 1576, 1588, 1589, 1648, 1740, 1807, 1834, 1846, 1847, 2001, 2104, 2190, 2209, 2382, 2584
School and Society, 1321
Schoolmaster, 335
Science and Society, 1404, 1501
Scribners' Magazine, 220, 224, 380
Scrutiny, *356, 377, *427, 432, 434, 487, 515, *575, 590, 611, *743, 771, 807, 865, *879, *920, 921, 929, 1002, 1067, 1208, 1270, 1336, *1398, 1401, 1464, 1465, 1493
Secession, 105
Senior Scholastic, 2507, 2508

Sewanee Review, *170, 252, 253, 347, *364, 428, 490, 510, *593, 663, 678, 725, 951, 974, 1042, 1061, *1073, *1074, 1133, 1251, *1258, *1267, 1291, *1433, *1445, 1544, *1581, 1602, 1614, *1655, 1659, *1705, *1750, *1769, 1790, 1863, 1913, 1977, 2074, 2143
Shama'a: a Magazine of Art, Literature, and Philosophy, 2029
Shenandoah, 2031
Sign, 856
Sketch, 492
Social Progress, 801
South Atlantic Quarterly, 425, 752, *992, 1210, 1221, 1455, 1513, 1597, 1690, 1739, 1751, 1778, 1864, 1986
Southern Review, *556, 603, 609, 620, *624, 626, *646, *772, *780, *798, 831, *860, 864, *897, 2237, *2257
Southern Review: an Australian Journal of Literary Studies, 2123, 2126
Southwest Review, 411, 1515, 1712, 1863, 2254
Spectator, 299, 304, 305, 324, 370, 441, 477, 524, 596, 766, 774, 1169, *1340, 1347, 1391, 1573, 1757, 1829, 1932, 2247, 2248, 2293, 2336, 2540
Spirit, a Magazine of Poetry, 753, 1266
Stage, 511
Standpunkte, *2208
Studia Germanica Gandensis, 2150
Studies, an Irish Literary Quarterly, 757, 896, 1038, 1064, 1914, *2194
Studies in Bibliography, *1523, *1777
Studies in English Literature and Language, 598, 1996
Studies in Philology, 523

Symposium, 222, 226, 231, 289, *298, 310, 321, 373

Tablet, 396, 717, 726, 893, 1040, 1182, 1223, *1285
Texas Quarterly, 1843, 1874
Texas Studies in English, *1961
Texas Studies in Literature and Language, 1991, 2019, 2063, 2142, 2220
Theatre Arts, 397, 569, 582, 622, 629, 632, 670, 1373, 1408, 1531, 1568, 1570, 1628, 1692, 2575, 2680
Theatre Programme, 2671
Theatre World, 2576
Theology, 398, 422, 869, 870, *909, 1088, 1341
Theology Today, 1341, 1452, 1481
Theoria, 1707
Thought, 808, 1023, 1033, 1077, *1441, 1466, 1676, 1813, 1448, 1917
Time, 91, 155, 546, 656, 657, 718, 719, 720, 779, 902, 903, 1044, 1101, 1102, 1204, 1205, 1206, 1301, 1302, *1303, 1304, 1305, 1306, 1307, 1308, 1359, 1439, 1503, 1629, 1773, 1814, 1815, 2116, *2179
Time and Tide, 318, 401, 443, 469, 491, 494, 500, 519, 520, 522, 530, 533, 535, 537, 538, 539, 540, 741, 1103, 1135, 1195, 1370
Times Literary Supplement, 7, 17, 18, 27, 28, 29, 30, 55, 77, 78, 92, 115, 139, 156, 172, 173, 174, 175, 182, 210, 250, 277, 337, 399, 486, *516, 547, 721, 722, 723, 724, 833, 834, 881, 1045, 1104, 1105, 1309, *1310, 1311, 1440, 1449, 1507, 1552, 1553, 1554, 1555, 1704, 1804, 2013, 2040, *2124, 2180, 2181, 2348, 2350, 2408, 2498
Today, 52

Town Topics, 2448
Trace, 1938
Transactions of the Royal Society of Literature of the United Kingdom, 1050
Transactions of the Wisconsin Academy of Sciences, Arts, and Letters, 1686
Tri-Quarterly, 2253
Tulane Drama Review, 1601
Tulane Studies in English, *1825, *1903, *2080, *2081
Twentieth Century, 1528, 1579, 1620, 1748, *1775, 1890, 1911
Twentieth Century Literature, 1738, 1774, 1919, 1972, 2153
Twentieth Century Verse, 769

Unity, 578
University of Colorado Studies, Series A, 292
University of Colorado Studies in Language and Literature, *1780
University of Denver Publications, Studies in Humanities, 1437
University of Kansas City Review, 1051, 1120, 1656, 1736, 1897, 1965, 2079
University of Toronto Quarterly, *350, 750, 1010, 1119, *1565, 1653, 1657, *2024, 2105

Vanity Fair, 93, 124
Verse, 554
Vice Versa, 787
Vogue, *121, 128, 1046, 2580, 2661, 2678
Voices, 599
Virginia Quarterly Review, *387, 479, 481, 567, 601, 1215, *1218, 1673, 1698, 1818, 2057, 2504

Wake, 1381
Walt Whitman Review, 1929, 2171

Washington Square College Review, 649, 2462

Washington University Studies, 1556

Week-end Review, 225, 300, 317, 357, 375

Weekly Westminster Gazette, 56, 112

Western Humanities Review, 2102

Western Review, *1231, 1232, 1378, 1543, 1960

The Wind and the Rain, 1268, 1397

Windsor Quarterly, *344

Wingover, 2683

Wisconsin Studies in Contemporary Literature, 2016, 2075, 2117

World Review, 1247, 1363

World Theatre, 2219

X, a Quarterly Review, 1976

Xavier University Studies, 2032, 2054

Yale French Studies, 1546, 1646

Yale Review, 95, 284, 389, 525, 612, 681, *758, 946, 1226, *2183

Year's Work in English Studies, 1085

SUBJECT INDEX

T. S. Eliot is abbreviated to TSE. Starred items are especially useful.

Adams, Henry, *The Education of* and "Gerontion," 1994

Aeschylus, influence of *Eumenides* on *Family Reunion,* 836

Agrarians, the, TSE a fellow traveler, 623

Aiken, Conrad, TSE's influence on, 59; Reciprocal influence of, 1635, 1761

Aldington, Richard, TSE's influence on, 2334

Anti-Semitism of TSE, 1202

Apollinaire, Guillaume, influence of *Les Mamelles de Tiresias* on "Sweeney Agonistes," 2148; influence, general, 1600

Aquinas, Thomas, relation to TSE, 165

Arnold, Matthew, and TSE as critics of society, 800; criticism and style compared with TSE's, *364; generalization in TSE and Arnold, 510

Auden, Hugh W., and TSE, 2643

Auditory imagination in TSE, 882

Babbit, Irving, and TSE, 1109; defended against TSE, 570, 667; influence on TSE's criticism, 2164; reply to No. 667, 693

Baudelaire, Charles, TSE on, 1096; influence of "Bohemiens en Voyage" on "Ash Wednesday," 2262; influence of

Fleurs du Mal on *Waste Land,* 2046

Beethoven, Ludwig van, influence of *Opus 132* on *Four Quartets,* *1793, *1921

Bennett, Arnold, conversations with TSE, 341

Benson, A. C., influence of *Fitzgerald* on TSE, 1221

Bibliographies of TSE's works, *1062, 1184, *1516, 1694, 2346, 2352, 2365, 2426, 2463; material concerning TSE, 905, 1184, 1312, 1694, 2382; concerning *Waste Land,* 1728

Bishop, John Peale, compared with TSE, 1061

Blake, William, influence of "London" on *Waste Land,* 1742

Bodelson, C. A., review of book on TSE, 1943

Bollingen Prize controversy *re* Ezra Pound, 1211, 1225, 1249, 1250, 1292

Broadcast of reading by TSE in Chicago, 2567

Bradley, F. H., influence on TSE, 1540, *2081

Brooke, Rupert, TSE's style compared with, 2307

Browning, Robert, compared with TSE, 61; influence of "Childe Roland" on *Waste Land,* 2238; influence of *Colombe's*

333

Birthday on *Family Reunion*, 1507

Buber, Martin, ideas similar to those of *Family Reunion*, 1088

Business, TSE's relation to, 1688

Buttle, Myra, identification of, 1774

Cather, Willa, ideology like TSE's, 1210

Catholic readers, attitude toward TSE, 1950

Children, TSE's attitude toward, 1905, 2687

Christian society, TSE's based on Anglicanism, 1831

Church, TSE's idea of, 1857

Classics, influence of on "Burbank with a Baedeker," *1581; place of in TSE's Christian humanism, *2119, *2186; use of by TSE, 1248

Coleridge, S. T., "Ancient Mariner" and *Waste Land* compared, 1940; influence of theory of organicism on "Ben Jonson," 1767

Communism, TSE's alternative to, 326; Marxist reading of *Waste Land*, 383; opposition of to TSE, 339, 378, 439

Compton-Burnett, Ivy, influence of *Men and Wives* on *Family Reunion*, 1069

Conrad, Joseph, influence of *The Heart of Darkness* on "The Hollow Men," 2063; influence on TSE, general, *1768

Corbière, Tristan, influence on "East Coker," 1414; influence, general, 1735

Crane, Hart, as antidote to TSE, 948

Crime fiction, influence on TSE, 1749

Criterion, effect of on TSE's creative work, *1927; notice of first publication, 77, 78; pass-

ing of, 713, 714, 719, 745; praise of, 609; review of July 1936 issue, 544; survey of, *763

Croce, Benedetto, TSE compared with, *566

Criticism of TSE's work, general: arid scholasticism in, 470; attacks on, 359, 1404, 1475; books and dissertations on, *206, 262, 291, 295, *302, *325, 444, *516, 867, 933, 971, *1029, 1055, *1062, *1083, *1086, 1094, 1108, 1153, *1191, *1196, *1217, *1231, *1239, *1281, *1323, 1382, 1405, *1412, 1475, *1516, 1519, *1524, 1527, 1551, 1599, 1622, 1625, 1641, 1650, 1717, 1725, 1741, *1766, *1768, 1776, 1799, 1805, *1824, 1828, 1873, 1892, 1904, 1906, *1930, 1954, 1966, *1967, 1969, 1982, *1988, 1992, 1995, 2011, 2022, *2035, 2044, 2049, 2058, 2060, *2061, 2062, 2072, 2085, *2090, 2091, 2108, *2109, 2112, 2114, 2115, 2125, *2128, *2130, *2132, 2137, 2138, 2140, 2146, 2150, 2162, 2167, 2168, 2204, 2211, 2264, 2463, 2645; career: *270, 815, 1139, 2212; survey to 1934, 453; survey to 1936, 600; survey to 1937, 641, 644; survey to 1941, 837; survey to 1947, 1075; survey to 1948, 1123, *1146; survey to 1953, 1558; cartoon concerning TSE, 2560; Christianity treated indirectly by TSE, 2082; comments on TSE, 1478; criticism good but poetry uncouth, 276; decline since leaving America, 708; defense of, 664; development of poetry and plays, *1196; difficulties in reading his work, 195; estimate of, 444, 1031, 1893, *1930, 2022; existentialism in, 2091; horror, vision of in, 195; humor in, 2505; importance of, 245; life and work, 971, *2035, 2090, 2494; introduction to for Indian readers, 2085; minor poet but great critic, 214; modernity of, 1272; morality and expression in, 1256; philosophical background of, *1281, 2049; popularization of work of, 2508; primness of, 380; prose snobbish, poetry fine, 1226; religion and tradition in, 1492; sacramental point of view in, 1597; students like work of, 2052; style of, 1372; summary of life and work, *170, 1017, 2507; three major attacks on, 1380; unity of theory and practice, *206, 567, 1092; work does not indicate withdrawal, 707. See also Criticism, Poetry, Drama, Biography, titles of individual works

Dante, influence on TSE, general, *646, *869, *2128, 2254; influence on images, 2044; relationship to TSE, *871, 1040
Dial prize, criticism of award, 122; reason for award, 73, 2299; essay on, 2074
Dickinson, Emily, compared with TSE, 1345
Dissociation of sensibility, adverse criticism of theory, 1505; meaning of term, 1540, *1796, 2041; use of by TSE in work, 1641, 2067
Donne, John, influence on TSE, 100, *206, 261, 1599, 1624; no real likeness to TSE, 100, 196; TSE's relation to, *1903, *1916
Doyle, Conan, influence on TSE, 1181, 1449, 1697, 1729, 1752, 1937, 1944, 2055

Drama, general, books and dissertations on: *1191, *1196, *1323, 1382, 1641, 1717, *1766, 1828, *1930, *1988, 2011, *2035, *2058, *2061, 2062, 2072, *2090, *2109, *2128, 2138, 2140, 2156, 2162, 2668; TSE's aims in, 2586; analysis of verse in, *1121; Christian dogma acceptable in, 563; Christian meaning in, *1705; clash between verse and naturalism in, 1701; classicism in, 2054; comedy in, 1713; conflict, diction in, 2027; criticism of, *1497, 1498, *1545, 1568, 1639, 1754, *1915, 1928, 2185; decline of, 1760; Euripides, contrast with, 1630; full study of, *1988; historical, critical, and textual analysis of, 1717; hocus-pocus manner of, 1050; Hugo von Hofmanstahl as influence on, 1986; humanism in, 1718; Alison Leggatt on playing two roles in, 1855; liturgy in, 2156; meditation in, 1535; melodrama in, *2068; mysticism in, 2135; myth in, 1707; myth and allegory in, 1461; nontheatrical, 1619, 1756; poetic drama, theory of, 393; poetry vs. verse in, 1604; production problems of, 1830; production of Murder and criticism of Family Reunion, 1127; realism in, 1936; rejection of human love in, 1763; relation to criticism and poetry, *1027; religious meaning of, 1933; rhyme and blank verse in, 2134; ritualism and realism in, *2203; steadily less dramatic, 1672; summaries of, 1504; theatrical craftsmanship of, *1313; themes of, *1753, 2042, 2162, 2167; themes and methods,

2072; theology in, 2032; theories of, 2280; theory and practice in, *2109; unity of, 1595; verse form of, 1058, 1727, 1737. See also titles of plays.

Eliot, Thomas Stearns

I. Biography: ancestors of, 1556; an evening with TSE, 685; appearance and manner of in 1917—*1179; appointment to National Arts Foundation, 2563; attraction of Europe for, 479; as banker, 1851; bad health and financial straits, 2299; Bel Esprit Fund for, 2306; birthday tributes to, 1160, 1161; British subject, 155; Commencement speaker, 1054; Dry Salvages and TSE, 2229; early years in St. Louis, 217; English Circle of Books across the sea, president of, 2498; encouragement of new authors, 1860; Harvard student, 1962, 2086; Harvard in 1932, 2368; health, 2299, 2660, 2675; honorary degrees, 2379, 2461, 2467, 2480, 2528, 2637, 2648; honors, 70th birthday book, 1828; honors and prizes, 73, 1046, 2116, 2659, 2686; Nobel Prize, 1100, 1102, 1164, 1171, 1266, 2514; Order of Merit, 1103, 2513, 2515, 2517, 2519; intellectual background, *2130; leaving America for Europe, 1926; memorial service for, 2233; lecture and reading in 1933, 2376; lectures on education, 2552, 2571, 2587; marriage, second, 1815; photograph of in 1957, 2678; poems in honor of, 1106, 1107, 1129, 1158, 1172, 1178, *1183, 1186, 1187, 1832, 1889, 2174; portrait of, 1205; portrait rejected, 657, 2466; as publisher, 1159; readings, 1053, 1531, 2237, 2510, 2564; relationship to C. W. Eliot, 1359; reminiscences of by Conrad Aiken, 1097, 1500, 2172; by Clive Bell, 1110; by Laurence Durrell, *2196; by William Empson, 1130; by Wallace Fowlie, 1787; by Desmond Hawkins, 1142; by H. G. Porteus, 1166; by Henry Rago, 2239; by Francis Russell, 2245; by Henry Sherek, 1408; by Robert Speaight, 1182; by Stephen Spender, 1484, *2252; by Igor Stravinsky, 2255; by W. G. Tinckom-Fernandez, 703; by Leonard Unger, 2258; return to America in 1932, 290; as schoolmaster, 1113; success of, 2261; summary of career, 290, 333, 574, 641, 718, 1303, *1323, 1723, 1732, *2265, 2342, *2494, 2536, 2574; tribute to in March and Tambimuttu, 1193; seminar at U. of Chicago, 1307

II. Characteristics: Americanism, 682, 1385, 2211; analysis of hand, 616; alleged anti-Semitism, 944; denial of anti-Semitism, 944; attack on, 1714, 2679; behavior with Wyndham Lewis and James Joyce, 640; classical knowledge, 1420; classicism, 106, *121, *142, *161; classicism and catholicism, 1299; classicism not associated with religion, 226; conformity, 20; conservatism, 231, 283, 312; courtesy and self-possession, 2031; criticism, 382; defeatism, 229; defense, 1502; domesticity, 1657; Europeanism, 2211; inhumanity, 1751; intellectualism, *121; intelligence and suavity, 127; as international hero, 1005; modern consciousness, *88; myth concerning, 1482; occult, interest in, 1658; paradoxes, 1644; pessimism, 1625, 2230, 2341; Puritanism, 150; as poet-critic, 1865; prejudices, remorse for, 1784; priestlikeness, 2223; as prophet, 674; qualities, 630; relation to his age, *935, *1536; remoteness, 1288; romanticism, 796, 1641; social charm, 832; solemnity, 146, 2353; traditionalism and classicism, 610; triviality, 1625; two selves, 1720; unamericanism, 1508, 1539

III. Interviews and conversations: 499, 995, 1118, *1267, 1278, 1589, 1593, 1674, 1708, *1842, 1846, 1938, 2039, 2226, *2234, 2381, 2438, 2465, 2470, 2509, 2547, 2551, 2610, 2684; re Cocktail Party, 1247, 1305, *1922, 2551, 2598, 2602, 2614, 2630

IV. Obituaries: 2173, 2176, 2177, 2178, *2179, 2180, *2183, 2216, 2219, 2222, 2256, *2257, 2263

V. Opinions: on athletics, 2378; on book clubs, 2378; on union of church and state, 2205; on civilization, 2136; views on culture rejected, 1407; on death, 2209; on ideal society, 1805; on impossibility of comprehending others, 1590; of magazines, 1702; of old age, 1487; of radio, 2378; on reality and poetry, *2080; anti-romanticism of, 1646; on science, *947, *1427; on suffering, *575; on television, 1439; on tradition and the individual, 493; on politics and religion, 1132; anti-democratic views of praised, 679; defense of his politics, 1220;

fascism of asserted, 1242; Hillyer's attacks on his politics, 1225, 1249, 1250; leftist attack on, 1198, 1199; liberal attack on his politics, *961, 1514; a liberal democrat, 587; Sandburg denounces, 2486; social and political views not Anglo-Catholic, 1510

VI. Religion and philosophy: Aquinas and TSE, 165; attack on, 1685, 1867, 2001; Bradley's influence on "Burnt Norton," 2112; Catholicism vs. communism in, 303; Christian belief not well handled by, 2084; Christianity treated indirectly by, 2082; church, TSE's chief interest, 1155; religion as alternative to communism, 326; TSE's cynicism becomes hope, *365; religion a solution for despair, 310; role of doubt in his religion, 1875; on Lambeth Conference, 1201; on his religious history, *694; no longer mocks at religion, 615; poetry vs. religion in, 379; general, 181, 843, *871, *885, *889, 910, 1850, 2340; religious progress of, 890, 1650, *1872; part of renaissance of, 675; report by on religious affairs, 1154; self-centered quality of, 300; should be Roman Catholic, 1019; sincerity of questioned, 2248; Anglo-Catholicism independent of his social views, 1510; sonnet to him concerning, 835; spiritual biography of, 1792; religion harms his poetry, 247; his philosophy, *1951; thought in his religion, 2511; style not harmed by his religion, 343

VII. Reputation: causes difficulty in reading, 698; declining, 417, 508, 2012, 2083, 2457; early, 60, 271; in age of fiction, 2175; international, 1156; is King of the Dead, 683; many critics of, 1224; probable posthumous, 1203, 1274; significance of, 1268

VIII. Writings

The Adventures of Huckleberry Finn, introduction to: TSE's approval of the conclusion, 2653; notice of, 1306, 1324, 2546, 2570

After Strange Gods: approval of, 437, 2389, 2405, 2431; decline in power shown in, 390, 434; defense of, 430, 2397; disapproval of religion in, 557; shows distrust of faith in, 2416; doctrine of original sin in, 478; economics ignored in, 447, 448, 449, 450; excellent but over-brief, 441; fascism in, 401, 475, 2397; freedom limited by doctrine in, 460, 480; liberalism and authority in, 454; notice of, 2400; opinions in eccentric, 400; orthodoxy not defined in, 413; prophecy is poor, criticism good, 424; qualified approval of, 445; religion as criterion for criticism objected to, 407; racial purity and tradition in, 428; rationalism and traditionalism in, 415; religious insight of, 392; review of, 422, 558, 2414; reviews, unfavorable, 394, 403, 404, 416, 421, 431, 2403, 2413; review of reviews, 2396; salutary chastisement in, 471; summary of, *418, 2389, 2398, 2400, 2411, 2417; traditionalism in, 414, 476; his unhappiness shown in, 426

Anabasis, translation: praise of, 232, 706; flatness of, 655, 2102

"Andrew Marvel": praise of, 76

"Animula": classical ideal of contemplation in, 222; Longfellow poem compared with, 671

Ara vos Prec: compared to Browning and Laforgue, 61; irony in, 40, 41; jazz in, 57; no synthesis in, 2283

Ariel Poems: notice of, 2344

"Ash Wednesday": acceptance of doctrine in irrelevent, *267; "aged eagle" in, 246; allusions in, 1456; "Bohemiens en Voyage" as source for, 2262; and Botticelli, 1642; and *Ecclesiastes,* 230; Christian poem, failure as, 1608; clarity of defended, 700; criticism of, *270, 558, 979; and Dante's *Purgatorio,* 1908; diction of, 1137; explication of, *223, 1352; explication of two lines of, 527; liturgy, importance of in, 1608; Mass for Ash Wednesday and the poem, 2038, 2043, 2232; meaning of, 241, *625, *689, *1059; narrowness of, 255; obscurity of, 212, 249; paraphrase of I, II, and V, *853; prosody of, 2210; relation to other English religious poetry, 225; religion in, 211, 495, 1799; religion of anticipated in *Waste Land,* 240; revolutionary quality of, *298; rhythm of, 239; sources of, *772, *1766; style of, 227, *1615; summary of, 2348; symbolism of, 1343, 1409, 1956; thought in, 232

"Aunt Helen": paraphrase of, 793

"Author and Critic": disagreement with idea of, 1706; report of lecture, 1704

"Ben Jonson": Coleridge's influence on, 1767; criticism of, *855

"The Borderline of Prose": discouraged the prose poem, 939

"The Boston Evening Transcript," explanation of, 1120

"A Brief Introduction to the Method of Paul Valéry": published in Échanges, 2493; too difficult a preface, 135

"A Brief Treatise on the Criticism of Poetry": false analogy in, 28; objection to doctrine in, 29; too much craftsmanship in, 31

Bubu of Montparnasse, introduction to: Toryism in, 283

"Burbank with a Baedeker; Bleistein with a Cigar": allusions in, 981; analysis of, 168, *1240, *1581, *2208; classical sources for, *1581; Ford Madox Ford as source for, 1839; sources for, general, *1766

"Burnt Norton": allusions in, 1456; Bradley's relation to, 2112; Christology in, 1997; compared with Rilke's Eighth Duino Elegy, 1743; criticism of, *794, 859, 864; meaning of, 850, 1087, 1260, 1566; relation to Collected Poems 1909–1935, 622; rose leaves in, 1660; St. Louis girls' school as influencing, 2064; sources of,

*1766; verbal pattern in, 1963. See also Four Quartets

"Byron": comment on, 635

A Choice of Kipling's Verse: criticism of, 915, 936, 944; defense of Kipling's imperialism in, 874; Kipling compared with TSE, 906; notice of, 2504; over-praise of Kipling in, 868, 884, 908; praise of Kipling, 904; summary of, 2497, 903

The Classics and the Man of Letters: criticism of, 968; narrowness of, 892; summary of, 875, 896

The Cocktail Party: acting in criticized, 1435, 2590, 2632; actors like play, 2612; allegorical interpretations of, 1379; compared with Alcestis, 1528, *1587, 2155, 2241; compared with Christopher Fry's plays, 1367; compared with Family Reunion, *1392, *1398; compared with Measure for Measure, 1342; compared with Murder in the Cathedral, 1400; compared with The Passing of the Third Floor Back, 2626; compared with Piers Plowman, 1425; attack on, 2534; Buddhism in, 1809; Christian meaning of, *1314, 2020; Christianity insufficient in, 1341; clarity of, 1411; comments on, 2666; criticism of, 1316, 1389, *1417, *1418, 1786, 1819; curtain speech by TSE at, 2573; decorum in, 1673; defense of, 1350, 2601; discomfort to audience caused by, 2591; dislike of, 1381, 1399, 1429, 2557, 2594, 2603; drama lacking in, 1373, 1393,

2595; Edinburgh production of, 2607; TSE sees in New York, 2553; financing of, 1302, 2555, 2579; first New York productions of, 2544; four levels of meaning in, *1340, *1348, 1391; Goethe as influence on, 1668; "happening" in, 1984; Harcourt-Reilly in, 1499, 1790, 1949, 2053; Hermes as archetypal figure in, 1363; humanism in, 1611; insight in, 1354; interviews with TSE on, 1247, 1305, *1922, 2551, 2598, 2602, 2614, 2630; Irish production of, 2636; is a brilliant lecture, 2644; is a Waste Land, 1466; London opening later than New York's, 2554, 2556, 2577; London performance of, 1548, 2549, 2604; London reception of, 1308, 2561, 2606; meaning of, 1330, 1355, 1396, *1483, 2613; Mexico City performance of, 2566, 2620; morality play, *1433; mythology in, 1543; New York performance of, 2550, 2588; not comic, 2543; not poetic, 2631; obscurity of, 1375, 2599, 2628; opening of Jan., 1950, 2531; pessimism of, 1333; poem on success of, 1406; politics in, 2617; praise of, 1276, 1522, 2532, 2533, 2578, 2623, 2624, 2628; prizes and awards for, 1304, 2558, 2559, 2565; production changes in, 1366; prosody of, 2140; psychology and religion in, 1925; publication of text of, 1264, 2568; reception of, 2627; recording of, *1344, 2593; relation to contemporary British theater, 1311; relation to earlier work of TSE, 1241, 1361, 1378, 1397, *1671; relation to Weston's From Ritual to Romance, 1434; relation to Poetry and Drama, 1806; religion in, 1327, *1387, 1518, 1598, *1616, 1653, 1662, 1676, 2020, 2037, 2163, 2541; sacrifice in, *2113; sources of, *1766, *2109; spoof of critics of, 1422; summary of criticism of, 1206, 1569; reviews of, 1257, 1279, *1285, *1310, *1315, 1317, 1318, *1319, 1321, 1347, 1349, 1364, 1368, 1370, 1384, 1388, *1394, *1402, 1436, 1476, 2540, 2542, 2569, 2572, 2581, 2582, 2583, 2584, 2585, 2592, 2596, 2597, 2600, 2605, 2608, 2609, 2615, 2616, 2618, 2626, 2628; summary of, 1300, 1301, 1356, 1477, 2527, 2537, 2576, 2611; summary and photographs of, 2576, 2580; television production of, 1821; unintelligibility of, 1328; U.S. tour of, 2642; verse form of, 1309, 1335, 1391, *1430, 1474; wit in, 2529; world premier of, 2535, 2538; worldliness of, 1341, 1452, 1465, 1470, 1481

Collected Poems, 1909–1935: attack on, 554; Burnt Norton, relation to other poems in, 622; clarity of, 577; dichotomy between earlier and later poems in, 596; influence of waning, 2457; later poems inferior to earlier, 546, 564, 601, 638; love of order and hatred of sham in, 595; minor poet

in, 612; notice of, 2453;
obscure but enjoyable, 550;
poetry praised and politics
disliked, 579; religious subjects disapproved, 562; review of, 583, 608, 2444;
stylistic changes in, 620;
suffering, attitudes toward,
*575; unity of the collec-
tion, 639; *Waste Land* a
failure; later poems better,
2451

Collected Poems 1909–1962:
exhilaration lacking in,
2104; intensity of, 2096;
poetry becomes music in,
2087; pretentiousness of,
2157; virtue of, 2187

Collected Poems and Plays:
reviews of, 1503, *1509,
1532

The Confidential Clerk: acting and staging of, 1771;
adverse criticism of, 1573,
1579, 1623, 1627, *1631,
1632, 1637, 1648, 1649,
1669, 1730, 2668, 2669,
2674; appraisal of difficult,
1638; as comedy of hu-
mours, 1661; casting of,
2650; relation to *The
Three Voices of Poetry,*
1698; content lacking in,
1620; criticism of, *1655,
*1750, 1819, 2652; letters
concerning, 2656, 2657,
2658; meaning of, 1700,
*1705; paradoxes in, 1785;
photographs of, 1628, 2647,
2649, 2661; praise of, 1665,
1666, 2664, 2665, 2667; relation to TSE's earlier work
*1671; reviews of, 1570,
1588, 1591, 1594, 1626,
1636, 1647, 1652, 1663,
1667, 1677, 2649, 2663,
2670, 2671; on reviewers of,
1692; sources of, *1766,

*2109; summary of, 1591,
1628, 2655, 2662

"A Cooking Egg": analysis of,
353; meaning of, 1517,
1559, 1560, 1561, 1571,
1574, 1617, 1618, 1634,
1687, 1840; sources of,
*1766; wit in, 18; struc-
ture of, 156

Coriolan: analysis of, *879;
satire in, 1488; sources for,
1488, *1766

"The Cultivation of Christmas Trees": appreciation
of, 1862

"Cyril Tourneur": attack on,
523

Dante: praise of, 237; review
of, 222, 228; summary of,
233

"A Dialogue on Dramatic
Poetry": confusion in, 176;
Dryden and TSE com-
pared, 174, 187

"Difficulties of a Statesman":
unity of questioned, 330

"Donne in Our Time": critical summary of, *1424;
idea of questioned, 320;
summary and praise of,
2358

"The Dry Salvages": and the
actual reefs, 2229; as intentional parody, 1748; de-
spair in, 878; Graham
Greene's influence on,
2144; humility in, 877; review of, 833; science and
Christianity in, *1427;
sincerity of questioned,
888; sources for, *1766;
stage in a pilgrimage, 887;
symbolism in, 1887; *see also*
Four Quartets

"East Coker": analysis of,
*1536, 2059; compared
with *Family Reunion,*
*993; criticism of, 857, 864,
894; gloom in, 807; musical

structure of, 1119; meaning of, 877, 951, *1025, 1033, 1563; *Essay on Man* as a source of, 2098; TSE on sources of, *845; reviews of, 825, 2491; rhetoric in, 1645; sonnet praising, 1076; sources of, *860, 1173, 1414, 1752, *1766. *See also Four Quartets.*

The Elder Statesman: clarity of, 1913; disapproval of, 1829, 1858, 1877; equilibrium in, 1883; ghosts in, 2005; mass audience, effect of, 1932; *Oedipus at Colonus,* parallels with, 2016; *Pillars of Society,* parallels with, 2246; *Samson Agonistes,* parallels with, 2016; praise of, 1931; reviews of, 1814, 1890, 1894, 1898, 1952, 1955, 2681; sources of, *2109; summary of, 1847

Elizabethan Essays: Anglican Church proud of, 2393; good Shakespearean criticism in, 432; provocative quality of, 420

Essays Ancient and Modern: criticism in first-rate, 560; criticism in impure, 585; defense of, 592; disapproval of, 590, 2462; dullness of, 542; importance of for Christians, 649; literary essays in preferred, 647; Marxist conclusions approximated in, 580; religious-liberal criticism of, 584, 613; remoteness from today, 565; summary of, 547, 552, 571, 597; unity of is religious, 591

"Euripides and Professor Murray": cavalier quality of, 32; notice of, 2284

Experience and the Objects of

Knowledge in the Philosophy of F. H. Bradley: summary of, 666

The Family Reunion: the Absurd, techniques of, 2182; acting and staging of, 1771; Aeschylus's influence on, 836; analysis of, 764, 1360, *1536; broadcast of, 2562, 2641; Browning's *Colombe's Birthday* as a source of, 1507; Cambridge, England, performance of, 901; character motivation lacking in, *748, 1270; comments on, 2666; compared with "East Coker," *993; compared with *Murder in the Cathedral,* 2481; Ivy Compton-Burnett's influence on, 1968; criticism of, 741, *794, *822, 1057; decline shown in, 771; defense of, 2107; dramatic failure of, 711, *758, 769, *780, *798, 2485, 2512, 2690; Eumenides in, 742, 754, 1983; excellence of, 1782; existentialism in, 2065; failure of, 721, 2050; Freudian analysis of needed, 725; Hamlet and Harry compared, 744; "happening" in, 1984; Harry, character of, 746, 1322; haunting quality of, 775; Hulme and Bergson in relation to, *1290; humor in, 740; irrelevance of, 738; language of praised, 737; meaning of, 982; moral confusion in, *1471; notice of, 774; a new TSE in, 729; New York 1959 production of, 2685; Orestes theme in, 1286; poetic style incongruous in, 1265; praise of, 731, 732, 735, 736, 750, 755, 759, 770,

831, 2484; praise of verse and character but not of plot, 762; production of in 1957, 2680; prosody of, 2141; "Prufrock," transition from, 730; psychoanalytic study of, 725, 852; relation to rest of TSE's work, 1331; relevance of, 728; reviews of, 710, 716, 2477, 2478; sources of, *1766, *2109; success, reasons for, 1089; summary of, 726, 2152, 2496; symbolism in, 751; Synge's dramas contrasted with, 858; teleology in, 752, *2251; verse good but plot poor, 2479; vulgarity and dullness of, 760.

"La Figlia che Piange": meaning of, 1018, *1065; paraphrase of, 793

For Lancelot Andrewes: as a retreat, 188; criticism of, 171, 198; development of TSE's thought toward, 194; effect of religion on, 200; a "flattering obituary notice" of, 175; grimness of, 199; Aldous Huxley's essays compared with, 190; importance of, 189; lucidity and force of, 171; order, love of shown in, 192; praise of, 205, 2347; *re* Edmund Wilson's review of, 208; religious bias in, 2345; religious position in unacceptable, 209; review of, 178; is beginning of TSE's career, 204

Four Quartets: Beethoven's *Opus 132* as influence on, *1793; Buddhism in, *1525; a Christian poem, 1608; detailed study of, *1029, *1063, 1551, *1824, *1967; contemplation in,

913; demands on reader made by, 929; diction in, 1137; diction, syntax, and rhetoric in, 1776; difficulty of, 922; essay on, 2002; exacting quality of, 900; experience and expression in, *1441; good students respond to, 1845; habit of analysis, effect of on, 1541; Heraclitean paradox in, *2015; hints and guesses in, 1656; history in, 1715; images in, *992; incongruity and irrationality in, 917; Indian literature as influence on, 2189; integrity and poetic sensibility of, *1036; interpretation of, *873, *879, *919, *1063, 1496, 1512, 1542, *1824, 2108, *2194; Italian translation of, 2010; levels of meaning in, *1011, 1332, 1348, 2075; Loyola and theme of, 1684; Guillaume Machaut as source for, 2191; musical qualities of, 914, 916, *1334; mysticism in, 1078; notice of, 2499; Orwell's attack, defense against, *889; paraphrase of, 2071; personal history of TSE in, 1621; praise of, 902, 922, *949, 953, *970, 999, 1551, 2503; prosody of, 1873; relation to modern art, 1081; religion and language in, *1463; relation to earlier work, 1002; religious and philosophical thought in, 1133, 1917; religious meaning of, *870, 1544; reviews of, 907, 1020, 1022, 2500, 2502; on reviews of, 927, 960; Rilke and TSE compared, *1721, 1946; St. John's Gospel in, 2264;

sensuousness in, 942; simplicity and subtlety of, 946; sources of, *1766; spiritual helpfulness of, 984; structure and symbolism in, *931, *1444, 1564; structure of, *1710; summary of, 1215, 2045; symbolism in, 1678; Tchelitchew's painting compared with, 991; Tennyson's *Maud* as a source of, 2151; themes in, 1007, 1010, *1095, 1149, *1699; themes and imagery in, *899, *1095, 1386; theology in, *2066; time and eternity in, *918, *972, 1041, 1386, 2692; two levels of, *1035; unity of, 1000, 1082; versification of, 940; *Waste Land* compared with, *1180, *1445, 1982; weakness of compared with "Prufrock," *885; Whitman's *Song of Myself* as influence on, 1863.

The Frontiers of Criticism: account of the lecture, 1744; summary of, 2677

The Function of Criticism: analysis of Winters's objection to, 978

"Gerontion": allusions in, 1004, 1456; analysis of, *727, *1090, *1844; analysis of two lines of, 633; *As You Like It* as an influence on, 1939; "boy" and "jew" in, 2093; collation of texts of, *1523; *Education of Henry Adams* as source for, 1994; TSE's reading of, 809; gutter, meaning of, 1836; history in, 1715; line by line analysis of, 1072; Marvell's "The Garden" as a source of, 1912; meaning of, 1015, 1230, *1885, *1886, 1978; meaning of lines 56–61, 1781; meaning of title, 1008, 1282; parallels with Newman's "Dream of Gerontius," 1079; Pope as a source of, 1791; *Portrait of the Artist* as influence on, 2026; proper names in, 1165, 1282; religion in, 1410; revolutionary poetry, *298; satiric and tragic quality of, 1455; sources for, *1766, 1791; spiritual decay in, *1961, unity of, *387

"Hamlet and His Problems": allusion to, 2290; Clutton-Brock's criticism of, 75, 80, 83, 2297; criticism of, *1234; denunciation of, 75, 2269, 2328; failure of, 39, 55, 83; objective correlative for TSE's Hamlet, 1693

"The Hippopotamus": allusion to, 5; meaning of, *962, *975; parallels to, 1468; symbols in, 1262

"The Hollow Men": and fertility rites, 1738; criticism of, *794; TSE's reading of, 809; "The Heart of Darkness" as influence on, 2063; *Julius Caesar* as influence on, 1353, 1981, 1991; meaning of, *1885, *1980, 2019; parallels with Virgil and Dante in, 1376; paraphrase of, 793; revolutionary poetry, *298; Santayana's influence on, 2009; set to music, 1816; sources for, *1766; Tennyson as a source for, 1738

Homage to John Dryden: precise but inconclusive, 117; praise of, 128, 137; quotation from, 134; summary of, 119, 126

"The Humanism of Irving Babbitt": essay attacked, 667; rejection of humanism in, 202; relation to Catholicism, 191, 224

"Humouresque": 1490

"Hysteria": explication of, 1972

The Idea of a Christian Society: attack on democracy in, 776, 777, 816, 817, 828; Coleridge's ideas compared with, 2143; confusion in, 823; criticism of, *811, *1770; defense of, 783; democracy defended against, 724; disapproval of, 784, 785, 786, 802, 803, 1244, 2488, 2489; education in, *811, 812, 813; gloominess of society in, *743; intellectual seriousness of, 791; laughed at, 2490; materialism and supernaturalism in, *826; medievalism of, *795; Murry's *Defense of Democracy* compared with, 797; a national church in, 717; not truly Christian, *761; political left condemns, 788; praise of, 781, 782, 789; Protestant criticism of, 810; Roman Catholic criticism of, 827; summary of, 712, 723, 757, 778, 779, 800, 805; summary and criticism of, *761, 801, 814, 818

John Dryden the Poet the Dramatist the Critic: criticism of, 355; reviews of, 343, 2359; summary, 332; praise of, 322

"The Journey of the Magi": and TSE's conversion, 2198; Christianity of, 2340; compared with other poems on the subject, 2133; the horse in, 1989; narrator in

egotistical, 1703; Rilke's influence on, 1973; sources of, *1766; three levels of meaning in, *1800; "Wee Willie Winkie" as source of, 1682

Knowledge and Experience in the Philosophy of F. H. Bradley: reviews, 2169, 2187. See also *Experience and the Objects of Knowledge in the Philosophy of F. H. Bradley.*

"Little Gidding": an allegory concerning, 1152; and Dante, 1947; criticism of, *969; essential and intimate quality of, 934; interpretation of, *909, *920; musicality of, 924; overpraised, 921; praise of, 881, 945; remorse, confession of in, 1784; requirements for appreciation of, 893; sources of, *943, *1766; Swift as ghost in, 1253; symbolism in, 1887; Tourneur as a source of, 1414; verse form of, 911. See also *Four Quartets.*

"London"; introduction to: praise of, 268; statements in questioned, 210

"The Love Song of J. Alfred Prufrock": absurdity of, 2; ambiguity in, 1251; amusing quality of, 6; analysis of, *662, *688, *1428, 1577, 1640; Christianity in, 1544; *Crime and Punishment* compared with, 1003, 1080; criticism of, *270, 1787; Dante contrasted with, 2033; diction of, 13, 2199; disapproval of from political left, 1501; disparaging reference to, 2293; epigraph of, 2036, 2099; fog in, 1958; Grail motif in, 2000; *Hamlet* as a source for, 1779; influence on Day-Lewis, Auden, and Spender, *419; introspective quality of, 1; Lazarus, source for, 1346, 1453, 1964; lesson in explication from, 1789; meaning of, 926, 1009, 1724, 2021; metaphors in, 637; meter of, 12; mythology in, *627; Prufrock not a lost soul, 1817; not obscure, 2343; not poetry, 7; praise of, 8, 9, 10, 14, 15, 44; *Prufrock,* etymology of, 2088; psychoanalytic interpretation of, 1294; publishing history of, 654; realism of, 3; rejection of society in, 1810; *rolled trousers,* meaning of, *1622, 1695, 1765; satire on St. Louis society, 2028; sensuousness in, 942; skepticism in, 347; sources of, 1486, 1549, *1766, 1779; R. L. Stevenson as a source for, 1549; strength of compared with later poems, *885; symbolism in, 1546, 2073; theme of, 1812; too clever, 4; verbalism in, *1795; Charles Williams as influence on, 1606

"Lune de Miel": called "disgusting", 5

"Marina": analysis of, *879, 2079; revolutionary poetry, *298; sound and rhythm in, 1654; technique of, 263

"Meaning in Poetry": account of lecture, 2385

"Metaphysical Poets": relevance of today, 2097; criticism of, 773, *855

"Milton I": analysis of, 360

"Milton II": modesty of manner in giving this lecture, 1043; notice of, 1526; quotation from, 1044. *See also* Milton.

"Mr. Apollinax": identified as Bertrand Russell, 111

"Mr. Eliot's Sunday Morning Service": interpretation of, 1537, 1733; painting mentioned in identified, 2165; Whitman's influence on denied, 1929

"Modern Tendencies in Poetry": hitherto unrecorded, 2008

The Moonstone, introduction to: praise of, 186

"Morning at the Window": explication of, *2208

Murder in the Cathedral: acting history to 1938, *669; acting the role of Becket, 856, 1881; action as passion in, *1060; apparatus for students, 1382; Becket's actual murderers, 2430; Becket's character, 613; Becket's Christianity, 2051; Becket's holiness ambiguous, 534; Becket a mythic figure in, 2118; Berlin reception of, 1223; Boston production of, 2474; broadcast of, 632; Buenos Aires production of, 956; characters abstract in, 532; chorus of, 1265, 2476; clarity of, 578; classical and medieval qualities of, *509; Columbia University performance of, 2640; comment on, *1240, 2666; compared with "Christabel," 2106; compared with Hardy's *The Dynasts,* *665; compared with *Family Reunion,* 2481; compared with Shaw's *Saint Joan,* *1726, 2459; compared with *Samson Agonistes,* 603, 1578; contrasted with

Tennyson's *Becket,* 2105, 2449; Conan Doyle source of a passage in, 1181, 1449, 1729; criticism of, 517, 521, 525, 574, 594, 599, *684, 691, *794, *1013, 1959, 1960, 2244, 2458, 2495; dramatically poor, 511, 658, 2446, 2468; dullness of, 2437, 2439; *figura* in, 2110; film of, *1538, 1848, 2638, 2646; Greek tragedy, relation to, 668; Harvard production in 1937, 2460; Hobart College production, 2506, hocus-pocus in, 2450; humanity of, 484; imagery in, *1073; influences on, 2138; influence on poetic drama, 524, 629; interesting but obscure, 2472; introduction to, *2061; Italian production of, 2548; London Mercury Theater production, 543, 2432; London 1941 production, 2492; London 1953 production, 1557, 2654; martyrdom in, *2078; medievalism in, 586, 606; murderers, character of, 1866; New York opening, 1936, 2455, 2456; New York production of 1938, 2469; not commercial, 581; not tragic, *1298; praise of 1936 production, 619; praise of 1938 production, 656; success of 1937 production, 621; productions of 1936 and 1938 compared, 705, 709; obscurity of, 2475; operatic version of, 1849; Paris production of, 1369; pessimism of, 576; political criticism of, 504, 526, 602; recording of, 1576; religion in, 529, *870, 2433, 2436; reviews, favorable, 545,

*549, 553, 569, 582, 2428, 2435, 2441, 2442, 2443, 2445, 2448; rich but narrow, 501; *sacrifice* in, *2113; sources of, *1766, *2109; spiritual meaning of, *963; staging in Feb. 1938, 2471; structure of, *697, *1235; style of, 486, 490; remoteness of subject of, 2434; summary of, 487, 506, 617, 2473; superior to TSE's other plays, 1602; symbolism in, 1979; theology in, 830, *2251; theme in, 735, *1073; tragic hero and salvation in, 628; transcendence in, Burke's theory of, 626; unity lacking in, 559, 572; use of sources for, 1747; verse of, 594, 614, 2454; vileness of world in, 548; virtues and defects of, 607; vitality of, 2454; world premiere of, 2427, 2429

The Music of Poetry: criticism of, 968

Nightwood, introduction to: summary of, 636

"Notes on the Way": attacked, 535, 537, 540; confusion in, 491, 500, 519, 520, 530, 538, 539; defended, 533; relation to encyclical on war, 522; religious assumptions in, 494

Notes towards a Definition of Culture: analysis and criticism of, *1218, *1770; arguments of interesting, 2525; assumptions in examined, *1209; attack on ideas in, 950, 958, 965, 966, 1233, 1237, 1243, 1259, 1273, 1280, 1336, 1395, 1401, 1489, 2539; Coleridge's ideas compared with, 2143; defense of,

1213, 1255, 1269; issues in, 1227; ecclesiastical fascism in, 996; education in relation to, 912, 2518; inconsistencies in, *1297; irrelevance of, 1582; place of the poet in, 1284; praise of, 1522; questions concerning, *1371; relation to earlier work, 1511; religion not important enough in, 1229; reviews of, 1005, 1104, 1169, 1177, 1204, 1207, 1245, *1271, 1325, 2526; sociological writing deplored, 2521; summary of, 1195, 1291, 1296, 1607, 2516; too pessimistic, 1163

Old Possum's Book of Practical Cats: Rawsthorne's musical settings for, 1740, 2673; reviews of, 722, 733, 767, 2483; theological meaning in, 1974

On Poetry and Poets: notice of, 1773; reviews, 1788, 1807, 1852, 1876, 1888, 2069

"On Teaching the Appreciation of Poetry": review, 2689

The Perfect Critic": questions concerning, 37

Poems [1919]: Byronism of, 27; clever but empty, 17; disturbing, 2268, 2274; favorable reviews, 2275, 2276, 2279; foulness of, 2278; freshness of, 21; irony in, 35, 45; obscurity of, 44; not romantic, 33; product of jazz age, 57; Silver Age poetry, 16; technique of, 34; unintelligibility of, 48

Poems 1909–1925: borrowings in, 148; content lacking in, 145, 307; dislike of, 2338; obscurity of denied, *143; powerful but ob-

scure, 133, *136, 2337; praise of, 141; quoted, 2335; rhythm and diction in, 131; search for a theme in, 151; spiritual sense in, *163; squalor in, 140; technique of, *163

Poetry and Drama: notice of, 1438; relation to *Cocktail Party,* 1806; summary of, 1440, 1454; reviews of, 1446, 1448, 1485

"Poetry in Prose": intelligence in, 66; praise of, 68, 69; reference to, 2288

Points of View: represents a stage in a pilgrimage, 887; review of, 833

"Portrait of a Lady": introspective quality of, 1; praise of, 3, 44; parody of, 132; "To His Coy Mistress" compared with, 1739; Wycherley's *Plain Dealer* as a source for, 1791

"Preludes": Phillipe as a source for, 1413; rhyme and meter of, 11; sources for, *1766

"Religion and Literature": defense of, 514

"Rhapsody on a Windy Night": clarity, defense of, 700; diction of, 637, 2199; influence on, mistaken assertion of denied, 663; obscurity of denied, *625; paraphrase of, 842; Phillipe as a source for, 1413; rhyme and meter of, 11; sources of, *1766

The Rock: chorus, praise of, 446, 485, 631, 2387, 2391, 2399, 2419; chorus, use of, 670; Christianity of, 438, 440, 477; clarity of, 2418; comment on, *1240; criticism of, *427, 525, *2109; diction in, 396, 398; disapproval of, 405, 2409, 2412; doctrine in, 391, 469; fails as drama, 459; imitative, 410; influences on, 399, *1766; a link between *Waste Land* and future work, *427, 2394; London production announced, 2420; mentioned, 483; originality of, 2408, 2422; pessimism of, 395, 2402, production of, 406, 2421; reviews of, 505, 2392, 2395, 2423; shows decline in power, 390; theatrical success of, 397

"Le Rôle Social de Poete": account of Paris lecture, 987

The Sacred Wood: allusion to, 64, 2287; cleverness of, 23; contemporary literature ignored in, 56; disliked, 39, 2282, 2294; dramatic theory in, 2280; essay on, 1051; explanation of, 65; explication taught by, 1970; honesty of, 87; humanity of, 24; humor lacking in, 26; impersonality of, 58, 120; inconclusiveness of, 49, 70; notice of, 67; obscurity of, 2281; over-compression of, 43; praise of, 36, *51, 71, 85, 116, 198, 2270, 2271, 2272; questions concerning, *50; right reason in, 52; significance of, 42; snobbishness of, 53; solidity of, 47, 2285; wholesomeness of, *22

Savonarola, introduction to: use of blank verse in drama, 139

Selected Essays 1917–1932: blemishes in, 278; brevity of, 277; Catholic objections to, 2425; classicism of, 314; compared with Dr. John-

son's criticism, 318; criticism, *374; critical summary of, 2360; doctrine of autonomy in art in, 315; healthfulness of, 361; humanism of, 288; literary better than moral essays in, 285; literary sensibility in, 377; little human sympathy in, 311; misunderstandings in, 2363, 2364; narrowness of, 2367; over-scholarly, 297; passionate but narrow, 273; praise of, 275, 313, 316, 319, 2355, 2357, 2362; praise, except for religion in, 2354; reviews of, 293, 343, 1324; static quality of, 286; style of, 308, 2369; summary of, 1473; unpopularity, reasons for, 2361

Selected Prose: earlier essays preferred, 1553; style of, 1605; unity of, 1572

"Seneca in Elizabethan Translation": approval of, 158, 159; scholarship in, 152

"*Shakespeare and the Stoicism of Seneca:* objection to thesis of, *184; praise of, 162, 173, 185

"The Social Function of Poetry": summary and criticism of, 2215

"A Song for Simeon": notice of, 2344

The Study of Shakespearean Criticism: reassuring quality of, 334; announcement of lecture, 2381

"Sweeney Agonistes": allusion in, 2121; banality of, 345; chorus, use of, 670; conversation with TSE concerning, 1124; dullness of, 388; "Les Mamelles de Tirésias" as a source of, 2148; interpretation of,

*369, 536; musical quali-
ties of, 1479; obscure but
impressive, 512; perfor-
mance of at Vassar, 2377;
performance at Westmin-
ster, 492; praise of, equivo-
cal, 338; religious meaning
of, *1722; sources of,
*1766. See also *2199

"Sweeney among the Night-
ingales": criticism of, 149,
1248; epigraph to, 1664;
correction of No. 1664—
No. 1716; interpretation of,
2127; meaning of "horn'd
gate," 925, 977, 1924; musical qualities of, 1479; not
obscure, 2343; relation to
"Tradition and the Indi-
vidual Talent," 2025; parallels with "The Song of
Solomon," 1584; sources
of, *1766

"Sweeney Erect": mythology
in, *627

Thoughts after Lambeth:
disagreement with thesis of,
264; TSE's passivity in,
260

The Three Voices of Poetry:
connection with The Con-
fidential Clerk, 1698; summary of, 1555, 2672

To Criticize the Critic and
Other Writings: review of,
2181; summary of, 2247

"To the Indians Who Died
in Africa": resembles the
Bhagāvad Gita, 2101; ver-
bal revisions in, 2154

"Tradition and the Individual Talent": criticism of,
384; praise of, 30; relation
to "Sweeney among the
Nightingales," 2025; sum-
mary of, 272

"Triumphal March": com-
ment on, 2350; paraphrase

of, 842; unity of ques-
tioned, 330

The Use of Poetry and the
Use of Criticism: asides are
valuable in, 342; clarity of,
409, 2380; criticism of,
*455; criticism of, adverse,
331, 425, 429, 481, 2372,
2373; criticism, favorable,
357, 411, 423, 436, *451,
2370, 2415, 2431; discrepancy between TSE's poetry
and criticism, 458; doctrine,
lack of, 366; TSE's beliefs
in questioned, *356; TSE's
unhappiness in apparent,
426; exposition of, *566,
2371; inconclusiveness of,
337, 346, *402, *455; notice
of, 2386; poetry and religion in, 385, 389; pom-
posity of, 2385; reviews of,
362, 433, 2384, 2388, 2404,
2407; Shelley essay annoy-
ing, 443; sincerity of, 367;
summary of, 335, 336, 351,
370, 518, 2383; value lies
in light on TSE's career,
482; views in questioned,
348

The Waste Land: advertisement of, 2291; allusions in,
328, 1338, 1456, 2121,
*2202; analysis of, *193,
353, *624, *1049, *1070,
*1189, *1326, *1536,
*2202; and modern mathe-
matics, 2057; and Moses'
candlestick, 1745; Antony
and Cleopatra and boudoir-
pub scenes, 1610; appreciation of, 179; Ash Wednes-
day anticipated in, 240;
attack on, 1911; Blake's
"London" as source for,
1742; cerebral quality of,
74; characters in, 1320;
Christian meaning of,
*2147; "Childe Roland to

the Dark Tower Came," as source of, *2238; "C.i.f.", meaning of, 1868; collection of essays on, 2137; commentary on, 938; communist interpretation of, 383; "Ancient Mariner" compared with, *955; *Four Quartets* compared with, *1180, *1445, 1982; Horace's "Ode to Pyrrha" compared with, 2213; conclusion of, 2095; condemnation of, 99, 108, 2320, 2328, 2330; continuity of mood in *Waste Land* and *Quartets*, *1180; critics of, 1613; criticism of, 92, 93, 102, 103, *193, *270, 558, *794, 895, *2202; *currants* and *currents* in, 2089; "death by water," meaning of, 1034; defended, 98, 1911, 2321, 2323; *Dial* award for, 105, 2074, 2295, 2301, 2314, 2317; diction of, 1460; difficulty of communication in, 568; difficulties in explained, *387; disillusioned cynicism in, 633, 804; "dog," meaning of, 2149, 2220; double sonnet in, 2018; TSE personifies himself as Tiresias in, 1248; emotion in, 95; emotional and musical effects in, 941; epic quality of, 2217; explanation of, *193, 1512, 2322; fails as Christian poem, 876; faith lacking in, 104; "Fleurs du Mal," as source of, 2046; form of, 85; formlessness of, 110; French symbolists, influence on, 203; Freud's influence on, 2007; genesis of, 598; greatness of denied, 2312; a hoax, 2303, 2304, 2305, 2313, 2325, 2329,

2331; homosexuality in, 1530; identification of literary references in, 862; imagery in, 1175; impact of, 1859; incoherence a virtue of, 90; Indian literature as influence on, 2189; influence on Auden, Day-Lewis, Spender, *419; interpretation of, 1808; interpretation of passage in, 861; Joyce as influence on, 1679, 2142; Jungian interpretation of, 408, 503, 990, *1231; Laforgue as influence on, 611; Larisch as a source of, 1681; *leman*, meaning of in, 1941; levels of meaning in "Hurry up please," 1176; London in, 2192; *Lyrical Ballads*, as important as, 327; *Madame Bovary* as source of an allusion in, 2100; Marxism, relation to, 650, 672; modern techniques of art in, 1990; music of, 112; mythology in, *627, 1864, 1995; notes, attack on, 2123; notes, defense of, 2126, *2231; obscurity of, 91, 296, 2296, 2319; opinions concerning, 2040; overfastidiousness of, 97; paraphrase of, 1719; pessimism of, 118, 153, 180, 1975; Petronius' *Satyricon* compared with, 1818; "Phlebas," meaning of, 1764; TSE a "poet in a cellar," 692; Pope as influence on, 1612; popularity of ominous, 371; praise of, 85, *89, 376, 1214, 2298, 2300, 2322; praise of ambiguities in, *221; publishing history of, *2170; purgatorial quality of, 78; quest in, 2030; quotations, purpose of,

1580; radio dramatization of, 673; relativism in, 2200; revolutionary poetry, *298; rhetorical figure of architecture in, 2117; *The Rubaiyat* as influence on, 1778; Samuel Johnson's presumed opinion of, 980; satire in, 2333; satire of, 2302, 2316; skepticism in, 347; soda-water lines, meaning of, 2406, 2410; song-hit of 1912 as a source of line 128—1801; *Sosostris,* meaning of, 1337, 1374, 1691; sources for, *624, 1338, 1390, 1467, *1766, 1818, 1833, 2060; a "sporting attempt," 2292; structure of, 156, 1432, 1519, 1746; symbols in, 295, 1254, 1283, 1357, 1409, 1415, 1494, 1909, *2202; Tarot cards in, 1680; technique of, 168; themes in, *1699; theology in, 830; Thomson's "City of Dreadful Night," as source of, 1778; structure of, *89: thought in, 498; too erudite, 230; typist and clerk in defended, 844; *Ulysses* as influence on, 2142; unconscious in, 687; unity of, 101, 107, 109, *387, 2327; verse form of, 86; Webster's *White Devil* as source for, 1833; world a waste in, 238; wryneck in, 2227

What Is a Classic?: analysis of, 983; a masterpiece, 997; review of, 989; sleight-of-hand trick in, 1038; summary of, 994, 1028

"Whispers of Immortality": meaning of, 1192, 1222, 1953; organization of, 1651; praise of ambiguities in, *221; sources of, 749

"Wilkie Collins and Dickens": allusion to, 84

Eliot, William Greenleaf; likeness to TSE, 2023

Elizabethan inffuences on TSE, 148

Elizabethan and Jacobean dramatists; TSE's attitude towards, 1405

Epigraphs, sources of, *1295

Euripides; influence on *Cocktail Party,* 1528, *1587

Everyman: compared with *Murder in the Cathedral,* 1934

Fascism: attitude toward in the *Criterion,* 645; general, 1197. *See also* TSE: politics

Faulkner, William: influence on early poems, 1585; a parallel with TSE, 2120

Fertility rites: influence on "The Hollow Men," 1738

Film of *Murder in the Cathedral,* 1264

Fitzgerald, Edward; influence of *The Rubaiyat* on *Waste Land,* 1778

Fitzgerald, F. Scott: parallels between *Gatsby* and *Waste Land,* 2153

Flaubert, Gustav: influence of *Madame Bovary* on *Waste Land,* 2100

Ford Madox Ford: influence on "Burbank with a Baedeker," 1839; and TSE, 38

French poets and English metaphysical poets: influence on TSE, *72

French influence on TSE, 148

French symbolism: influence on TSE, *321, 588, 1586

Freud, Sigmund: influence on TSE, 1822; influence of *Totem and Taboo* on *Waste Land,* 2007; theory of applied to all of TSE's work, 2006

Gardner, Helen: review of book on TSE, *1348, *1362, *1457

Gesture: as symbol in TSE's poetry, 1711

Goethe, Wolfgang von: influence on *Cocktail Party*, 1668; misrepresented by TSE, 363; TSE's relation to, 1562

Gourmont, Remy de: influence on TSE, 604, 1540, 1907

Greene, Graham: influence of *The Man Within* on "Dry Salvages," 2144

Guiness, Alec: as actor in *Cocktail Party*, 2545

Hermes: as archetypal figure for Alex in *Cocktail Party*, 1363

Hofmannstahl, Hugo von: influence on TSE's drama, 1986

Hopkins, Gerard Manley: and TSE, 2114, 2115; influence on TSE, *372, 957

Horace: "Ode to Pyrrha" compared with *Waste Land*, 2213

Hulme, T. E.: philosophy compared to that of TSE, *157; his position like that of TSE, *350; relations with TSE, *1131

Hulshoff, Annette von Droste: influence on "Rhapsody on a Windy Night," 663

Humanism: attack on TSE as a humanist, 220, 234, 244; Irving Babbitt and TSE, 191, 218, 570, 667, 693; defense of TSE as a humanist, 219; dynamic form of needed, 2048; TSE undermines, 213, 215; TSE's attack on, 183; TSE the only good humanist, 216; in *Selected Essays*, 288; study of TSE's, *2119

Huxley, Aldous: essays compared with TSE's, 190, 243; mysticism compared with TSE's, *1491; novels compared with TSE's poems, 2501

Ibsen, Henrik: parallels between *The Pillars of Society* and *Cocktail Party*, 2246

Images: Dante's influence on, 2044

Imagism: relation to TSE, 792, 1450

Imitations of TSE's poetry, 1116

Impersonality in poetry: TSE's theory of, 1871, 2048

Indian literature: influence on *Waste Land* and *Four Quartets*, 2189

Influence of TSE on others: adverse, 734; on aesthetic analysis, 1200; on American criticism, 1731; on H. W. Auden, *419; on H. W. Auden and Stephen Spender, 1690; in Bengal, 1115; in Cambridge in the 1920s, 236, 1170; in Ceylon, 1148; in 1938, 690; on Hart Crane, 1194; on Nancy Cunard, 123; on C. Day-Lewis, *419; on dramatists, *1313; of *Waste Land* on William Faulkner, 2131; of *Waste Land* on F. Scott Fitzgerald, 1772, 2131; in France, 1032; general, 561, 659, 660, 680, 1168, 2228; in Germany, 1125; in Greece, *1174, *2158; *Waste Land* on Ernest Hemingway, 2131; in India, 1126; in Italy, 1099; *Waste Land* in Japan, 2034; on literary criticism, 115; on literature of his time, 1834; on Malcolm Lowry's *Under the Volcano*, 2218; on Cambridge in the 1920s, 227, *1131; in 1926, 1150; on James Picot, 1683; on H. G. Porteus, 306; on regeneration of English verse, 1185; in revolutionizing nineteenth-century English poetry, *298; on I. A. Richards, *1131; a poem on TSE's influence, 1006; of

Waste Land on J. D. Salinger, 2131; encouraged sciolists, 470; since the 1930s, 1826; on Stephen Spender, *419, 1690; of *Waste Land* on John Steinbeck, 2201; on Wallace Stevens, 2092; on Allen Tate, 2092; made writers more self-critical, 834; on younger poets diminishing, 768, 1111

Influences on TSE: *The Education of Henry Adams* on "Gerontion," 1994; on all work, *1412; to 1956, *1766; Guillaume Apollinaire, general, 1600; of *Les Mamelles de Tirésias* on "Sweeney Agonistes," 2148; on "Ash Wednesday," *772; Irving Babbitt on criticism, 2164; Baudelaire's "Bohemiens en Voyage," on "Ash Wednesday," 2262; *Fleurs du Mal* on *Waste Land*, 2046; Ludwig van Beethoven's *Opus 132* on *Four Quartets*, *1793, *1921; Blake's "London" on *Waste Land*, 1742; F. H. Bradley, general, *2081; Browning's "Childe Roland to the Dark Tower Came," on *Waste Land*, 2238; Browning's *Colombe's Birthday* on *Family Reunion*, 1507; classical on "Burbank with a Baedeker," *1581; on a line in "Burnt Norton," 1275; a St. Louis girls' school on "Burnt Norton," 2064; caution in identifying influences, *1901; Coleridge's theory of organicism and "Ben Jonson," 1767; Ivy Compton-Burnett's *Men and Wives* on *Family Reunion*, 1968; Conrad's *The Heart of Darkness* on "The Hollow Men," 2063; many, on the *Coriolan* poems, 1488; crime fiction, general, 1749; Dante,

general, *646, *869, *2128, 2254; on images, 2044; Donne, 100, *206, 261, 1599, 1624; Conan Doyle's *Hound of the Baskervilles* on "East Coker," 1752; general, Doyle, 1697, 1937, 1944, 2055; *Musgrave Ritual* on *Murder in the Cathedral*, 1181, 1449, 1729; "East Coker," influences on opening of, 1173; Tristan Corbière on "East Coker," 1414; Elizabethan and French, general, 148; epigraphs, sources for, *1295; Euripides on *Cocktail Party*, 1528, *1587, 2155, 2241; William Faulkner, on early poems, 1585; fertility rites on "The Hollow Men," 1738; Edward Fitzgerald's translation of *The Rubaiyat* on *Waste Land*, 1778; Gustav Flaubert's *Madame Bovary* on *Waste Land*, 2100; Ford Madox Ford on the epigraph to "Burbank with a Baedeker," 1839; French poets and English metaphysicals, *72; French symbolists, *321, 588; Sigmund Freud's *Totem and Taboo* and *Waste Land*, 2007; Goethe on *Cocktail Party*, 1668; Remy de Gourmont, 604, 1540, 1907; Graham Greene's *The Man Within* and "The Dry Salvages," 2144; Hugo von Hofmannstahl on drama, 1986; Horace's "Ode to Pyrrha" and *Waste Land*, 2213; Indian literature on *Waste Land* and *Four Quartets*, 2189; Joyce's *Portrait of the Artist as a Young Man* and "Gerontion," 2026; Joyce and *Waste Land*, 1679; Joyce's *Ulysses* and *Waste Land*, 2142; Jules Laforgue and *Waste Land*,

611; general, Laforgue, 1603, 1735, *1768, 1835, 2214; Marie Larisch on *Waste Land,* 1681; "Little Gidding," sources of, *943; Guillaume de Machaut's rondeau on *Four Quartets,* 2191; Marvell's "The Garden" on "Gerontion," 1912; medieval, 819; Saint-John Perse on TSE's poetry, 1835; Petronius's *Satyricon* on *Waste Land,* 1818; Charles-Louis Philippe on "Prelude" and "Rhapsody on a Windy Night," 1413; Alexander Pope on *Waste Land,* 1612; *Essay on Man* on "East Coker," 2098; *Dunciad III* on "Gerontion," 1791; Ezra Pound on TSE, 2254; on Prufrock's name, 1486; of Renaissance on TSE, 829; Rainier Maria Rilke on "Journey of the Magi," 1973; general on *The Rock,* 399; George Santayana on the theory of the objective correlative, 1802; of Santayana's *Three Philosophical Poets* on "The Hollow Men," 2009; Shakespeare's *As You Like It* on "Gerontion," 1939; *Julius Caesar* on "The Hollow Men," 1353, 1981, 1991; R. L. Stevenson on "Prufrock," 1549; Tennyson on "The Hollow Men," 1738; Tennyson's *Maud* on *Four Quartets,* 2151; James Thomson's "City of Dreadful Night" on *Waste Land,* 1778; Cyril Tourneur on "Little Gidding," 1414; *Sosostris* sources for name, 1691; John Webster's *White Devil* on *Waste Land,* 1833; "Wee Willie Winkie" on "Journey of the Magi," 1682; Walt Whitman, influence of *poly-*

philprogenitive denied, 1929; Whitman's *Song of Myself* on *Four Quartets,* 1863; Charles Williams on "Prufrock," 1606; William Wycherley's *Plain Dealer* and "Portrait of a Lady," 1791; W. B. Yeats on TSE, 2249

James, Henry, and TSE, 1899, 2129
Jazz, use of rhythms, 1513
Johnson, Samuel, compared with TSE, 318, 2150; TSE's criticism of praised, 2243
Jones, David E., review of book on TSE praised, 2013
Joyce, James, and TSE, 1151, 2115, 2207; TSE's admiration for, 2355; influence of *The Portrait of the Artist* on "Gerontion," 2026; influence of *Ulysses* on *Waste Land,* 1674, 2142; *Ulysses* compared with *Waste Land,* 164
Juvenal's parodies and TSE, 1856

Kennedy, John, quotes TSE, 2688
Kenner, Hugh, editor of collection of essays on TSE, 2058; review of his book on TSE, 1977

Laforgue, Jules, compared with TSE, 61; influence on *Waste Land,* 611; general influence, 1603, 1735, 1768, 1835, 2214
Language, TSE's attitude towards, 2260
Larisch, Marie, influence on *Waste Land,* 1681
Lawrence, D. H., and TSE, 1902; compared with TSE, 2355; TSE's attitude toward, 1464, 1465, 1493, 1675, 2355
Leavis, F. R., attack on TSE, 1854, 1920; TSE's influence on, 928; review of Leavis's

New Bearings in English Poetry, 279, 289

The Listener and TSE, 2250

Literary tradition and TSE, 1904

London, in TSE's poems, 1823

Lucy, Séan, review of book on TSE, 2013

Literary criticism and poetry by TSE: analysis of, *177; anti-religious criticism of, *967; appreciation of, 2103; are complementary, 63, *72; criticism of, *170, *206; criticism better than poetry, *129, 555; criticism poor, poetry great, 676; introduction to, 169; poetry reconciliation of opposites, *556; praise of, 138; in romantic-symbolist tradition, *1797; sketch of, 846; split between, 2289; survey of to 1951, 1443

Literary criticism by TSE: books and dissertations on, *206, *302, 444, 1055, *1083, 1094, 1153, *1191, *1217, *1323, 1405, 1828, 1892, 1904, 1906, *1930, 1992, *2035, 2049, 2058, *2090, 2125, 2159, 2204; analysis of, *50, *270, *1769, 1906; attack on, 838, 866; attacked by Rebecca West, 323, 324; and defended against her, 299, 304, 305; Irving Babbitt's influence on, 2164; Catholic element in, 1023; changes in, *1217, 1458, 1965; classicism, evidence of dichotomy in, *2160; compared with that of Coleridge, 1094; compared with that of I. A. Richards, 292; critic and society in, 457; defense of, *452, 841, 1042; development of, *1780, 1458; doctrine in, 1383; disapproval of, *531; dramatic convention, doctrine of, 1686; impersonality, theory of, 1871; impersonality,

weakness of the theory, 435, 2236; inconsistencies in, 2159; influential since 1939, 1066; interest in literature in, *177; introduction to, *193, 964; literary judgment, belief in, 1965; meaning in poetry, insistence on, 1320; meaning of *poetry* in, 1055; method of, *256, *1048, *1134, 1277; moral and aesthetic position of, 160; morality and criticism in, 648; narrowness of, 130; order, love of, 1882; overestimated, 1896; over-literary, 62; over-theoretical, 375; poetic sensibility, doctrine of in, 1794; poetry vs. religion in, 379; praise of, *50, 2225; radical conventionality of, 1854; reason in poetry, insistence on, 1320; religion in, 280, 563, 573; religion has harmed, 1140; soundness of, 373; split between poet and critic, 301, 883; standards for, 765, 2125; summary of, 1077, 1480, 1819; style of, 411; survey of, 207, *270, *302, 2069, 2204; tolerance in, 1451; tradition in, 154, 1145, 1992, 2056; unity of, 411; workshop character of, 1892. *See also* titles of separate books and essays

Machaut, Guillaume de, influence on *Four Quartets,* 2191

MacNeice, a passage from compared with one of TSE's, 891

March and Tambimuttu, review of anthology on TSE, 1182, 1431, *1457

Maritain, Jacques, likeness to TSE, 1024

Marlow, Fanny, may be a pseudonym for TSE, 2014

Marvell, Andrew: influence of "The Garden" on "Geron-

tion," 1912; "To His Coy
Mistress" compared with
"Portrait of a Lady," 1739
Marxism: TSE a potential marxist, 650
Matthiessen, F. O.: review of book
on TSE, 643, 1085
Maugham, Somerset, praise of
TSE's poetry, 2487
Mesterton, review of book on
TSE, 954
Metaphysical poets: influence of
on TSE, *72; TSE's relation
to, 854, *1916
Milton, John: consistency of TSE's
attitude toward, 1092, *1825;
controversy concerning, 1064,
1071, 1320; TSE should appreciate, 973; new attitude toward shows retrogression,
*1258; and 1936 and 1947 at-
titudes toward compared,
1045; refutation of TSE's
criticism of, 634, 702, 820,
863, 985; Milton shadow figure of TSE, *2024
Montale, Eugenio: affinity with
TSE, 1167
More, Paul Elmer: opinion of
TSE, 651
Musgrove, Sydney: review of book
on Whitman and TSE, 1550,
1552
Mythology: use of, 986

Nature: TSE's interest in nonexistent, 551
New Criticism: attack on, 2070;
danger in, 1670; TSE's relation to, 1228, 1365, *1447,
1945
New English Review, TSE will be
contributor to, 715
Nietzsche, Friedrich: and TSE,
*1209, 2139

Objective correlative, theory of:
Washington Allston as source
of, 2076; compared with San-

skrit critical theory, *2240;
contradictions in, 1757; Edmund Husserl as source for
the term, 1884; influence on
TSE's poetry, 2254; meaning
of, 1897, 2188; Walter Pater
and, 2193; George Santayana
as source for, 1802, 2145; theory unintelligible, 976
Occult, the: in TSE, 1948
"Old Possum": gaiety of, 824;
Lear and Lewis Carroll, resemblance to, 720
Ortega y Gasset: Compared to
TSE, *1209

Parham, Mr.: composite hero including TSE, 242
Parodies: 132, 281, 354, *472, 589,
642, 678, 1030, 1047, 1783,
2315, 2318, 2339, 2524; of attacks on TSE, 653
Pater, Walter: likeness to TSE,
*1565
Perse, Saint-John: influence on
TSE, 1835
Petronius: influence of the Satyricon on Waste Land, 1818
Philippe, Charles Louis: influence
on "Prelude" and "Rhapsody
on a Windy Night," 1413
Pirandello, Luigi: contrast with
TSE, 1891
Poe, Edgar Allen: comparison of
style with that of TSE, 201
Poems, general: allusions in, 473;
allusion to, 2296; analysis of,
*177, *879, 1056, *1622; ap-
preciation of, *344; architecture, lacking in, 938; aspects
of theory and practice in, 605;
attacked, 652; autobiography
in, 747; beauty, not concerned
with, 147; belief divorced
from form in, *144; books
and dissertations on, *206,
262, 291, 295, *325, *516, 867,
933, 971, *1029, 1047, *1083,
*1086, 1108, 1153, *1191,

*1196, *1231, *1239, *1281, *1323, *1412, 1475, 1519, 1527, *1524, 1551, 1599, *1622, 1625, 1641, 1725, 1741, *1766, *1768, 1776, 1799, *1824, 1828, 1873, *1930, 1954, 1966, *1967, 1982, 1995, 2011, *2035, 2044, 2058, 2060, *2090, 2108, 2112, *2128, *2132, 2137, 2168, *2202, 2263; Catholicism of, 262; characters lack life, *531; Christianity in, 1026, 2264; Communist-Freudian interpretation of, 867; condescension toward, 502; critical background of, *1524; criticism of, *170, *270, 456, *516, *2132 (see also Poems, general: books and dissertations); decadence in, 358, 368; detachment of, 54; diction of, 291, *464, *1469, 1521, 2003, *2259; difficulty of defended, 988, 998; disapproval of, 309, 496, 821, 1843, 2273; dislike of later poems, 839; doctrinal approach in opposed, 1592; early poems as anticipations of later, 677; comment on, 93; rhetorical figures in, 2267; study of style of, 1459, 2146; TSE finished as poet, 704; epigraphs, sources of, *1295; estimate of, 1098; ethical interest in, exaggerated, 643; evolution of, 1811, 1971; explanation of, 257, *325, 1339; fusion of music and meaning in, 1506; genius of, 46; good for school boys, 1837; highbrow language of, 2691; imagery in, *1073, *1093, 1289, 2003, 2206; imagination required to read, *488; influence in America in the 1920s, 1731; integrity and poetic sensibility of, *1036; intellectual

acceptance of irrelevant, *593; introduction to, 265, *381, *756, 932, 964, 1803, 1999, *2004; Jungian interpretation of, 990, 1012, 1016, *1231, 1725; lack of catholicity in, 489; linguistic study of, 1966; living language recovered by, 681; love in, 1136; man in, *1246; minor but fine poetry, 695; modernity of, 1976; moralist, not poet, 2452; music of ideas in, *235; musical structure of, 1001; myth in, 1741; as Nonsense Poetry, 1878; obscurity of, 349, 959; obscurity of denied, *72; and explained, *365; offensive to morality of students, 2633; over-intellectual, 386; patronizing essay on, 1091; permanance of, 294; Perse's influence on, 1835; personae in, 2011; personal tribute to, 1114, 1838, 1870; personality in, 474, 1112; philosophical background of, *1281; preference for earlier, 247, 515; poetry is not plain sense, 259; praise of, 19, 79, 197, 317, 1861; prosody, statistical analysis of, 1108; psychological patterns in, 1633; quotations, objections to, 847; religious evolution in, *1533, 2190; revolutionary effect of, *298, 1185; rhyme in, 2040; rhythm and sound in, 696; rhythm and meaning in, 1910; romanticism of, *2160, *2161; satiric, 25; science, effect on, 1162; seventeenth century, relation to, 442; sibilance in, 2235; spiritual dryness in, 181; style of, 166, 172, 1689, 1734; survey of, 266, 287, 412, 461, 513, 608, *1472, 2122; symbolism in, 497, 1138, 1212, 1954, 1956; technique of, 269,

*365, 880, 1037, *1084, *1086, 1329; themes in, *897, *898, *1073, 1609; themes and techniques in, *898, 1495; thought and sensibility in, 930; time and eternity in, 1709; tradition and orthodoxy in, 2094; unity of, 1143, 2266; verse form of, 1935; Yeats's dislike of, 618. *See also* names of separate poems

Poems and drama: Christian doctrine in, 937; criticism of, *1238, 1762, *2128; development of religious ideas in, 1437; language in, 1813; poems better than dramas, 2195; theme of evil in, 739; the sibyl in, 1283; survey to 1950, 1496; textual variants in, *1777

Poems in French: TSE's French is incorrect, 125

Pope, Alexander: *Dunciad* III and "Gerontion," 1791; *The Essay on Man* and "East Coker," 2098; influence on *Waste Land*, 1612

Pound, Ezra: Bollingen Prize controversy, 1211, 1225, 1249, 1250, 1292; collector of Bel Esprit fund, 2306; compared with TSE, *794, 1462; contrasted with TSE, 541; dramatic monologue in Pound and TSE, 1919; TSE has outrun, 699; TSE reproved for praising, 799; friendship with TSE, 1147; influence on TSE, 2254; letter from *re* TSE, 1804; letters to TSE, *1403; reference to TSE, 686

Predecessors of TSE: his superiority to, 528

Prose, general: attack on nonliterary prose, 2645; essays on religion praised, 952; style of, *1014; philosophical prose,

1969. *See also* titles of separate works

Quinn, John: friend of TSE, 2077

Rajan, B.: collection of essays on TSE, *1083; review of, 1067, 1287, 2520

Rascoe, Burton: *Waste Land* as a hoax, 2324, 2325, 2326, 2374

Recordings by TSE: analysis of, *1263, 1351, 1575; praise of, 1421

Renaissance: influence on TSE, 829

Revolution in poetry: TSE's place in, 1874, 1985, 2248

Richards, I. A.: TSE's relations with, *1131

Rilke, Rainer Maria: differences from TSE, 1614; influence of *Sonnette am Orpheus* on "Journey of the Magi," 1973; likenesses to TSE, 1547, 1743, 1946

Robbins, R. H.: review of book on TSE, 1515, 1534

Rose garden theme: *897, *1073, 1596, 1678, *1696

Rutherford, Mark: novel compared with *Cocktail Party*, 2682

Sandburg, Carl: attack on TSE, 974, 2486; defense of TSE against, 787

Santayana, George: contrasted with TSE, 2168; influence on TSE, 1802; *Three Philosophical Poets* as influence on "The Hollow Men," 2009

Sartre, Jean Paul: compared with TSE, 1416

Sayer, Dorothy: parallel between *Gaudy Night* and TSE's images, 1798

Scandinavian myth in TSE's work, 2221

Schwab Eliot Collection: to University of Virginia, 2440

Seferis, George E.: influenced by TSE, *1755

Sensuous thought: meaning of the phrase, 282

Shakespeare: compared with TSE, 507, 2619, 2625; influence of As You Like It on "Gerontion," 1939; influence of Hamlet on "Prufrock," 1779; influence of Julius Caesar on "The Hollow Men," 1353, 1981, 1991

Shakespearean criticism: TSE's influence on, *2124, *2166

Shelley, P. B.: defense of against TSE, 182, 753; TSE's attitude towards, 2062; likeness to TSE, 840

Short-story writer: TSE a potential, 1157

Smith, Carol: review of book on TSE, 2111

Song hit of 1912: influence on Waste Land, 1801

Song of Solomon: influence on "Sweeney among the Nightingales," 1584

Stevens, Wallace: compared with TSE, 1144

Stevenson, R. L., influence of on "Prufrock," 1549

Still point: in TSE's poetry, 2047. See also books on poetry

Sweeney: as Emersonian hero, 1998; identity of, 1190, 1529, 1618

Sweeniad: poetry bad in, 1876

Sybba, Jeremy Pratt: an ironic portrait of TSE, 248

Symbolists, French: TSE's relation to, *321

Tennyson, Alfred: influence of Maud on Four Quartets, 2151; influence of Maud on "Prufrock," 1546; influence on "The Hollow Men," 1738

Texas, University of: list of TSE holdings, 1879

Thomson, James: influence of "The City of Dreadful Night" on Waste Land, 1778

Tiresias: TSE's use of, 1923

Tourneur, Cyril: influence on "Little Gidding," 1414

Unger, Leonard: review of anthology, 1117, 1128, *1252, 2523

Unified sensibility: contradictions in theory of, 1757; obscurity of phrase, 2029

Venice: as a symbol in TSE's poetry, 1969

Vers libre: TSE's views on, 258

Webster, John: influence of The White Devil on Waste Land, 1833

"Wee Willie Winkie": influence on "The Journey of the Magi," 1682

Weston, Jessie: relation of From Ritual to Romance to TSE, *89

Whitman, Walt: compared with TSE, 1527, 1895; influence on "Mr. Eliot's Sunday Morning Service," 1929; influence of Song of Myself on Four Quartets, 1863

Williams, Charles: influence on TSE, 1419; influence on Cocktail Party, 1606

Williams, William Carlos: compared with TSE, 1736; references to TSE, 1377

Williamson, George: review of book on TSE, 1567, 1643

Williamson, H. R.: review of book on TSE, 340, 2356, 2366

Woolf, Virginia: and TSE, 1993

Wordsworth, William: and TSE, 1423, 1900; misunderstanding of by TSE, 363

Wright, George T.: review of book on TSE, 2013

Wycherley, William: influence of *The Plain Dealer* on "The Portrait of a Lady," 1791

Yeats, W. B.: comparison with TSE, *849, *1775, 2197, 2249; contrast with TSE, 1841, 2253; influence on TSE, 2249